# STUNTWOMEN

# STUNTWOMEN

## The Untold Hollywood Story

MOLLIE GREGORY

UNIVERSITY PRESS OF KENTUCKY

Published by the University Press of Kentucky

Scholarly publisher for the Commonwealth,
serving Bellarmine University, Berea College, Centre College of Kentucky,
Eastern Kentucky University, The Filson Historical Society, Georgetown College,
Kentucky Historical Society, Kentucky State University, Morehead State
University, Murray State University, Northern Kentucky University, Transylvania
University, University of Kentucky, University of Louisville, and Western
Kentucky University.
All rights reserved.

*Editorial and Sales Offices:* The University Press of Kentucky
663 South Limestone Street, Lexington, Kentucky 40508-4008
www.kentuckypress.com

Library of Congress Cataloging-in-Publication Data

Gregory, Mollie.
  Stuntwomen : the untold Hollywood story / Mollie Gregory.
    pages cm. — (Screen classics)
  Includes bibliographical references and index.
  ISBN 978-0-8131-6622-3 (hardcover : alk. paper) —
  ISBN 978-0-8131-6624-7 (pdf) — ISBN 978-0-8131-6623-0 (epub)
  1. Women stunt performers. 2. Women in the motion picture industry—
California—Los Angeles—History. I. Title.
  PN1995.9.W6G744 2015
  791.43'6522—dc23                                      2015025673

This book is printed on acid-free paper meeting
the requirements of the American National Standard
for Permanence in Paper for Printed Library Materials.

Manufactured in the United States of America.

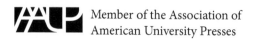   Member of the Association of
American University Presses

Character gives us qualities, but it is in the actions—what we do—
that we are happy or the reverse. . . .
All human happiness and misery take the form of action.

—*Aristotle*

# Contents

## IV. The Digital Age: 1995–2010

# Preface

Before I wrote this book, I didn't realize that being athletic is as much a gift as having a musician's perfect pitch. Whether athletes are male or female, that physical talent shapes and leads them, and they ignore it at their peril. I learned that many stunt performers in movies past and present were champion gymnasts, acrobats, riders, or swimmers. I learned that dealing with physical challenges is a skill and that taking risks builds self-confidence. A great stunt person is an athlete and an actor who has a quality known as heart—a blend of courage and endurance. They have guts and grace.

The story of stuntwomen is a classic come-from-behind, risk-it-all saga. Their arena is one that few know—a community of gifted athletes whose work makes movies thrilling. Like all stunt performers, stuntwomen risk injury or even death, but over the years, they have also faced institutional discrimination, unequal pay, and sexual harassment. The professional environment has improved, but the ultimate praise for a stuntwoman is still the same: "She hits the ground like a man!"

I never expected to write this history. Then, stuntwoman Julie Ann Johnson asked me to write a book about her life in the business and to include other stuntwomen in it. As she extolled the joys, sorrows, professional pride, prejudices, and hair-raising stunts, I was hooked. I began to interview stuntwomen, and I realized the combination of action, women, and the movies was a largely unexplored topic that was more than just enlightening. Eventually, a book about a few stuntwomen became an action-packed history of the profession.

Stunt communities are found wherever movies are made—Canada, Australia, China, France, Great Britain, India, and Japan. But this book is about the American film industry, located primarily in New York and Los Angeles. I interviewed sixty-five stuntwomen and a few stuntmen. The oldest worked in the 1930s; the youngest began in 2005. My questions covered their personal backgrounds; their best stunts (hilarious or scary) and how they were done; professional conflicts, such as race or sex discrimination; and what they'd like to change about the stunt business. Occasionally they went off the record, but 98 percent of the information they provided was available for publication (with a few exceptions for clarity, quotations from these interviews are not cited in the notes).

These interviews chronicle a history of individuals in a unique line of work. At some point, I became fascinated by the attitudes that shape our beliefs, expectations, and legends, all of which are reflected by the stunt community. Since the advent of motion pictures at the end of the nineteenth century, audiences expected to see men jump from moving cars or drive wagons over cliffs. Back then, no one imagined that women could do the same—and more. When women performed such stunts onscreen, they confounded all expectations of proper feminine behavior. Their exploits opened a new view of the modern woman and her astonishing possibilities. In fact, stuntwomen have been a source of inspiration since *The Perils of Pauline* in 1914. They've traded punches in knockdown brawls, crashed biplanes through barns, and raced to the rescue in fast cars.

*Stuntwomen* begins in the era of silent films. Before World War I, athletic actresses played famous action heroines in serial dramas that brought audiences back to theaters week after week. In those years, women also wrote, directed, edited, and produced movies. Then, almost overnight, movies became big business. Men pushed in for the profits, and except for popular actresses such as Mary Pickford, women were eased out—and that included stuntwomen. Donning wigs and dresses, stuntmen took over their jobs. Ignored and marginalized, a few stuntwomen (maybe ten or fifteen) performed from the 1930s into the 1960s. But men dictated what these women were and were not allowed to do. The struggles of this pioneering generation of stuntwomen went on for years.

Then, in the late 1960s and early 1970s, the movie business changed dramatically, and so did America. Activism by women and minorities increased, and a public clamor against discrimination and injustice exploded. Boosted by that dynamic decade, young women's attitudes began to change: they had aspirations, not just hopes; their mothers often worked outside the home; some of their fathers supported their unusual career choices; and more stuntwomen became members of the Screen Actors Guild. By the 2000s, stuntwomen had won some recognition and respect. However, they still face daunting challenges, such as a fair distribution of stunt work and the consequences of digital visual effects.

Stunts are an engine of the movies. Onscreen, a stunt—called a *gag*—seems like a spontaneous physical feat, but it is actually a carefully planned set of actions, and that's the art of it. In the early 1800s a gag was defined as a joke, an invention, or a hoax; then it became a theatrical term; and by the 1920s, a gag was a daring or showy feat that involved skill or cunning. Another meaning of a gag was a false story told for gain, which is, in a way, what stunts are. They create an exciting action that appears to be more spontaneous or dodgy than it actually is. And when a stunt person dons a costume—a disguise—to surreptitiously replace or "double" an actor, the gag enhances the movie star's reputation.

What is a stunt? In the interviews, veteran stunt performers offered vivid examples, but a stunt is more than just a daring act; it's a significant contribution to the story as a whole. A stunt has character, conflict, and resolution. It can be a woman swimming in the ocean when a shark attacks or hanging from a hot-air balloon 200 feet in the air or leaping over a 9-foot wall to freedom. Is a rider on a horse galloping through a meadow a stunt? It is when the meadow is full of gopher holes and it's a challenge just to stay in the saddle. Only an expert can make that look easy. These represent actual stunts in movies, carefully planned and performed by stuntwomen with the skills required to achieve great moments on film.

Are stunts important? They are more than that. They are fundamental to the mystery, excitement, and thrills provided by action movies, and stuntwomen help create that experience. John Steinbeck once wrote that entertainment is one of the major endeavors of life. "That's the business of Hollywood," a friend of mine (a vice president of business affairs at Warner Bros.) added. "We work here to bring delight. We're the delight makers, and humans have a need for it. It's not as stringent as our need for food, but it's an absolutely necessary part of life. It's the roses of the bread and roses."

So, in that vein, I believe the story of stuntwomen is central to the magic of the movies. Their firsthand accounts of trials, victories, determination, and excellence are an indispensable part of the history of entertainment, just as their successes against the odds are part of the history of women. Stuntwomen *are* the roses.

# Introduction

# Opening Shots

For the first fifty years of movies, stunt performers secretly doubled the stars in action movies. In the late 1960s they began to come out of the shadows and receive credit for their work, but many more years passed before stunt players were deemed eligible for industry awards.[1] Their status changed in May 2001 when billionaire Dietrich Mateschitz, CEO of the company that makes Red Bull energy drink, came up with the idea to honor stunt performers and funded the Taurus World Stunt Awards. "He also wanted to create a foundation for injured stunt people," said Jeannie Epper, who had been doing stunts since she was a child. "That's what hooked me. I agreed to serve on the board."

The categories of the Taurus World Stunt Awards included best coordinator, best fire work, best specialty stunt, best high work, and best overall stunt, but each year, men won most of the awards. Most women were still denied access to positions of power such as stunt coordinator and second-unit director. That incensed stuntwomen, including Epper, who understood their outrage. "But being on the board," she said, "I knew we had to strike at the right time." That time finally came in May 2007 when sixty-six-year-old Epper, a five-foot-eight-inch blonde, became the first woman to win the Taurus World Stunt Lifetime Achievement Award. The live outdoor show, staged on the Paramount lot, was surrounded by tall movie sets designed for stunts—running, falling, jumping, rappelling. Jeannie was introduced as "the mother of all stuntwomen, a groundbreaker, a legend, and 'our Wonder Woman'"—a role she had doubled for years. Film clips showed her in action: riding, slugging it out, being clobbered with a bar stool. In a shot of her as Wonder Woman, she seemed to leap from the ground to the nose of a plane—her back straight, arms up, right leg raised in a graceful arabesque. In fact, it was a perfectly executed backward high fall; the footage had been reversed in editing. As the clips played, Jeannie,

1

in voice-over, said that, as a woman, she had felt "a lot of opposition, but my dad told me if you commit and do your homework you will make it in this business." The lights went up, and from both wings of the stage a procession of gowned, stately women emerged until there were almost a hundred of them. Respected stuntwoman Debbie Evans stepped out and handed Jeannie the glistening twenty-six-pound, thirty-one-inch Taurus statuette. "I've always been proud to be a stuntwoman," Jeannie told the audience, "but never more than right now." After trying to juggle the award and her notes, she turned to Debbie and said, "Here, take this thing. My Wonder Woman days are kind of over." Evans, a motorcycle champ who'd been teased in school for her muscle-bound arms, hefted the award in one hand as if it weighed next to nothing.

Many different kinds of stuntwoman were there that night, including Julie Ann Johnson, an impatient firebrand who was not onstage with the other women; she was applauding in the audience. Both Jeannie and Julie had performed in hit TV action shows in the 1970s, and Julie had been one of the first women to serve as stunt coordinator of a major TV show. Both women were raised in Southern California, and both their dads had encouraged their athletic abilities. As kids, they were a handful: Jeannie jumped from trees to bulldog her sister—knocking her off her horse. Julie leaped from the garage roof and broke her wrists. They had a lot in common, but they were quite different, too. An only child of divorced parents, Julie lived with her mother and stepfather, who never turned down a cocktail. Jeannie grew up with five brothers and sisters in a close-knit stunt family. Julie knew nothing about stunts and had no support system, but she excelled in many sports. Thanks to one of those skills, she aced her first stunt. Could she leap over an ironing board? Easy—she'd been a long-jump champ in high school.

Julie's career started when she doubled Doris Day in *Caprice* (1966). The production manager said, "You'll be hanging from a rope ladder with a stuntman about forty feet in the air." At the location, Mammoth Mountain, stuntman Freddy Waugh assured her the stunt would be "a piece of cake." Wardrobe outfitted her in ski attire and boots, and she was taken to a snowy area where the rotor blades of a hovering helicopter beat at the stiff wind. The sliding door of the helicopter had been lashed open; a rope ladder bolted to the cabin wall trailed from it, flapping against the struts. An assistant director yelled, "The copter will come down, you'll get on the ladder, and the copter will go up to about 400 feet."

"Four *hundred*? I was told forty!"

"Nah!" he shouted. "Those office guys don't know."

This was Julie's welcome to the world of stunts, where the players quickly learn to expect the unexpected.

Freddy hooked a leg on one rung of the ladder, then attached himself to it with a spring-loaded carabiner lock. He reached for Julie, who flung a leg through the lowest rung and grabbed the ladder's side rail. Someone fastened a pair of skis to her boots. "We'll go up about twenty feet," Freddy said. He was cabled to the ladder; Julie was not. "He better hold on to me," she muttered. When her boots and skis left the ground, the sudden weight pulled at her, and she gripped the ladder. They swiftly rose to 100 feet. The draft of the helicopter rocked the ladder, and Julie felt herself slipping. "I can't hold on!" Freddy shouted at the pilot. "Down! Down!" But the pilot couldn't hear him. Finally, they were back on the ground, and a special effects guy rushed out. "I can't hold her," Freddy said. "Hook her up." When it was done, she straddled the bottom rung, Freddy put his arm around her, the camera rolled, and the helicopter lifted off again. Tied by cables, they both felt more secure as the copter swooped up and down and circled 400 feet over the mountain. Back on the ground, a relieved Julie flopped flat on her back in the snow. But if they had to go again, she'd jump at the chance. She was exhilarated.

Forty years later, at the 2007 Taurus World Stunt Awards, Julie congratulated Jeannie. Over the years, the two had had their differences, but their friendship endured. "I was so happy for Jeannie the night she won, happy for all of us," Julie said. "We'd really gone a distance since we did *Wonder Woman* and *Charlie's Angels*. We did more than just survive. I hope stuntwomen today will preserve the power we acquired for them, and pass it on."

Quietly, and mostly unrecognized, American stuntwomen have been passing it on for a century—since silent movies began. Back then, women were considered too delicate to survive the hazards of the voting booth, but in the movies they dodged speeding cars and dived eighty feet off bridges. Those images were inspiring. They gave women ideas and opened up possibilities. Decades passed, and their early exploits were overlooked and forgotten, but the uncommon courage of these stunt pioneers established an essential place in movies for daring women with exceptional physical skills. How had that come about? That amazing story began only because actresses wanted to be in motion pictures.

# I

# The First Stuntwomen

## *1910–1960*

# 1

# The Rise and Fall of Female Stunt Players in Silent Movies

I used to shoot at her feet with real bullets. Didn't bother her none.

—*George Marshall*

Helen Gibson's strong, handsome face and dark hair gave her the look of someone who would try anything. In 1915, while in her early twenties, she was doubling for the star of the hit serial *The Hazards of Helen*. In one stunt she was supposed to leap from the roof of the station to the top of a moving train. Years later, she called it her most dangerous stunt. "The distance between the station and the train was accurately measured," she said, and she had practiced the jump several times while the train was standing still. But for the shot, the train would be picking up speed for about a quarter of a mile. "I was not nervous as it approached and I leaped without hesitation," she recalled. She landed safely, but the rocking motion of the train rolled her straight toward the end of the car. Just before being pitched off, "I caught hold of an air vent and hung on." Then, with a sense of the dramatic, Gibson let her body "dangle over the edge to increase the effect on the screen."[1] She brought the same strength and flair to scores of other action scenes.

Silent movie actresses like Helen Gibson were the first stuntwomen. They were actresses who could ride horses, drive cars, and do high dives. From about 1910 to the early 1920s, they proved that the "weaker sex" could perform surprising physical feats. During that time, the overlapping

7

Helen Gibson in *The Hazards of Helen* (1916), episode 59, "A Boy at the Throttle." (Courtesy of the Margaret Herrick Library, Academy of Motion Picture Arts and Sciences)

advent of movies, automobiles, and airplanes, as well as the possibility of women's suffrage, set in motion a major cultural transformation in America and around the world. For women who, up to this time, had been restrained by limited opportunities, these brief, innovative, exuberant years must have felt liberating.

When motion pictures were created in the 1890s, the movie trade improvised an identity as it went along. The "flickers" were considered trashy amusements, no more respectable than the Jewish entrepreneurs who set up storefront nickelodeons (named for the five-cent price of admission) or the immigrants and urban poor—mostly women and children—who made up the audience. But movies were cheap, entertaining, and exciting. Nickelodeons spread through working-class neighborhoods, where they became ideal places to take the kids, meet friends, and escape life's grimmer realities. It wasn't long before movies became a very profitable business and an influential social phenomenon.

Before they worked in movies, many stuntmen had been boxers, carnival performers, cowboys, or soldiers. Their female counterparts were actresses, dancers, and singers, but most of them had no training or experience in physically demanding performance skills. At this time, Victorian constraints still dictated women's behavior, morals, and aspirations. To "proper" society, actresses were hardly better than prostitutes. And except for women who performed tough work on ranches and farms, feats of strength were generally not associated with women. If they had been, mothers of such "mannish" daughters would have felt shame and fear that the marriage market for their daughters would dry up. Science had declared women mentally and physically weaker; they had few financial rights, were excluded from significant education (it was considered a waste) and from most professions, and were denied even the basic right to vote. "When Woodrow Wilson was inaugurated president in 1913," journalist Eleanor Clift wrote, "a married woman was considered the property of her husband. Women couldn't serve on juries, or in the event of divorce gain custody of their children."[2] "Proper" women were discouraged from appearing on the street without a chaperone, but of course, no one escorted the women who worked day after day in factories and shops. Escorted or not, they went to the movies to be entertained and inspired. The onscreen adventures of the female characters, particularly in "chapter plays" or serials, were propaganda of the first order. Imagine the impact on the women sitting in those cramped storefront theaters, watching brave girls named Grace or Pearl fight the odds, week after week, and succeed.

Early on, movies became a force for social change because they reflected the concerns and interests of their largely female audiences. Besides love stories, dramas, and action serials, moviegoers watched films promoting the vote for women, such as the popular *What 80 Million Women Want* (1913).[3] Since 1848, the movement for women's suffrage had been found, lost, and found again. As many actresses and future movie stars made their first films in 1910, the state of Washington voted for female suffrage, joining Wyoming, Utah, Colorado, and Idaho. Clift called it a watershed year, noting that Washington State "paved the way for California in 1911, Oregon, Arizona and Kansas in 1912."[4] At the same time, America was on the move, and more and more Americans were taking the wheels of new, affordable automobiles—and that meant women, too. Debate raged about women's "fitness" to drive, with some trying to connect it to their inability to master the technicalities of the ballot. Despite this, cars gave women mobility and independence and opened up the possibility of radically different lives.[5] All this was encouraged by the action captured on movie screens.

Racing, crashing, and overturning cars became essential to movie production, and major stars like petite Mary Pickford set the pace. Who wouldn't be impressed by "America's Sweetheart" leaning into a curve as she hit fifty miles an hour or Helen Gibson hunched over on her speeding motorcycle? A surprising number of silent movie actresses were fully engaged in the action. Historian William Drew described the stars' close relationship to cars, down to the models they preferred and how fast they drove. "After all," he noted, "it was the actresses, not the actors, who were shattering Victorian ideals of gender roles through their yen for driving fast cars. Indeed, driving became a virtual prerequisite for actresses in action-filled films produced when car chases in those pre–back projection days could not be faked in a studio."[6]

Actress Helen Holmes wanted to race cars competitively, but that career wasn't open to women. So she took her motoring skills to movie star Mabel Normand and comedy producer Mack Sennett at their Keystone Company in Edendale, California, near Hollywood.[7] There, she was welcomed with open arms. The filmmaking mayhem at Keystone was good training for Helen's later stunts, including driving her car at top speed off a dock at San Pedro harbor and making a thirty-foot jump onto a barge for an episode of *The Railroad Raiders*. Fearless, she succeeded on the fourth try, and the press hailed the stunt as a "hair-raising ride."[8] Helen's driving skills would become part of all her serials.

Despite Holmes's daring, women's contributions to silent movies were largely unappreciated and ignored for decades. Then, film historian Anthony Slide's archival research rescued women from oblivion and completely altered our understanding of their influence on the movies.[9] For instance, the movie industry hired many people excluded by other businesses, such as women, immigrants, and Jews. In the burgeoning film studios, women's jobs ranged from the bottom of the ladder to the top—plaster molders, set designers, film editors, writers, directors, even producers and production executives. "The simple fact that all the major serial stars of the silent era were female demonstrates the prominence of women at this time," Slide wrote, "as opposed to the sound period when serial stars were men, and women were reduced to simpering and generally incompetent supporting roles." Before sound, "of the 500 top silent screen performers,

Helen Holmes ready to roll in episode 9, "A Leap for Life," *The Railroad Raiders* (1917). (Courtesy of the Robert S. Birchard Collection)

including both stars and below-the-title leading players, some 287 were women."[10]

Another forgotten pioneer was Nell Shipman.[11] She was "a remarkable woman" who became "a dramatic actress, scriptwriter, novelist, and film director."[12] Shipman sold the rights to her book *Under the Crescent* to Universal in 1915, wrote the screenplay, and kicked off her career. Two years later, she wrote and starred in the successful *Back to God's Country* (1917). She was the first to shoot her films entirely on location in the wilderness (including the wildlife there), and her resourceful heroines often rescued the men in her films.

At a time when few actors owned production companies, a number of women began to form them. Some men helped finance these companies, but to a great extent, silent movie stardom was the realm of women. According to Slide, more than twenty female stars formed and controlled their own independent production companies from 1912 to 1920. In addition to serial stars, they included preeminent directors such as Alice Guy

Lobby card for *The Girl and the Game* (1915), written and produced by Helen Holmes and her partner J. P. McGowan. (Courtesy of the Robert S. Birchard Collection)

Blaché, who developed the narrative film in the 1890s and was the first to set up her own production company in 1910, and Lois Weber, who formed her company in 1917 and was as famous in her time as D. W. Griffith. "Power was in the name, and the name was woman," Slide concluded.[13]

American movie production was centered mostly in the East, around New York, until a few producers fled to Southern California in 1910. There, they found "every variety of natural scenery from the Sahara Desert to the Khyber Pass"—mountains, deserts, ocean beaches—and constant sunshine. Bustling Los Angeles, a religious and conservative little town, offered a supply of cheap labor as the "nation's leading open-shop nonunion city."[14] The rural suburb of Hollywood had acres of inexpensive land, and it wasn't long before the movies moved in. The locals viewed outsiders with suspicion, and they saw actors as undesirables with no moral compass. Soon, film production had turned Los Angeles into one big movie set, with horses, cars, and wagons careening up and down the once-quiet streets. Citizens complained loudly, but by the end of World War I, West Coast moviemakers were cranking out 80 percent of the world's movies, and *Hollywood* became synonymous with the art and business of motion pictures.[15] A famous English critic, H. Sheridan Bickers, described the spectacle: "An attack in the street, a fracas with a policeman outside a saloon, the hurried moving of traffic to make way for a fire-alarm with an engine-load of wildly gesticulating souls in torment and uniform—all mean 'merely the movies. . . . ' America's great Carnival City on the Pacific is full of thrill-ums and 'fil-ums.' . . . The camera will get you in his grind somehow—somewhere—sometime."[16]

Across the country, in tiny towns and big cities, thousands of adventurous young women sat in darkened theaters, yearning to join the action onscreen, but "if Venus rose from the sea again tomorrow right outside the casting director's window he wouldn't give her anything but an extra part in a production," Frances Denton wrote for *Photoplay*. "Getting into the movies nowadays . . . isn't much different from getting into a laundry. You go and apply for work. If you look like you can deliver, you get a chance to prove it—nothing more." To make it in the movies (or "to movie," as it was called), a would-be actress had to ride, swim, and dance; supply her own wardrobe and makeup; drive a car, preferably recklessly; and do any fool thing asked of her—such as leaping out a third-story window and praying the guys holding the rug below would catch her. The pay, Denton reported, was $7.50 to $15 a day.[17] Women lined up outside Hollywood casting offices, dreaming of wealth and fame. But as former vaudeville child star Esther Ralston found out, the movie factory wasn't all sunglasses and swimming pools. The application form asked the usual questions: Can you ride, swim, dance? Do you own a tuxedo? To each she wrote "no" until another girl told her, "You'll never get anywhere in pictures saying no." Ralston couldn't swim and "had never seen a horse, but she answered yes, yes, yes, and found herself on horseback, hanging on to the animal by his mane and her teeth."[18]

Performing in silent films could be as dangerous as it was glamorous. The movies were turned out fast, and there were no safety guidelines. Stunts were experiments in action—someone thought up a car crash and had no idea if it would work until someone else actually tried it. The hazards were real. Film historian Kevin Brownlow described it best: "Stunting in the silent days meant walking on tigers' tails. It was an occupation with few veterans."[19] For example, in 1916 actress Mary MacLaren appeared in a film for Universal that required her "to drive an automobile backward down an incline at the rate of twenty-five miles an hour, which she did, losing control and going over an embankment." MacLaren sued the studio and named her mother as a codefendant, seeking "to break a contract that forced her to undertake dangerous stunts while placing her salary under her mother's control."[20]

In *What Happened to Mary,* serial star Mary Fuller did a scene that was "so absurd . . . nobody should have bothered to chance her life on it." Mary was playing a mermaid, so her legs were encased in a tail. She was posed on a rock jutting out from shore, thirty feet above the pounding surf, with a bunch of lilies on her chest when she noticed that the tide was coming in fast. "I called out in alarm to my director and cameraman," she recalled, but they were some distance behind her. "The cameraman was fascinated with the picture and continued to turn the cranks," Mary said. Her heavy mermaid tail made it impossible for her to get up and run. Spray, then waves, washed over her and swept away the lilies. "I began to move but not towards the shore. My direction was out to sea. I was gasping with fear." At the last minute, the men looked up from their artistic preoccupations, fished her out, and carried her back to shore. The sea took the camera.[21]

A report on injuries among thirty-seven movie companies from 1918 to 1919 stated, "Temporary injuries amounted to 1,052. Permanent ones totaled eighteen. There were three fatal injuries." The report called this "a surprisingly low rate of accidents, considering the risk." But more than a thousand injuries a year does not reflect a safe or trouble-free profession.[22] The industry's attitude was exemplified by Pathé (dubbed "The House of the Serials"), where Louis Gasnier advised his writers, "Put the girl in danger."[23] They fulfilled that mission with vigor.

Serials had two main formats: the cliffhanger or holdover, which ended at a pivotal moment in the action—a ploy designed to woo the audience back to the theater every week—and the chapter serial, each installment of which was a complete story that could be shown in any order. The weekly serials delivered rivers of cheap thrills. Though wildly popular and profitable, they were low-budget factory-line products with little prestige in a studio's production lineup. Most of the leading serials of this period starred women: *The Adventures of Kathlyn, The Hazards of Helen, The Perils of Pauline, The Red Circle,* and *The Purple Mask.* Their gutsy heroines dodged danger every week, and whether they escaped traps set for themselves or saved others in peril, their actions redefined what women could do. They did the "gags"—vaudeville slang for "stunts"—and the term came to be associated with risk, action, and promotion.

Long before there were movies, newspapers described clowning around on a ship as a stunt.[24] In the 1880s the term "stunt girls" was applied to women engaged in sensational journalism.[25] Referring to a literary promotion, author Samuel Butler explained in an 1878 letter, "It was a stunt for advertising the books."[26] The movie studios' first foray into mass-market cross-promotion was itself a stunt to emphasize the serial's risk- and action-filled story and promote it with breathless advertising and over-the-top marketing schemes.[27] Most serials appeared both onscreen and in newspaper installments, a potent promotional campaign that began with the Edison Company's *What Happened to Mary* (1912). The weekly serial played in theaters, and McClure Publishing issued "chapters" of it in *Ladies World* magazine. Author Shelley Stamp described the vigorous interlocking marketing maneuvers: "Newspapers reached 'a class of people who are interested in the pictures,'" and magazines encouraged "movie fans to read newspaper installments, then see it at the theatre."[28] This turned out to be a successful scheme that made unknown actresses into stars.

Another early marketing device was to fuse serial star and story, giving the lead character the actress's real name to encourage the audience to believe in her adventures. Of course, the star didn't chase bandits in real life, but this contrivance revealed the first canon of moviemaking—forget reality; fire up profits. The success of *What Happened to Mary* and its sequel *Who Will Marry Mary?* spurred "Colonel" William N. Selig to produce *The Adventures of Kathlyn* (1913). His company, Selig Polyscope, was based in Chicago, but the new serial was produced at his Los Angeles studio. As the onscreen episodes were released, the *Chicago Tribune* issued print installments. The LA studio became known as the "Selig zoo" because of the wild animals he kept caged there. They added exotic drama to his films, and Selig made money renting them to other producers.

Serial star Kathlyn Williams had worked at Biograph for D. W. Griffith before moving to Selig's studio in 1910. She played dozens of roles, including Cherry in the first movie version of *The Spoilers*.[29] Williams was described as a "golden-haired" beauty, genteel, dignified, and "fearless"—a fascinating combination that was perfect for her frequent tussles with beasts from Selig's zoo. When she wasn't facing down tigers, Kathlyn wrote and directed movies of her own, proudly stating, "Women can direct just as well as men," and they "often had a keener artistic sense and more of an eye for detail."[30]

Most of the early movie stars—Kathlyn Williams, Mary Fuller, Pearl White, Ruth Roland, Grace Cunard, Ann Little, Helen Holmes—had been on the stage or with theatrical companies before circumstances forced them to take movie work—considered a big step down for stage performers. Some, like Ruth Roland, grew up in middle-class families; others, like Pearl White, escaped cruel childhoods for the uneven rewards of stock companies. They were skilled riders, swimmers, or acrobats who were willing to do almost anything. Some had good business sense and invested their money (Roland); others spent it (Gibson). All suffered injuries that affected some of them for years and may have shortened their lives (White and Roland).[31]

In their prime, these serial queens belonged to a special society: they were brave, they performed stunts, and they were wizards behind the wheel of a car. Grace Cunard fit right into the club.[32] She was a force—she drove like a maniac. "No speed is great enough to please me," she declared.[33] Although Pathé Studios was the leading purveyor of the serial genre, Universal avidly competed for gold with its own stable of athletic overachievers. One example was the partnership of Grace and writer-director Francis Ford, the older brother of director John Ford.[34] Universal contracted them to cowrite *Lucille Love, Girl of Mystery* (1914), which expanded into the studio's first serial and starred Grace and Francis. Grace

Grace Cunard in *The Purple Mask* (1916). (Courtesy of the Robert S. Birchard Collection)

wrote the scripts for many films and eleven serials, and the partners took turns directing.

The period from 1914 to 1918 was the zenith of serials starring women, but Pearl White, Ruth Roland, and Ann Little kept turning them out long

A tense but calm Pearl White in *The Black Secret* (1919), with Walter McGrail. (Courtesy of the Robert S. Birchard Collection)

after the vogue had crested. Pearl was known for her bravado, generosity, and good humor, despite a rough childhood in Springfield, Missouri. She began acting at age sixteen with a resident stock company in her hometown. From 1907 to 1910 Pearl traveled with a road company and appeared anonymously in films for the Powers Company.[35] About seventy films later, she began her famous work at Pathé, starring in *The Perils of Pauline*

Ruth Roland and her horse in the serial *Ruth of the Range* (1923). (Courtesy of the Robert S. Birchard Collection)

(1914). Sequels and other serials followed.[36] Aided by Pathé's exciting story lines, its ceaseless publicity machine, tie-ins with newspapers, and her own determination, Pearl's fame and salary soared. Ironically, as soon as actresses became well-paid stars, the studios hired men in wigs to double them, cutting them out of most of the stunt work that had made them special.[37]

Ruth Roland doing an aerial stunt. (Courtesy of the Robert S. Birchard Collection)

Ruth Roland rivaled Pearl White's popularity. She was dubbed "one of the nerviest girls in pictures."[38] George Marshall (*Destry Rides Again*) directed two of the serials produced by her company. Marshall said, "She did everything herself. I remember I used to shoot at her feet with real bullets. Didn't bother her none. Sometimes I wonder what would happen today if actresses had to do what Ruth did."[39] After headlining in vaudeville, Ruth switched to movies in 1908; later, thanks to her riding skills, she was cast in westerns, but her career took off in the serial drama *The Red Circle* (1915). She starred in eleven serials and produced six of them.[40]

Like everyone else in the serial queen club, Helen Holmes was an ardent driver of fast cars before starring in the Kalem Company's first serial, *The Hazards of Helen*.[41] *Hazards* retained the chapter format, serving up a complete story every week for a record-setting 119 episodes from 1914 to 1917. Trains were integral to the story line, and Helen, a telegraph operator, was at the center of the action. In the first episode she almost didn't get the job "because women lose their heads" in emergencies. But one man spoke up for her, and she was hired. For scores of episodes, Helen took on bandits, saved people in need, and never lost her head.

Helen Holmes jumps onto a train in "The Midnight Limited," an episode of *The Hazards of Helen* (1914). (Courtesy of the Margaret Herrick Library, Academy of Motion Picture Arts and Sciences)

Occasionally a handsome man rescued her, but usually the writers found some ingenious way for Helen to take action against the evil forces they'd dreamed up.

Although Holmes did many of her own stunts, Edward Sutherland or Gene Perkins sometimes doubled her, as did Helen Gibson, one of the first women (if not *the* first) to double a female action star.[42] Gibson (born Rose Wenger) was one of five daughters, and her father encouraged her to be a tomboy. In 1909 she and a friend went to a Wild West show. "Enraptured," they asked how they could get jobs on the show, which certainly seemed more appealing than their work in a cigar factory. They were told the Miller Brothers' 101 Ranch in Ponca City, Oklahoma, "wanted girls who were willing to learn to ride horses." Gibson made the cut, and in 1910, at age eighteen, she not only learned to ride a horse but also mastered the trick of "picking up a handkerchief from the ground" at a full gallop. When veteran riders warned her that she might get kicked in

Helen Gibson, ready to ride. (Courtesy of the Robert S. Birchard Collection)

the head, she didn't believe it would happen to her—a confidence stunt-women have shared for decades.[43]

Rodeos ran from spring to fall, and the Miller Brothers' Wild West Show ended its 1911 season in Venice, California. This allowed its riders to work in the movies during the sunny Southern California winter.[44] That was how many riders got their start in the movies, including Tom Mix and Will Rogers. The Kalem Company hired Helen Gibson in 1912 to appear in one-reelers such as the memorably titled *Ranch Girls on the Rampage*. She earned $15 a week—"a big salary for a beginner." She also rode in the Los Angeles rodeos, which is where she met future cowboy star Hoot Gibson.[45] They didn't consider marriage until they were performing in the Pendleton rodeo and needed to find overnight accommodations. Married couples were given preference when it came to hotel rooms, so, Helen recalled, "we decided to get married."[46]

Back in Los Angeles, Hoot doubled Tom Mix at the Selig studio, and Helen (still known as Rose at the time) began to double Helen Holmes in *The Hazards of Helen*. When Holmes retired after forty-eight chapters, Gibson replaced her, and the studio made her change her name to Helen. After the longest-running serial ended in 1917, Universal offered Gibson a

Theater marquee for *The Wolverine* (1921), one of Helen Gibson's last starring roles. (Courtesy of the Margaret Herrick Library, Academy of Motion Picture Arts and Sciences)

three-year contract at $125 a week to appear in two- and five-reel pictures. By the time she formed her own production company, the business was changing. Prospects for women were dwindling as men recognized the profits to be made in the once underestimated movie business. Helen ran out of money before completing her first film, *No Man's Woman* (1921); she obtained loans to finish it and then went bankrupt.

Hoot was at the top of his career, but the marriage had ended, Helen said, and he avoided her. She scrambled to find jobs in a Wild West show, with the Keith vaudeville circuit, and in movies. She took "anything I could get, character parts and extra work." Stunts saved her when she began to double stars such as Marie Dressler, Marjorie Main, and Ethel Barrymore. She worked for the next thirty years, securing her reputation as a stuntwoman. As she said, "Screen acting was often a matter of guts." She certainly proved that.

Today's stuntwomen are the direct descendants of these silent movie actresses. In the glory years before the 1920s, their action roles in early movies—put in motion by automobiles and powered by demands for suffrage—changed the image and direction of women. Winning the vote in 1920 capped the brief period in which women dominated the film industry.[47] Movies gained more respect in the 1920s as the onscreen stories and the audiences changed. After 1927, talking pictures increased production costs and profits until motion picture production was the fifth largest industry in the United States. The rash, risky exuberance of the silent era had vanished. And in many ways, so did the opportunities for women at all levels of production. For those who survived the 1920s, the 1930s would be even harder. But the story of stuntwomen was just beginning, and like the plot of a great movie, it had everything: humiliation, injustice, injury, death, determination, courage, excitement, and, finally, hard-fought success.

# 2

# Blackface and Wigs

## Men Take over Stunts

In the fifteen years I worked in films, I never heard of a
stuntwoman. The men wore wigs and women's clothes.
—*Jewell Jordan*

An enterprising *Los Angeles Times* reporter went around town in 1935 asking, "Are women braver than men?" He hit pay dirt when he asked director Eddie Cline, who had started in 1913 with Mack Sennett's Keystone Company. Cline knew what women could do. "They didn't have to be asked twice to leap from 40-foot masts on ships or from bridges 60 feet above the water," he said. "Those ladies had courage. . . . And they did all this not for glory but for $3 a day." Lack of bravery was not the reason why so few "girl stunt players" worked in Hollywood. As Cline observed, "So many stunt men of small stature can double perfectly for feminine stars that we simply don't need women in stunts."[1]

The exit of women from many levels of the motion picture business began in the 1920s, as "the big tent of the institutionalized circus"—the movies—became the most prominent industry in Los Angeles. Metro Goldwyn Mayer (MGM) billed itself as "a city within a city." To the savvy author Carey McWilliams, a studio was more like "a beehive or a community."[2] By 1925, MGM's beehive consisted of forty-five buildings and seventy-four stages on forty-three acres in Culver City. In a short promotional film, the studio boasted that it hired 100,000 extras a year, offered 200 dressing rooms, and operated a restaurant on the lot that served 2,000 meals a day. Its laboratory developed and printed 40 million feet of film a year—enough celluloid to stretch across the nation three times.[3] MGM had organized all aspects of movie production into departments—publicity, story, wardrobe, camera, sets, props. Most of the department heads and all the directors were men. According to film historian Anthony Slide, departmentalizing the work may have slowly stripped women of their positions by making it harder for editors or writers to move into directing and producing. Slide does not believe that sound, which arrived in 1927, shut women out. "It cost more to make films and producers were unwilling to take risks with female filmmakers."[4]

In society and in the film industry, the attitude toward women had shifted. As a result, onscreen stories and actresses' roles in them changed. These were lean times for stuntwomen; their positions were precarious, they earned less money, and the stunts deemed suitable for them to do were often silly.[5] From the 1920s on, the central distinction was this: action women were *not* stars; they *doubled* stars.[6] One writer of that time got it right: "Insurance companies issue no risks on their lives; their employment is irregular and uncertain, yet without them motion pictures would be like a country band with the brass and drummer missing."[7] Although men performed most stunts, a few daredevil girls slipped through. The best of them were champion swimmers or riders; most have been forgotten, but they were the "fearless girls" who built the bridge between the action-actresses in silent movies and the stuntwomen of later decades.[8]

"Queen of the Hollywood doubles" is what acclaimed journalist Adela Rogers St. Johns called ninety-pound, five-foot-tall Winnie Brown. Winnie was "the best stunt rider and broncobuster and horse wrangler ever to wear chaps. The idol of real cowboys." She leaped from the ninth story of a burning building and "rode a whirling, threatening jam of logs."[9] She did 100-foot falls over cliffs on horseback, for $5 a fall. "If you fall limber, you can't get hurt," she told a reporter for *Picture Play*; what she probably meant was, "Don't tense up to do a stunt."[10]

Before her colorful movie career, Winnie broke mounts for the U.S. Army and was the only female member of the Mexican Border Patrol. At Universal she played Indian girls riding bareback, but she couldn't make a living doing that, so she fell back on her other talent—dancing. According to a 1925 article, "She joined a dance academy as the paid partner of one and all, and for five hours a night after riding all day she danced." In the 1920s drugstore cowboys were ubiquitous in Hollywood, and Winnie disdainfully described them as "short on horses and long on bull."[11] Great

John Ford's "Wild Bunch." Winnie Brown is in the first row, third from left. Next to her is western star Harry Carey; Carey's wife, Olive Fuller Golden; and Jane Bernoudy, champion horsewoman. (Courtesy of the Kevin Brownlow Collection)

western riders and actors were part of John Ford's "Wild Bunch" at Universal, and so was Winnie.[12]

Even though stuntwomen didn't get much work, a few stood out. A Universal casting director proclaimed that swimming champion Janet Ford "did things a man would not attempt." Another, eighteen-year-old Loretta Rush, dived from the roof of a house into a blazing tank of water laced with gasoline. "The edges of the tank had been camouflaged to represent the banks of a stream"; a submerged partition divided the tank in half, and the gasoline had been poured into one side. Once Loretta was "into the blazing fuel, her body passed down into the cool water, under the partition, and up on the other side."[13] High-diver Mary Wiggins was cheered as the "best all-round performer, a real daredevil—she crashes cars and motorcycles, flies and stunts her own plane, she's a tumbler and a parachute jumper." An appealing brunette with a confident air, Wiggins came to Hollywood at age seventeen. Her feats included diving eighty-six feet from the Ocean Park pier, and if that wasn't enough, she was tied up in a mail sack and thrown into a swimming pool.[14]

These women, born in the early 1900s, would have seen the serials starring women, but there are few records of what they knew or felt. Maybe their limited opportunities as athletes and stuntwomen seemed normal to them. What they were up against is exemplified in a little 1933 film, *Lucky Devils,* which reflected the attitudes of the 1930s and the kinds of roles women were offered. *Lucky Devils,* a cinematic ode to stuntmen, starred Bill Boyd two years before he achieved fame as Hopalong Cassidy. It was produced by RKO, whose reputation was far less refined than that of MGM. David O. Selznick (who made *Gone with the Wind* seven years later) was stuck supervising forty pictures a year at RKO, most of them budgeted at $200,000 to $375,000. *Lucky Devils* was on the low end of that scale. One year into his job, drowning in the "gorilla film" *King Kong,* Selznick escaped to MGM on February 2, 1933, the day before *Lucky Devils* was released.[15]

The film starts with a bank robbery—men crash through windows, swing from chandeliers, fire guns, and terrorize customers.[16] One robber manhandles a switchboard operator, shoving her to the top of a staircase, where he punches her. The battered woman rolls down a dozen stairs and lands hard at the bottom. "Cut!" A young woman on the set rushes to the actress lying at the foot of the stairs. "I didn't know girls could do such dangerous things!" the fan pants. "Will you sign my autograph book?"

"Sure, honey, with love and kisses." The "stuntwoman" grabs the girl, kisses her, and rips off his curly blonde wig.

"You're a man!" she gasps.

"A *stunt* man! I double for the leading lady!"

A man performed that stair fall, even though a number of women could have done it. For instance, Crete Sipple tumbled down a flight of eighty stairs in *The Wanters* (1923), and Aline Goodwin performed Scarlett's big fall in *Gone with the Wind.* But in casting and in story lines, movies projected the proper place for both women and minorities, onscreen and off. Producers and directors hired white actors and stunt-men for almost every job, including roles that could have gone to African American actors, who had worked in movies since *Uncle Tom's Cabin* in 1903.[17] In *Lucky Devils,* a black actor could have played Al, an aspiring stuntman with a monumental stutter, but actor Roscoe Ates was "painted down" with black makeup on his face and hands. White actors in blackface were so common that even Shirley Temple was painted down in *The Littlest Rebel* (1935). Like everyone else, African Americans were influenced by the movies, but the message in films "perpetuated the vision whites had of blacks" and condoned outright "racial bias by retaining a tradition of demeaning blacks."[18] Painting down and men doubling for women were not denounced by members of the Screen Actors Guild until the late 1960s. Both practices continued into the 2000s.

In *Lucky Devils,* the stuntmen gather at their favorite bar and grill. The character Slugger (William Bakewell) is about to be married, but Skipper (Bill Boyd) says marriage and stunts don't mix; married stuntmen worry about their wives instead of their hazardous work, so to stuntmen, "women are poison." In separate incidents, as both men are about to do difficult stunts, their wives "lose their heads" and show up on the set, wailing and carrying on. As a result, the men's stunts go wrong and people are injured. Women are weak and emotional, the film seems to argue. Though made before the Motion Picture Production Code delivered "morals" to movies in July 1934, the female roles in *Lucky Devils* do not resemble the dominant dames in other pre-Code movies such as *Torch Singer, Frisco Jenny, Baby Face, Blood Money,* and *Blondie Johnson.*[19] These independent female characters went after what they wanted, whether that was high-level corporate work, a bank heist, an affair, or an abortion. Administered by Will "Deacon" Hays, a former postmaster general, the Code shut down controversial topics and ushered in studio-controlled censorship. The movies' "circus-carnival atmosphere completely vanished."[20]

The first decade of talking pictures hummed with pivotal changes and opposing contests: pre-Code versus post-Code; New Deal social programs; the growing influence of labor unions versus the increased power of movie studios; and studios' huge profits in the midst of the grinding Depression. One historic change was already in play: motion picture workers became part of the American labor movement. At first, the studios controlled everything from talent to exhibition. Actors took whatever roles were assigned to them, whether they boosted or undermined their careers, and their fees were not negotiable. There were no rules for how long actors, directors, or crews worked each day and few safety regulations. Then, in 1933, five men and one woman risked their careers to form the Screen Actors Guild (SAG) to represent actors and stunt players who appeared in front of the camera.[21]

"Hollywood tycoons had the notion that the industry was theirs to rule as they saw fit," Carey McWilliams wrote. "Resourceful strategists, they fought the unionization of the industry by every trick and stratagem known to American employers."[22] But the rebel guilds took them on. When thousands of stars and contract players voted to strike on May 9, 1937, Louis B. Mayer of MGM and Joseph Schenck of 20th Century–Fox recognized SAG as the collective-bargaining representative for actors. The basic contract set the crucial minimum wage—the "scale" performers would earn—plus overtime and stunt pay; the number of hours performers could work; wardrobe allowances; and required meal breaks. The SAG minimum daily rate was $25 for actors, $35 for stunt players, and $5.50 for extras.

The first SAG office on Cherokee Avenue in Hollywood was across the hall from the newly minted Screen Writers Guild (later the Writers Guild of America).[23] Stuntman Gil Perkins cheerfully recalled that for weeks, the line of people waiting to join the guild stretched from the door of the building and down the street, "like you were going to a great movie."[24] Stuntwoman Loretta Rush became member number 3766 on October 13, 1934, two years before SAG was fully recognized.[25]

Now known formally as SAG-AFTRA (Screen Actors Guild-American Federation of Television and Radio Artists), SAG's long history attests to its rugged battle for artists' rights. However, one consequence of the labor movement was not immediately apparent. The new guilds became part of the institutional demotion of women. For the next forty-five years, the male-dominated guilds and unions did not recognize or confront widespread discrimination in the industry until women and minorities forced the issue in the 1970s.[26]

In the fifteen years she worked in films, Jewell Jordan never heard of a stuntwoman, even though she was one of the few women who actually performed stunts.[27] "The men did the stunts," she said. "They wore wigs and women's clothes." Jewell was a teenager in the 1930s, and she heard all the conflicting talk about the unions battling the wicked studios versus the genial family atmosphere of the studios headed by princes of the realm like Jack Warner and Adolph Zukor. "I'll tell you this," she said, "there was order" in the studio system. "Sam Goldwyn's company produced *Wuthering Heights* and we knew who to go to with a problem. I'm sure the studio wanted to make money, but it had an artistic side and everyone wanted to make a good movie. We were in the terrible Depression, we were looking for opportunity, contract players could take dancing, singing, elocution, and we took a *personal* pride in doing a good job." Jewell worked in the studio system from 1927 to 1943. "I earned three dollars and fifty cents a day as an extra or a performer. I handled 'special action,' the rough stuff."

Jewell Jordan did the "rough stuff." (Courtesy of the Jewell Jordan Mason Collection)

She wasn't athletic and didn't like to take risks, but she did it anyway. In *Tarzan Escapes* (1936) she had to fall off the limb of a tree onto a mattress. "I dislocated my hip," she said, "but they grabbed hold of my leg and pulled it right back in place. It hurt only for the moment."

Jewell and her sisters grew up in a neighborhood near MGM. The school they attended, St. Augustine, offered a pool of eager youngsters and became a prime source of casting for the studio. "Father O'Donnell got me a job at age ten at MGM," Jewell said, and these acting jobs helped her and her sisters "pay for our education." Jewell entered the realm of movie stars. "They had a mystique about them because they didn't let it all hang out. Laurence Olivier was very cold and aloof on *Wuthering Heights,* but David Niven was a joy to be around. Marlene Dietrich was funny—she made fun of herself. In *Destry Rides Again* she wore a skin-tight beaded gown. When asked if she'd had lunch, she said, 'Of course not. If I had an olive, it would show.'" One night, Jewell was one of the few actors present for a shoot at the train station on MGM's Lot 2. "The picture was *Camille* and it was Robert Taylor's twenty-fifth birthday. He was so enthused about his career and working with Garbo. She was gorgeous, such a mystery person. I liked not knowing everything [about her]. We don't have to."

Jewell Jordan doubled child actress Sarita Wooten in *Wuthering Heights* (1939). In one scene, a huge dog attacks young Cathy as she tries to climb over a garden wall. She screams when the mastiff's jaws clamp on her leg and the dog drags her off the wall. "I wasn't scared," Jewell said. "I'm not of that nature. I felt things were going to work out. I never thought about being hurt" (much like Helen Gibson, who wasn't afraid of being kicked in the head by a horse). The next day, Jewell's leg was black and blue from the pressure of the animal's jaws, but she arrived at the studio for a fitting. "Merle Oberon, who played the adult Cathy in the film, noticed my leg, even though I had on hose and high heels. Merle couldn't figure out why I was at the studio. Even though my leg hurt, I put up with it because in those days you could build a career. I loved every minute of it. I didn't have any bad experiences. If I had, I would never have sued or complained. This was my job. You went forward."

Two other stuntwomen who worked in the thorny 1930s had influential careers. In 1937 twenty-seven-year-old Lila Finn was in Pago Pago, Samoa, doubling for Dorothy Lamour in *The Hurricane*.[28] "She jumped at the job," her son Barry Shanley said. "She loved to travel. She was adventurous, incredibly persistent, and absolutely opposed to giving in or giving up."[29] That film swept Lila and another young diver, Paul Stader, into the work they would do for the rest of their lives.[30] "My mother did all the swimming and diving for Dorothy Lamour," Barry said, "but the producer and the director were concerned about the Hays Commission and its industry censorship guidelines, because in one scene, after she drops the sarong, they shot footage of her naked, diving into the lagoon."

Blonde, five-foot-three Lila came from Venice, California, a beachfront recreational area near Santa Monica. It had been founded in 1907 as the American version of the Italian original. The Venice Hot Salt Water Plunge, a huge pool fed by fresh filtered seawater, could hold 2,000 bathers. As a child, Lila dived off the spectators' balcony for coins tossed by tourists. "We banked them in our mouths," she said. Later, as an accomplished stuntwoman, she branched out from water work to do other stunts. Stair falls were her favorite. Sometimes a director knew what he wanted, she said, "but usually you thought out how to do it, or asked someone. . . . They are the most rewarding because everyone thinks they look great. They're quite simple, actually. I shouldn't say that. You're at the top of the stairs . . . you get down and start rolling this way, then that way. I've done at least fifty of them."[31] Lila was not a daredevil, but she once let a man throw knives at her; he outlined her body "with knives, then cross[ed] the hatchets, one on either side of my head."[32] That was one scary stunt. "He told me to look at the ceiling so I wouldn't move and you can bet I didn't budge a millimeter."[33]

Acrobat Helen Thurston met Lila Finn in the 1930s. They were the same age, they each had a son, and they became single moms after their husbands' deaths. Their first stunt jobs were lucky career boosts, doubling for stars (Dorothy Lamour and Katharine Hepburn) in big films (*The Hurricane* and *Bringing Up Baby*) with major directors (John Ford and Howard Hawks). This allowed them to join SAG immediately instead of toiling as extras. They had something else in common: Lila had dived for coins in the Venice Plunge, and Helen began "her acrobatics by trick dives into the Sacramento River."[34] Helen was one of eight children, and her father, a Baptist minister with a drinking problem, regularly uprooted his family. Finally they settled in a tiny house in Redding, California. "They always had some meatless stew on the stove," Helen's grandson Sean Fawcett said. "The kids were always looking for something to eat. Helen craved meat and when she was older, doing acrobatics, she'd fry up a steak or pork chop, sit down, and eat it without vegetables or side dishes." She ran away as soon as she could, probably at age sixteen or seventeen, joined a traveling acrobatic troupe, and married acrobat Jimmy Fawcett.[35] Helen "mothered a son and saw Europe and the United States from a trapeze bar."[36]

As the Depression deepened, vaudeville acts started to fail. Helen, Jimmy, and their son moved to Los Angeles sometime around 1936. They hung out with acrobats and stuntmen on Muscle Beach in Santa Monica. "Helen was blonde, pretty, about five-six, quite strong, but very feminine," recalled Paula Dell. Nine years younger than Helen, Paula was a teenage acrobat and future stuntwoman. Helen "could do all kinds of stunts," she noted. "Later, she doubled Lucille Ball in movies and on TV. When you see Lucy fall, that's Helen!" In the 1930s Paula and Helen were performing outside the norm. "Helen inspired me," Paula said. "Today, women are much more athletic, but back then girls did not do stunt work. My sister was a really good tumbler; there probably weren't six women in LA that tumbled as well. She got married and had five kids. I was the one that had a burning desire to be the performer."[37]

Helen and Jimmy headed to Republic Pictures in the San Fernando Valley. The studio operated like a hard-up repertory company, turning out

Helen Thurston working out on Muscle Beach. (Courtesy of Michele and Sean Fawcett)

low-budget B pictures with experienced but often irreverent production teams (for instance, on the day after Pearl Harbor, someone commented at a staff meeting, "Anyone who quits Republic to join the army is a coward").[38] Herbert Yates had formed Republic in 1934 by merging several "poverty-row" companies, including Mascot, Monogram, Liberty, and others specializing in mysteries, serials, and westerns.[39] A small staff of writers, directors, and producers relied on a rotating stable of actors and stuntmen. These included actor-stuntman David Sharpe; Yakima Canutt, soon to be a celebrated second-unit director (*Stagecoach*); and "Breezy" Eason, who would direct a second unit on *Gone with the Wind*. Stuntwomen at Republic included former serial star Helen Gibson, Babe DeFreest, and Nellie Walker, said to be the only stuntwoman under contract to Republic.[40] Republic's "Hollywood Colony" was an interconnected group of pros who had worked in silent movies or were related to families in the business. One of the writers was Barry Shipman, the son of Nell Shipman, famous for her wildlife sagas.

At first, Republic director William Witney wasn't too keen on an act involving three acrobats. "It started with two men and a girl doing a ball-room waltz," Witney wrote in his autobiography. "They twirl the girl around gracefully, then something goes wrong, she lands in a chair and goes over backward." The men pick her up and start the routine again, but "she spins one of the guys off the stage into the pit. He crawls back and the free-for-all is on with the gal coming out the winner." The performers were Ken Terrell, a former Mr. America; Jimmy Fawcett, a "great high fall man and all-around athlete"; and Helen Thurston, who "became the number one stunt girl in the entire picture business."[41] Witney made them part of his stunt team for serials.

Anyone looking for work had to hustle all the studios. When Jimmy snared a bit part in *Living on Love* at RKO, someone noticed that Helen Thurston was about the same height as Katharine Hepburn and asked her, "Are you afraid of wild animals?" Helen said she didn't think so, and she was hired. *Bringing Up Baby*, a comedy directed by versatile, stone-faced Howard Hawks, starred Hepburn, Cary Grant, and "Baby," a leopard.[42] The film used split screen, rear-screen projection, and other optical effects to misrepresent the leopard's actual distance from the cast. Surrounded by the nonsense and tumult of a movie set, Baby had her moods, but Helen was deft and up for any challenge.

By this time, the career path had been set for stuntmen, but not for stuntwomen. The studio system involved a maze of departments, most of which impacted stunt work. In production, the "first unit" films scenes with dialogue and actors; the "second unit" augments the first unit by film-ing stunt sequences, landscapes, animals, and objects—scenes without dialogue. The second unit includes a smaller camera crew and the action director, a position well above that of first assistant director. The work of the two units is edited together to create the finished film. In this hierarchy, a stuntman could move up to "gaff" stunts, or coordinate the stunts of a movie; later, he could direct a second unit. The gaffer planned the action of a stunt, such as deciding the direction and speed of a car that flips into a lake.[43] In the late 1960s the gaffer's job became more powerful, taking on the functions of a "stunt coordinator," who selected and hired the stunt players. These management positions were ideal for older stuntmen who didn't want to keep hitting the ground. Second-unit director, a major promotion, brought membership in the Directors Guild of America.

In 1939 the studio system was at its pinnacle. "All the elements of a popular art coalesced at a moment of maturity," film executive Steven Bach wrote, "sharp and fresh, without cynicism for the audience."[44] Ninety percent of all films made in America came from Hollywood, but unlike other industries, movie production inflicted no environmental blight on the land. That year, the studios produced 376 films, employed 30,000 to 40,000 workers, spent about $190 million to manufacture the films, and paid $90 million in salaries.[45] And they released some of the best movies of all time: *Dark Victory, Destry Rides Again, The Hunchback of Notre Dame, Gone with the Wind, Ninotchka, Stagecoach, The Wizard of Oz, Wuthering Heights,* and many others.[46] Along with these legendary movies came legendary stunt sequences, including the one Helen Thurston performed, doubling for the star, in *Destry Rides Again.*

All stunt people dwelt in the long shadows of the "doubles." In movie productions, the stars, directors, producers, writers, and sometimes cinematographers are known as "above the line" contributors, or those who influence the creative direction of a film. Wardrobe, set design, technical crews, and stunts are "below the line." Stuntwomen worked not only below the line but also under the radar.

According to historian Kevin Brownlow, the need for stunt doubles began right after *The Great Train Robbery* in 1903. That movie used stopmotion: the cameraman stopped filming, "a dummy was substituted for the engineer," the camera started rolling again, and the dummy was "thrown from the train. The audience was unfamiliar with such tricks, but they caught on so quickly that a stuntman or stuntwoman had to be employed for such scenes."[47] The use of doubles developed to protect stars from injury, but since this arrangement was a trade secret, it enhanced the stars' box-office appeal. For example, because a sixty-foot dive off a boat appeared to be done by the star, the actor reaped the benefits. "The secret of who doubles whom, and when, is one of the most jealously guarded of studio mysteries. Nobody wants the facts known," wrote reporter Florabel Muir.[48] A big, brusque redhead, Muir specialized in writing about Hollywood celebrities and underworld figures, and she broke the code of silence about doubles in her 1945 account of stuntwomen.

A stunt double is selected for her physical resemblance to a star as well as her ability to perform the stunts required by the script. In *Gone with the Wind* Vivien Leigh had three doubles—Aline Goodwin, who worked on the film for a year; Lila Finn; and possibly Hazel Hash, a horsewoman from Montana.[49] Lila Finn did the fire scene, depicting the burning of Atlanta. "My mom is on the horse-drawn carriage as the buildings are collapsing near them," Lila's son revealed. "She also told me she was used as a body double for Leigh in the 'I'll-never-be-hungry-again' scene—a silhouette shot with her hand raised against the sky. When she saw the finished picture she wasn't sure if the shot was of her or Vivien Leigh. They may have shot Leigh doing it, too. You can't really tell." Aline Goodwin did Scarlett's tumble down the stairs, but Hazel Hash claimed credit for it. Important scenes were sometimes shot more than once with different doubles, and any one of those versions could end up in the final cut. That's part of the mystery of stunt work.

In the pantheon of 1939 films, *Destry Rides Again* contributed its own doubling mystery in "the champion cat fight of all film history." The "amusing little western" began shooting without a budget and only half a script on September 4, 1939. "Hitler was taking Poland as Marlene [Dietrich] was taking the San Fernando Valley," Bach wrote.[50] Throughout the 1930s, European camera and sound technicians, actors, producers, composers, and authors had found work and refuge in Hollywood. They brought culture to what those on the East Coast considered a cultural wasteland.[51] Once war broke out in Europe, casts and crews on sets all over Hollywood, including *Destry Ride Again,* anguished about friends and family trapped abroad.

From the first shots of Marlene Dietrich rolling a cigarette in a noisy saloon, then throwing a drink in the face of a cowboy, it's clear that Dietrich's character, Frenchy, takes no prisoners. George Marshall, who had been directing comedies, westerns, and serials since 1916,[52] hired Helen Thurston, known for her fighting skills, to double Dietrich. Marshall and his stunt coordinator, Duke York, had cooked up a knockdown saloon brawl between Frenchy and townswoman-with-a-beef Lily Belle, played

On the set of *Destry Rides Again* (1939). (Courtesy of Michele and Sean Fawcett)

by Una Merkel.[53] The two women are like wrestlers on speed, tussling on a table, rolling on the floor, growling, kicking, and punching until Destry (James Stewart) pours a bucket of water on them. When Lily Belle flees, Frenchy grabs a gun and aims it at Destry. She lobs the gun at him, jumps on his back, rides him like a bronco, falls off, and flings a chair as he slides out the door.

According to Dietrich's daughter, Maria Riva, her mother had tried to persuade Marshall "to let her do her own stunt work for the saloon fight. He said no! The stuntwomen had been hired, rehearsed, and would deliver on film a wild and rowdy brawl with their usual expertise. Dietrich and Una Merkel, properly bloodied and disheveled, would then take their places" for the close shots. Universal's top producer, Joe Pasternak, might have gone along with Dietrich's request, except for the risk of injury—the fight had been planned for professionals. "But the prospect of the enormous publicity that would be generated . . . finally outweighed any objections the worried studio could come up with." Besides, Marshall could always reshoot later with the stuntwomen, if necessary. On the day of the shoot, the set was jammed with press from *Life, Look,* the wire services, and fan magazines. A first-aid station had been set up outside the soundstage. The stuntwomen were on the "sidelines, ready to take over," Riva wrote. "Merkel and Dietrich took their places, the cameras rolled, my mother whispered, 'Una, don't hold back—kick me, hit me, tear my hair. You can punch me too—because I am going to punch you!' and with a snarl, jumped on Merkel's back, knocking her to the floor."[54] When it was over, the spectators on the set burst into applause. The fight became part of movie lore. Merkel said she and Dietrich had no rehearsal; they just did whatever Marshall wanted: "We punched and slapped and kicked for all we were worth!" Later, she said, "I looked like an old peach, green, with brown spots. And I felt rotten, too."[55]

The object of the studios' doubling game was to have it both ways. While publicly denying that their stars were doubled, they secretly used doubles to protect their actors. For *Destry,* Universal could declare that "no doubles" were used and be backed up by the press. But six years later, *Variety* reporter Florabel Muir outed Dietrich's double in the *Saturday Evening Post.* "When you saw Marlene Dietrich's historic barroom brawl in *Destry Rides Again,* you were not looking at Marlene, but at Helen [Thurston]. That fight, incidentally, made such a hit with fans that fistic brawls involving girls have been favorites with producers ever since."[56]

It's hard to imagine that a pro like Helen Thurston would tell a reporter she'd doubled Dietrich if she hadn't. The Dietrich-Merkel fight might have looked great to the reporters present during the filming, but how did it look to the camera? After seeing the rushes, Marshall and Pasternak may have decided to reshoot with doubles to improve the punches, the falls, or the timing. If the scene was reshot, technicians on set would know who was doubling, but revealing such a secret could have serious repercussions.

"On the screen, we are shapes, and not faces," stuntwoman Frances Miles said.[57] Going over the fight frame by frame, in some shots Dietrich's slender, oval face appears to be round, like Helen's; in other shots Merkel's face looks angular, unlike her own. At normal speed, a stunt goes by so fast it's impossible to tell whether it's the star or the stuntwoman being punched. Stunt doubles learn how to hide their faces. "The whole idea is not getting noticed, not being identified," stunt coordinator Conrad Palmisano said years later. "You get good at not letting your face be seen in a stunt."

To insiders, that fight became a stunt within a stunt, and as the story about it spread, Helen Thurston's reputation grew. After *Destry,* she went back to Republic. A year later, director William Witney was planning a serial "around a girl," the first since the advent of sound. *Jungle Girl* starred Frances Gifford, and in terms of history, Helen was the best double around. She became a superlative stuntwoman, one of the few in the 1930s whose skills sustained the onscreen position created by Winnie Brown, Helen Gibson, and the action serial actresses.

# 3

# Television

## More Stunt Work—If You Can Get It

Now, girls, please be very careful. I don't want any of you hurt.
—*New director quoted by Florabel Muir,*
*"They Risk Their Necks for You,"*
Saturday Evening Post, *September 15, 1945*

"These girls sometimes have more guts than any man," stunt veteran "Breezy" Eason declared. He directed the second unit on a 1945 swash-buckler called *The Spanish Main* and had hired Betty Danko and Helen Thurston to do the fencing stunts, which RKO paid them to learn. Betty, who also wrote poetry and composed music, had twenty years' experience doing stunts; Helen had eight.[1]

"Actor Paul Henreid thought all this talk about Helen being a toughy was a lot of nonsense," wrote one reporter. When he stepped up to Helen, she "grabbed his arm, boosted him onto her shoulders, got the proper balance, gave him the old spin—and deposited the surprised actor right on the floor . . . Helen turned to 212-pound Eric Alden, a stuntman standing nearby, laughing. Before Alden got the smile off his face, he was up and over—beside Henreid."[2]

As Helen was up to her old tricks, twenty-six-year-old Polly Burson was facing facts in Denver, Colorado. Her grandfather had been a champion bronc buster, her parents owned a riding and roping show, and she had become a rodeo champ in Europe and the United States, including four years playing Madison Square Garden in New York City.[3] But Polly was no longer at the top of her game. "I was going back down to the fifteen,

Helen Thurston lifts Bud Abbott over her head in *Abbott and Costello Meet the Keystone Kops* (1955). (Courtesy of Michele and Sean Fawcett)

ten, and five shows where I'd started. I didn't want that. I had to change my life."[4] Polly had no real education and few options, but her mother had worked in rodeos with Babe DeFreest, who had left the circuit for the movies. "I figured maybe I could use my trick riding and sort of fall back on the movies. I called Babe about my chances, and she said, 'Get in! There's room for you!'" Polly had lots to learn about stunts, but she had style—she was a genial, self-deprecating, wisecracking athlete with enormous appeal. She and her new husband, Wayne Burson, arrived in Los Angeles in the spring of 1945. She recalled, chuckling:

> Now in those days the Screen Actors Guild was closed, and what that meant I had no idea, but you had to have a card to get a job and you had to have a job to get a card. I kept bugging the studios until one day Babe recommended me for a serial, *The Purple Monster Strikes* [1945]. She doubled the star, Linda Stirling, and I doubled Mary Moore. At that time she was married to Clayton Moore, who was not the Lone Ranger yet. Babe and I had to do a fight on the edge of a cliff and then fall off it, but when we got up there, I looked down and said, "Babe, there's no damn way we can get there from here." It was about seventy-five feet to the bottom. They'd built a platform down there and the grips and all the men held up a round firemen's net. Babe said, "Don't bounce, grab something and go to your back." I don't know if the wind blew me off, Babe pulled me off, or I stumbled off, but we both hit right on the X. I made $150 and thought, my God, this is the gravy train! Then I didn't work for a month.

Polly had no idea she would soon board the big gravy train—Paramount Pictures' *The Perils of Pauline.*

Compared with Pearl White's 1914 serial, the 1947 movie directed by George Marshall was child's play. Marshall had boosted Helen Thurston's career in 1939 in *Destry Rides Again,* and he would do the same for Polly when he hired her to double Betty Hutton. Marshall asked Polly if she had ever done a "transfer" onto a train. "I said, 'The only way I ever got on a train was I handed a porter a quarter and stepped on.' Mr. Marshall just stood there looking at me, so I said, 'No, I haven't, but here we go.'"

Back then, directors knew the kinds of stunts they wanted and the players to do them. In this case, Marshall didn't want Polly to ride up to the boxcar on her horse, grab the bar, and pull herself onto the train. He wanted her to leap from the horse to the train.[5] "I'm up on a hill a couple of blocks away from the train and the railroad tracks," Polly said. "It's straight downhill and I have to judge the time I'll need to get to that first boxcar behind the coal car. I had to get in position to reach it. I wasn't behind, but I was whipping the horse to get to my ladder on the car. And that's timing. I had the best darn horse under me, I hated to admit it, but she was a mare. I reached the boxcar and—I jumped onto it!" Polly and her galloping horse seemed fused together until she rose up in a graceful, liquid leap toward the moving train, and as she sailed off, the horse kept racing with the same unbroken rhythm. She landed perfectly. "I had to stay between cars and shoot back at the Indians chasing me," she said. "Then I had to crawl up and run along the boxcar into the coal car, run along it into the engine room, around the engineer, and up to the cowcatcher. I did that three times. I couldn't figure what the hell was wrong. When I came real close by the engineer, it was George Marshall! He said he'd been a frustrated engineer since he was a kid. I said, 'Mr. Marshall, I wish you'd have practiced with somebody else.'"

Polly Burson quickly became known as "a fearless, peerless stunt rider." One stuntman said she had the best timing he'd seen "in a woman." Timing is crucial to any stunt, and it can't be taught. Polly developed it riding relay races. "You're on three head of horses, you ride each one half a mile. When you come into the stretch, you must be in position to get into your station to change horses. If you're not, you won't make it. Your head has to tell you how to do it, and you have to start thinking about it after a quarter of a mile. That's timing and I found I had it on the transfer from my horse to the train."

That was the only riding stunt in *The Perils of Pauline*. According to Polly, she couldn't have done the other stunts without the help of the men on the set. "Betty Hutton playing Pauline is onstage singing and dancing," Polly related, "but the audience is hollering, 'We want a stunt!' She runs up a catwalk behind the curtain to a landing high above the stage where great big ropes, darn near eight inches in circumference, hung alongside the curtains. She grabs one, swings across the stage and back, across again, and drops to the stage." As Hutton's double, Polly was expected to do the action, but Marshall was still working out how to do this stunt with the men. "Back then, a lot of little men were wearing wigs" and doubling for actresses, an irritated Polly recalled. After two stuntmen tried it and failed, the prop men urged Polly to tell Marshall that she wanted to do it. "They forced me, almost. So I did and he said, 'You really want to do it?' I said, 'Yes, sir, I do.' I was so scared if you'd asked me to spit, I wouldn't have been able to."

The stuntmen's mistake, Polly realized, was that they couldn't complete the full swing because they hadn't let the prop and effects guys help them. "It was the macho in the men, that's all I could figure," she drawled. "When you swing through the first time, you have to turn, come back, then turn around again, but by that second time you've lost your momentum. When I did the turn, two men put their hands right on my butt and pushed me. I went way up again, turned, went down about thirty-five feet, dropped off, landed on my back, and it was done! But I didn't have the clothes on!" she shouted, laughing. "I wore the Betty Hutton wig, but no one thought I could do it so they hadn't shot it! I had to get in costume and do it again."

After World War II the studios were minting pictures in all denominations—*Two Years before the Mast; The Lost Weekend; Sorry, Wrong Number; The Trouble with Women.* In 1916 canny, farsighted Adolph Zukor (Famous Players) and Jesse L. Lasky (Lasky Feature Play Company) had merged their businesses, forming a film distribution company called Paramount Pictures. Today, the Paramount studio on Melrose Avenue in Hollywood looks as stately and picturesque as it did in 1947. That year, on the studio's back lot, Polly Burson met Lila Finn. They were different in many ways, but they shared a love of travel and were friends for the next fifty years. At the time, Polly had two years in stunts; Lila had ten years. Polly, a brunette, was an accomplished horsewoman; Lila, a blonde, was an expert swimmer and a volleyball champ. Polly loved a rowdy good time with friends and told great stories with wry humor; Lila, more reserved, was "a lady who knew what she wanted, planned for it," and went after it. Polly spent her money; Lila invested hers. When they met on the lot, Lila had joined the swirling hordes in Cecil B. DeMille's extravaganza *Unconquered* (1947).[6] Polly became Paulette Goddard's second stunt double.

One major sequence of *Unconquered* was shot in Idaho on the Snake River, according to Polly, Lila, and others who spoke to Bill Mayer of *Variety* in 1977. Downriver by the falls, where the water was choppy, canoes full of Indians chased the one bearing Lila and Ted Mapes, Gary Cooper's double, heading for the steep drop ahead.[7] As they went over the falls, DeMille wanted them to grab onto a tree limb. "But when they tried it," Mayer wrote, "the branch broke threatening to hurl them into the current and dash them against the rocks. Camera angles and other strategies could have eliminated the danger, but DeMille insisted on realism in all its fine-spun and constantly visible detail."[8] Special equipment was brought in to secure the limb. "My mom [Lila Finn] and stuntman Ted Mapes were in a canoe shooting through some pretty significant rapids," Barry Shanley

Polly Burson riding high on her beloved horse, Pat. (Courtesy of Polly Burson)

said, "and then the picture cut to a long shot of the waterfall." As the canoe is perched on the crest, Ted grabs the branch of an overhanging tree, Lila grabs him, and the canoe plunges over the falls. Onscreen, they hang from the limb and then swing forward into the sheet of water. The scene cuts to Ted and Polly bursting through the curtain of water and landing on a rocky ledge behind the falls, soaked but safe. "They hired Polly to be the stunt double under the waterfall," Barry said, "and that scene was done on a soundstage." Lila, Polly, and eleven stuntmen worked on *Unconquered*. At a time when stuntmen often doubled actresses, "Polly showed that horseback riding is a great equalizer between the sexes," Lila wrote. "She was so versatile and so popular, it was a wonder the rest of us got a chance to work!"[9]

In 1945 movie attendance was at an all-time high, but soon the blows came fast and hard from different directions. First, the dream factory lost its control of theater chains in the 1947 Paramount Decree, which radically changed the way studios had operated for the past thirty years. By 1950, a new home-entertainment gadget called television began stealing away their audiences. The movie industry fumbled for a magic key—it tried 3D and Cinerama—to bring audiences back. Producers resurrected ideas from old low-budget movies, such as crime or love stories, and they produced feature-film knockouts like *High Noon* and *Shane* (westerns were safer than stories of social problems during the regressive 1950s). When every stratagem failed to halt the growing appeal of the small screen, the studios went into the TV business.

Meanwhile, the House Un-American Activities Committee (HUAC) scoured the nation for Communists and then narrowed the hunt for Reds to Hollywood. Many individuals from the film industry, mainly writers (including the "Hollywood Ten"), were forced to testify at congressional hearings. The result was the notorious blacklist, which lasted into the 1960s. In these oppressive years, fear and cowardice reigned, friends betrayed friends, and guilds and unions adopted a more conservative mode to avoid any hint of the militancy they'd embraced since the 1930s. Although the turmoil was nationwide, the effects on Hollywood set off a chain of reactions.

The old studio production system was forced to change, given the studios' loss of theater ownership and the growing number of independent film productions. A flood of B picture producers and directors moved to television. They created weekly comedies, mysteries, and westerns that, in a way, resembled longer versions of silent movie serials.[10] TV shows were considered second rate, but they gave everyone in the movie business, including stuntwomen, a whole new market for their work.

Whether they played on small black-and-white screens at home or on wide-screen Technicolor in darkened theaters, most movies and TV shows focused on men's adventures. Behind the scenes, men controlled the studios, the productions, and the film crews, and stuntmen orbited action stars such as John Wayne, Gregory Peck, Kirk Douglas, and Robert Mitchum. Stuntwomen, in contrast, often worked alone on the set, limited to performing whatever little action the female star might do. Now, thanks to television, at least there were more sets.

Stuntwoman May Boss attributed her early success to the numerous TV westerns being shot all over Los Angeles. "I could fall a horse. That's where you come flying towards the camera and boom! The horse goes down." Agile, tough, and pretty, with sharp blue eyes, May said, "If I stick my tongue out, I'm five-four." Her father had owned and trained racehorses in New York, and she really wanted to be a jockey. "I was a great size for it," she said, "but those jocks did not like women on the racetrack. They told me, 'We'll box you in, we'll knock you over the rail.' They don't fool around. They're nasty. It was a hostile environment and they still don't like women." Once May realized she had no future as a jockey, she went to the rodeos. "There the guys treated you like a sister," she said. "I pretty well taught myself trick riding and I got lucky. I rode a horse that had just one speed—full on. Very quickly I got the reputation." She worked all the big shows in the United States, and she liked "never know[ing] for sure what's going to happen next." Trick riding involves showmanship, and according to May, she "learned that from Dick Griffith, the classiest trick rider ever. He went around the arena in the opening parade and all he did was take off his hat and brought the whole crowd with him. He had dark skin and his wife made him white clothes with no fly! I don't know where he put his equipment in those costumes and I didn't know him well enough to ask. I had long blonde hair and when I did a drag my hair swept the ground. It looked really dangerous. Showmanship."[11]

May earned a living, but she was divorced and had a son, Clay, to support, so money was tight. She rented a house in the San Fernando Valley that happened to be near the home of John and Frances Epper. John, a former member of the Swiss mounted cavalry, had immigrated to America in the 1920s, where he became a renowned stuntman. The Epper children—Margo, Jeannie, Stephanie, Tony, Gary, and Andy—followed him into the stunt business. In fact, everyone in the neighborhood seemed to be in the "picture business." May's next-door neighbor was Roy Rogers's trainer. He helped her get work as an extra, and May began to learn about stunts.

She had some close calls. "I was driving wagons. I don't remember what TV show it was, but the director said, 'I want you coming flying

May Boss hoisting a stuntman up and over. (Courtesy of May Boss)

around this corner and I want you'—I love it when directors do this—'I want you to stop your wheels right there.' That's virtually impossible with two head of horses. I kept my mouth shut. If it works, great, if it doesn't, can't be done. I was lucky that day, nobody got hurt and I stopped 'right there.'" She learned to be wary of a stunt when part of it was out of her control. "You can be hurt when you have to leave part of a stunt to someone else," she said. On another occasion, she learned that stuntmen know what to do in a crunch:

> I was almost burned to death on a TV show when too much fire-retardant gel was applied to my back and ran down my legs. Too much gel feeds the flames. On the other side of the door I was supposed to come through, one fireman had a blanket and the other held an extinguisher. Two stuntmen were on set just to watch. I was set on fire and I'm a torch! I go through the door, I'm supposed to scream and I'm screaming for real. The firemen freeze, but the stuntmen go into action. One grabs me by the throat and knocks me out. The other grabs the hose and sprays it on me. Next week I'm in the mountains with my son, lying in the snow, and it sure felt good.

Before pagers and cell phones, anyone who needed to contact stunt people called Teddy O'Toole's, a 24/7 answering service in Hollywood. Teddy's staff could track them down. They also helped new producers looking for specific types, such as "a stunt girl about five feet tall who can do high falls." The women answering the phones knew the height, weight, hair color, size, and specialty of all Teddy's clients, which included fifteen stuntwomen and eighty-one stuntmen in December 1954. The male-female ratio of six to one hasn't changed much today.[12] Stuntman Paul Stader, who had worked with Lila Finn on *The Hurricane,* adapted his sister-in-law's answering service exclusively for stunt players and told all his friends to sign up for it.[13]

When May Boss heard that a woman named Polly Burson was the ramrod (stunt coordinator) on a feature titled *Westward the Women,* she called Teddy's to find Polly:

> She answered in that gruff voice of hers and I said, "I hear you're looking for trick riders."

"Are you a trick rider?" Polly said.

"Yes."

"You got your SAG card?"

"No."

Polly hangs up! Well! I sure don't want to know her!

May got her SAG card, but not in time for that show.

*Westward the Women* (1951) told a very different story of the West, and it employed practically every working stuntwoman around.[14] This unique experience must have given the women a fleeting sense of the camaraderie stuntmen enjoyed on every job. *Westward the Women* covered the 2,000-mile cross-country trek of 100 women on foot, horseback, or prairie schooner. Buck (played by Robert Taylor), the leader of the wagon train, says, "'Take a load of good women across hell? If we're lucky we'll only lose one out of three!'"[15] Crusty William A. Wellman directed a cast led by Taylor, Denise Darcel, and Hope Emerson.

Stuntwoman Bonnie Happy grew up on a horse. Her mother, Edith, was an expert rodeo rider.[16] "Mom drove a four-up for Polly," Bonnie said, "and on that show [when] you . . . hear somebody say, 'Okay, Hap'—they're talking to my mom. The women got together, named Polly their stunt coordinator, and Wellman agreed. She took care of the women's stunts and the men on it took care of theirs. So she was the first woman to stunt coordinate. Polly was a pistol."[17]

"Wild Bill" Wellman—good-looking, brilliant, and sometimes irascible—had directed movies since 1920. His most famous, *Wings,* won the first Oscar for best picture in 1927. It is hard to imagine him saying, "You girls decide who's coordinating," but *Westward the Women* was a unique picture. "Oh, yes, Polly stunt coordinated," said the director's son, actor William Wellman Jr.:

My dad liked stunt people. Frank Capra wrote the story, but his studio wouldn't let him make it because it was a western, so he took it to my dad who liked it and MGM made it. For two weeks before shooting, dad set up training for the women, how to handle the wagons, the shooting, and the bull whips. The men did stunts the women didn't want to do or my dad wouldn't let them do, like the falls. He cast actresses who were good riders and stuntwomen, like Evelyn Finley. He thought she was the best rider of all.[18]

Tragedy hits in *Westward the Women* when they cannot slow the first wagon descending a steep incline. (Courtesy of the William A. Wellman Collection)

Shot on location for eight weeks in Utah, *Westward* is an exciting, warmhearted story that focuses on the women's determination and courage. When the wagons are forced to go down a steep incline—more cliff than hill—the script calls for the first woman who attempts it to die. In the ensuing silence, Buck yells, "All right, who's next? C'mon, it's been done before, the only difference was it was done by men!" One of the women, six feet tall and about 200 pounds, says, "By men, huh?" She breaks the moment of defeat, the women get back in their wagons, and she's the first in line.

Little has been written about the remarkable stuntwomen who worked on that movie. "Sharon Lucas was a great rider," said stuntman Loren Janes, "and she was the first stunt girl I ever worked with." He did his first stunt—an eighty-foot dive off a cliff—on *Jupiter's Darling* (1954). Sharon was Esther Williams's riding double. Loren recalled one incident when Sharon proved her mettle:

> After dinner, Sharon and I were walking down the street, when two stuntmen came out of a bar, walked behind us saying, "Look

at the butt on that gal." I turned to get them to shut up, but Sharon said, "No, no, don't." They kept making these remarks and she kept telling me, "No, no," so we kept walking and all of a sudden she spun around! One was a great big guy and the other was a little guy with a big stuntman reputation. She hit him first, then the other. They both went down and just lay there. She turned around and kept right on walking with me. I'll never forget that. She was a fantastic gal.[19]

The families of Stevie Myers and Lucille House were in the business of supplying horses and livestock to the movies. Short and dark-haired, Stevie looked like "a leather saddle," one stuntwoman said with affection. Respected for her expertise, she trained and rented horses and ran her father's ranch in the San Fernando Valley. "She had a real direct manner," May Boss said. "Lots of stuntwomen then were female-ish, which put Stevie off. Horses are men's work, herding, cleaning, currying." Other

Stevie Myers, a real horsewoman. (Courtesy of Julie Ann Johnson)

young stuntwomen said Stevie's forthright manner influenced them to speak up in the tough, liberating 1970s.

Lucille House's father owned one of the world's largest movie-livestock supply companies. The year before *Westward the Women,* Lucille had doubled Maureen O'Hara in *Tripoli* (1950), which, according to stuntman Chuck Roberson's autobiography, was filmed in "the sand dunes of Indio, California, known as Hollywood's Sahara. It was hot before the sun came up."[20] A World War II veteran, Roberson was new to stunts, as were the other men who worked on *Tripoli*—Little Chuck Hayward, Terry Wilson, and Bob Morgan. Their leader, Cliff Lyons, had been a stuntman since *Beau Geste* in 1926. Lucille was the only stuntwoman on the film.[21] Costumed in robes and burnooses, each man had been assigned a camel to ride, and Roberson's camel snatched the burnoose off his head and tried to eat it. "I was tugging and pulling when I heard a feminine voice behind me. 'Watch out! Get that camel away from the horses! Bill told me he gave you Henrietta,' she said. 'She's in heat.'" Roberson had been told the camel's name was Clyde! "I saw this girl, who seemed to know so much about the mating habits of the female camel, was dressed in an Arab costume complete with veil. 'My name's Lucille House.' I recognized the name," Roberson wrote. "Next to Polly Burson, she was the best stunt girl in Hollywood." Lucille gave him advice as they rode up and down the dunes. The temperature climbed to 120 degrees, and then "someone turned on forty wind machines. Suddenly, a real Santa Ana wind roared up from the south and blew the machines away. Instead of packing up and heading for cover, the director [Will Price] decided to take advantage of the sand storm. I stuck by Lucille."[22]

Kidding around is part of life on the set and on location, and whether the target is male or female, it's both a joke and a test. May Boss and Polly Burson could certainly take a joke, but their first work had been in the more female-friendly and egalitarian rodeos. The stunt culture was quite different. In the 1950s "about ten or twelve stuntmen—'boss stuntmen'—ran the business. If they didn't know you, you didn't work."[23] The women, few in number and relatively powerless, competed intensely for the one job open to them—doubling for actresses. "A gal I met doubled girls in westerns," May said. "I was new. I'd tell her I heard of a job on X, and she'd say, 'I've got that job.' And I believed her! Then I began to catch on. If that woman couldn't handle a stunt, she'd take the job anyway and give it to a boy. She'd never hand it off to a woman." A stunt could be taken away from a woman for any reason; maybe the director thought it was too dangerous for her, or the stunt coordinator decided to replace her with his girlfriend. Stuntwomen also had to contend with the "girls on location," who couldn't do stunts but were hired from the stunt budget to sleep with the crew. "The business is all about who you know, and in some cases who you blow," one reporter said. "One stuntwoman said she had to bring her kneepads when she wanted to get a job."

Roberson described how some stuntwomen were hired. Director Raoul Walsh was hunting for "stunt girls" to double Jane Russell in *The Tall Men* (1955), starring Clark Gable and filmed on location in Durango, Mexico. "Walsh picked the girl by reputation, not by her ability as a stunt girl," Roberson wrote:

> Joe Behm, the production manager on the picture, brought three girls to Walsh to be interviewed. "This is Polly Burson," he said. "Best stunt girl in Hollywood. She can do anything—rear mounts, drags, transfers, falls, you name it."
>
> "What kind of home life does she have?" asked Walsh.
>
> "She's a model wife and mother, faithful to her husband. . . ."[24]
>
> "Okay," sighed Walsh, "I get the idea. . . . Bring in the next girl."
>
> Joe ushered in Sharon Lucas, who stood smiling sweetly before old Walsh. . . . Joe whispered to him, "She's not as good as Polly but she can still stunt pretty well."
>
> "How is she *off* the horses?" asked the old man.
>
> "She's been married about eight years and has a couple of real cute kids."
>
> Walsh waved his hand in dismissal. "Bring in the last one."
>
> "I don't think you want this one," warned Joe, ushering in Sue Brown [not her real name]. Sue had big boobs and an "easy" look about her that made the old man sit up. . . . "Tell me about this one."
>
> "As a stuntwoman she stinks. . . . About the only thing she's got going for her are those boobs."
>
> "Couldn't tell it wasn't Jane [Russell], from a distance," the old man smiled.
>
> "Yeah, but she's not worth a shit as a stuntwoman. The only thing she knows how to do is screw," Joe concluded.
>
> "That's good enough for me!" said Walsh. "We gotta keep the crew happy, you know."

"The end result," Roberson wrote, " was that the crew got happy and I got a stuntwoman who didn't know whether to ride her horse or kiss it."[25]

Skill and talent didn't count. Polly and Sharon may not have known at the time why they weren't hired for *The Tall Men*, but they probably found out.[26] The budget could have afforded both stunts and sex—a good stunt-woman *and* a good-time girl. But supplying sex to the guys trumped everything. And if the girl who was hired couldn't do a stunt, no problem! A man would put on a wig, do the stunt, and earn the extra pay. No one has calculated the financial loss to the skilled stuntwomen over the decades who were passed over for women who were willing to "keep the crew happy," or the impact on the women who were, in effect, prostitutes.

May Boss tackled the "location girl" tradition when she doubled Suzanne Pleshette on *Nevada Smith* (1966). This was her first time working for director Henry Hathaway, and one of the locations was in the bayous of Baton Rouge, Louisiana. May recalled:

> They'd hired about six women for "night work." They were called "rice paddy girls." The assistant director tells me to go to wardrobe to get my rice paddy outfit. I said, "No. I'm hired to double the girl." He went off. Soon Mr. Hathaway yelled, "May!" I went up to him and he said, "Why aren't you a rice paddy girl?" "Because I wasn't hired for that." I walked away. The crew was standing around, trembling for me. The next day he did it again. "Why aren't you a rice paddy girl?" I told him, "I wasn't hired for that kind of work and besides, I'm being *paid!* Those girls are doing the night work for free."

May took a big risk. Stunt people, and particularly the women, were expected to be cordial and to comply with the director and the key stunt-men. A ramrod had the power to hire, and he could give a woman's stunt to a man with no explanation. Almost no one bucked the system, for fear of not being hired again and for fear of losing her colleagues' trust, which is crucial in stunt work.

More often, May and Polly were well respected. "But we were females making a living," May said, "and some guys gravitated to women like us to get into pictures. About a dozen men are working because Polly helped them," she said with a resigned chuckle. "We were good friends and we went on interviews together. One job was to dance with a bear," May said. "The director said to the trainer, a Russian, 'Show the girls what to do.' He opens the cage, jerks the bear out, says a few words to him, the bear raises his paws, gives him a bear hug, and pretty quick the trainer's turning real red, the bear's not letting go, and Polly says, 'It's your job, Bossie!' That's what she called me. 'Just take off your panties and toss 'em under his nose!' She's laughing her head off and she walks out!"

It may have been easy to refuse the job with the bear, but work was hard to find. And even the best stuntwomen earned less than men for almost all stunts, a fact that was rarely reported until Florabel Muir brought it up in 1945. "Thrill directors agree that stunts are worth more than they cost, and that the studios get off very cheaply indeed, considering the risks the girls run. Over the years, the girls do not average more than $100 to $150 a week."[27] The gnawing inequity came up again and again, but in the 1950s there wasn't much they could do about it. "There were so few stuntwomen," Polly groaned. "We had Helen Thurston, who couldn't spell horse, but she was a hell of a trampoline artist, and we had Lila Finn, a hell of a swimmer."

Then came Lila's big coup, doubling for Sandra Dee in *A Summer Place* (1959). Stuntman Regis Parton (widely known as Reggie) doubled Troy Donahue.[28] As Lila's son recalled:

She and Troy were supposed to take a sailboat out, turn it over, and get washed up on the beach. The director waited for a big enough storm to make it look realistic. When it finally came, it was so big the Coast Guard, which was supposed to accompany their sailboat, refused to go out. As a swimmer, my mom was confident she could handle anything. She and Reggie took this little boat out. They were completely on their own. They got past the breakwater, but one of the first waves dashed the boat on the rocks. They tried to push it off, but waves kept coming. They dived in, swam through the waves and back through the breakwater. When she came home she told me it was the biggest one-day payday a stuntwoman ever had. Because she and Reggie had done the same stunt, she'd demanded the same adjustment pay—and she got it. I think it was $2,500 or $3,000. She figured that if the Coast Guard wasn't willing to go out it had been really dangerous, so she and the stuntman hung together and got themselves a really nice adjustment.[29]

An "adjustment" is the amount over the SAG daily rate that all stunt people receive. In the past, when a stuntman and a stuntwoman did a gag together, the man negotiated the adjustment for both of them with the director or gaffer. Even when taking the same risks on the same stunt, the woman usually received a lower fee, presumably because she had less physical strength or less experience. Most women accepted whatever was offered because complaints could get them labeled as troublemakers. Lila had to speak up for herself, but Reggie held the key to her triumph when he supported the equal split. Today, women are more likely to speak up for their fair share.

A year later, an off-the-cuff idea from Mickey Rooney increased the stuntmen's control and management of their work—the first stuntmen's association was formed. A few years after that, stuntwomen formed their own association. Though never as powerful as the men's, it clarified the action they had to take to improve their standing. Not one of those changes would be easy.

# II

# Taking on the System
# and Fighting for Change

*1960s – 1980s*

# 4

# Stunt Performers Organize

We were fighting for basic recognition as stuntwomen.
—*Jeannie Epper*

On an episode of the 1950s TV series *Your Show of Shows,* star Sid Caesar played a "stunt double being beaten, hanged up and blown up in a series of gags. The handsome leading man steps in for the hero in close-ups, followed by the fawning adulation of the director and leading lady, while the dazed, bloodied and broken stuntman staggered about in the background, totally ignored. That's show biz."[1]

Movie folklore praised them, but Caesar's skit showed their real status. "The industry's plebeian jocks, the stunt men," producer Saul David wrote, "have always seemed special and pure—a kind of gentle warrior caste like Kurosawa's samurais, menacing, high-principled and comfortingly for sale. Stars and executives who will rage if you speak discouragingly about Hottentots will talk about stunt men as if they were Arabian horses."[2] Even today, one stuntwoman said, "the industry's perception is that we're dumb, reckless daredevils, and we don't read books. No one assumes I went to college and studied Shakespeare."

In 1960 stuntmen greatly improved their position. Of all the changes that engulfed the movie industry, the resignation or retirement of long-time studio heads, producers, and directors was one of the most significant. They had known every aspect of the business, and their departure left a vacuum that was hard to fill. In the shifting sands of what had once been terra firma, corporations began to take over the studios, and talented young producers, directors, and entrepreneurs mounted their own independent productions.

Twenty-nine-year-old Loren Janes and thirty-five-year-old Dick Geary each had about seven years of stunt experience in 1960.[3] That's when they agreed to work on a film called *Everything's Ducky,* which it was not—not on that movie and not in the industry.[4] However, change and confusion often lead to opportunity. One scene in the nutty comedy starring Mickey Rooney, Buddy Hackett, and Jackie Cooper was frustrating Dick and Loren. "After three days trying to work out a big fight between twelve marines and twelve navy guys," Loren said, "Mickey Rooney takes me aside and says, 'Why is this so bad? These guys don't know what they're doing.' I said they weren't stuntmen, they were extras. Dick was the only stuntman on the navy side and I was on the marine side. *We* knew what to do; the other guys didn't." The moguls who had run everything since the 1920s were gone, and the corporations that had taken over the studios "were managed by new guys or independent producers who didn't know a stuntman from a farmer. The producers on that show had hired extras because they were cheaper. They couldn't do the job."

Stunt fights always work better when the pros do them. "The extras really punched and kicked," Loren recalled, and "some were getting hurt. Mickey Rooney's asking me, 'What are we going to do tomorrow?' I said, 'Let me hire twenty guys and we'll do it in half a day.' The next morning Dick and I brought in real stunt guys, we did it in a half a day and it was perfect. Rooney was really pleased. 'You stunt guys ought to get a group or something together.' Dick and I talked it over for weeks. Nobody knew who the real stuntmen were, but if we had a group, producers and directors would know where to call. Six other guys helped us pick out the stuntmen, we had a meeting at the Screen Actors Guild, forty guys showed up, and every one was a real stuntman."

Loren and Dick cofounded the Stuntmen's Association of Motion Pictures in 1961. No one could have predicted its success. The organization of stuntmen, stunt coordinators, and second-unit directors became a powerful group, wired to different levels of the industry, and it began to control most of the stunt work. Membership was by invitation only; to join, a member had to earn at least $10,000 a year (a few made as much as $50,000). One writer called it "a sort of elite fraternity of pros that keeps a watchful eye on the benefits of the trade."[5] The association became a one-stop shop for the services of stuntmen; this increased their paychecks and solidified their place in the industry. The organization's unspoken, unwritten practice of hiring its own members built its true power. In 1969 membership totaled 135.

The Stuntmen's Association was openly discriminatory: women and minorities were excluded. According to Dave Robb, a reporter with *Variety*, one stuntman admitted (off the record) that the association didn't want women because "they would create sexual problems. If women were part of the group, then they'd be hooking up with other people. If women were not there, they [the men] wouldn't have to explain things to their wives." One stuntwoman said, "If I'd been a stuntman then I would have been ashamed to look a stuntwoman in the face."

Some of the excluded still got work on the 300-plus movies made each year and on TV shows. The basic requirements were agility, coordination, style, and timing. A sense of humor helped lighten the strain of working with groups of different, often eccentric individuals. Later in his career, Loren Janes researched stuntmen from the silent movies to the 1980s and found that "the top all-round stuntmen, without exception, were gymnasts, acrobats, and divers. Many had college degrees, often in engineering. Those guys knew how to design an action because they had studied how to get a stunt done."

Stuntmen still doubled women, and white stuntmen were still "painted down" with makeup to double black actors. Beginners had a hard time breaking into the business. There were no stunt schools or SAG regulations regarding who qualified as a stunt person. The best way to join the ranks was to be born into or marry into a stunt family or to know someone in the movie industry. For example, May Boss had no connections, but her neighbor did, and he helped her get work; her riding skills did the rest. No one had to bend the rules to let her work—there were no rules. Other professionals, such as teachers and engineers, need credentials, but stunt work has always depended on physical ability, and the only real stunt school was the set. Hopeful neophytes worked because they were talented, made friends, wangled jobs as extras, did small stunts, and learned by trial and error. In this informal, unregulated way, they got a foot in the door and expanded their skills. One stuntwoman summed up: "Some girls got stunt jobs because their boyfriends or husbands were in it. Others knew from day one what they wanted and went after it; some fell into it by accident, and a few girls were born into stunt families."

Jeannie Epper was born into a stunt family, and Julie Ann Johnson fell into it. They both became leaders in the challenging years ahead. Jeannie's father had performed stunts since *The Charge of the Light Brigade* in 1936. Thanks to his relatives in Switzerland, Jeannie had the opportunity to

Jeannie Epper at about age twenty, before she became the stuntwoman's stuntwoman. (Courtesy of Julie Ann Johnson)

attend a convent finishing school there. For two years she learned new languages and made new friends. But Jeannie had grown up in the San Fernando Valley doing acrobatics and riding horses, and when she returned home, she was determined to become a stuntwoman because action was her real language.

In the late 1950s Jeannie worked as an extra, doing little stunts. As a rookie, she didn't immediately jump off a building; she had a chance to learn the craft by watching Polly Burson and May Boss do stunts that were usually done only by men. "As a woman, when you pull off something only men do, it raises respect for all women—it opens the door for women to do all kinds of things."[6] According to Jeannie, Polly and May "were my mama chickens, they taught me the ropes." Jeannie also had a lot of support from her father and her siblings. More often, stuntmen trained their sons, not their daughters, but Jeannie recalled, "My dad saw that I was serious. When you're young, you let people boss you around, because you think you don't know enough, but my dad said, 'You're not doing that stunt. Go easy.' He was really strict. He also said, 'Don't sleep with anybody in the business, because you'll ruin your reputation.' And I didn't." For years she listened to her father's counsel shared at the dinner table. "His words saved my life a few times. The best advice he gave me was 'you can tell a lot by looking in their eyes. A horse with bad eyes would buck you off. It's something wrong inside them.' I remember that when I talk to actors about doing a stunt. I really look at them and I can tell if they're going to be okay or not with what I'm asking them to do. I was lucky to have a wonderful dad, but it was tough for me, too, because I had to be as good as a guy."

By 1967, Jeannie Epper had been doing stunts for about ten years. The six-year-old Stuntmen's Association had a lock on the business, but the fundamental distribution of stunt work had not changed. Skilled white stuntmen, especially members of the association, worked frequently, increased their experience and their income, and could advance to stunt coordinator or second-unit director. A few skilled white stuntwomen worked often and made a living, but they never earned as much as the men, nor could they graduate to positions of greater authority. Talented black stuntman worked, but not very often, which meant they lacked opportunities to increase their experience. Talented black stuntwomen rarely found work.

The decade of the 1960s delivered free love, flower power, the youth culture, Black Power, marches, and sit-ins. Young and old, black and white, sought to break down closed doors and seize long-denied opportunities. Stuntwomen and black stuntmen started to talk about forming their own stunt groups, and two separate incidents sparked their respective resolve.

For the stuntwomen, the catalyst was Julie Johnson, who was on the hot seat for taking a "horse job" in the TV series *Hondo* (1967). "Some stuntmen did not want women doing stunts at all," Julie said. "They didn't mind making a girl look bad so they could say, 'See? A girl can't do it, we have to replace her, we have to put the wig on.' They relished it. The horse job I did was one of those." In the silent movie era, women didn't get anywhere by saying no to a stunt, so they said yes to anything and then improvised. Fifty years later, experienced stuntwomen knew that saying yes could make their problems worse. They had to prevent rookies from taking jobs they couldn't handle. A botched stunt reflected badly on all stuntwomen, and it justified the ongoing practice of men doubling for women.

The women met in April 1967 at the Malibu home of Marilyn Moe and her husband, stunt coordinator Paul Stader.[7] All those present had strong bonds to the community: Jeannie and Stephanie Epper; Patty Elder,

Julie Ann Johnson.
(Courtesy of
Robert Young)

who had married stuntman Eddie Hice;[8] Regina Parton, whose father had once agreed to an equal fee split with Lila Finn.[9] Lila was among the senior stuntwomen; Helen Thurston, Loretta Rush, and Stevie Myers had been working in the business for thirty years and were still at it. Polly Burson and May Boss were less senior but no less talented. Pretty Julie Johnson was considered promising, but no one knew much about her: she'd come out of nowhere, wasn't related to anyone, and had barely five years experience.[10]

It was a beautiful spring night, and the women got right down to the problem—Julie's horse job. "Why are you taking jobs you can't handle?"

"They lied to me about it," Julie said.

"If you say you can ride a horse," May Boss warned, "you better be as good as a jockey."

"I know that," Julie said, "but the stuntman just asked, 'Can you ride a horse?' I can, and I asked him to tell me exactly what he wanted. He said, 'Just ride into town.' So I agreed to the job." What she hadn't been told was that when the two cowboys accompanying her went inside to rob the bank, she was supposed to stay outside and control their horses. Just before the director called "Action!" a prop man handed her a heavy shotgun. She was expected to hold on to all three horses, as well as the shotgun, until the men ran out of the bank, threw her a bag of money, and leaped onto their horses. Then she had to mount her horse, carrying the gun and the moneybag, and gallop out of town. A minute later she was supposed to "race the horse," and a rope was pulled across the street, where she would fall. They had put sand on the ground for her to land on, but the sand worried the horse; he bolted left and dumped Julie over his head onto the ground. She missed the sand. Disgusted, a stuntman yelled, "We're running out of time for you to keep trying this. Let me have your clothes and wig. I'll do it myself!"

The few women who could have done it in one take were in Marilyn's living room. "It was a royal setup to prove that a woman can't do the job!" Stevie Myers yelled. The women groaned and jeered. "When are they going to hire a real horsewoman?" Polly grumbled. Cool, calm May Boss said, "No, I understand. Don't we all understand?" They nodded, but it was hard to let go of their anger. Julie didn't have the skills to do a horse job, especially one that changed just before it was shot.

Jeannie Epper was eight months pregnant and had difficulty focusing that night. "Back then you were either a horse person or you weren't," she said. "If you were not really great at it, you were looked down upon. That happened to Julie. The other horse girls, Stevie, May, Polly, felt she took a job that was over her head. Today we have stuntwomen's organizations. We bring the younger girls in to show them the ropes. No group did that for us. We were fighting for basic recognition as stuntwomen. We warned the girls that if they took jobs they couldn't do as well as a guy or *better,* they were going to put a guy back in the clothes. That was the issue we were fighting—too many men were doubling women." The senior stuntwomen wanted to select the best girls for certain jobs, just like the men did, but stuntwomen had no control over either stunts or hiring. Further, the new stuntwomen resented the older women's interference and insisted on taking jobs they thought they could do. "It was a breakthrough time," Jeannie said. "That's why the girls were upset with Julie because they didn't want her or anybody to set us back." At the end of that meeting, the group decided to organize the first stuntwomen's association.[11] Julie was relieved when she was invited to join.

The event that sparked the creation of the Black Stuntmen's Association (BSA) came in 1963. Edward Smith had been an extra and an actor since the 1950s.[12] While working on *It's a Mad, Mad, Mad, Mad World* (1963),[13] he saw a white stuntman being painted down to double Eddie "Rochester" Anderson. He complained to director Stanley Kramer, "Why isn't a black stuntman doubling Rochester?" Kramer replied, "Well, find me one." Smith tried, but, he said, "I couldn't get no brothers nowhere."[14] As a result, Smith and Calvin Brown came up with the idea, and with the firm support of Marvin Walters, they formed the Black Stuntmen's Association in 1967.[15]

"The nature of the times catapulted the movies' problem people of old into militants of new," film historian Donald Bogle wrote. "No longer were sad-eyed black people trying to prove their worth in order to fit into white worlds. . . . Instead the headstrong militants appeared. . . . It started with sit-ins, boycotts and marches and ended with riots, demonstrations and a series of horrifying assassinations. In 1960, Negroes were quietly asking for their rights. By 1969, Blacks were demanding them."[16]

Racism in the film industry was so ingrained that the studios were called "plantations." In 1943 Oscar-winning actress Hattie McDaniel had asked the Screen Actors Guild to form a committee to discuss the problems faced by black performers in films. "Los Angeles was a particularly cruel mirage for Black writers," wrote social critic Mike Davis. Specifically, he was referring to Chester Hines, who got "a fresh start as a screenwriter for Warner Bros." in the early 1940s. "Despite his formidable reputation as a short story writer for *Esquire,* Hines encountered an implacable wall of racism in Hollywood. As his biographer describes the incident, 'he was promptly fired when Jack Warner heard about him and said, "I don't want no niggers on this lot." After that Hines retaliated, writing two blazing novels about Los Angeles 'as a racial hell.'"[17] SAG did not act on McDaniel's request until 1972—twenty-nine years after the fact.[18]

In the 1960s television and films began to feature more black actors— Sidney Poitier, Cicely Tyson, Bill Cosby, Ruby Dee, Harry Belafonte, Gloria Foster. The TV show *I Spy* (1965–1968), starring Cosby, was a hit. But according to reporter Tod Longwell, the struggle of the Black Stuntmen's Association "is a lost piece of civil rights and Hollywood history." Poitier observed that the BSA's contribution "is all too often not remembered . . . they were quite a force."[19] The newly formed BSA did not go unnoticed, however. "White stuntmen were wary of its formation, concerned that they would be losing jobs to African Americans."[20] Early BSA members included Alex Brown, Henry Kingi, Ernie Robinson, and a few women who trained with them on weekends. "We'd look across the street and there'd always be cops in unmarked police cars, watching," Kingi said, laughing. "We figured they thought we were another Black Panther group forming."[21]

"The guys worked with us girls just like we were guys," Evelyn Cuffee said. "They didn't slack up on us. When they got beat up, we got beat up." Evelyn was separated from her husband and raising five children by herself. She eventually joined the Stuntwomen's Association in the 1970s, but she was working as an extra when Eddie Smith "got the stuntmen together in a park in the late 1960s. I was the only girl, but soon Louise Johnson, Peaches Jones, and, later, Jadie David joined. Peaches was a cute little girl, very agile, and shy, too, but if she did something, she did it right. We all became friends, but back then stuntwomen hardly ever worked together. The guys in BSA showed us how to do fights, how to fall. I could throw a punch and I could take one—a *good* one." She had grown up with six brothers in Mitchell, South Dakota, where her father worked in a bank. "We were the only black family in town. I did everything the boys did, track, football, basketball. It was rough, but they were my guardians."[22] In 1972 Evelyn worked on *Buck and the Preacher,* directed by Sidney Poitier. "Peaches did utility stunts—that's when you do a lot of everything," Evelyn said. "Louise and I did horseback riding. On one stunt, the bad guys were burning up the wagon train, trying to catch the women. I ran through a burning wagon when the guy chasing me slashed at me with a machete. I thought it was a prop, but it sliced right through a rope close to my face. Sidney said, 'Oh, great, really good stunt!'" Being an African American and a woman "did not help my stunt career," Evelyn said, "not on anything. We had a hard way to go. I'm sure the white girls had a hard way, too—those guys doing the hiring didn't want women in there at all."

"We were members of everything—PUSH, CORE, the NAACP," said Kingi. "Eddie [Smith] would call studios and say he was the Black National Congress leader of the African Society of Whatever-It-Was, he'd heard there was a problem, then we'd go in as the group and follow up. Every time Eddie would tell us, 'We've got another situation,' we'd say, 'Okay, who are we today, Eddie?' We were either going to do or die. We were not going to sell out or be bought out. . . . We all stuck together." Some BSA members were "branded as troublemakers" because they competed for work with other "black stuntmen who did not make waves." The white stuntmen "resented that we were taking money from their pockets," Kingi said. "They also didn't like taking orders."[23]

Evelyn Cuffee, tough and optimistic. (Courtesy of Evelyn Cuffee)

Another "paint down" gave the BSA added momentum in 1971. Roydon Clark (James Garner's regular double) was the stunt coordinator for *Skin Game,* and he hired white stuntman Jerry Brown to drive a stagecoach for Louis Gossett Jr. "'It was a safety issue, not a black-and-white issue,' said Clark, but he acknowledged 'my decision almost cost me my career.'"[24] Eddie Smith went on a mission and "complained to Warner Bros., naming a qualified black man—Tony Brubaker, later a top stuntman—called the NAACP, the Equal Employment Opportunity Commission, and the Screen Actors Guild. Warner Bros. responded by including black stuntmen in all scenes involving general stunt work, and invited black stuntmen to train with veteran white stuntmen."[25] When requests for black stuntmen started to increase, Smith warned newcomers, "If you can't do the job, don't do it, because it just takes one guy to screw it up for everybody."[26] It was the same issue facing stuntwomen: each person in a marginalized group must prove that he or she is as good as or better than those on the inside. White stuntwomen had to scale a wall to get work, but it was a much higher obstacle for people of color.

In these years, two other changes affected all stunt performers: the end of secrecy surrounding the use of stunt doubles, and the advent of stunt coordinators. Steve McQueen and other stars broke the old studio-enforced code of silence. Loren Janes, who doubled McQueen for twenty-three years, recalled: "I'd be on the set wearing a long coat so no one saw I was doubling him until I took it off to do the stunt—all because he told everyone he did the stunts. After *Nevada Smith* [1966] he said to me, 'You tell everyone you do it and that's it.' Roydon Clark doubled James Garner for years and around that time Garner told everyone, 'I wouldn't get on a chair without my stuntman.'" And so, stunt players began to be credited for their work.

Meanwhile, the position of ramrod or gaffer became known as stunt coordinator. "Directors, assistant directors, and others hired stuntmen," Loren said, "but in the 1950s that job started being called the 'ramrod.' A director hired a stuntman as the ramrod and asked him, 'Who do we hire for this?' The ramrod told him and the director hired the men. In the mid-1960s, a ramrod became a 'stunt coordinator.' He managed the stunts and hired the stunt people. The first time I was called a stunt coordinator was on *The Sand Pebbles* in 1966. We were in Taiwan, Hong Kong, and China for eleven months. The director, Robert Wise, told me what he wanted. I found the stuntmen to double the stars and worked out the stunts we needed. Back then, coordinating wasn't as complex as it is now." Nor was it as powerful. Today, stunt coordinators break down the script, design and budget the stunts, and hire the players. It is a multifaceted job that requires managerial skills, creativity, stunt experience, and knowledge of cameras and special effects, as well as a balance of action and people skills. A coordinator must make the stunts exciting while ensuring the safety of cast, crew, and stunt players.

Around this time, the great Polly Burson said yes to a dreadful movie. She was fifty years old, she needed the money, and she'd been hitting the ground for twenty-three years.[27] She had coordinated the female roles in *Westward the Women,* but that one job meant nothing; the position of stunt coordinator was not open to her or any other woman. "I think it was Julie Johnson's first big action picture—as big as it was," Polly said scathingly. Neither Polly nor Julie knew the film had ever been released. "I believed the scuttlebutt," Polly said, which was "that it was [financed with] Mafia money from Florida and they didn't take out any taxes. My checks were always good, but some of the crew's—those checks were hot!" The low-budget movie starred James Caan, Stephanie Powers, Sammy Davis

The "somersault thing" in the Polly Burson–Julie Johnson fight scene. (Courtesy of Polly Burson)

Jr., and Aldo Ray. Finally released as *Gone with the West,* it is, by any standard, a terrible movie.[28]

Unofficially, Polly and Julie coordinated a great stunt sequence in that terrible movie. They called it "the fight to die for." It takes stunt knowledge to create a fight that tells a story through physical actions, and it takes talented stuntwomen to execute the stunt so that every punch looks real. That's the essence of a gag—it's a trick, and it's an art. "The fight started in a bedroom above a saloon," Polly said, "went out the door, down the stairs, into the bar, onto tables, through a window, down on the street, and ended up in a water trough. I have a photo—I'd thrown Julie over in a somersault thing and you can't tell who's who except I've got my legs and arms in the air."

In a room above a saloon, Aldo Ray's character is lounging in bed with Little Moon (doubled by Julie) when his jealous girlfriend (doubled by Polly) bursts in and literally flies at her rival.[29] "That's when Polly hit her knee on the side of the bed," Julie said. "I heard the impact." (Polly's knees had already taken a lot of punishment jumping on and off horses.) In the next setup, Polly punches Julie and throws her to the floor. Julie staggers to the landing, where she falls into a breakaway railing and onto the stairs below. Polly leaps over the railing and hits the stairs; they both roll down, clobbering each other. Polly slams Julie into a breakaway table, tosses her into the "somersault thing," and breaks a chair over her head. When Julie gets to her feet, Polly's punch gives her the momentum to crash through a big breakaway window.

That's when a disagreement ensued. According to Julie, "a stuntman told me how to go through the window. He'd made advances to me, I'd said no thank you, and now he insisted I fall through the window a certain way. It felt really wrong so I told Polly and she said in a loud voice, 'You'll break your bloody neck if you do it that way. We're too high off the ground. That ass wants to make you look bad 'cause you turned him down.' Polly said the best way to hit the window and survive was to run at it, hit the pane with my right shoulder and land flat on my back outside on the boardwalk." After Julie breaks through the window, Polly pitches through the open space and lands nearby. Julie lurches up, but Polly brings her down with a flying tackle. Julie kicks Polly, puts her in a headlock, punches her hard in the face—bam! bam!—and knocks her into the water trough, but Polly drags Julie into the trough with her.

Odds are almost no one saw that remarkable stunt fight, but in 1969 millions saw *True Grit*. "I loved John Wayne," Polly purred. "I doubled the girl, Mattie, played by Kim Darby." Written by Marguerite Roberts, it was directed by the dour Henry Hathaway.[30] The film preserves a lasting vision of Polly riding a horse named Little Blackie hard and fast, plunging into a river, and swimming across it. As Polly recalled, "The SPCA was standing

Polly Burson and Little Blackie in the cold, cold water. (Courtesy of Polly Burson)

there" to ensure the animal's safety. "They'd only let me ride a horse once into that cold water. They didn't give a damn if I got in and froze stiffer than a plank."[31]

But in Polly's opinion, the best thing that happened on *True Grit* was this: "Robert Duvall and his gang are at the top of a hill holding me down as the girl, Duvall's got his foot in my back, I scream, he gets mad at something, Mr. Hathaway gets mad and says to Duvall, 'You owe me an apology.' Duvall says, 'I don't owe you a damn thing.' Mr. Hathaway says, 'You owe my *crew* an apology.' Duvall yells, 'I don't owe them anything either!' Three women were up there—the hairdresser, the script girl, and me. Mr. Hathaway says, 'You owe the women an apology.' Duvall says, 'Fuck the women.' The hairdresser raises her hand and says, 'Me first.'" Polly whooped with laughter. "Even Mr. Hathaway laughed—he *hollered*—and believe me, he didn't do that very often."

The increasingly visible struggles of women and minorities to obtain stunt work coincided with two unexpected opportunities in film and television. In different ways, both revealed the best-kept secret in the business: stuntwomen of any color were tough and competent. Their athletic performances in the rebellious 1970s helped change the image of women on television and in the misnamed, short-lived, but effective blaxploitation movies.

# 5

# Social Turmoil Brings New Opportunities for Women and Minorities

We are what we are *perceived* to be.

—*Congresswoman Barbara Jordan*

Of all the obstacles stunt performers faced—real and metaphorical—the most difficult ones were those faced by African American women. In the TV series *Get Christie Love* (1974–1975), stuntwoman Jadie David had to jump over a nine-foot wall. "I didn't think I could do it until they sicced this huge dog on me. I was surprised how fast I got over that wall, but the goddamn dog came right over behind me!"[1]

Four years earlier, Jadie had been a college student studying to be a nurse. Having grown up in Burbank, California, near the Equestrian Center on the edge of Griffith Park, she often took breaks from her studies to ride horses in the park. "A man used to ride by me sometimes," she said, "and one day he stopped to say he needed a tall black woman who could swim and ride a horse to double an actress in a film. He did give me a job on the movie—I hate the name of it—*The Legend of Nigger Charley*. Isn't that amazing? Back then people didn't think about a title like that. For a scene in it Denise Nicholas and Fred Williamson were to jump off a rock, swim to shore, and fall in love, or whatever."[2]

The man in Griffith Park, Bob Minor, became a friend and influenced Jadie's career. He had been a record-holding track athlete in college and later won bodybuilding titles, including "Mr. Los Angeles, best chest, best back, best arms." He had been working out at the California Gym when

Jadie David, about to become a stuntwoman. (Courtesy of Jadie David)

someone asked him if he'd ever considered stunt work. "I had not," he said. "That seemed kind of far out of my reach." But he looked into it, joined stuntman Paul Stader's gym in Santa Monica, and even took acting classes. By 1970, at age twenty-six, he had a whole new set of ambitions. "Being an African American, I knew the opportunity was there and I had to try to take it."

To stay in shape, Minor rode in Griffith Park. "I saw this cute girl," he recalled, "but she acted stuck up like she thought she had it going on." He had just been hired to double football player Fred Williamson in a western. "I rode up to her like a guy in a sunset. 'Hey, little girl, do you want to be in movies?' She said, 'Yeah, right.' I said, 'I *am* doing a movie.'" She didn't believe him, but he managed to wangle her name and number, and she was hired. "And that's how I met Jadie."[3]

Minor recalled their swimming scene in detail. He and Jadie, doubling for Williamson and Nicholas, were supposed to swim to shore, where they embrace and kiss. "That's when the director always says 'Cut!' and the actors come in," Minor explained. "Stunt people do the rough stuff, not love scenes. Jadie and I are on the beach, but the director's still rolling camera and I don't hear 'Cut.' I didn't know what to do, so I gave Jadie the big-

78

Outgoing Bob Minor, confident and ready to work. (Courtesy of Bob Minor)

gest kiss. And we're kissing and kissing before I hear, 'Come on. . . . ' Everyone started laughing. The director had said he wasn't going to holler 'cut,' but it was nice, two stunt people on the beach kissing, a scene I'll never forget."

Jadie hadn't known what to expect on her first movie. "I thought I was acting," she said, "but that wasn't my job." She took the kissing scene with good humor: "Here's the new girl, let's do the whole kiss, a little joke. If it had been malicious, I would have picked that up." When the production wrapped, Jadie realized "they were going to pay me to have fun!" She abandoned her plans to be a nurse.

*Sweet Sweetback's Baadasssss Song* and *Shaft* were box-office hits in 1971, and they were among the first films made by and for African Americans in this era.[4] At the time, the film industry was interested only in making movies for the masses, which were perceived as white. Jadie's athletic skills and the changing times made her career possible. "That was the beginning of the black exploitation film era," she said. "There was a need for someone like me, and people started giving me jobs."

Before that time, black stuntwomen hardly seemed to exist at all. Back in 1954, Joyce Jones, an actress in New York, had been hailed as "the only

Negro stuntwoman in television." According to *Jet* magazine, Jones took on "tough TV roles other girls refuse. She has been pistol-whipped, shoved down stairs, kicked from a ladder and beaten in a bar room." Jones said the secret to being a "stunt girl" was "learning how to fall. 'You've got to be completely relaxed at it.'"[5] In the 1920s stuntwoman Winnie Brown had said the same thing—"fall limber."

A year after the *Jet* article on Joyce Jones, the civil rights movement gained traction. Rosa Parks refused to give up her seat on a bus in Montgomery, Alabama. The cultural upheaval and the demonstrations that followed in the 1960s and 1970s (soundtrack by Bob Dylan, the Four Tops, Ray Charles, Motown, and the Beatles) mushroomed and enveloped other causes and groups such as voting rights, freedom riders, the Black Panthers, and Vietnam War protesters; these issues merged with the galloping influence of the new women's movement and the national debates over race and sex discrimination. The appalling assassinations of Martin Luther King Jr. and Robert Kennedy had fired up the social stew of shock, unrest, and opposition. All over the country, people expressed the frustration later heard in Paddy Chayefsky's movie *Network* (1976): "I'm mad as hell and I'm not going to take it anymore." These turbulent times racked up divisions, bloodshed—and opportunities.

The powerful exchange between movies and audiences, which both reflected and influenced social reality, triggered new onscreen stories. Real stories about black women and men had not been seen since the work of Oscar Micheaux (1884–1951), who directed and produced forty-four films between 1919 and 1948. But in mainstream movies, black actors were usually relegated to roles as porters, slaves, servants, laborers, dads, moms, or friends of the stars. By the 1960s, some mainstream films featured a few black actors: *Take a Giant Step, Raisin in the Sun, Lilies of the Field, To Kill a Mockingbird, Guess Who's Coming to Dinner?* Other movies made by or about African Americans included *One Potato, Two Potato; Nothing but a Man; The Split; The Riot; Slaves;* and *The Cool World.*[6]

In April 1971 Melvin Van Peebles's *Sweet Sweetback's Baadasssss Song,* an insolent little movie that made big money, caught the industry's attention. Black Americans "were laying claims to the screen for the first time." These films "gave black people a sense of self, which had been stolen from them. . . . It was the first time a black could make it to the end of the movie without being killed by white folks," said Van Peebles. "Just like Sweetback— he gets away!"[7] *Shaft* and others followed—*Super Fly, Black Caesar, Uptown*

*Saturday Night, Friday Foster, Let's Do It Again.* Many of these movies with predominantly black casts were labeled blaxploitation films, a controversial term. In Isaac Julien's documentary *Baadasssss Cinema,* actor, director, and producer Fred Williamson explains that the term *blaxploitation* came from middle-class black organizations such as the NAACP. "But who was being exploited?" he asks. "Actors were being paid, audiences got to see things they'd longed for, so I don't understand where the term fits." For decades, low-budget films of all types had been the turf of entrepreneurs looking to make money by exploiting some taboo—sex, nudity, violence— but many so-called blaxploitation movies were stylish and fresh.

The social turmoil of the 1970s had an impact on stuntwomen. Gloria Hendry had stage and screen roles to her credit, including being the first African American to play James Bond's girlfriend in *Live and Let Die* (1973). But for some of her roles she felt "put down by the theater community and by my family. The teachers, the mothers, the organizations, the churches were tired of 'these stereotypes.' They were right," she said, "but we were beginning to make our own stars, our own movies, the door to filmmaking was wide open and that was brand new! It was so exciting. Some movies were on the periphery of society's no-no's, but part of that was, 'How dare you make a career out of acting?' Women still couldn't do things like make more money than a man, and college for us was a privilege—but *acting?*"[8]

Until this time, the business of stunts had been a closed white shop. Some white actors still performed in blackface, but it wasn't cool anymore. A few African American men had done stunts in the 1960s: Wayne King, Eddie Smith, Marvin Walters, Calvin Brown, Ernie Robinson. They were joined in the 1970s by stuntwomen Peaches Jones, Jadie David, Evelyn Cuffee, and Louise Johnson, as well as by Henry Kingi, Richard Washington, Alan Oliney, Bob Minor, Tony Brubaker, and Jophery Brown, followed by Greg Wayne Elam, Wayne King Jr., and Henry Kingi Jr.[9] They were hired because the 1970s blaxploitation films made money, and the stories by writers such as Richard Wesley, Ernest Tidyman, and Jack Hill changed movie roles. Hill created characters that stuntwomen could double, such as Coffy, who sought revenge for her sister's death, and Foxy Brown, "a woman who can handle herself in high society," Hill said. She "knows the street, too, can discuss philosophy and hit someone with a bar stool!"[10] Pam Grier brought style and vigor to the heroines she played, and Jadie David doubled her.[11] "Coffy was my mom, Foxy was my aunt," Grier said.

Left to right: Jadie David, Pam Grier, Bob Minor. (Courtesy of Yolanda Minor)

"They were independent women."[12] When trouble was brewing, Coffy and Foxy didn't wait around to be rescued; they saved themselves, saved others, and got payback, too. Their characters' motivations echoed not only the silent movie serial *The Hazards of Helen* but also *An Auto Heroine* (1908) and remakes of that story by Mary Pickford and Mabel Normand, who portrayed women willing to take action to save someone in need.[13]

Bob Minor, who stunt-coordinated *Coffy* and *Foxy Brown,* recalled that "Jack Hill was always a fair man. He wanted to give an African American a chance to coordinate *Coffy,* and with a lead like Pam Grier, he figured the combination would be good." Those movies had fight scenes galore, and some were real brawls. "I was the one with the short hair that goes to Foxy and starts the fight," said Jeannie Epper. About thirty-three then, the sullen, tough-looking Jeannie makes the move that drags a dozen women into the melee, punching, kicking, and breaking up furniture. "Fights are like a big play day," Jadie rejoiced. "You're not really putting your life on the line, but in *Foxy Brown* Jeannie got hit over the head with a picture frame that wasn't scored properly and she ended up getting some stitches."[14]

Props that break with a satisfying pizzazz are a big part of stunts. But improperly designed props can cause injuries. In Jeannie's case, the wood of the picture frame should have been partially cut through so that it would break easily, not clobber her. Other breakaway props are deliberately constructed to fall apart, such as chairs made of balsa wood that shatter on impact. When stunt people crash through windows, they're really shattering sheets of hardened sugar called "candy glass," which breaks harmlessly, with no dangerous shards. Stuntwoman Evelyn Cuffee, who "ran like hell" in *Buck and the Preacher*, barely escaped injury in *The New Centurions* (1972). She played a customer in a bank that's robbed by stuntman Calvin Brown. "Cal's holding me hostage in front of him, waving the gun, and we're supposed to go out the door, but he's backing up, misses the door, hits a plate glass window and it breaks! He wasn't supposed to go through it, but he did and I went with him." That window was not made of candy glass.

Other African Americans hired to stunt-coordinate included Tony Brubaker, Alan Oliney, and Richard Washington, who had quit his day job as a deep-sea diver to devote his life to stunts. "In the beginning you do what you're told," he said, "but as you get older, you might say to the guy hiring you, 'What if I did this instead?' He looks at you, you don't know if he'll say 'Okay' or 'Get out of here.' If he says it's a good idea, he tells the director and the director thinks he thought it up, so he gets brownie points and you get to create a little bit of action. When you're the coordinator, you create it all. On *Buck Rogers*, I wrote every fight, blow by blow."[15] On one of his first stunt-coordinating jobs, Washington hired Jadie David to double Pam Grier in the 1975 movie *Sheba Baby*.

For Universal's TV series *Get Christie Love*, stunt coordinator Paul Baxley hired Peaches Jones, the first successful black stuntwoman in Los Angeles, to double Teresa Graves in the title role as an undercover policewoman. Peaches had worked on shows like *The Mod Squad* in the 1960s; she and her dad, Sam Jones, were among the first members of the Black Stuntmen's Association.[16] "Patty Elder and Peaches excelled as stuntwomen, they were really well liked," Jadie said. Jeannie Epper agreed, "but Peaches would disappear, then turn up and step right back into the work because she was so talented." Jeannie was alluding to drug use, which increased significantly in the 1970s. According to Rich Washington, Peaches began to show up late or didn't show up at all, and Jadie replaced her on *Get Christie Love*. "If Peaches hadn't gone off the deep end," Jadie said, "my career would not have gone as well as it did. I slipped in because

Stunt coordinator Richard Washington with Don Adams on the set of *The Nude Bomb* (1980). (Courtesy of Richard Washington)

she left a void. I'm real clear on that." Drugs wrecked many careers, including those of talented stuntwomen Peaches Jones, who died at age thirty-five, and Patty Elder, who died at forty-eight.

The rush of independent black films lasted from 1970 to 1975. "Then the door shut tight," actress Gloria Hendry said. "We all fell off the track for years, except a black star here or there. *Sounder* or *The River Niger* didn't come around too often." Only a few stars and stunt people of color were able to build long careers based on their early work in those special films.

By the 1970s, the Stuntmen's Association had about 140 members. The Black Stuntmen's Association had 100 members, including 8 to 10 women. Rich Washington estimated that 20 BSA members made a living; of those, 10 did very well. The newest of the groups, the Stuntwomen's Association, had 18 members.[17] Respected horsewoman Stevie Myers was its president in 1971; Lila Finn presided in 1972. Most members agreed that although the stuntwomen's group was helpful, it could not get them access to stunt-coordinating positions. Those years were frustrating and contentious. In February 1972 the Stuntwomen's Association planned to release its first directory to publicize members' abilities and credits, but a few members fought against the proposal. Two wanted to disband the organization altogether; the motion was voted down.[18]

These internal quarrels reflected a small, powerless group fighting itself. In time, the organization did improve its members' professional standing, but it could not increase their employment. The association could only advise members not to take a stunt unless they could do it "as well as a man—or better." The group promoted its members' abilities, provided a place for them to vent, and gave them a chance to feel like a sisterhood.[19] "I don't know if it really helped us in our careers, unfortunately," one stuntwoman said. Another pointed out that the men's groups argued too and were "just as petty, trying to steal jobs from each other. You'd think the guys would go toe-to-toe, duke it out, but they were very nonconfrontational, they were just as bad as the girls. You can't get ten stunt guys to agree on anything. Or stuntwomen."

The male leadership of the Stuntmen's Association ruled like an oligarchy, and some members were grumbling. In 1970 "about fifteen stunt coordinators had a stranglehold on the stunt business," stuntman-director Hal Needham wrote in his autobiography. "They ran most of the features and a major portion of the TV shows being shot. They would hire each other first, and then if there were any crumbs left over, they would dole them out to their closest friends. The only way to get work was to have a talent nobody else had—or to suck up to them and politick your ass off."[20] Members wanted to "modernize" stunts, instead of reworking old gags originated by Yakima Canutt and Jock Mahoney.[21] Westerns were fading; horses were out, bikes and cars were in. The dissidents weren't happy about the money either. For every stunt, the coordinators negotiated the fees, but the rates had been set in the 1960s, and the rebels wanted a raise.[22] Needham, Ron Rondell, Glenn Wilder, and fifteen other stuntmen decamped to form Stunts Unlimited in 1970. "Longtime friends hardly spoke to each other," Needham wrote. "Stuntmen's Association members would not hire Stunts Unlimited members, and vice versa. The Association thought—and hoped—Unlimited would fail. They could not have been more wrong." Two years later, Stunts Unlimited had twenty-five members.[23]

Five years after that split, May Boss, Julie Johnson, Jadie David, Jeannie

Epper, and Stevie Myers left the Stuntwomen's Association and formed the Society of Professional Stuntwomen.[24] Membership was limited to the top twelve stuntwomen, and the group's goals were to increase safety, "help train new stuntwomen, and gain recognition for women as courageous and adventurous souls," Janet Chase wrote for *Cosmopolitan*. "Facing perils unknown to their male colleagues, stuntwomen have had to wage war on the industry tradition of using men in drag to perform stunts for actresses, just as they've had to struggle for equal pay."[25]

Stuntwomen were in the first stages of a classic David and Goliath confrontation. They and minority stunt players fought on parallel battlefields for similar goals, but in different ways. Dave Robb, who covered legal and labor issues for *Variety* and the *Hollywood Reporter* for twenty years, described what they were up against: "In the industry, if anybody had a problem, I was the complaint department. If you got a call from me, it meant you had labor or legal problems. Basically, I wrote about people getting screwed by Hollywood—in the unions or the minority groups. Of all the groups that seemed to be getting screwed the most, it would probably be a tie between stuntwomen and American Indians. For instance, both stuntmen's groups didn't allow women. One guy told me, 'We don't allow women, because it's called the Stunt*man's* Association,'" Robb recalled. "'It's not the Stunt*women's* Association or the Stunt *Person's* Association.' He said that on the record. I think he was president of the Stuntmen's Association."[26] He was. As Bill Lane (*Dirty Harry, Ghostbusters*) told Robb, "'It's a California corporation. It was set up that way (for men only) 22 years ago. At that time, they didn't have the ERA (Equal Rights Amendment) or any of that other **** like that.'"[27] "But they were not just fraternal organizations," Robb said. "They were also hiring halls, which had to be licensed by the state, which they were not, and by law, hiring agencies are not allowed to discriminate based on gender or race or age. I don't think they thought they were a hiring agency until I first brought it up to them. That they were doing something illegal never occurred to them. They would hire their own members. If you weren't a member, you were boxed out. Women were actively being discriminated against right up through the 1990s."[28] But as Robb pointed out, "not all stuntwomen feel they are discriminated against. These women say they have their own stunt organizations . . . they don't want to join the men's groups, are treated well by the men and frequently hired by them. Others say that women are often the victims of sexual harassment by stuntmen and coordinators and that the only way to be hired by them is not to rock the boat. Minority and independent stuntmen have also complained that they are 'locked out' of Hollywood by the stuntmen's organizations, few of whose members are black, Hispanic or Asian."[29]

To improve their position, stuntwomen had to find a way to raise their professional standing, stop the practice of men doubling for women, and contest their near-total exclusion from another significant work category called "nondescript"—ND for short, which also stood for "no dames"—such as being part of a crowd scene that employed not only extras but also stunt people for a street brawl, for example. A stunt person in a crowd is only a blurred face, but coordinators didn't hire women or minorities for those scenes. ND work might last for half a day or a week, and the SAG minimum rate in 1977 was $172.50 a day. "We almost never got any nondescript work," said stuntwoman Evelyn Cuffee. Julie Ann Johnson charged that "cronyism among stunt coordinators contributes significantly to the dismal employment record of stuntwomen."[30] In the twenty years May Boss had done stunts, very few had been nondescript. "That was the worst," she groaned. "They get an order for fifteen drivers, call up all the men they know, and then say, 'Gee, we didn't think of a woman for this.'"

The Screen Actors Guild's 1963 nondiscrimination policy directed studios and producers to make "every effort to cast performers" in suitable roles "and in a manner where 'the American scene' may be portrayed realistically." The "American scene" implied hiring people of different races, but the mandate to make "every effort" had no teeth; it did not specify women and was not enforced. "If you keep giving jobs to people who look like you," Jadie David said, "they will get more experience and that qualifies them for the next job." She knew she was sometimes hired because someone wanted to do the right thing; other times she knew she wasn't hired because of her color, her gender, or both. "We fought that all the time. All the time. Stunts were dominated by people who did not look like me."

Members of the BSA took on the system. "If a production painted a white stuntman black, it had to answer to a lot of people, and I was one of them," Rich Washington said. "I was into affirmative action with the studios. That was the only way we could secure jobs." In terms of approach, he and Eddie Smith were polar opposites, but they worked in tandem. "Eddie would rush in," Rich said, and "he might threaten to cut your tires. I might talk about a lawsuit with the federal government. We played off each other, good cop, bad cop, and it worked." But the more Washington spoke up, the more jobs he lost. "Finally, my wife said, 'You've got to shut up.'" So he went to meetings and sat in the back row. One day at Universal he was pressed to speak up, and that led to another stunt-coordinating job.[31] Washington had already developed a job-hunting strategy that consisted of "walking the corridors"—going to the studios' production offices and asking about stunts on that week's TV episodes. "I'd be told there was no one for black actors to double. That was my cue to say, 'Okay, maybe next show,' but I'd ask, 'What about ND work?' Nondescript wasn't as good, but for a picture in the U.S., crowd scenes were supposed to be a mixed racial group. The guy hadn't thought of it and sometimes he agreed I could work in a crowd scene. I saw it as a negotiation, like chess."

Meanwhile, Bob Minor targeted the all-white Stuntmen's Association and became its first African American member in 1972. "I wanted to and I did break the color barrier. I also wanted to be in the group that was well established. The BSA asked me to join, but I wanted to learn from experienced stuntmen who had made their mark, like stunt coordinator Carey Loftin, who did *Bullitt,* Terry Leonard, Roydon Clark, and Max Klevins. I was always a big supporter of the Black Stuntmen's Association and later as a stunt coordinator I hired many African American stunt people from the group."[32]

Jadie David ticked off the problems faced by women "in this male-oriented business. Stuntwomen double only when there's a scripted stunt for an actress, but there aren't nearly as many roles for us as there are for men." Women weren't hired for nondescript work because the men doing the hiring preferred guys. Jadie and other women also lost jobs when the actors didn't want to risk "hurting women." On other jobs, there might be "the macho thing" in addition to "a money factor. A big stunt might yield a $2,000 adjustment fee and another might yield $200," Jadie said. "A guy would rather have his friend make the $2,000 and so-and-so can make the $200. Finally, though I have not personally run across this, sometimes I've had the feeling a guy would rather do a stunt because he'd hate to see a woman do it as well as he could."[33]

Women were virtually stalemated: if they remained silent, nothing would change, but speaking up could have serious consequences. In the stunt community, someone who made "disloyal complaints" could be labeled a troublemaker, and that could end a career. According to Joe Ruskin, first vice president of the Screen Actors Guild and cochair of the Stunt and Safety Committee, the stuntmen's group was "a community unto themselves. The women are blackballed for complaining. I've heard it out of the mouths of the stunt ladies."[34] Nonetheless, the women did speak out—at the Screen Actors Guild and to the press. "It just came to a point when we realized we were not in the Dark Ages anymore, and we said, 'Give us a shot, let us try at least,'" Jeannie Epper said. "It took a while. . . . We had to really get our actresses to say, 'Hey, we don't want some hairy-legged guy doubling us.' And we began proving that we could do what we said we could do."[35]

Women and blacks had to fight for a chance to work and for the opportunity to fail. "A black person has to be perfect just to be equal," Bob Minor said. "When you're black, you cannot make mistakes. If I wasn't perfect, they'd say, 'I gave him a chance and he failed.' But when you fail, you learn! The next time I'll drive at this speed instead of that speed." One stuntwoman said, "It was like we had to be Olympic-class athletes on every single stunt"—an impossible standard. "Often when people try to do their jobs under great adversity and discrimination they become stronger," Dave Robb noted. "They become real heroes and heroines. Stuntwomen weren't only brave to do the stunts, they were brave to be working in an industry that really didn't want them."

In 1964 Charlton Heston, president of the Screen Actors Guild, had appointed Kathleen Nolan to the Hollywood Screen Actors board.[36] Peppy and tenacious, she jumped into battles that involved actresses, minorities, and stunt people. She had been acting since age five and had appeared in many television series (*The Real McCoys, Burke's Law, The Big Valley*); she knew "the stunt community—the best of the bunch." In 1972 she formed the first SAG Stunt Committee. The year before, Writers Guild of America member Diana Gould (*Family, Sisters, La Ciociara*) had petitioned her organization to form an official Women's Committee. She argued that female writers needed to discuss and act on their professional concerns, and the WGA agreed. Kathleen Nolan and Norma Connolly also created the SAG Women's Conference Committee in 1972 "to erase ways women are stereotyped on and off the screen, work for equal opportunity for employment, regardless of sex . . . [and] reshape the media image of the American female."[37] That year, SAG established the Ethnic Minorities Committee as well.

These committees rocked with arguments—and action. They made underemployment of minorities and women a central issue. The Screen Actors Guild, along with groups like the NAACP, worked hard to desegregate Hollywood.[38] The guilds turned out riveting statistics to wake up the industry and the public. The numbers proved what women and minorities already knew: they did not write, direct, or act in nearly as many shows as white male guild members did. Bolstered by a Brigham Young University study, SAG claimed that 81.7 percent of TV roles were male, and only 18.3 percent were female.[39] Norma Connolly, chair of the SAG Women's Conference Committee, said, "The underemployment of actresses, especially those over forty, is emotionally and financially devastating. It's a disaster." A later survey found that actors and actresses aged twenty to twenty-nine shared equally in jobs and earnings; however, at age thirty to thirty-nine, women's wages and jobs declined by about half, and by their forties, almost three times more men than women were employed.[40] The careers of actresses and stuntwomen were also much shorter than those of their male counterparts, who always seemed to be working. "According to the casting director of one of Hollywood's top TV series, stunt coordinators do indeed hire the stunt personnel for their respective shows. 'The stunt coordinator does all of that (the hiring). . . . They are the ones who know all the guys. They run their own small empire. It's the most incredible fraternity I've ever seen.'"[41]

Even when proven stuntwomen were present on the set, men still put on wigs and did the stunts.[42] "Get the wigs off men" became the slogan the women took to the SAG board, the Stunt and Safety Committee, the studios, and the press. "Oh, yes, I was out there running my mouth about getting the wigs off the men," Jadie said. "Being a stuntwoman wasn't just a job to me—it was a way of life. I was a woman and a person of color, and I used to wonder where my allegiance lay. When we addressed the lack of work for people of color, it seemed that men benefited most from our efforts. When we addressed the lack of work for women generally, women of color were overlooked. Many times that was disheartening for me." The crusade to amend the guild contract to prevent stuntmen doubling for women and to stop "paint downs" went on for years.

In the summer of 1975 Kathleen Nolan ran for president of the Screen Actors Guild on an independent ticket—the nominating committee had refused to recommend her. Even her strong supporter Charlton Heston had told her, "President is not a job for a woman."[43] After a noisy and malicious campaign, Nolan won by a landslide on November 3, 1975. "Irish Street Fighter Wanted SAG to Be Part of the Cultural Revolution," one headline cheered.[44]

A year later at the Democratic National Convention, a chance meeting revealed the crux of the women's struggle in Hollywood, and a remedy. Nolan was backstage in the green room with Mayor Richard J. Daly of Chicago, a few other politicos, and lobbyist Tom Boggs (brother of another female pioneer, journalist Cokie Roberts). In walks Barbara Jordan, the first African American congresswoman from the Deep South. "A young woman was offering coffee or tea," Nolan recalled, "and Barbara Jordan said in her incredible voice, 'I will do that. I will pour my own.' Then she explained. 'They say we're making tremendous progress. We will never make the progress we are after until things change for *her*.' She put her arm around me. I was blown away because she's this powerful presence. Mayor Daly asked, 'What did you mean by that?' Jordan said, '*She* represents the women that appear on screen, and we are what we are *perceived* to be. Until things change for *her*, they will not change immeasurably in the United States for any of us.' She was talking about the influence of film and television," Nolan said. She was pointing out "that roles and attitudes on screen have to change before anything else will change. That stuck with me, 'We are what we are *perceived* to be.'"[45]

In the volatile 1970s actresses depicted women who took charge of their own lives. Audiences had not seen that for a long, long time. One example was *Black Belt Jones,* which offered a surprising and comic view of these changing perceptions. When four badass guys in a pool hall ridicule and threaten Sydney, played by Gloria Hendry, she wipes them out and leaves them on the floor.[46] According to Gloria, director Robert Clouse came up with the idea for another pivotal scene that wasn't in the script—what she called "the bit about the dishes."[47] In that scene, Sydney's boyfriend (played by Jim Kelly) gets a call from a friend in trouble. He takes out his gun, ready to go help, and Sydney expects to accompany him, as usual. He's on the phone and doesn't see her checking her revolver, but her presence distracts him. He waves an arm and orders Sydney, "Do those dishes or something." She gives him a look—click!—do those *dishes?* She takes aim and fires a few shots into the china on the kitchen counter. Shattered bowls and plates fly into the air. "They're done," she says. The message: when demeaned, don't do the dishes—blast them off the drain board.

These hilarious scenes blew away the image of acceptance and obedience. Action roles in the 1970s changed the view of women onscreen and off, and they had a cumulative effect. We are what we are perceived to be.

# 6

# The Women's Movement and Female Action Heroes

Who's getting screwed the most?
—*Dave Robb*

Film critic Molly Haskell's influential book *From Reverence to Rape* examined "good girls and bad girls"—the enduring, conflicting, damaging images of women. "The big lie perpetuated on Western society is the idea of women's inferiority," she wrote, "a lie so deeply ingrained in our social behavior that merely to recognize it is to risk unraveling the entire fabric of civilization." She indicted the movie industry, which "was dedicated for the most part to reinforcing the lie." She wondered "how women will break through barriers of a commercial cinema more truly monolithic in its sexism than it ever was in the old days of Hollywood."[1] Stuntwomen were a microcosm of that larger issue. How could they prevail against the challenges they faced? Fortunately, *recognition* was the watchword of the 1970s.

The social and political tidal wave set off by the modern women's movement roared ashore in the 1970s. It swept up women's expectations and ambitions, influenced entertainment, and changed social attitudes. It reinforced and broadened the civil rights laws established in the 1960s— the Equal Employment Opportunity Commission, Title VII to prohibit employment discrimination, and Title IX to level the playing field for girls in sports. On the tennis court, the "Battle of the Sexes" slammed the message home in September 1973 when Billie Jean King beat Bobby Riggs in a "man's" game.

To the traditional soap operas and female-oriented daytime programming, TV networks quickly added slates of "women's programs" in prime time. TV executives recognized that women constituted a wider, more diverse audience than previously supposed, and this promised new viewers and bigger advertising revenues. The first programs for women were "soft" shows and comedies such as *Honey West* (1965–1966), *That Girl* (1966–1971), and *The Mary Tyler Moore Show* (1970–1977), featuring more independent heroines.[2] Soon the networks whipped out female-driven action series: *Police Woman* (1974–1978), *Get Christie Love* (1974–1975), *Wonder Woman (1976–1979)*, *Charlie's Angels* (1976–1981), *The Bionic Woman* (1976–1978), *Private Benjamin* (1981–1983), and *Cagney & Lacey* (1982–1988). Jeannie Epper, Julie Ann Johnson, and newcomer Rita Egleston doubled the leads in *Wonder Woman, Charlie's Angels,* and *The Bionic Woman*. "Today, people forget that era," Jeannie Epper said. "There were many women's roles in television, and that meant more stuntwomen worked." Most of them didn't become major stunt performers, "but they were all important," said Rita Egleston. "They contributed to the range of what women did. The Stuntwomen's Association had about fifteen members, and some of the new girls had different skills like circus trapeze work. If they were good, if they hung in, put up with the bullshit, had a good attitude and some people skills, they had a better chance in the '70s."[3]

Audiences never seem to tire of watching women in jeopardy. Weekly episodes of these new TV series, studded with beautiful, take-charge action heroines, mirrored the old silent movie serials. Shows of the 1970s owed much of their popularity to the talents of stuntwomen, who were the descendants of daring serial actresses from decades ago. Now, adolescent girls were glued to their TV sets, engrossed in the exhilarating world of female action stars.

When twenty-two-year-old Rita Egleston saw stuntwomen being interviewed on local television, her life took a new direction. "One of them was Jeannie Epper, and that's when I decided," she said. Rita had grown up in Los Angeles and was very good at sports. Her mother, a teacher raising three children alone, had no money to spare, so Rita was fortunate to win a scholarship to Occidental College, where she played intercollegiate sports. Later, while taking a judo class, "I was suddenly thrown, found myself airborne, and knew that I loved flying," she recalled. "It was a brief moment in the air—but, oh, what a cool feeling." In the future, she would be in the air quite a lot. A serene, five-foot-eight blonde, Rita didn't know anyone in the movie business until she found a stunt school run by Paul Stader, the swimmer who had worked with Lila Finn on *The Hurricane* in

1937. Now a respected stunt coordinator, Stader taught Rita what she needed to know to work in front of the camera. "Fighting is one thing," she said, "stunt fighting is another. Back then, it was mainly for guys, but Paul taught us how to throw a punch and make it look real." She learned that sports and stunts are quite different. Jeannie Epper agreed: "A stunt performer has to adapt to constantly changing situations and surroundings," she said, but "as an athlete, you practice the same routines a million times, which does not directly translate into being able to react quickly to changes on set. Stunt performers are challenged every day—different scenes, people, vehicles, or circumstances."[4]

Rita worked the graveyard shift at a Seven-Eleven and hustled stunt jobs during the day. Stader recommended her to double Linda Lovelace, who had starred in the infamous X-rated *Deep Throat*. The new film was tamer—a comedy titled *Linda Lovelace for President* (1975). The stunt involved jumping from an energetically trotting burro into the open door of a moving bus, a mini-version of Polly Burson's leap from a galloping horse onto a train. Rita's next job was more demanding: doubling for star Lindsay Wagner on the new TV series *The Bionic Woman*. "Jeannie Epper doubled Lindsay on the two-part sequence of *Six Million Dollar Man*," Rita

Rita Egleston. (Courtesy of Jonathan Exley)

Lindsay Wagner and her *Bionic Woman* stunt double Rita Egleston. (Courtesy of James Marchese)

said, "the show that introduced *The Bionic Woman,* which was a midseason replacement series. . . . After *Six Million* wrapped its season, their crew switched to *Bionic Woman,* various people were replaced, and I came on the show. Doubling superheroes was mainly running and jumping," Rita remembered, "leaping tall buildings in a single bound—falling frontward and backward." Rita, Jeannie, and others performed these free falls twenty years before safety concerns and new technology led to the use of wires and harnesses.

A backward high fall is against every instinct. "The next time you're at the top of a staircase," Julie Johnson said, "turn around, hold onto something, look back down the staircase and think of falling backwards. It takes a lot of mental concentration. Mental tells the physical what to do."[5] To double superheroes, Jeannie and Rita had to perfect the backward high fall. In the editing room, the footage was then played backward to achieve the illusion of the superhero leaping from the ground to the top of a building. Rita would stand at the top of a structure, her back to the edge, and jump off, looking up as she went down. To perfect the illusion, Rita had to get her takeoff and landing just right, which wasn't easy. "I fell into boxes or airbags," she said, "but going backwards you want to land feet first. If you pull your feet up too soon, the camera will show that. The falling time is only a few seconds before landing, so I kept my feet down until they actually touched. Then I sat backwards, which puts you into a roll and the safety pad takes all that energy. If you stick it, land on your feet, you run a good chance of messing up your back." The stunt was tricky, and Rita was new at it. She had to know where she was in the air, but she couldn't look down. Soon her body automatically knew how long she would fall and when she would land. The fall was usually about thirty-five to forty feet; at sixty-five feet, the illusion didn't work. "As I stepped backwards from a sixty-five-foot height," Rita explained, "I traveled out from the building until gravity took over and pulled me straight down. When that fall was reversed in editing, it looked like I'd jumped straight up and then magically traveled over to where I landed." Rita doubled Wagner until the series ended in 1978.

Stuntwomen faced other challenges besides staged fights and free falls. "I spent three years in that Wonder Woman costume not eating," Jeannie Epper said, laughing. She never liked being in the air, but she mastered the backward and forward jumps and did them for years. Jeannie's leaps and landings for shapely Lynda Carter as Wonder Woman had to be done with "grace and ease." Jeannie couldn't just jump over a fence; she had to do it "with style, do it with heart, have a good attitude, never settle for the mediocre—and that's what separated the girls from the women!"[6] "When you're working with actors," she said, "you have to really watch them because they're not trained, but some of them are really athletic. Lynda Carter did a lot of the fight work herself, but today she wouldn't be allowed to do as much. Sometimes we take our wonderful job for granted. When I look back at that Wonder Woman costume, and I have for several decades now, I know it was an unbelievable experience to wear that costume. Kids wanted to touch my lasso or my wrists or the bracelets. They didn't care if you're Jeannie Epper or Lynda Carter. To them, you are Wonder Woman."[7]

The purpose of using stunt doubles is to protect the precious stars from injury and to protect the studios from costly production delays. A double is selected for her resemblance to an actress, based mainly on height and body type. If the star is five-foot-eight and the stuntwoman is five-foot-one, that might not work, but it did in *Thoroughly Modern Millie* (1967), when acrobat Paula Dell doubled the notably taller Carol Channing. "When you're going through the air," Paula explained, "your height doesn't matter!"

Doubles are also chosen for their particular skills. For example, if the lead character is a race-car driver, the double must have driving skills; if the lead has to ski in just one scene, a second double is hired to hit the slopes. Doubling requires acting ability, observation, and an instinctive knack for imitating how another person moves. When she was working on *Wonder Woman*, Jeannie Epper noticed that when Lynda Carter ran, "her arms kinda flail up a little bit. I had to train myself to run like a girl."[8] Jeannie, who also doubled Kate Jackson and Tanya Roberts in *Charlie's Angels* and Linda Evans in *Dynasty*, said a good stuntwoman "will stay on the set to study the physical style and emotional motivation of the actress she will be doubling, just as a good actress will study the stunt for which she will receive credit."[9]

Jadie David, who regularly doubled Pam Grier, noted that Rita Egleston "walked, talked, and moved just like Lindsay Wagner. She studied her, took on her characteristics. You must do that. I was amazed how Rita could *be* Lindsay."[10] Julie Johnson doubled Doris Day in *Caprice* (1967), and the first time she put on a gray suit and blonde wig she amazed even herself when she looked in a mirror. "I was so surprised! I looked just like her, I moved like her. You become the person you double. It's eerie."

A constant obstacle for stuntwomen was men's urge to protect them. That relic from the past cast doubt on women's capabilities and judgment as professionals, restricted the stunts they were allowed to do, and limited their income. The notion of protecting a woman can be commendable, but not when it's a ruse to replace her. "It had nothing to do with protection,"

Paula Dell in the air, doubling Carol Channing in *Thoroughly Modern Millie* (1967). Ted Delrayne is at the bottom, Russ Saunders is catching, Ray Saunders is spotting, and Darryl Ferges is on the hit board. (Courtesy of Russ Saunders)

May Boss stated plainly. "These guys wanted to do the stunt." Sometimes even the male stars stepped in as protectors. For *McLintock!* (1963), starring John Wayne and Maureen O'Hara, Polly Burson was hired to do a stair fall for actress Yvonne De Carlo. "I'd just done one the day before," Polly snapped, "no carpeting, badly constructed stairs, and I skinned myself from rear end to teakettle. On this fall the steps were carpeted, a piece of cake. But Duke [Wayne] wouldn't let me do it! I asked why, because he was going to cost me money. He said, 'Somebody's foot might kick your breast or your neck. You're not doing it.' He really felt he was protecting me."

Newcomer Jean Coulter got a job on the TV miniseries *Captains and Kings* (1976). One scene took place on a magnificent staircase. "I was wearing some dinky outfit," Jean said, "and I had to fall down about forty hardwood stairs with no pads on my legs or elbows. The actor, Vic Morrow, was supposed to hit me at the top of the stairs, but he didn't want to. He was a fine actor and a nice guy. When you're standing on a staircase it's hard to start a fall if you're not pushed, because you can't look like you're going for it. Vic couldn't bring himself to hit me. I kept telling him it was okay. Finally he hit me!" she cheered. Afterward, Jean suffered from the lack of padding. "I had huge lumps on my legs and elbows," she said. "They looked like an egg was under my black and blue skin."[11] In the 1970s actresses' alluring costumes tended to be tight and skimpy, so even a small pad would show, and Jean's scanty costume simply didn't allow it.

In contrast, stuntmen are rarely asked to take hits in their underwear. Fully clothed, they wear pads underneath, and no one knows the difference. An amusing and telling example occurs in the opening credits of *Hooper* (1978): a stuntman gets ready to go to work; he puts on form-fitting pads that cover practically every inch of his body and walks out wearing a jacket, shirt, pants, boots, and helmet. But the wardrobe department dresses women "in shorts or negligees, not to mention high heels," Julie Johnson said. "Then they tell us to fall down a flight of stairs. Even when a scene calls for long pants they're usually too tight to allow padding. We're made more susceptible to bruises, rug burns and splinters than the boys are." When the costume consists of a short skirt and a tank top and the gag "require[s] the body to be mashed and mangled, I'd say 'shoot the rehearsal,'" Julie advised. "That's your most spontaneous take, and on a lot of stunts I don't want to do a second take unless I have to. You don't want to do stair falls twice, you don't want to do car hits twice."[12]

Stuntmen would agree. "There isn't a stuntman in the world that would look forward to the work stuntwomen do, because they go down flights of stairs in a bathing suit," said New York stuntman Vince Cupone. "The men pad up, padding protects you a lot, but nine times out of ten women don't have that luxury. I know several girls that have done car hits in tight dresses with nothing protecting them from that car except technique. Not only do they work in spite of their wardrobe, they're in a completely macho field where they have to constantly prove themselves," he said. "They don't have girl-to-girl communication because most stunt coordinators are *not* women. Stuntmen and coordinators understand as best as we can what the women face. A good coordinator will try to protect them, but at the end of the day, they're not padded. They're not protected."[13]

Julie's wardrobe was not the only problem on the TV series *Starsky & Hutch* (1975–1979). Producers, directors, and crews had fresh ideas and eagerly churned out the action, but they often didn't realize that even simple stunts could be dangerous. Julie's stunt involved a "near miss"—a car was supposed to *almost* run her down. "The director kept saying the near miss didn't look close enough," she said. "His camera was in the wrong place. To see how close the car was to me, the camera had to face the car, but he had it on the other side." Julie suggested that when the car got close, she could turn and dive onto the hood. "The director agreed, but he still wanted the driver to come in really close. He was a new director. They were all nervous and hyper, trying to make a name. As I dove for the hood of the car, the right front fender tagged my leg, the impact spun me off the hood and set me on my butt on the ground. They got the shot, but my leg started to swell up, and by the time they drove me to a hospital, it was the size of a telephone pole. I had a huge hematoma on my shin. The doctor said, 'Lady, I don't know what your legs are made of, but this leg should be shattered in a million pieces.'" Ignoring the grim compliment, Julie went home on crutches.

Stuntmen commonly worked together like a band of brothers, doubling the lead and the other male characters, playing villains, dads, soldiers, cops, lawyers, and pals. This allowed them to assess who was good, who wasn't, and who could be trusted. In contrast, stuntwomen were often isolated. Before the 1970s, having more than one or two stuntwomen on set was rare. But as Rita Egleston observed, "The only way to be able to judge yourself as a stunt person is in comparison to others, by watching them work." For stuntwomen, this period offered them the opportunity to work together.

In the spirit and practice of the times, Donna Garrett and Regina Parton doubled the actresses and did other stunts on *Fantasy Island, Hart to Hart, Police Woman,* and *The Rockford Files;* on *Wonder Woman,* Jeannie Epper might do Lynda Carter's car scenes one day, and Regina Parton might drive the next day.[14] But "when a script called for a motorcycle stunt," Jeannie said, "they brought in the best woman cycle rider in the world, Debbie Evans, because Wonder Woman should ride a motorcycle as well as she does everything else."

Motorcycle champ Debbie Evans explained why doubles are needed: "A lot of the jobs we do are just things the actress shouldn't be doing, or she'll get hurt—but they're easy for us. I also feel if a woman is doing the acting, a woman should do the stunts." On *Deathsport* (1978), while doubling for lead actress Claudia Jennings, Debbie jumped her motorcycle across a ravine that was about thirty feet deep and ten feet wide. Another scene required a close-up shot of Jennings, but the actress had no experience on a motorcycle. She was supposed to be going only about five miles an hour as she rode past the camera, which had been placed "really high on a tripod," Debbie recalled. "The director said, 'Now Claudia, whatever you do, don't hit the camera.' Claudia's all nervous, pops the clutch, and heads straight for that camera. . . . The bike knocked out one of the legs, the camera and cameraman came flying down, Claudia crashed, and someone had to catch the camera. . . . There's no way an actress can do what we do."[15]

Debbie's skills made her a preeminent stuntwoman, but she was a champion long before that. "They used to call me Motorcycle Arms in high school," she said. "You got teased a lot if you even liked sports. I was always on my bicycle, skateboard, unicycle, playing football, baseball, basketball, surfing, water-skiing, and I loved climbing trees! But I was ridiculed for the muscles on my arms. 'You think you're a boy?' Getting teased frustrated me, but looking back, it's funny because now biceps are *in.*" While still in high school, Debbie was a factory-sponsored rider for Yamaha and performed in shows before the championship races at the Houston Astrodome, the Silver Dome, Texas Stadium, and Anaheim Stadium, as well as at Super Cross races and the AMA Camel Pro Series races. "I'd do wheelies, ride over some obstacles, and [do] my balancing act—I'd stand on my head on the motorcycle. It wasn't moving, but no kickstand or anything held it up. It was done just by balance. You turn the handlebars and lock the front wheel with the brake. I've done balancing since I was about eleven—standing on the bike seat and do[ing] a 360 balance, swing[ing] my legs around the side to the back, then to the other side, and com[ing] back to the front."

Later, when Yamaha wanted her to ride in the national championships, she didn't expect any flak because she'd grown up competing against boys, and they seemed to accept her as that girl from Southern California who rode motorcycles. But "the national organization guys from Michigan or Ohio wouldn't let me ride," she said. "It was 1976. They could not fathom how a girl could do it. Finally, they let me in and they put in their best girl rider, because it was kind of an East-versus-West contest. She didn't finish, but I was right up there with the men. That's the way I pictured it. I don't set boundaries for myself. I don't say 'only guys can do that.' My dad helped me to see beyond boundaries. When I was six, he taught me how to ride a motorcycle, how to throw a baseball, and how to throw a punch—not like a girl. He wanted me to be able to protect myself, do some damage. He taught me a lot."

In 1977, on an episode of *CHiPs,* Debbie was part of a group of bikers that was supposed to go around the track at Indian Dunes. "I'm on my trials bike," she recalled. "I was going to do a wheelie and I asked the transportation guy if I could use the air on his truck to do my tire pressure. He was acting like I didn't know anything because I was a girl, so I got out my gauge, started to let air out, but he's trying to push me away. I said, 'It's okay, I know what I need.' He goes, 'How much air you gonna put in there?' I said, 'Eight pounds.' 'But it says thirty on the side of the tire. You need to put in thirty pounds!' He was all huffy and puffy about it." So, Debbie continued, "I get the air down, start the bike up, took off, went about six feet, pulled it up in a wheelie and wheelied all the way down the road. I looked back at him, and he's standing there, mouth wide open, and I went— Yesssss!" Small or large—a triumph is undeniable.

Stunt players know that routine is not their strong suit, and they know their work is outside the norm. And even if they've done hundreds of falls, they know that every stunt is different. Christine Anne Baur came to know that well.[16] In the 1970s the athletic, humorous, outspoken, five-foot-four-inch blonde surfed, skateboarded, and rode horses. She was no stranger to movie sets: her grandfather, George Marshall, had directed many Hollywood hits, including *Destry Rides Again* (1939), and her father, director Frank Baur, was a production manager on Mel Brooks's *Silent Movie*

Debbie Evans wheeling away! (Courtesy of Debbie Evans)

(1976). Her dad had no idea he was helping to launch her career when she threw herself into her first stunt, doubling for Bernadette Peters. "I had to swing back and forth across a stage in my lingerie," she recalled. Until that moment, Chris had planned a career in stable management—show horses, hunters, and jumpers. "That stunt changed my life, because in those days I felt I could do anything athletic. Second, I'd grown up on movie sets, and as I swung across that stage, I realized how perfect I felt doing something physical in a film. For years I'd heard about how movies were made, I understood artistically what was being created, I was on familiar territory—a movie set—and it all came together for me. I'd found the best work I could do." But her father had principles. "Nepotism was a dirty word," Chris said, "and he didn't want anyone to think I got special favors. He opened a door for me, but I had to walk through it."

Her dad referred her to a woman in the wardrobe department, the wife of Paul Baxley. After surviving Iwo Jima, Baxley got into stunt work in 1947 and became a stunt coordinator in the 1970s. He regularly hired stuntmen he knew and trusted, and they became known as the Baxley Bunch—a band of about eight stuntmen "and one girl, Beth Nufer, a terrific circus acrobat."[17] Christine became the second girl in the Baxley Bunch. Since his shows involved much more car work than horse work, Chris learned stunt driving from fellow stunt performer Jerry Summers. "Paul Baxley was very, very old school," she said. "He believed girls in stunts were nice-looking, maybe can do a few things, [but] it was still a man's world."

When Baxley signed on for a new TV series produced by Warner Bros., he didn't think it would last six episodes. "It was so schlocky!" Chris laughed. The show was *The Dukes of Hazzard*, which ran from 1979 to 1985. The first year of the series, Chris drove cars and even doubled some of the actors—small men and boys. "We worked as a company, and that was fun. The girls didn't get to do the big jumps—they'd wig Jerry Summers—but at times I was wigged up to double a guy." Then there was some trouble. "After I'd had a great time driving a car," Chris recalled, "one of the guys accused me of penis envy, like I was showing up the boys. And he was a friend! I'd been working hard, hanging it out there, and I was shot down for it. Alan Wyatt, Jerry Summers, and Henry Kingi weren't like that. After the penis-envy thing, we were on location to finish a race sequence, and some Warner Bros. people were there. I didn't know Paul had told them he'd found a great stuntwoman. For him to gush about a stuntwoman was unheard of." Chris, doubling for Cathy Bach (Daisy Duke), was supposed to drive a truck through barricades of hay bales. Just before the stunt, Chris saw a police car parked beside the road. She told Paul's nephew it made her uncomfortable, but he assured her that no one would see it. "We did the stunt, I slammed into the hay bales, broke through the first barricade, but as I went through the second one, hay and straw made the road slick as ice. I went around the corner and the car hydroplaned on the straw. That would have been okay, but I hit the police car—not a huge wreck, but not pretty. I managed to control it, drive out of the shot, and save it." For Chris, that was another career-changing moment. "Paul went into a tirade, 'You can't trust stuntwomen,' and on and on. It was awful. All the months on that show and on other shows for years after that, I'd seen the boys wreck boats, wreck cars, and nothing happened. But I go from hero to zero. 'See? You can't trust stunt girls, got to wig the guys.'" Chris's work for Baxley fell off sharply, but he was soon forced to rehire her because she had grown up on a skateboard, and there were almost no skateboard experts in stunt work. "After all those wasted hours of my youth skateboarding," she crooned, "I finally went to work with my board under my arm and made money."

Baxley was stunt-coordinating *In God We Tru$t* (1980), a film written and directed by comedian Marty Feldman, who also starred in the movie, playing a monk. Chris was going to double Feldman and was supposed to teach him enough skateboard basics for his close-ups, which turned out to be almost impossible. "They made a curly wig," Chris said, "a mask of his face that wasn't prosthetics, a brown friar's robe, and shoes that looked like sandals with painted toes on them. He and I were the same size, and I strapped down my little bosoms." In the relevant scene, Feldman's character tangles with a paperboy on a skateboard and winds up riding the board down a hill while being chased by six motorcycles, two limousines, and a crowd. He then crashes into the back of a boat mounted on a trailer attached to a parked truck. As the truck starts to pull into traffic, Feldman (doubled by Chris) stands up on the skateboard, holding on to the water-ski towline, and races through the streets of Los Angeles—a water-skier on asphalt. Eventually, the truck and the boat go one way, and Chris on the skateboard whizzes the other way. "I go through a parking lot and hit a wall. Marty and I thought it would be cool to hit the wall with my arms out in that crucifixion look. That was the kind of stuff I was into. It wasn't just about doing the stunts; it was about the artistic connections. Take one of the scene was too slow, so on take two, I really whipped it. Halfway through I knew I was going way too fast. Arms out, I smacked into that wall *hard*." It's one thing to see a woman in a bikini take a header off a building. To watch her willfully slam face-first into a concrete wall is unforgettable. At least the crazy gag didn't break Christine's nose. "I was very proud of doing that whole sequence," she said. "Another kid in the business skateboarded, [and] he might have been able to do it. I thought it was pretty cool for a woman to pull it off."

"You've got to have an attitude to do stunts," said May Boss. "I always love it when the guys brag, 'I've never been hurt.' If you've never been hurt, you haven't done much. You try not to get hurt, you try to save your life. You can't be a coward mentally to do stunts. The attitude is, 'We're going to get on with it.'"

Before doing a stunt, the performers go over the moves they plan to make. They dream about it. No one speaks about being afraid; they talk about a stunt that "gets their attention." "Stuntmen have been broken from neck to toe," said Sherry Peterson, a novice stuntwoman in the late 1970s. "When the guys get hurt, they get a card, the stuntmen's groups make sure their bills are taken care of, and they mentally and physically help them, but when the girls get hurt it's like everybody flees from us."[18] Stuntwomen don't want to let anyone know they're injured because they don't want to be replaced. That applies to stuntmen, too, because there's always a line of guys behind them ready to move in. The 1970s and 1980s were times of both peril and opportunity. But the injuries kept mounting.

# 7

# Disaster Movies and Disastrous Stunts

You're not supposed to kill the stunt people either. We're all supposed to go home.

*—Conrad Palmisano*

Television offered action shows of all kinds, and disaster movies (aka event films) bristled with victims and mighty male stars. Any catastrophe anywhere would do—on land, at sea, in the air, even meteors from outer space: *The Poseidon Adventure, King Kong, Logan's Run, The Hindenburg, Apocalypse Now, 1941, The Black Hole, Meteor.*[1] Ape and airport themes were especially popular throughout the 1970s.[2] A disaster movie could be a blockbuster, but not all blockbusters were disaster films. *Jaws* and *Star Wars* were blockbusters with zeitgeist.[3] Most of these movies generated elaborate stunt gags in search of bigger box-office receipts. The combined pressures of profit and peril raised the odds of mishaps, culminating in the terrible stunt accident that occurred during the filming of *Twilight Zone: The Movie* in 1982, which forced everyone to stop and rethink (see chapter 10).

In particular, 1974 was a blowout year for stunt-heavy movies: *Earthquake, The Towering Inferno, Airport 1975,* even the rowdy *Blazing Saddles.*[4] Stunt coordinator Paul Stader hired more than seventy stunt people for *Towering Inferno.*[5] The thrilling elevator sequences were shot at the Fox ranch or in downtown Los Angeles. As the fire rages in the doomed high-rise, one scene depicts the slow descent of an external glass-paneled elevator bearing a fireman, eight frantic women, and a child. Rocked by violent explosions, the elevator jerks to a stop, while inside, the women are tossed around like dice. Lisolette (played by Hollywood star Jennifer Jones) clutches her child. A glass panel behind her falls away, and one of the other women grabs the child just before the stuntwoman doubling for Jones takes what looks like an eighty-story fall. Accounts vary about who the stuntwomen in the elevator were, but most agree that the one who took the fall was new to the business. Glynn Rubin, an appealing blue-eyed blonde, was one of the two stuntwomen in the elevator. "I think the rest were extras," she said. "The elevator hung from cables above a concrete parking lot in downtown LA. *The Hollywood Reporter* said the fall was eighty feet—so not true! It was about two stories into the airbag. The other stunt girl hadn't worked much, but she took the fall—young, pretty, and scared to death. When we were cued for the fall, she didn't go, and finally I pushed her out."[6]

Giant disaster movies needed lots of "extra bodies," and that's how stunt people of all kinds got their start. Sandra Lee Gimpel said, "*Towering Inferno* was my real introduction to the stunt business." Later she became a fourth-degree black belt, a stunt coordinator, and a second-unit director.[7] On *Inferno* she was one of five people hired to do "a little swimming" when the high-rise's glass elevator blows and water pours into the dining area. She recalled, "I brought my eight-year-old daughter to the set to see that mommy's stunts were not dangerous. Five of us were on a platform in front of the elevator. The assistant director said, 'When the elevator blows, you guys jump off the platform and make sure you're in front of a camera.' Underwater cameras had been set into the floor to film us struggling in the water. The glass elevator blew and the water literally knocked us off the platform and into the air. We weren't thinking about the cameras, we were trying to save our lives. Later they admitted they 'kind of blew in too much water.' Oh, yes. That was the last stunt my kid saw me do for a long time."

*Earthquake* reportedly hired 141 stunt people—more than ever before for one film.[8] They were hit by cars and dropped into cracks in the earth, narrowly escaped drowning (or not), were enveloped in flames, fell from rooftops, and ran for their lives. Evelyn Cuffee vividly recalled "the feel and the sound of the effects they created—scary, just like an earthquake."

Acrobat and dancer Paula Dell returned to stunt work in the 1960s.[9] In her long career, she had been afraid only a couple of times—once on *Earthquake*. Pointing out the dangers of stunt work in disaster movies, she said, "Usually, if we needed something to make a stunt safer, we knew the prop and special effects people would fix things for us, but these big movies hired many nonunion, inexperienced people. In one scene, the crews

Veteran stuntwoman Sandy Gimpel, age sixty-six, practices her kicks in preparation for an upcoming workout video. (Courtesy of Sandy Gimpel)

were supposed to throw things off a roof to make it look like the building was falling apart, but some guys up there were throwing real rocks. They thought it was funny because we were down on the street and we were supposed to be dead! All this stuff came down on us and we couldn't move. That was scary."

Regina Parton and Julie Johnson were among the many "victims" caught in a "flooding underground sewer" that was actually a long tunnel constructed on Universal's back lot. It was open on top and about thirty feet deep. The water came from a nearby lake. "At one end, a gate could open to release thousands of gallons of smelly lake water on us," Julie said. "At the other end, a gate would close so the water backed up to fill the tunnel." Regina, an expert swimmer, doubled actress Genevieve Bujold as the rising waters washed away a dozen people. "The film crew was positioned on either side of the drain, unaware that a gate had failed to operate and the water was spilling over the sides toward the power outlet. Regina was alert, traced the power source and forced the electrician who was numb with panic to pull the plug."[10] Her quick action averted what could have been a disaster. "At first it was true Regina was hired because of her dad [stuntman Reggie Parton]," Rita Egleston said, "but she was a legitimate working stuntwoman, and so were others who got those breaks—they were good stuntwomen. In the stunt community the kinds of shows you worked sort of depended on your specialty. There were the cowboys and the non-cowboys. Usually they don't mix, but in the 1970s the cowboys were learning how to drive cars and how to swim. Regina was really good with cars and underwater work."

On the same underground tunnel set, Julie doubled famous movie star Ava Gardner as part of a desperate crowd trying to climb a ladder and escape the rising water. The person on the ladder ahead of Julie was supposed to step on her hand and cause her to fall about fifteen feet into the rushing water below. "Charlton Heston was not being doubled for this scene," she said, "and he was below the ladder. The cameras rolled, the water began to rush in, the director yelled 'Action,' Charlton yelled at me: 'Jump!' But I couldn't drop fifteen feet—the water barely came up to his knees, not high enough to buffer my fall, and I knew a six-inch curb ringed the base of the cement floor." It was decision time: ruin the shot by not going on cue, or slam into the concrete? "The scene was in full progress and Charlton kept yelling 'Jump!' I hit the bottom, my legs buckled instantly, my knees hit the curb hard. I'd been cued too early, one of the greatest hazards of our business." Soaking wet, she grabbed a bag of ice and hobbled painfully to the dressing room, where she was told Miss Gardner wanted to see her. Astonished, Julie tottered off to the star's trailer. "Ava hugged me and asked, 'How badly are you hurt, my dear?' She poured me a shot of brandy. All I could think of was my knees hitting the concrete, and here was Ava Gardner insisting I drink brandy, which I welcomed."

*Earthquake* almost ended Polly Burson's career. Back in 1947, she and Lila Finn had been working on *Unconquered* on Paramount's back lot when a gag drenched Polly with hundreds of gallons of water. Now they were both on Universal's back lot, which was being demolished by *Earthquake*. Polly stood on the porch of a house, and special effects dumped 3,000 gallons of water on her. The porch collapsed. "The water was supposed to go somewhere else," Lila said, "but it hit her and she hit the wall."[11] "I broke my left leg and some bones in my face and I decided it was time to quit," Polly said.[12] She later found out the water drop was only a test. "They weren't even filming! What a waste." Polly worked on a few more films, one of them aptly titled *Last of the Great Survivors* (1984). Then she indulged her wanderlust on a "salty old forty-two-foot gaff-rigged schooner," sailing it to Hawaii and New Zealand. She and the friend accompanying her "had no previous sailing experience," Lila said. "They took a 'shakedown' cruise to the Channel Islands just off California and headed for Hawaii!"[13] They didn't know anything about celestial navigation or, apparently, much else about sailing, but Polly could do almost anything. After all, she was a stuntwoman.

Along with female-driven TV action-adventures, the huge disaster movies of the 1970s changed stunts. Explosions were bigger, falls were higher; horses were out, cars were in. Yet some things remained the same: fights and car work were still considered guys' work. Women had seldom taken the wheel like bandits on the lam since the silent movies. In the fractured, frenzied 1970s they began to make up for lost time.

Within a short period, three movies celebrating stuntmen were released: *Stunts* (1977), *Hooper* (1978), and *The Stunt Man* (1980).[14] *Hooper*, Hal Needham's jovial ode to stuntmen, was his generation's version of *Lucky Devils* (1933)—highlighting the work that's really more like play.[15] One stuntwoman called *Hooper* "a whole lot of everything—fights, motorcycles, car races, chariot races" performed by about sixty stuntmen and eleven stuntwomen.[16]

The title character is aging stuntman Sonny Hooper (Burt Reynolds), who is challenged by his disintegrating vertebrae and by an eager young stuntman (Jan-Michael Vincent). Hooper's vision of his future is epitomized by revered elder stuntman Jocko (Brian Keith), who tells Sonny, "You oughta drink more. Nothing hurts when you're numb." Unlike *Lucky Devils*, *Hooper* doesn't blame women for causing their men's trouble, although stuntmen and marriage still don't mix. Hooper and his girlfriend Gwen (Sally Field) talk about marriage, but it's a distant possibility. Other spirited, savvy wives or girlfriends are merely satellites to the action. At the stuntmen's hangout, a fight erupts with a visiting SWAT team. Gwen is unmoved by the mayhem: when Hooper lands on the table, she merely shifts her plate and then breaks a bottle over a SWAT guy's head. If stuntwomen are in the crowd, they're not identified, but a beautiful babe at the bar does throw a solid punch. Then, outside, a car slams down the street, goes into a roll, and—surprise!—two women pop out of the upended vehicle, waving to the crowd. They were Janet Brady and Sammy Thurman. It was one of Sammy's first stunts.[17] "That car roll was on a wooden ramp," Janet said. "You run the left or right wheels of the car up a ramp and you had to be very precise to roll a car from that. The guys were betting I couldn't do it. That made me stubborn enough—*man* enough—to show them I could do it."

Janet may have been one of the first women to roll a car, but she was not the first to recognize that her stubbornness was a boon to her stunt work. "In those days it was hard for the guys to accept girls doing car stunts," she said. "The guys didn't say anything, but I could feel it, and if you did one thing wrong, they'd want to stick a guy in the car while you're saying, 'Wait, give me another shot.' Girls didn't get another shot. They were tough on us." Janet learned car work from an expert, stunt coordinator Alan Gibbs.[18] "He was an incredible stuntman," she said, "and his timing was so right on the money that he could actually tell you at what point to crank the wheel. If you followed what he said, you had no problem." On the pilot for the TV series *CHiPs* (1977–1983), Janet did a difficult car roll up an embankment. "I didn't realize motorcycles could go faster than cars. I was trying to stay up with a motorcycle that was supposed to make me go off-road. The timing was hard. I had to reach about seventy miles an hour to go up the embankment and get the car to roll. Instead of keeping the car straight, I had to go to the left at a forty-five-degree angle, then crank the wheel at the right angle and at the right time [to] roll the car. That was a ride."

In *Hooper,* Janet Brady takes the wheel to start the car roll. (Courtesy of Janet Brady)

And she's into the roll. (Courtesy of Janet Brady)

All through school Janet had trained in gymnastics, and then she became a hairdresser. She never thought of doing stunts until her brother-in-law, a stuntman, asked her to do a bit on *Won Ton Ton, the Dog that Saved Hollywood* (1976), because "they couldn't find a girl small enough." Janet was supposed to walk through a doorway as explosions went off and the walls of the building collapsed around her. This was quite similar to Buster Keaton's dangerous stunt in *Steamboat Bill, Jr.* (1928), when the wall of a house fell on him but left him untouched, standing in a perfectly placed open window frame. If Keaton had moved a few inches in either direction, he would have been crushed.[19]

Janet wound up marrying her driving teacher, Alan Gibbs, who was also president of Stunts Unlimited, the group that had split from the Stuntmen's Association in 1970. Likewise, stuntwoman Kitty O'Neil married Stunts Unlimited member Duffy Hambleton.[20] It's not surprising when stunt people marry each other, but it *was* surprising when Gibbs, Needham, and stunt coordinator Bobby Bass proposed Janet and Kitty for membership in the all-male Stunts Unlimited in September 1976.[21] "I never thought of being a member," Janet said. "Some guys didn't want a woman in the group and it was probably as hard on them as it was on me. I had to earn their respect." Kitty and Janet were called the group's "token women," which they were. Although they benefited from having the inside track, Janet and Kitty were also skilled professionals.

Years later, looking back, a few stuntwomen wished they had reacted differently to the conflicts of the 1970s. "I would have been a lot stronger," said Janet Brady. "For a long time I was the only woman in Stunts Unlimited, but they put other women in spots they should have offered me as a member. I didn't tell them how much it affected me personally, and my career. Today the guys are like my brothers. Back then I told myself I was lucky to be in Stunts Unlimited, lucky to be working, that was all that mattered, and I let it go. If I had it to do over, I'd speak up." If Janet's and Kitty's admittance to the group had opened the door to other women, the history of stuntwomen might have been very different.

The late 1970s has been seen as a turning point in stunts. Accidents increased, and safety became an issue; nonunion crews were inexperienced, and the crucial trust among stunt people began to crack. African American stuntman Jophery Brown (Morgan Freeman's regular double) remembered *Hooper* as "a watershed." He had followed his brother Calvin (Bill Cosby's stunt double) into the business. Other than Cal, Jophery had no mentors, he said, "until I met Hal Needham. Hal took me under his wing," and Alan Gibbs and Bobby Bass taught him "finesse." "After *Hooper*," he said, "so many came out here wanting to be stunt people," and they were listed as stuntmen "when they didn't have a clue. Also, you had 'briefcase production companies' that would do their movie and leave. They wanted to hire their friends, like the director's brother's son or his daughter's boy-friend, and put them in our spot. You can't take somebody out of college, put him in a fire-suit and light him up. That guy doesn't know what to do or how to move. It's like, 'What do I do when I get hot?' When you get hot, it's too late—you're dead! You have to anticipate it and hit the ground so the guys can put you out. A guy like that gets everybody in trouble because it's a snowball effect . . . and it's unsafe for everyone. That's what we lost. We lost that comfort zone of knowing who's around you."[22] For this reason and oth-ers, stunts became riskier, but many failed to notice the critical changes in the business. As a result, one stuntwoman working on *King Kong* narrowly escaped injury, only to be hurt on her next stunt.

In 1976 Dino De Laurentiis decided to resurrect *King Kong*.[23] Acrobat Sunny Woods had done trapeze work with and without nets, but she was new to stunts when she doubled Jessica Lange (Dwan) on the remake of the giant gorilla movie. To film scenes of Dwan clutched in Kong's hand, a huge mechanical arm had been constructed that, suspended from a crane, could be lifted at least thirty feet from the ground. De Laurentiis, his staff, and executives from Paramount filed in to see the apparatus in operation. Ronnie Lippin covered the event for *American Way:* "In the trial run, the hydraulically controlled hand reached out and picked up a few large wooden boards, the enormous fingers closed around them and . . . crushed them into a thousand pieces." For the next shot, Sunny was in the gorilla hand. "With the film rolling . . . the fingers closed gently around her slim body, the arm moved and Sunny was lifted high above the ground. The monster seemed to stare at the delicate blonde girl who was pretending to struggle in terror. And then, without warning, the mechanism broke. The hand suddenly tipped over backwards and, with Sunny's head aimed directly at the ground, the monster's enormous fist smashed into a large pile of rocks on the set. Everyone thought Sunny's head had been crushed." But luckily, one of the gorilla's knuckles had "caught on a rock, twisting the hand slightly" and saving Sunny's life. She squeezed out, "visibly shaken, crawled around the rocks in time to see the terrified studio executives rushing out the door. Only *Kong* producer, Dino De Laurentiis, waited to make sure Sunny was not injured before he left the set."[24] She even had the guts to climb back into the unpredictable motorized paw for a second take.

Sunny had had a close call, but she wasn't as lucky on an episode of *The Bionic Woman*. Rita Egleston had fallen backward dozens of times on that show without incident. "Long before *Crouching Tiger, Hidden Dragon* reintroduced being 'flown' in a harness, it was a circus thing," Rita said. "Sunny was a really good aerialist, but the design of the stunt on *Bionic Woman* was—iffy. She was to fall from a theater balcony into breakaway tables, but they were not constructed as breakaway tables. She landed on them and crushed both her heels." That's how fast everything can change. Sunny recovered, but her stunt career was over.

Creating and shooting a stunt can involve many experts in different departments doing different tasks. The stunt coordinator, who bears ultimate responsibility for the safety of a stunt, works with the second-unit director, the special effects and prop departments, and others. But people make mistakes, especially when a stunt is considered simple or easy. In Sunny's case, she was new to stunts and just assumed the tables were breakaway, but no one checked to see that they were made of balsa wood or some other flimsy material that would collapse on impact. Perhaps someone in the prop department, too new to know better, simply brought the wrong tables. It was a costly mistake. That's why Jeannie Epper's dad had advised her to learn about everything, "be involved in all aspects of stunts, the ropes, the mechanisms" and to question everything: "why use a handheld camera, which lens, why it's being shot this way."[25]

Other factors can complicate stunts as well. They are usually the last scenes to be shot at the end of the day, when everyone's tired. The shots may be rushed, especially on TV shows, which often don't have time for rehearsals. For instance, a well-designed and safe car stunt can become perilous if no one realizes the road is icy or if no one considers the effects of blinding lights on the driver. Or disaster can ensue if someone changes a tiny part of a stunt after rehearsal, just minutes before filming. That's what happened to one stuntwoman working on a *Jaws* sequel.

*Jaws* decimated the competition in the summer of 1975. In its unforgettable opening sequence, a young woman splashes into the ocean for a moonlight swim. As she treads water, her body suddenly jerks violently, and she disappears beneath the surface; she pops up again, eyes wide with horror, as she's wrenched through the water from side to side by something unseen. Then she vanishes. The beauty gulped down by the shark was Susan Backlinie. According to Rita Egleston, "Beneath her in the water, a stunt diver yanked her down by a rope tied around her waist. That's how Susan said it was done." When she resurfaced, the underwater diver began swimming back and forth, pulling her sideways as if she were in the grip of the great white shark's powerful jaws.[26]

On *Jaws 2* (1978), six-year stunt veteran Jean Coulter was alone in a wooden V-bottom boat when the mechanical shark attacked. "Jean hurled gasoline cans at it, spilled gas on herself, fired a flare gun that ignited her costume and the boat, which finally exploded. 'That was a pretty good gag,' she said. 'My wig caught fire, I lost my eyelashes and brows. But they cut out my best close-up where I'm in flames and tears are streaming down my face. They said it was too morbid.'"[27] On another take, a different problem wormed its way into the stunt. "The mechanical shark was to hit the boat hard enough to make a hole in it," Jean said. "In rehearsal, when the shark hit the boat, everything was fine, but then someone moved the boat closer to the shark. No one told me. The shark hit the boat really hard, jerked me to one side, my foot got wedged in the bottom of the boat, I tore the cartilage in my knee, and the boat almost went over." She ended up in a cast from the waist down. She sawed it in half so she could take it off for the rest of her shots.

Janet Brady, Jean Coulter, and Glory Fioramonti were among the new stuntwomen who proved themselves in the 1970s. Glory was not a trained acrobat or swimmer, but she was daring. She once asked her dad, a location manager at Warner Bros., if he ever thought she'd become a stuntwoman. Then he reminded her of a pony ride when she was about five years old. While riding one of the supposedly docile animals around in a circle, Glory said, "my pony broke free, darted out of the gate, and galloped down the yellow line on the road that had a few cars going both ways. My parents were running after me so fast that my mom lost her shoes. I was having the time of my life, yelling, 'Go pony, go!'" When the pony headed into the woods, Glory thought it would be a good idea to stop riding, so she just jumped off. When her parents caught up to her, she was sitting on the ground grinning. From that auspicious beginning, Glory found a place in stunts.[28]

In 1972, after college, she was training young horses that, according to Glory, "were trying to kill me on a daily basis." Her father told her they needed someone to double Ann-Margret "and ride next to John Wayne for three months in Mexico." Not impressed, Glory wanted to know what it paid. Her father told her she'd get into SAG, but at the time, Glory had no interest in movies. "Then he told me SAG's rate was $125 a day. I was making $50 a week." Because she'd been riding "those rank horses," Glory was hired and got to ride next to Wayne on *The Train Robbers*. "It felt like a family because Wayne carried the same crew with him on every picture."

Glory had planned to be a psychotherapist, and she said, "My degree in psychology helped my new career a lot because this is a game of personalities and egos more than stunts."

Even though anything can go wrong, most performers go into a stunt confident that it has been set up correctly and safely. But that's not always the case, as Glory found out in Texas while performing a stunt for *Soggy Bottom U.S.A.* (1980). "About eight of us were hanging onto the back of a Model T pickup truck," she said. "The driver was Tony Epper, a big man who had to cram himself into the cab. We were to career down this hill, jump the embankment onto a ferry that was floating on the swampy water about thirty to forty feet off. Once on the ferry deck, Tony would stop the truck, but in case it was hard to stop, they had set up a bunch of props—boxes of live chickens, bales of hay, a parked truck—to slow us down. Maybe Tony came in too fast or the brakes went out, but we barreled right through all the props, off the end of the ferry, and sank like a rock. It had to be hysterical to watch, like a Mack Sennett comedy. Suddenly we're all in the water trying to figure out what the hell is going on, swimming for our lives, wondering where's Tony, because he's so big he's hard to miss. He almost didn't get out of that truck. That was *not* funny." Glory paused. "I have to mention one of the towns we were shooting in was called Uncertain, Texas." In this case, no one could have guessed that all those props wouldn't stop the truck.

In other situations, stunt people's instincts tell them that something is wrong. This can save them—if they pay attention. If they ignore their instincts and squeak through, the experience becomes part of their stunt wisdom. On the TV series *Lancer* (1968–1970), Jeannie Epper was standing in for a young actress trapped in a burning building while clutching a doll. The director had told Jeannie, "Whatever you do, don't let go of the doll." Before the house was set on fire, she felt like something wasn't quite right with the gag. "As the cabin began going up in flames, beams started falling all around her. 'When I woke up in the hospital, all my hair was burned off,' she said, 'but I still had that doll in my hand. You should have seen that doll, too. It was all fried up. We both were.'"[29] After that, Jeannie became much more careful. "When you're young, you just crash and burn, crash and burn. But you can't keep slamming into the ground forever without getting hurt."[30]

Experienced stunt people listen to their instincts; they assume nothing. But sometimes even a veteran can be talked into a gag. Jadie David

Later, Jadie David did a burn without injury, but as this magazine cover shows, these gags can be very tricky. (Courtesy of Garry Brod)

had "slammed into the ground" for five years without being seriously hurt—until *Rollercoaster* (1977).[31] The big Universal "Sensurround" movie was being shot at several locations, and Jadie's stunt was taking place at the Ocean View Amusement Park in Norfolk, Virginia. Three cars on the roller coaster were supposed to derail and toss out the vacationing joy riders. "We were to jump off one of the cars," Jadie said, "but we weren't comfortable with the way the stunt was set up." Some of the stunt players were to jump into a breakaway building with pads in it, while others, including Jadie, were supposed to land in the sand. "I often think about that stunt. The women didn't really want to do it. They felt it wasn't safe. I understood that we had decided as a group *not* to do the stunt, but then the company renegotiated with us. Three men decided to do it and so did I, but two women would not do it the way it was set up. I was stubborn enough to say, 'Oh, you know, if the guys can do it, I'm going to do it,' which wasn't very bright. That was probably the most difficult stunt I ever did because I don't think it was physically possible." One car jumped the track and "sailed into a balsa wood building."[32] Jadie and stuntman Diamond Farnsworth were thrown from another car, jumped to the right, and hit the sand hard. "Farnsworth ended up splitting his pelvis," Jadie said, "and I broke my back." They were out of work for months, but they healed. The next year Farnsworth worked on *Deadman's Curve,* and Jadie was supposed to double Madge Sinclair, driving a big rig on the truckers' revenge movie *Convoy.* But according to Jadie, unlike the stuntmen on the show, "I was not given the chance to get my CD [commercial driver's] license, so a stuntman in a wig replaced me."

Debbie Evans's skill on motorcycles was well known, but she was comparatively new to stunts in 1978, and while working on *The Jerk* (1979), she let herself be talked into a job she didn't feel right about.[33] Conrad Palmisano, an actor and stuntman since 1970, was stunt coordinator for the film, as well as Steve Martin's double.[34] Conrad's relaxed air of experience comes with a jovial sense of humor. He recalled that "Carl Reiner was a wonderful, creative director to work for. Debbie did the motorcycle stuff and played a girl in a circus act that crashed through a wall of fire. She was wearing some kind of Styrofoam shark fin thing on her helmet. She didn't have a lot of clothes on." The wardrobe department had dressed Debbie in a bizarre outfit—a one-piece bathing suit, fishnet stockings, a helmet crowned by that "shark fin thing," gloves, and boots that came up past her knees. Her shoulders and back were bare for her motorcycle ride through a wall of fire. She was supposed to break through a wall made of thin pine slats that were attached on either side to two other walls that held the crash wall upright. She didn't know the crew had stapled the crash wall to the main frames. When she asked if they were going to score the wood, or par-

Conrad Palmisano, stunt coordinator and second-unit director. (Courtesy of John Stephens)

tially cut through it, she was told, "Oh, no, you'll break right through that." Debbie thought the pine would bend rather than break, so someone finally scored part of the crash wall. She then asked if she could wear Nomex, a fire-retardant fabric. "Oh, no," a crew member said, "you can't because they'll see it. Do you want us to get a guy to do it?" She knew the guys had been doing it in nylon jackets at thrill shows all week long. She recalled, "I was new and I thought maybe I was making a bigger deal out of this than it really was. I thought they probably knew better." However, she did get a Nomex hood that hung beneath the helmet, and she applied flesh-colored makeup gel to protect her throat and chest.

Next, Debbie was rigged up to a "ratchet," a device that would make it look like she was thrown off the motorcycle while inside the wall of flames. Under her costume she wore a jerk vest that was attached to the rig by a cable. On cue, the ratchet would yank her into the air. "That was the gag," Conrad said. At one time, doing a stunt with a ratchet could be quite dangerous. "They called them nitrogen jerk ratchets," Debbie said, "and they could jerk your head off. You have to have your chin tucked into your chest, and you have to be pressed back against the cable. Today, a ratchet isn't exactly dangerous, but it takes training, timing, and the stunt person has to know when to lean back just before she's catapulted into the air. They say they are 'going for a ride.'"

Just before the stunt was shot, the crew distributed hay in a circle around the wall supports, doused it with diesel fuel, and lit it up. "I revved up the bike and went for it," Debbie said, "but when I crashed through the wall, a couple of slats broke, the rest pulled out of the frame, all bent, and the staples popped right out. I was through the wall, but the burning frame was all around the motorcycle and me. I saw smoke coming from my back and thought I had a piece of it on me. I couldn't push it off, so I bailed off the back of the motorcycle and rolled." Conrad added, "We were told that Debbie's costume had been treated with fire retardant, but sadly, the foam shark fin had not been done sufficiently. Debbie paid the price when it caught fire and caused her burn. I should have tested it in advance. She was then and is now one great performer, her gender never mattered—except the girls almost always have far less to wear. It's easier to do [a stunt] yourself than to put friends out there running around like they're burning to death," he said. "They're acting, of course, but where does the performance end and reality begin? It's a blurred edge. As a stunt person, we all care for each other. When it comes down to it on the set, it's a very tight-knit community. Between 'action' and 'cut,' we're all brothers and sisters." Debbie spent two awful weeks in a burn ward and didn't work for two months, but she learned an important lesson. She would never again let anyone talk her into a stunt she didn't feel right about. Later in 1979, Debbie tied for second at the CBS Sports Spectacular stunt competition, where she was the only female competitor.[35]

In the risky world of stunts, women pushed to "get wigs off men," blacks challenged the bulwark of discrimination, and everyone pressed for safer stunts, driven in part by the escalating rate of accidents. These complicated uphill efforts came to a head in the 1980s—at the Screen Actors Guild, on the set, and finally in the press.

# 8

# Stunt Safety and Gender Discrimination

What's that mean, he had the last of the Coca-Cola?

*—Jean Coulter*

Performing stunts well is the key to professional success, but coordinating them confers more prestige and control. Not all stunt performers are cut out to stunt-coordinate; in addition to stunt experience, it requires the ability to create and set up stunts, knowledge of cameras and special effects, and good people skills. It's an important job with major, sometimes life-and-death, responsibilities.

In the late 1970s, more than two decades after Polly Burson coordinated stunts in *Westward the Women* (1951), a few other women began to coordinate, including Donna Garrett, *The Streets of L.A.* (1979); Julie Johnson, *Charlie's Angels* (1976–1981); and Sandra Lee Gimpel, *Mrs. Columbo* (1979–1980).[1] On *Mrs. Columbo,* Sandy managed to snatch victory from the jaws of defeat. "On the third or fourth episode we couldn't finish a big car thing," Sandy said. "I was called to the office and told they were hiring 'Bob Someone' through the DGA [Directors Guild of America]. 'You know the show, you've been on it, he hasn't so we want you to help him through.' I said, 'No, I'm not.' They looked at me like, 'What do you mean, no?' I said, 'I want to direct second unit and if you don't want to let me do it, then let him do it, but I won't come in that day.'" Sandy then left the office, got in her car, and began to cry. "I figured they'd tell me not to come back. An hour later the production manager called. 'Tomorrow morning, eight o'clock, Black Tower, sign your contract, they're buying you the DGA card.' Then I really cried." Among other duties, a second-unit director designs and films a show's stunt sequences. The job requires knowledge of camera work (decisions involving lighting, angles, and lenses), the character of the actor's role in the stunt, and how the sequence being shot tells the story, as well as ensuring that the stunts are exciting. The next day, Sandy met with Universal's head of production. "He asked if I had my shot list. I did. 'You have eight hours. Make sure you get everything you want and they want.' I guess I did pretty well. Best of all were the guys I had worked with who always helped me, like Charlie Picerni and Mickey Gilbert."

However, the stunt business was still a man's world, and a stuntwoman was still considered to be doing a man's job, especially when she worked as a stunt coordinator or second-unit director. "You had to know how to talk to them [the men]," Sandy said. "If you didn't, you were going to be eaten alive. You could not alienate them. If someone had a suggestion, you listened to it, said 'thanks very much,' and if you didn't like it, you did it your way. So much of our business is politics. Most of life is." To prove they could handle the job, women walked a thin line between leading and following; they could not tackle the work the same way their male counterparts did. "There were absolutely no role models for us," said Beth Kennedy, a director of information systems and the first female executive on the back lot of Universal Studios. "The models we followed were the guys we worked with in the divisions. Sometimes they'd yell, but they didn't like it when a woman yelled at a man."[2] Early in her career, producer Gale Anne Hurd (*The Terminator* [1984], *Aliens* [1986], *The Hulk* [2003]) realized that to be successful, she had to be "strong, better prepared, and less emotional [than men] so that I wouldn't be judged or dismissed as a female. I saw the way men interacted—they were tough, forceful and firm. If they got emotional, they didn't cry or apologize. A lot of men were not prepared, but they were men, they knew the lingo, they were part of the boys club, and they could get away with it. As a woman, I could not."[3] Stuntwomen who wanted to coordinate needed all the usual skills plus others that had little to do with stunts.

Ron Rondell was the Spelling-Goldberg supervising stunt coordinator and second-unit director for *Charlie's Angels* (1976–1981). The son of Ronald Rondell Sr., a respected actor and second-unit director, Ron was handsome and outgoing. He had been a skilled gymnast at Hollywood High School and started doing stunts in the 1950s. He quickly became known for his agility and daring, such as his stunt on *Kings of the Sun*

(1963): He clung "to the top of a flaming 50-foot ladder as it was pushed over, rode it down until unseen wires caught it half-way to the ground. He continued on, crashing through the thatched roof of a hut."[4] In 1978 Ron hired Julie Ann Johnson as assistant coordinator on *Charlie's Angels.* Julie was one of several women who regularly doubled the lead actresses on the series (others included Jean Coulter, Jeannie Epper, Darlene Tompkins, and Hilary Thompson).[5] When Julie became a stunt coordinator, the press took notice because *Charlie's Angels* was a top-rated TV series. From that high point, no one—certainly not Julie or Ron—could have imagined what was to come.

Participants at the show's weekly production meeting dissected the script, which included a breakdown of all the stunts. Julie was worried that the cars supplied by the Spelling-Goldberg production company frequently had no seat belts or brakes; she'd "had words" about other safety issues with the cameramen and directors. In addition to being new to the job, she was the first female stunt coordinator on the show, and her forthright manner was not in sync with the way women were expected to behave. Jean Coulter, who worked with Julie and often doubled one of the Angels, said, "In our business, when a woman came in to coordinate, it was like you were not supposed to be there. Julie called talented people to work for her, she was alert on set, stood right by the camera, and cared about the safety of everyone. I saw no difference between the way she did the job and other coordinators I worked for." Jean knew the business: she came from an industry family. Her grandfather had been Claudette Colbert's chauffeur and lived on her estate; her father, Russell Menzer, was a commercial artist and art director at Warner Bros. for forty years and helped design the Disney Worlds in France, Japan, and Florida; her sister, Lori Martin, had been a child star on the TV series *National Velvet* (1960–1962). Jean was an athletic horsewoman and scuba diver, as well as being a very pretty blonde who had won her share of beauty contests. She "fell into" stunts in the 1970s, and she did some rugged ones, including the pilot of *Flamingo Road* (1979). While doubling for Morgan Fairchild, Jean was stranded in a small boat sinking in choppy waters. A rescue helicopter hovered overhead, with stuntman Glen Wilder hanging off the last rung of a ladder suspended from the aircraft. "I grabbed onto his belt," she said, "pulled myself out of the boat, climbed up and over his body to his hands, grabbed the ladder, climbed over the rest of him as the helicopter took off, shimmying and shaking. To bring up your body with your arms takes strength. I think

The "Angels" Jean Coulter doubled: Tanya Roberts, Jaclyn Smith, and Cheryl Ladd. Inset: Coulter and Ladd. (Courtesy of Ray Marek)

we did that stunt five times. What a tough show."[6] But Jean and Julie were about to be involved in another stunt that didn't go so well.

Filming a stunt successfully and safely takes the cooperation of everyone involved—director, unit manager, first assistant director, camera operators, crew, stunt people, and actors. The women who were hired to coordinate had solid stunt experience, but as one of them said, "She got the job of coordinator. Now she has to find a way to be allowed to do it." For instance, for one stunt on *Charlie's Angels,* Jean Coulter was supposed to climb a six-foot ladder, grab a rope, and "bulldog" a man—fly through the air and knock him down. "We had to fall quite a distance on to a marble floor," she said. "Julie insisted we have a pad. The director didn't have time. He said to her, 'You've told me what you want, now go over there and sit down. We're going to shoot this.'" Safety problems can arise when a director won't listen to the stunt coordinator, but that's not what happened in January 1979.

Jean and Julie were in the backseat of a car on a dirt airstrip near Magic Mountain, thirty-one miles north of Los Angles. Julie, doubling for Farrah Fawcett, sat on the left side behind the driver; Jean, doubling for Cheryl Ladd, was on the right. Simultaneously, they were supposed to jump out the rear doors of the moving car. The driver, Bobby Bass, was an experienced stuntman and coordinator; in the passenger seat, stuntman Howard Curtis would cue the women when to jump.[7] Each time they drove around the track, Jean prepared for the jump; the car doors were very heavy, she recalled, and her seat right next to the door barely gave her enough room to launch herself out of the car. Rehearsals were mainly to set the speed of the car—ten to fifteen miles per hour. They didn't feel safe jumping at higher speeds. "During the rehearsal Bobby was kind of in a daze," Jean said later. "I don't know what the problem was but he wasn't reacting to what I said to him. . . . I'd worked with Bobby before on many jobs. He was very good in cars."[8] They took a break at 10:30 a.m., and Bobby and Jean left the car; Julie stayed inside and worried about the camera placement. The shot was supposed to show both women leaping from the car's back doors—a dramatic sight—but earlier, Julie had argued with first assistant director Blair Gilbert and cameraman Richard Rawlings Jr. that the cameras were not correctly placed to film both sides of the car.[9] "Blair was standing next to our car before we did the stunt," Jean said. "Julie was upset and said to Blair that she was doing the stunt for nothing. . . . The cameras were on my side of the car, so I knew the camera would not see Julie jump out. There was no camera on the left side simultaneously filming the action with the camera on the right side. I am absolutely positive of this. . . . The cameras were not changed."[10]

During a later break, Julie, still in the car, heard the walkie-talkie squawk: "Where are you guys? Get back here!" From different directions, Jean, Howard, and Bobby hustled back to the car. As Jean got in, someone passed the driver's side of the car. "I heard him say, 'Bobby got the last of the coke this morning,'" Julie said.

Jean asked her, "What's that mean, he had the last of the Coca-Cola?"

"No, Jean, coke."

"Oh, now I get it."

"Bobby sped back to the filming site real fast," Julie said, "got into position, and the director on the walkie-talkie yelled, 'Action!'" According to

Jean, "Bobby floored it." Both she and Julie shouted at him, but he ignored them. The jump point was only a quarter of a mile away. "We were supposed to start out at 15 mph, then drop back to 10 or 12 miles per hour," Julie said. "Howard was to give us the cue to jump, but we got a hesitant cue." She felt the car's speed decrease a little and saw that Jean was ready to jump. But as Julie crouched on her seat, one hand on the door handle, the car sped up. "That threw us totally off."[11] Julie and Jean looked at each other, and despite the speed of the car, they decided not to spoil the shot. Jean jumped first, then Julie. But as they tried to make their exits, "we were pinned between the heavy doors and the ground," Julie said. "I pulled up my legs so the wheels wouldn't run over them. Bobby hadn't waited for us to get out before he stepped on the accelerator." Jean told Julie that the instant she opened the door, she knew "the car was going three times the speed we were supposed to go, not the way we rehearsed it at all."[12]

The stunt was over in seconds. "After I jumped, I thought I was going to die," Jean said. "I went up into the light. It was dead quiet." She started running. "Cheryl [Ladd] grabbed me because I did not know what I was doing. I saw Julie on the ground in convulsions, lying face down on the dirt. I thought she had been very badly injured."[13]

"They said I was flopping like a fish," Julie said, "and in my mind I guess I felt like I was continuing my work of getting up and running. . . . I do remember a heaviness about me and I thought, 'Oh, boy, I broke my back.' I wondered why can't I get up? I realized someone was on top of me to keep me from violent jerks that can really injure you." Ron Rondell was holding Julie down. Neither Jean nor Julie knew what day it was or even their own names. There was no nurse or other medical personnel at the airstrip. Ron commandeered a station wagon to take them to the hospital in town. "When Jeannie and I got into the back seat, we said, 'What happened?' Then there was a pause and we both said, 'He sped up instead of slowing down.' We were both in shock, physical shock."[14]

"Bobby did not do what he was supposed to do," Jean said. "This was the reason we were hurt."[15] They both had concussions, but no broken bones. Julie also had a hairline fracture in her neck. The emergency room doctor advised them to go home, but they returned to the airstrip to complete the scene. As professionals they knew "it was important to do the last shot of us getting up and running to a car." That's part of the stunt code—finish the scene, don't complain about injuries unless you can't walk. In other words, real stuntwomen don't cry.

The crew was on a lunch break. Jean and Julie hadn't eaten for hours, so they got in line at the buffet. Julie noticed Bobby in line. "I thought I'd go up to him, but he turned, looked at us, turned away real fast. He looked depressed and glazed . . . and as he looked away he sneered."[16] Jean recalled, "Bobby . . . didn't even come over to ask how we were and this was not like him."[17]

At about three o'clock, Jean and Julie were waiting to finish their scene after Bobby Bass spun out a car. "I mean, anybody can spin a car," Jean said, tartly. "He'd done it before, but he couldn't do it. Ronnie Rondell got in the car to show him how! I couldn't believe it. I mean, that was terrible, Bobby should never have been working. To this day I can't imagine why he'd put us in that position. But he wasn't jumping out of the car, we were." She sighed. "What a mistake. At least we're alive."[18] According to Jean, no one talked to her about reporting her injuries; nor did she know whether Spelling-Goldberg Productions investigated the "circumstances that caused" the accident.[19] Julie and Jean completed their scene and went home.

The next morning, in a screening room at Fox Studios, Julie, a few production people, and assistant director Blair Gilbert watched the footage shot the day before. Aaron Spelling was there too, which was not unusual.[20] Julie knew the footage wouldn't show her jump from the car. "I wanted to explain to them . . . especially to Blair," Julie said. "She still insisted I would be seen. 'You have a low camera and a high camera,' she told me. I said, 'I'm on the other side of the car. You're on Jean's side of the car.'"[21] Julie was right. Jean saw the footage later. "At the very end of the video taped sequence," she said, "the person lying on the ground in the center of the screen was me. Julie was on the other side of the car. She was not seen in the film."[22] On Julie's side of the car, only the open door was visible. Julie apologized to Spelling. "He only said to me, 'Who was driving the car?' He said it very emphatically. I said, 'Bobby Bass.' He sort of grumbled, got up and walked out."[23]

Every bone and muscle in Julie's body ached, and she was angry. She had asked Ron Rondell to stop by her home. "The footage was bad, the cameras were not placed right, and I wanted to mention what I'd heard about drugs." She was nervous about speaking to him, and their meeting was short. "I said, 'I have to tell you what I saw and heard,' and he said, 'What?' I told him and he said, 'I didn't know that.' I told him that Jeannie and I were almost killed, that I didn't mind losing my career, but if I had to lose it over someone's cocaine use, that was pretty sad. Ron said he would look into it." As he was leaving, she asked "if it was known in the industry about cocaine, did he realize what would happen to all of us if it got out? If one goes, everyone goes. He said, 'Oh, I know, I'll take care of it.'"[24]

At that time, television series went on hiatus from March to September. Julie was invited back to stunt-coordinate the fourth season of *Charlie's Angels,* which ran from September 1979 to March 1980. She broke down the stunts in scripts, devised ways to do them, organized the work, hired the stunt people, and doubled the actresses in some episodes. March 24, 1980, was the last day of shooting for that season. It started with "a big second unit sequence—five stunt people to drive five cars, near misses, sideswipes, maybe some crashes. No acting, just action," Julie said. "I was driving a car, Jean Coulter, Regina Parton, and two stuntmen were in others." The Fox Hills location was a few miles south of the studio. Everyone was there at 8:00 a.m., but there were no cars. They all had to be back at the studio by 3:30 p.m. to finish the last shot, a car turnover by Regina Parton. When the cars were finally delivered at 11:00 a.m., Julie and Ron found that three had no seat belts, no brakes, and no emergency brakes—they were junkers. In a production meeting a few days earlier, Julie had asked the head of transportation to make sure the cars were properly equipped for the stunts. Of the cars delivered that morning, only two could actually be used in the scene, "which made Ronnie even madder," Julie said. "He decided to park three of the cars, have Regina do some sideswipes with them, 'and then we'll just improvise from here on.' That's what we did. We improvised from there on."[25] Jean Coulter said this was a common problem: many times "we'd go out to do a driving job and the emergency brakes weren't working . . . there were no seat belts . . . I'd tape myself in or get a rope and make do with that." Jean didn't get a car that day "because there wasn't one of them good enough to drive."[26]

Back at the studio at 5:00 p.m., daylight was going, and the pressure was on to finish the scene. Julie checked the car Regina was supposed to use for the turnover. It didn't have the five-point harness needed for a turnover, but special effects had already started drilling to put one in. Regina didn't have a helmet or her wig, either. Julie checked on those and then went to the set, where she found that the "special effects [guy] was still not set up with his explosion stuff, and he was working fast to try to pull it together. The ramp [for the car turnover] was not totally lined up either. Ron was out there eyeballing it and the greenhouse that the car was to turn over on." Julie was afraid that everyone was "rushing too much," which can cause accidents. She wanted to do the shot the next day, since there wasn't enough time to prepare the equipment and do the stunt properly. "But it costs money, a few thousand dollars, to go back a second day. In my opinion it doesn't cost that much compared to what can happen if something goes wrong. Naturally you're a hero if you get it in on time—wow, you saved us half a day! They don't know we went through hell to save half a day." Regina was under a lot of pressure, even though "her stunt didn't require that much skill," Julie said. "No one else was involved in it, just her and the ramp, and as soon as she hit that ramp she had no control anyway. The ramp props up the car and gives her a nice landing."[27] Regina was an expert driver, but this time, Julie had to push her. "She seemed afraid to drive the car she was given," Julie said, "and she delayed the stunt, which wasn't like her. Later she denied it. I know she felt rushed, and she was, but she was kind of blanking out. I didn't know why." In the end, Regina turned the car turned over, the explosion went off as planned, and it all worked out. Years later, Julie learned why Regina had hesitated: she was pregnant.[28]

That was the last stunt of the season, but Julie wasn't celebrating. She went off to find Bob Thetford, the head of transportation. She took him aside and, out of earshot of the other men, criticized the condition of the cars. She reminded him she'd asked for better-equipped cars in the weekly production meetings. He said, "Belts and brakes are expensive." Julie lost it. "I spun around and said, 'You're telling me belts and brakes are expensive? My God, what's that compared to a day's shoot, compared to a person's life?' I wanted us to talk to Aaron [Spelling] right then, but Bob was in a hurry, so I said, 'Okay, we won't go now, but things had better change for next season with this car situation.'" Right after that, she went to the production office to speak with Kim Manners, the unit production manager. Kim and Bob were good friends, but according to Julie, "We were all friendly. I mean, you live with all these people on a show like that for four years and you are all very close." She apologized for chewing out Bob, but the day's events had affected everyone. "I felt there was no excuse, and I wanted some changes for next season," she explained. Manners didn't say very much. "He sat back in his chair and threw his pencil on the desk."[29]

Production of *Charlie's Angels* went on hiatus, and six weeks later, Ron Rondell told Julie she would not be rehired as coordinator, although she was welcome to come back and perform stunts. Stuntman Gary Epper, Jeannie Epper's brother, was the new coordinator. On long-running TV series, stunt coordinators tend to come and go, but Julie wanted to know why she wasn't being asked back. Ron told her, "The producers said I'd overpaid, and something [negative] about the work. 'How can I overpay? I don't control that.' He said, 'If it was up to me, you'd still be there.'" Julie learned that one of the producers on the show, Elaine Rich, had had the "heaviest hand" in the decision, and Julie wanted to talk to her. "Ronnie said, 'Go ahead. Maybe it will help.'" In a meeting with Rich, Julie asked how she had overpaid for stunts. Rich replied, "No, I can't go into it, it would take too much time. It's just that we thought you were too high, you overpaid." Julie pointed out she didn't control the budget, but Rich said she couldn't go into it. When Julie asked about her work being "substandard," Rich said, "Some of the shows are just not good." Julie asked for specifics, but Rich said she "couldn't go into it." Julie asked her "to consider what . . . it will do to my career." Rich said, "There's nothing I can tell you. That's it."

Julie then called Norm Henry, the supervising unit manager for Spelling-Goldberg Productions, and asked about her rate if she returned to the show as talent: would she get the weekly SAG rate or the lower daily rate? He said, "You'll only come back when Gary wants you to come back."[30] Next, she wrote letters to Henry and to Spelling. The latter responded that if she had creative differences, she should settle them with the producers. Julie wrote back several times but got no reply. In the summer of 1980 she asked the Screen Actors Guild to help her reach Spelling, and SAG agreed to try. "After that, I tried to hang in there at SAG and hammer at the problems of the women, regardless of how devastated I felt about not being with *Charlie's Angels*."[31]

The Screen Actors Guild became a real center for action. The rising toll of injuries caused the Stunt Safety Committee to draft new proposals for contract negotiations, and the press picked up on the increase in stunt-related accidents. Issues that had simmered for years in the stunt community boiled over in the early 1980s. How dangerous had stunt work become? "When SAG sanctions someone to do a stunt," Rock Walker, president of the Stuntmen's Association, told reporter Dave Robb, "they don't care if you can fly a 747 or roll a car. All they want to know is if your dues are paid. It's possible to have a complete production crew who knows nothing about action films, a stunt coordinator whose only qualification is that he's a friend of the producer, and a stunt man whose only credits may include 22 speeding tickets. And the first thing you know, you're reading that another stuntman's been killed."[32] As the nation's premier union representing actors, SAG had a long history in the American labor movement. It had stood up to the studios in the 1940s and continued to fight for artists' rights, but now stunt players felt that SAG didn't grasp the enormity of the safety problems they faced.

Amazingly, the contract between the Screen Actors Guild and the Alliance of Motion Picture and Television Producers (AMPTP) included few safety provisions for stunt work. Stunt players were trying to make the unregulated system safer. For instance, the people who drove stunt cars—notorious for being nothing more than "buckets of bolts"—wanted contracts to specify that producers were to supply cars in "good working condition." In addition to safety, stuntwomen and minorities were equally concerned about the blatant discrimination that often truncated their careers. The only rule that even came close to addressing affirmative action stated: "women and minorities shall be considered for doubling roles and for descript and non-descript stunts on a functional non-discriminatory basis."[33] That wording was nonspecific, noncompliance carried no penalties, and efforts to strengthen the rule had been postponed or rejected.

The procedure for adding a clause to a contract was rigorous. SAG was a bureaucrat's dream, studded with members' committees and layers of executives that, some groused, guarded the board and delayed action. A motion to add or change a clause had to be written, voted on, and passed by a committee before it was sent to the SAG board. If approved, it then went to the Wages and Working Conditions Committee, where it might eventually become a demand in contract negotiations with producers. These negotiating sessions could be daunting. From 1977 to 1982 Julie Ann Johnson, representing the Society of Professional Stuntwomen, served on negotiating teams. "We weren't talking to producers, we were talking to attorneys, rows three-deep of attorneys around a table that ran a mile. Talking about our concerns as stuntwomen in front of all those men, it wasn't easy." Only when the AMPTP and SAG agreed on the final wording of a clause did it become part of the contract and thus an enforceable principle. Rejected motions languished for three years, the term of the next negotiating period. Given the long, drawn-out process required to make changes, stunt players were frustrated. They felt that SAG didn't recognize their needs, and "nothing ever happened."[34]

Two years before Julie and Jean were injured in the *Charlie's Angels* car stunt, twenty-nine-year-old Vic Rivers had died while doing a stunt. "Vic had been part of the coordinating team on *Grand Theft Auto*," stunt coordinator Conrad Palmisano said, "but on *High Riders* Vic coordinated himself. He jumped a car into a lake, but he didn't take an air canister with him. He got stuck in the car and he drowned." Conrad was a member of the SAG Stunt Committee, which met every three years when a new contract was being negotiated. After Rivers's death, Conrad convinced SAG to transform the Stunt Committee into a full-time, year-round committee and to add the word "Safety" to it. Chaired by Conrad, the Stunt and Safety Committee devised and pushed hard for a new system to rate stunt people based on their experience. "There are no qualifications whatsoever to be a stuntman," he said. "If you have a Screen Actors Guild card, you're as qualified as Lassie. I had one fellow tell me he was a stuntman, and all he'd done was a voice-over on radio."[35]

The committee's proposal was known as the A, B, and R classification system. An "A" rating denoted a fully qualified stunt person, including anyone who had stunt-coordinated in the past; a "B" rating applied to a stunt person with at least three years experience; and an "R" rating was given to a new stunt person, who was eligible to work only when a class A stunt person was on the set. But because the system was based on the number of days worked per year, many women and people of color, who had fewer credits, felt it was unfair. Both the stunt community and SAG had mixed reactions to the ratings system, and in the 1980 contract negotiations, the producers turned it down because the proposal had not been finalized.[36]

"Unless something is done to regulate the qualifications required before a person can become a stunt coordinator," stuntman Henry Wills wrote, "many who carry the title are actually walking accident-makers." In Wills's first thirty years of stunts, only six people were killed, but from 1967 to 1984, "over twenty stuntmen, new members or actors, [were] killed, and an untold number of life-time, crippling injuries [occurred]. Intelligence and knowledge-through-experience is the answer to safety. Know the people who are placed in control of lives!"[37] "They treat race horses better than us," Julie Johnson stated in 1981. Changes should be made "immediately, not two years from now . . . all we want is a system and the producers are standing in the way."[38]

The ratings system was only one of many efforts to make stunt work safer. But a related and more dangerous threat had been growing throughout the 1970s. Few talked about it, but it soon became clear that the stunt world had taken a disastrous turn.

# 9

# Danger, Drugs, and Death

You don't want to toss up a Hail Mary to get a stunt done. The goal is to work, not end up in the hospital.

—*Rita Egleston*

As stunt people continued the battle to expose the lack of safety regulations, a stream of fights, falls, crashes, and burns jazzed up many 1980s film productions. These included action comedies, which delighted an increasingly young movie audience. In *Airplane!* (1980), two stuntwomen—Sandy Gimpel and Paula Moody—delivered a fight of lasting popularity.[1] "Sandy Gimpel is one of the stuntwomen who has a DGA card," stunt coordinator Mary Albee said. "She's a second-unit director. We call her 'The Midget.' She's five feet tall, about sixty-five years old now, and a black belt." Six years after Sandy's frantic swim on *The Towering Inferno* set, she and Paula let loose for the "Girl Scout fight" in *Airplane!* "Paula and I were both short," Sandy said, "dressed in the uniforms, our hair in pigtails, our boobs flattened—Girl Scouts! We're playing cards in the bar and bang! We go into a knockout, drag-out fight and we had so much fun bashing it out."

"We wanted a unique fight that looked like the kind guys do," said stunt coordinator Conrad Palmisano—a movie buff who's particularly fond of westerns. "I wanted that fight to be an homage to the Dietrich-Merkel fight in *Destry Rides Again,* so I designed it from what I recalled—in 1980 we couldn't rent videocassettes of old movies. We needed to find two petite girls that were tough as nails and could take the punches. They weren't all padded up, either." Sandy tosses Paula over a banister; she lands on a table and smashes it. Paula gets Sandy in a chokehold, breaks a bottle over her head, and then they pound each other with punches. "In the middle of the fight," Conrad said, "I wanted real punches like John Wayne's haymakers, a sort of 'Wayne meets Dietrich' fight. We have an expression: 'can of peas off the shelf.' You reach back, grab the can, and hurl it at a guy's head. Well, Wayne pulls his arm back, shows you the punch coming at you, and wham!—that kind of real fight. And those girls delivered!" When Sandy flings Paula onto a bar lined with sullen drinkers, she sails past them on her belly, head-first, straight into the jukebox. Conrad laughed. "Who knew the fight in *Destry* and the Girl Scout fight would end up on YouTube?"

That fight had few dangers, other than the usual ones, but some larky comedies provided rafts of perilous scenes. In hindsight, these unfettered free-for-alls and high-spirited, wacky romps represented a kind of fiddling-as-Rome-burns folly. Instead, the guilds should have been dealing with matters that would deeply affect the pattern and progress of the athletic art of stunts.

On the slapstick comedy *Honky Tonk Freeway* (1981), skateboard wizard Chris Baur was driving a car, along with a dozen others.[2] In rehearsal, they were all going very fast, and she was worried about doing her stunt: a guy slides in front of her, and she swerves around him and does a 180. "We go back for the take," she said, "they call 'Action!' and suddenly they turn on big arc lights and rain machines. We're speeding around trying to make our moves, but we're literally blinded by the light and rain. I couldn't see anything. That scared the hell out of me. No one was hurt, but I don't know how we did it." It's not always possible to rehearse with wind and light effects, but someone should have told the drivers what to expect. Fortunately, Chris's stunt driving on *Dukes of Hazzard* had seasoned her. That TV show—known for its car stunts—had a reputation of prioritizing "spectacle over safety, creating hazardous working conditions [on] dysfunctional sets."[3]

Now, a new danger had been added to the risky business of stunts: drugs. The seemingly benign recreational drug use of the 1960s had morphed into the more hard-core drugs of the 1970s and the cocaine-riddled 1980s. Slurred speech and forgotten lines were annoying and wasted time, but stunts were different. One stunt person said, "When the drug stuff started," *Dukes* was "a terrible work environment. Everyone was on cocaine—scary times—because we'd be doing car work with people who were high as kites." In these years, that description could apply to any number of productions.

While *Honky Tonk* tore up the road, *The Blues Brothers* (1980) busted up the Dixie Square Mall, setting the tone for irreverent, wacko mayhem and dark humor buried in a riot of action and music. John Landis directed, and Gary McLarty stunt-coordinated.[4] Stuntwoman Janet Brady was part of the melee that took weeks to film inside the shop-lined mall.[5] Speeding cars crashed through plate-glass windows, and glass flew everywhere—very dangerous. "They even did a rollover in that mall. We *destroyed* that mall," stuntwoman Jean Coulter said gaily. "John Landis was directing, so anything went." After a day's work, the scuttlebutt was all about big parties and "bowls of coke."

Drug use in Hollywood was one of the worst-kept secrets in the world. In early 1981 *TV Guide* printed what many insiders already knew but the public did not. "Coke was all over the place, directors, writers, producers, everyone," a top network official told Frank Swertlow, writer of the two-part article. "It's horrendous." Tension, late nights, bone-deep fatigue, pressure to rush the shot, and screaming directors were not new in Hollywood. Drug dealers on the set *were* new. "In many cases, the producer said, the pusher was a technician who set up shop in a corner of a sound stage. 'It's very easy,' he said. 'It's dark. A pocket is opened and one hand passes the money and another drops the coke.' On other occasions ... dealers blended into a production by simply putting on a T-shirt with the name of the show written on it."[6]

Cocaine had become a currency of exchange. Another producer said, "You might not be able to pay a writer or an actor or a director a bonus, so you pay him in cocaine." And when someone wanted to be paid in drugs, failing to do so had consequences. Swertlow quoted one producer who had refused: "'You see, the way the intimidation works is that if you don't play, you are cut out. A guy like this will tell his boss the rewrites of the script were not good enough. He can do that at any point, so you really are at the mercy of these executives.'" Refusing to negotiate in cocaine could cut anyone "out of parties," where "plenty of deals are made." Thousands of dollars for cocaine were buried in budgets under the headings of "miscellaneous or food or entertainment. One studio head joked about his creative bookkeeping. 'There are three kinds of costs: above-the-line, below-the-line and cocaine-line,' he said."[7] One producer's reaction to the news that an actor was stoned: "So what?" he screamed, "we created the show stoned, we cast it stoned. He fits right in."[8] In Hollywood, fitting in is essential. Everyone counts on relationships and coworkers for cooperation, for favors, even for employment; it's a time-honored exchange that gets the work done and builds careers. Cocaine created an inner circle within industry groups and within stunts.

After "snow" had already "kidnapped the industry," the Los Angeles Police Department formed an Entertainment Squad in 1985 to investigate narcotics use. One undercover detective estimated that 80 percent of the people contacted—from "top management" to individuals at all levels of production—used cocaine.[9] *Variety* later reported that 35 percent of all people working in motion pictures and television had substance abuse problems; of those, 75 to 80 percent worked in below-the-line jobs.[10]

The press reported the drug use of actors, producers, executives, and directors—but not stunt performers, even though that's where drugs could do real damage. When a writer who is high on coke is talking script changes with a producer who is high on coke, "That's not a meeting," one said, "it's bedlam." But the writer's job doesn't involve driving a car, missing a stunt person standing in the road, and crashing into another car. "When you mix high-risk explosives, car crashes, and drugs, you're going to have a bad result," reporter Dave Robb said.

The pervasive use of drugs worked against stunt performers' efforts to impose better safety measures. It may have been the real reason behind Jean Coulter and Julie Johnson's car accident on *Charlie's Angels*. "Many people were so lost in cocaine they didn't know how to relate to anyone," Julie said. "If you can't communicate with them on a set, you're in trouble." And drugs were very easy to get—just show up for work. That's what Julie did in January 1980 when she was doubling Farrah Fawcett in a trap-door sequence on *Charlie's Angels*. Outside the sound stage, which was close to the front gate of Fox studios, Roy Harrison, a stunt coordinator on that series and other Spelling-Goldberg shows, offered Julie cocaine from his van parked nearby. She declined.[11]

In addition to the combustible combination of stunts and drugs, there was another layer of influence. The studios and audiences both exhibited an increasing appetite for movies that glorified thrills. This increased corporate demand, intensified pressure, complicated stunts, and strained trust.

The bond of trust among stunt people had been unraveling since the 1970s. "Trust is everything," said Loren Janes, cofounder of the first Stuntmen's Association. "When you're doing a stunt, you've got to trust the other guy's going to do it right. May Boss or Polly Burson, if they had to land there, you could always trust them to do that. When someone's on dope, that trust is gone. A lot of people hired guys on dope because they were on dope themselves." But drugs alone did not fracture the trust among stunt performers. "There are so many elements in trust," Jeannie Epper said. "It relates to who you are, who you work for, and who you work with. A few times I got that gut feeling that I had to be really, really careful." She never walked off a set, but sometimes she insisted on making changes to a stunt, even when everything had been checked. When she stepped up to do a stunt, she waited for a complete peace to come over her. "If I don't feel that, I step back," she said. "I won't do it or I'll change something. It took me years to get to that place. Trust is a big issue, but things can go wrong." For a long time, stuntwomen avoided doing or saying anything that might disturb that implicit trust among stunt people, including speaking up about sex discrimination or unequal pay and even when their instincts warned them that a stunt didn't feel right.

Stunt people are not daredevils. They are, according to John Baxter, "hard-thinking technicians who squeeze between the apparent danger of their situation and an infinitesimal margin of safety they built into it."[12] The erosion of trust narrowed that margin of safety, but when accidents occurred, there was usually not one cause but several. Whether those factors included unfamiliarity with colleagues, drug use, lack of safety regulations, the inherent danger of stunts, or simply stunts that "went wrong," more people were being badly injured and even killed in the 1980s.

On November 14, 1980, forty-year-old Odile "Bebe" Astié, a preeminent stuntwoman from France, was killed while doing a stunt for the CBS children's show *The Treasures of Althea Alpheus Winterborn*.[13] Like other stunts that have ended tragically, it was supposed to be a simple one: a roll off a steeply pitched roof onto an airbag twenty-five feet below. Glory Fioramonti reported the fatal accident to the new SAG Ad Hoc Stuntwomen's Subcommittee in December 1980: "An 18 × 20 × 5-foot air bag had been placed on the ground, ample for a fall of that height. Boxes were placed to fill in around the air bag. The problem of the gutter at the bottom of the roof was anticipated." Removing the gutter or filling it with sand had been considered, but "Bebe felt fine about leaving the gutter as it was." Someone suggested that the stunt might be safer if it were done in two shots: "have her come down the roof, then cut and do the high fall onto the pad." But in the end, it wasn't done that way. The hard plastic tailbone pad Bebe was wearing got caught on the gutter. "She hit the ground between the airbag and the boxes. It is not clear if the boxes were tied to the air bag or if there were qualified safety men to catch her."[14] Her death had nothing to do with drugs or rushing the shot. It showed how easily something could go wrong.

Other injuries and deaths could be attributed to the lack of industry safety measures. Three camera assistants were killed in 1980–1981: Rodney Mitchell was crushed to death when a car overturned on him during a scene for *The Dukes of Hazzard.* In December 1980 Robert Van Der Kar was killed on the set of *Magnum P.I.* Two months later, in February 1981, a driverless stunt car killed Jack Tandberg on the set of *The Five of Me.*[15] "How can safety standards improve when a director wants you to stand behind a camera as a car comes flying off a ramp toward you at 80 miles an hour?" asked Bill McCreary, a former cameraman on the TV series *CHiPs.* "You just cross yourself when they say 'action' and get ready to run in case something goes wrong. You're helpless. They have guys from the Humane Society out there to protect dogs and horses, but they don't have jack crap for us."[16]

Brianne Murphy, the first woman admitted to the cameramen's union, and two other cameramen formed an Ad Hoc Safety Committee of Local 659 in association with Stunts Unlimited and the Stuntmen's Association. According to a reporter for the *Los Angeles Times,* it was "the first time that camera and stuntmen have joined forces for a common goal." On February 23, 1981, they placed a notice in the trades: "DEAD . . . Due to a total lack of common sense, three of our people are dead . . . There is no shot worth a life."[17]

One of the worst stunt-related injuries had occurred a few months earlier. *The Cannonball Run* (1981), starring Burt Reynolds, Roger Moore, and Farrah Fawcett, tracked a coast-to-coast race jammed with cars and stunts. Veteran stuntman Hal Needham directed; Bobby Bass coordinated the stunts.[18] Beautiful six-foot-tall Heidi Von Beltz, a gymnast, model, and champion skier, had grown up in the movie business, helping her actor-father, Brad, learn his lines. Bobby Bass and Heidi were an item, and according to her autobiography, he wanted to marry her. Heidi had acted in a few television shows, including *Charlie's Angels;* she aspired to produce and direct, but she had little stunt experience. Bobby had taught her the fundamentals of the car work she had used on *Cannonball!* (1976) and *Smokey and the Bandit II* (1980). "The trick," she wrote, "is to create the illusion of danger, without exposing the stunt people to real danger, and most of the time it works."[19] For Heidi, the danger became reality on June 25, 1980.

The production team was on location in Boulder City, Nevada. Heidi had just finished a car stunt—a 180-degree spin—and she felt pumped, so she asked Bobby what else she could do. The only person he needed was an extra to ride as a passenger in a car chase, and he had already hired newcomer Eurlyne Epper (Jeannie's daughter) to do it. He suggested that Heidi go back to the hotel and enjoy the sun and the pool, but she wanted to be part of the action. Bass gave in and called Eurlyne. "I was supposed to ride passenger in the car," she said, "but Bobby told me he had it covered. So I didn't go." The stunt was big enough, but it wasn't considered complicated. An Aston Martin—like the one James Bond drove—was supposed to speed down the highway, chased by the bad guys. A switch in the car turned on a device to make smoke pour out the back and blind the pursuers. The smoke was also supposed to fill the interior of the car, making it hard for the driver to see and causing him to swerve all over the highway to avoid oncoming traffic. Jimmy Nickerson, a stuntman for fourteen years, was doubling Roger Moore in the Aston Martin. Heidi doubled Farrah Fawcett, but at six feet tall, she must have had to squeeze herself into the small car. Hidden on the floor of the backseat was special effects man Cliff Wenger, operating the smoke machine. Nickerson had practiced with the Aston Martin, which had many problems, including a "faulty suspension [and] smooth tires." The steering didn't work, and neither did the clutch; "it had no speedometer, and no seat belts." The car was sent to the mechanic. "The next day we got the car back and the steering was fixed to only a bare minimum," Nickerson said. "They told me the parts from L.A. had not arrived and they had had to 'make do.'"[20] It still had no seat belts.

It was late in the afternoon, so the light was fading. It was the last shot of the day, and everyone wanted to get back into town. Take one: Nickerson accelerated to about thirty miles per hour, but the car "handled like a truck." Needham didn't like what he saw; the action was too slow, and there wasn't enough smoke. He wanted Nickerson to "double his speed," do more "side to side action," and weave between each oncoming car instead of just one. Nickerson told him he didn't think the car could handle it, but he went ahead and tried anyway.

Take two: Heidi braced herself, left hand on the dashboard, arm stretched out. With the cameras rolling, someone on the radio in the car was yelling, "Faster! Faster!" Nickerson was cursing, struggling against the steering, but he got "up to a speed of 45–55 miles per hour. He made it past the first on-coming car, but when he tried to cut back in to weave past the second car, the front end went to 'mush' and, in trying to abort the stunt, crashed head-on."[21] "The impact," Heidi wrote, "slammed the engine toward us with the force of a freight train." She described what happened next:

> Jimmy, Cliff and I kept moving forward until we were stopped by the pieces of the fragmenting car. A jagged shard of glass or metal tore free and sliced into Jimmy's head, scalping him and splashing us both with hot blood. Cliff shot stiffly out of the back as if fired from a cannon, and he rolled across the ground to a stop. . . . The force continued through the dashboard and into the hand I had braced there, driving my straight left arm like a pool cue into the vertebrae in my neck. When the top of the long humerus bone struck my spine, two vertebrae shattered like china cups and my shoulder jerked viciously out of its socket. The impact traveled up my leg and snapped the heavy bone in my thigh, popping the femur. My entire body shut down instantly.[22]

Heidi was paralyzed from the neck down. In addition to his head wound, Jimmy Nickerson had a shattered hip, a compound fracture of the left arm, and numerous lacerations. Even though Cliff Wenger had been thrown from the car, he suffered no serious injuries. Stuntman James Halty, driving the van that hit them, had a few cracked ribs and other minor injuries. He had been wearing a seat belt and harness.

Needham, Bass, and Nickerson were all top stuntmen. They knew the Aston Martin had severe problems; they knew the dangers inherent in rushing to get the last shot. The stunt had several obvious warning signs: the rush to avoid losing the light, the lack of seat belts, and a change in the stunt without a rehearsal—Needham's direction for Nickerson to weave in and out of all five cars.[23]

Another change had been made to the stunt, but that didn't come to light until later. Conrad Palmisano replaced the hospitalized Jimmy Nickerson, and a fairly new stuntman told Conrad that in earlier takes, he'd been driving the van off the road onto the dirt shoulder. But fearing the van might stick and flip over, they had switched the van for another vehicle—a station wagon. Afterward, the young stunt guy thought the wreck might have been partly his fault because in that millisecond, Nickerson could have been confused. "Hal Needham was pushing to do it faster," Conrad summed up, "but on the next take the station wagon and the van had swapped positions, and the driver's going, 'Do I go left? Do I go right?' I know in the mind of a stunt person when things are coming at you, closing in at sixty miles an hour, you're clocking the *cars*—the station wagon, the van—and one moment of indecision is enough to cause a wreck. A last-minute change can cause a real problem just because two stunt guys are trying to help each other out. Generally, it's not one thing, it's a series of events that turn a situation sour."

Heidi's terrible injury hit the stunt community hard, reverberated in the press, reinforced the inherent danger of stunt work, and highlighted the risk of using an inexperienced performer even on a "little" stunt. Annie Ellis, an expert horsewoman who became a stunt driver, knew the risks. "When you're new, you figure, 'Oh, I'm just riding passenger in this car,'" Annie said. "I tell the new people they have to watch everything going on around them. Many times in a car chase, there might be a collision, or something comes through the windshield. You've got to be ready for anything even when you're 'just a passenger.'"

Ultimately, stunt people are responsible for saving their own lives. If they're lucky, they learn that early in their careers. When rodeo champ Marguerite Happy married stuntman Clifford Happy, she joined a family of stunt performers and became a stuntwoman herself. Each time Marguerite left for work, her father-in-law, Don, a stunt veteran, reminded her: "Don't let them set a trap for you." He meant that even though a show had a stunt coordinator, "it was up to each of us to watch our own back." The value of that advice came home to Marguerite on the set of *Throw Mama from the Train* (1987), which was coordinated by Vince Deadrick Jr. While doubling actress Ann Ramsey, Marguerite wore a harness hooked onto a T-bar to secure her inside the compartment of the train. Marguerite said, "I was hanging half in and half out of the train while Billy Crystal and Danny DeVito were fighting over me. On the next stunt, the train went across a trestle on the bridge. I looked at the trestle, it seemed narrow, and I asked Vince if there was enough space for my body hanging outside the train to clear that. He said, 'Yeah, there is, but we'll measure it.' Sure enough, there wasn't enough space. If I hadn't asked, it might have been a horrible wreck. That's [what Don meant by] 'don't let them set a trap for you,' and it's the sign of a good coordinator who does everything to make sure we're safe."

Heidi Von Beltz accepted her role in her accident: "I was the one who

In the thick of it, Marguerite Happy doubles Jane Seymour in *Dr. Quinn Medicine Woman*. (Courtesy of Marguerite Happy)

had wanted to work on the movie," she said. "I considered it a privilege, and I had loved every second until I stepped into that car. I was an adult, a paid stuntwoman, and I knew that stunt work could be dangerous. I had agreed to do the stunt in the Aston Martin mock-up. In fact, I had begged to do it. Maybe I should have asked more questions or insisted on having seat belts in the car. Maybe I should have left the scene to a more experienced stuntwoman. But the stunt coordinator and everybody on the set, the pros, told me the stunt wasn't a big deal and that it certainly wasn't dangerous. I believed them."[24]

Jimmy Nickerson also acknowledged his role: "If I'd said, 'Wait a minute, we've got to do this, we've got to do that,' I would have been home," he said.[25] Three years after the accident, in a pretrial deposition, Nickerson said, "If we all had seat belts, ladies and gentlemen, we all wouldn't be sitting here today. I would have dusted myself off and we would have got a new car."[26] In 1980 seat belts were not a contractual requirement in producer-supplied stunt cars.

That summer, however, stuntwomen got their act together. To communicate the biases they faced on the job and to improve their position, they had to be united. That was a difficult undertaking in a group of competing individuals, but they had allies: Norma Connolly, a polished stage and screen actress and a SAG board member, and former SAG president Kathleen Nolan, who had initiated the guild's first Stunt Committee. On August 19, 1980, they announced the new Ad Hoc Stuntwomen's Subcommittee. "YOU WANT WORK—MONEY—RESPECT—ACKNOWLEDGEMENT OF YOUR UNIQUE SKILLS," declared a fact sheet distributed by Connolly. "As a community of stuntwomen—FIGHT for it—nobody else will! United you stand—divided you fall. SIMPLE. Come and express this at your union and at your committee meeting."

In 1980 SAG's membership included 85 stuntwomen and 544 stuntmen.[27] Twenty-nine women showed up for the December meeting, where Rita Egleston was elected chair and Julie Johnson was elected cochair of the subcommittee; Jadie David, Mary Peters, Janet Brady, and Stevie Myers were at-large members.[28] The agenda: to add clauses to contracts preventing men from doubling women and to require equal pay, more opportunities to coordinate stunts, and more access to nondescript work.

Another issue that was rarely mentioned in public (but soon would be) was sexual harassment. In a report by the SAG Women's Committee, Connolly stated, "The amount of sexual harassment has been unbelievable. Women bring their complaints to the Stunt & Safety Committee [of SAG], but the people who hear them are the ones that hire them so they [stuntwomen, actresses] are punished either on the job or by not getting hired." Connolly suggested that stuntwomen bring their complaints directly to her, not to the male-run committee. She would then submit them to the board, without mentioning names.[29] The guild had also set up a twenty-four-hour hotline to deal with any problems, including sexual harassment. But in this case, the women were up against an unregulated system over which they had no control. "The stuntmen dictate who will work," a Stuntwomen's Fact Sheet stated, "because the Screen Actors Guild and the AMPTP refuse to adopt the necessary rules and regulations to protect us."[30] Women had to work without complaint for stuntmen—their employers. Thirteen years later, in 1993, Jeannie Epper repeated, "Every time you talk, you don't work. We're in a Catch 22."[31] Julie Johnson's take on the situation: "Keep your mouth shut and you might work."

"A lot of stunt guys had been working since the cowboy movie days in the 1950s," Dave Robb said, "and some of them had that John Wayne attitude, you know, we're white men in America and we'll do whatever we want. A lot of them were employers." Stuntmen put on wigs or were painted black not because a stunt was "too hard for girl" or they couldn't "find any black stuntmen." They wanted to keep the work for themselves or their friends—and they did.

There was another excuse to exclude women. Off the record, one stuntman revealed that the Stuntmen's Association didn't allow women because "they'd be hooking up with people." If the group didn't have any female members, then "the men wouldn't have to explain things to their wives." Brianne Murphy, the first woman admitted to the American Society of Cinematographers, knew firsthand the difficulties faced by women in a field dominated by men. She once asked a male colleague why the guys didn't want women running the camera. His response: "It's very hard for us to go home and tell our wives we work for a woman, because we've convinced them we're top dogs, we do a very difficult, complicated job. How would we ever explain that to our wives? They would never understand it."[32] Was that a good enough reason to shut women out? What if a woman did the job as well as a man? What if a stuntwoman could roll a car as well as or better than the guys? Stuntwomen who were just trying to make a living faced the same challenges as other women in the industry, but the stuntwomen's conditions were much harder to change. That's what they set out to do, with help from SAG.

Julie Ann Johnson knew her protests about unsafe cars and her visible role on SAG negotiating committees had made her decidedly unpopular with some stuntmen. She had been tagged as a troublemaker. Julie was a hot, in-demand stuntwoman, but she declined to do stunts when "my instinct told me to turn them down," she said, particularly if "I didn't trust the stuntman who asked me, or I didn't like his tone. I didn't take melees because someone in there could be designated to hurt you." She did work on *Raging Bull* (1980), even though it involved being part of a crowd rampaging around a boxing ring. Martin Scorsese directed and Alan Gibbs coordinated the stunts. "I put on pads and a protective vest," she said, "but just before the shot Gibbs looked at me in a way I'd never seen him do before, like 'it's your turn in the bucket.' I knew I was in trouble. I was trampled. It felt like every stuntman there was tromping on my head, my feet, and my back. Martin Scorsese saved me because he began screaming, I could hear the panic in his voice, 'STOP! STOP! CUT! CUT!' Oh, I was so grateful to him."

After failing to be rehired to stunt-coordinate *Charlie's Angels,* Julie had tried and failed to talk with producer Aaron Spelling. She had asked SAG to intercede with Spelling, but after several months a SAG staffer told her, "'We can't reach Mr. Spelling either. Sorry, that's all we can do.' I was angry and amazed. I mean, when was she going to tell me?" Then Julie made a decision that would alter her life. She contacted attorney Gloria Allred, who advised her to go immediately to the Equal Employment Opportunity Commission (EEOC), because her time to file a complaint had almost expired. "The EEOC was one of our main allies," Julie said. "SAG told us to go there when all else failed." At the EEOC offices, Julie told a clerk her complaint involved Spelling-Goldberg Productions. "The clerk stepped back, put her hand to her mouth, and said, 'Oh, no.' I asked her what was wrong. She said, 'You're the seventh one in the last few weeks.' I told her I didn't feel so bad now." But filing with the EEOC began what Julie called a "thirteen-year trek through no-person's land."[33] Eventually, Julie's daring legal actions gained almost as much publicity as the rollout of a much-anticipated movie.

# 10

# Breaking the Code of Silence

As time went on, stuntwomen found that if the injuries didn't get them discrimination would.

—*Julie Ann Johnson*

During the 1980s, big, brash, stunt-filled movies "redefined the very nature of screen entertainment," Stephen Farber and Marc Green wrote in *Outrageous Conduct,* "placing the emphasis on massive special effects, graphic violence and apocalyptic horror."[1] These forces would detonate in the summer of 1982.

In February of that year, the activist Stuntwomen's Subcommittee elected Julie Johnson chair and Lila Finn cochair. Their advocate and supporter Norma Connolly repeated her warning: the history of stuntwomen had been "one of divide and conquer. It is time to put aside competition. The strength of this group can become enormous, but as individuals there is no strength at all."[2] Meetings at SAG and in the stuntwomen's associations were stuffed with grievances about unsafe stunts, unequal pay, coordinators hiring their girlfriends rather than professional stuntwomen, and being shut out of nondescript stunt work. The men's power to hire ignited friction, divided loyalties, and pitted women against each other. At work, the atmosphere "became jungle rules, which meant no rules," Julie Johnson said. "Everything and everyone was fair game, and the game was dirty." Norma knew all about the stuntmen's code of silence—don't complain, don't sue—and the punishment if it was broken—loss of work, even blacklisting. She reminded members of the subcommittee to keep what was said in the meetings confidential "so that individual grievances can be aired without fear of retaliation."[3]

Norma and Julie met privately, and Norma insisted that the bickering in the subcommittee had to stop. It kept them from "getting the facts about their working conditions" and identifying where "the problems really came from." She suggested a perfectly logical way to report their work experiences: a survey of stuntwomen in Los Angeles and New York. When the idea was presented to the subcommittee, the members voted in favor of the survey. Looking back on the rugged terrain of that year, the survey stands out like a diamond chip in an empty field. But it turned out to be a volatile issue.[4]

The subcommittee had sixty-four members. Most were aged twenty-five to forty. Julie was forty-two, and Lila Finn was seventy-one and still swimming vigorously. In a business that valued good looks and youth, Lila didn't work much, but director Robert Aldrich wanted an older woman to do a stunt in a boxing ring on *All the Marbles* (1981). "There were three girls in the ring," Lila said. "I come out of the audience, get into the ring, they throw me against the ropes, I bounce off over and over, finally fall down and crawl out." She went to some of her best friends, who were stuntmen, for advice. They told her, "As you hit the ropes, you check yourself just a little, you grab the rope, lock it in, and then you bounce off. If you don't grab the rope, you can really hurt yourself. It keeps you from going out of the ring. That was the key to the job."[5]

Along with Lila and Julie, Leslie Hoffman would take part in an upcoming drama within the Stuntwomen's Subcommittee. When Leslie (from Saranac Lake, New York) first arrived in Los Angeles in the early 1970s, she had looked up "stunts" in the phone book. By 1982, she had worked on *Charlie's Angels, Fantasy Island, Private Benjamin,* and *The Fall Guy,* and her commitment to the stuntwomen's efforts to achieve equality had already drawn her into the sizzling politics of the guild. Leslie was even contemplating a run for the SAG board, which for years had included only stuntmen. In 1984 she would become the first and only woman to play slasher bogeyman Freddie Krueger on *Nightmare on Elm Street.* "They were filming the scene with the body bag," Leslie said. As Nancy, the heroine played by Heather Langenkamp, runs down the hallway, she knocks Leslie to the floor. For the next shot, Leslie's pretty hands were outfitted with razor-like claws. Director Wes Craven told her, "I want you to say, 'Hey, Nancy, no running in the hallway,' and then do a sinister laugh." As Leslie said, "Everyone wants to be remembered for being in a special movie. I didn't expect mine to be a horror cult classic."

Leslie Hoffman, a new
stuntwoman in town.
(Courtesy of Leslie
Hoffman)

"Lila and I were members of SAG committees," Leslie recalled. "I
didn't know her well. She was pleasant, demure, rather quiet. I do not
remember when we began to think Lila might be telling the stuntmen
what we discussed. We were finalizing the survey questions, and one dealt
with sexual harassment. Lila said she'd never been sexually harassed.
Maybe not, but in the meeting I felt it was a blanket statement that [it]
couldn't happen to any woman." Later, some of the women heard that
members of the Stuntmen's Association had been talking about the wom-
en's discussion of sexual harassment. "After that," Leslie said, "some of us
felt [Lila] might have told them what we said and who said it." Two other
subcommittee members said they thought Lila might have told the stuntmen about their discussions, but they didn't recall any repercussions.
Another said she didn't remember much about the meetings and wasn't
sure who had talked to the stuntmen; for all anyone knew, someone on the
committee could have told her boyfriend. But Julie Johnson also thought
it was Lila. "She kept her cool," Julie recalled, "but she didn't seem to believe
the problems we discussed existed, like sex harassment. I don't think she
understood that." "Maybe Lila thought she was doing right," Leslie said,
"but the survey was a way to improve our working conditions. Lila was

A confident Leslie Hoffman goes right out the window. (Courtesy of Leslie Hoffman)

from another generation, men were the authority, what they did was right, and if she heard something detrimental about them, she'd tell them." The SAG-sanctioned survey was also supposed to be anonymous. The women were concerned about any breach of confidence because the stuntmen in charge of hiring could replace or even blacklist those who had created a survey about drug use, sexual harassment, and other sensitive matters.

During this time, Julie told both the Stuntwomen's Subcommittee and the group she had cofounded, the Society of Professional Stuntwomen, that she planned to file a lawsuit against Spelling-Goldberg. "Jeannie Epper was very concerned," Julie said. "She said I had to stop pursuing it, that they'd been told if they associated with me, they were not going to work. I asked her who was telling her that? She said something about guys. I wanted to know which guys—Spelling's people, guys at Unlimited, who? We were both getting angry. I said I didn't want anybody to lose work because of me . . . but I have to continue with this. My rights were violated." So Julie left the group and pursued her suit. If she had dropped the lawsuit, she might have salvaged her career.[6] "I was afraid Julie was going to ruin herself in the business," Jeannie said. "I remember talking to her back then, because I'd been trained that you never, never sue and you never turn anybody in. It was a mind-set my dad gave me when I was a little girl." But Julie's dad had taught her that when she saw something wrong, she shouldn't be afraid to speak up. Julie broke the code of silence. "She spoke out," Leslie said, "and she really paid for it."

In April 1982 subcommittee members were finishing the survey and, of course, doing stunts. On May 6, 1982, the Screen Actors Guild mailed the survey questionnaire to eighty-five stuntwomen in Los Angeles and New York. Responses were still being received in July. By then, a time bomb was ticking.

Indian Dunes, about forty miles north of Los Angeles, was a popular location site for film productions. On July 23, 1982, at about 2:30 a.m., director John Landis, best known at the time for his raucous comedies *Animal House* (1978) and *The Blues Brothers* (1980), was preparing to shoot the last scene of his segment of *Twilight Zone: The Movie* (1983), which featured a spectacular explosion.[7] Everyone was exhausted. Landis ordered the pilot of a helicopter containing a camera crew to fly lower than planned over actor Vic Morrow as he ran across a shallow stream with two small children. When the explosive blast went off, it threw up debris that blew the tail off the hovering helicopter, sending it into the path of Morrow and the children, killing all three.[8]

The catastrophe stunned America and the movie industry, and previously suppressed calls for safety turned into screaming front-page headlines. Speaking up for stunt safety became respectable because Morrow and the children had died during what was, essentially, a stunt. "Someone put actors and children where they shouldn't have been," said stunt coordinator Conrad Palmisano. "Afterwards, people were saying that Morrow and the kids 'should have been stunt performers.' We are there to take the risks. However, you're not supposed to the kill the stunt people, either. We're all supposed to go home at the end of the day."

Groups of all kinds "demonstrated their concern through a time-honored Hollywood ritual—they had meetings," Michael London wrote for the *Los Angeles Times*. "The Alliance of Motion Picture and Television Producers hosted a joint labor-management committee instructed to 'review, investigate, interpret and give recommendations on safety.'" Cameraman Bob Marta, outspoken chair of the safety committee for Local 659, weighed in passionately about the new safety committee at the Directors Guild of American (DGA), which had "refused to even acknowledge that a safety problem existed."[9]

The DGA agreed to "look into the *Twilight Zone* incident and formulate safety policies for the future," according to Farber and Green's definitive book on *Twilight Zone*. "The Screen Actors Guild participated in hearings before the California legislature for the purpose of introducing legislation [to] safeguard its members. James Nissen, safety director for the Screen Actors Guild, noted in dismay that the maximum fine for a safety violation was only five thousand dollars. 'Producers spend more than five thousand on coffee and doughnuts!' he said bitterly."[10] As everyone scrambled to be on the right side of safety, the A, B, and R rating system for stunt performers took on a new urgency.

Unfortunately, meetings and hearings often blunt momentum and dissipate the sense of urgency following a crisis. The dangers highlighted by the accident on *Twilight Zone* were already well known. "Only rarely does anyone on a set have the nerve or authority to challenge a headstrong director about the hazards of a proposed scene," Farber and Green wrote. "To understand why Morrow took the risks he did, one must apprehend the particular desperation of an actor over fifty who fears that every job could be his very last chance to prove his mettle and recoup his standing." As Morrow had said about an earlier risky scene: "That's the way John [Landis] wants it. And I want to give him as much as I can."[11]

At the time, Dave Robb had recently started reporting for *Variety*. "People said that if they'd been using a stuntman it wouldn't have happened. It wasn't Vic Morrow's fault, he was just doing the job, which was carrying those kids across the river, but when the situation changed so drastically, he wasn't prepared as a stuntman would be to see that something was wrong and to change with the situation." A stunt double might have reacted differently, but essentially, the helicopter pilot had been ordered to fly too low, about 25 feet, and too close to the explosions, which sent it into a spiral that caused the death of the children and Morrow.

Two weeks later, on August 5, there was an incident on the set of *The Thorn Birds*, a TV miniseries based on the best-selling novel by Colleen McCullough. One scene involved a fire around the family homestead. "The director [Daryl Duke] and the producers wanted actors rather than stunt doubles to participate in the sequence," wrote Farber and Green. "'We felt it would be more effective if we could get the principal players close to the fire,' producer Stan Margulies explained. 'We had checked out all the problems beforehand.'"[12] Stunt coordinator Kim Kahana had hired Julie Johnson to double Jean Simmons and a new stuntwoman, Irene Lamothe, to double Rachel Ward. Both stuntwomen were ready on the set. "Then the director wanted the actresses to do it," Julie said. "The wind whipped up the flames around them. The director said the fire wouldn't get out of control, but it did. Rachel Ward's hair was singed; the actresses were scared, and I didn't blame them. What were they doing in there? As stuntwomen we knew how to handle it. Kim and his crew walked off the set. We backed him. We went to SAG about it. We had warned the director and producers of our concerns, but they were trying to save time and money because when an actor does the stunt, the adjustment fees for the job do not have to be paid to the stunt people." According to actor Richard Kiley, "The problem was if a director said to an actor, 'Look, I can get a stuntman to do this, but we're really going to be able to see your face,' nine times out of ten the actor will say, 'I'll try it.' In a way, it's a kind of unfair seduction of the actor. It's also a kind of macho challenge." Many believed that was why Vic Morrow had agreed to do the stunt that killed him.

Stunt safety collided with the growing authority of directors, some of whom were young and inexperienced. In the 1980s Hollywood was betting on big budgets to attract audiences, and "hot" directors often overruled producers, who no longer wielded the power "to rein them in" and thus avoid dangerous situations. "You have to operate with the idea that what can go wrong will go wrong," said seasoned director Sydney Pollack (*Out of Africa* [1985]). "So you have to be like a judge in a courtroom, deciding whether or not to approve the stunt." The director should take the advice of the stunt coordinator, but "in the deepest ethical sense, the one person 'answerable' is the director."

Leslie Hill had been the only female member of the camera crew the night Vic Morrow and the two children died. A few days later, she was at a union meeting when cameraman Stephen Lydecker said he had warned Landis "that the explosions coming off the cliff might damage the helicopter. Landis's flip reply: 'We may lose the helicopter.'" For Leslie, that's where it all "coalesced, the impression we had that this really was a man who didn't care."

People all over Hollywood dissected the parallels between *Twilight Zone* and Heidi Von Beltz's injury two years earlier on *Cannonball Run*. Some crew members had worked on both films. The scene that paralyzed Heidi had also been the last shot of the day, and just before the car crash, someone had yelled "Faster! Faster!" According to Farber and Green, cameraman Lydecker was the one who had pulled Heidi from the demolished car. "When he went to work on *Twilight Zone*, he was still bitter about the dangerous conditions that precipitated her accident. In his mind, the fatal helicopter crash was a consequence of the whole pattern of recklessness that he'd seen overtaking Hollywood in the previous decade. 'It's always cheaper to shoot real than to shoot illusion,'" he said. "The *Twilight Zone* case, coming so soon after *Cannonball Run*, was really the coup de grace."[13]

The *Twilight Zone* accident underscored a concern that many had felt for years. "Before *Twilight Zone* we were dispensable commodities," stuntwoman Glory Fioramonti said. "We were just stunt people, and if we got hurt, they'd get another one. Safety is better today, but that wasn't motivated by what we told SAG about the unsafe conditions. It was motivated by lawsuits. They realized safety measures could save *money*, not that they could save lives. Very sad."

In June 1983 the Los Angeles County grand jury indicted director John Landis, associate producer George Folsey Jr., production manager Dan Allingham, special effects coordinator Paul Stewart, and pilot Dorcey Wingo for involuntary manslaughter. The case dragged on for the next five years, culminating in a long, contentious trial in May 1987. All five men were exonerated of the charges.

Accidents had been piling up even before *Twilight Zone*, and they continued to do so afterward. In 1981 the Screen Actors Guild had 74 accident reports, according to the minutes of the Stunt and Safety Committee.[14] In 1982 SAG recorded 214 accidents involving actors or stunt players. On

July 28, 1982, stuntwoman Victoria Vanderkloot, a fireman, and another stuntwoman were burned on an episode of *Fantasy Island*. On May 13, 1983, a police car in *Blue Thunder* blew up, catching two cameramen in the fireball. In February 1985 SAG reported "that of the 596 injuries from January 1, 1982 to December 31, 1984, 316 were suffered by stunt persons."[15] Those figures were not the complete picture. Reporters Deborah Caulfield and Michael Cieply wrote, "Movie and TV veterans claim that such accident statistics are seriously misleading, because stuntmen observe a 'code of silence' that prevents many from reporting injuries."[16] The code of silence was carved in stone: don't complain about cars with no brakes, unworkable stunts, or being hurt. The code was (and still is) based on pride, on tradition, and on machismo: finish the job, even though you broke your shoulder. One stuntwoman explained: "When I walked on a set, the guys said, 'You want to be a man? You're going to be a man on this stunt.' They meant I was going to hit the ground pretty hard and I better be tough enough to take it—like a man." Unless injuries were very serious, they were not reported. They were dealt with in other ways, at little cost to the production.[17]

By August 1982, as the industry scrambled to respond to the *Twilight Zone* calamity, the stuntwomen's survey results were in. Norma Connolly met with subcommittee members Stevie Myers, Jadie David, Leslie Hoffman, Jean Coulter, and Julie Johnson to discuss tabulating the results and releasing them to the press. They all recognized that the survey was an eye-opening documentation of the realities of working stuntwomen— what they had seen, experienced, or knew to be going on. Norma asked for a sacrificial lamb. "Who is going to fall on her sword?" Silence. Just filling out the survey could get a stuntwoman blackballed.[18] Julie had already traded her career for the stuntwomen's battles and her suit against Spelling-Goldberg. She had nothing left to lose, so she raised her hand. "Norma wanted me to help write the final report, sign my name to the survey, and help get it distributed." In short, Julie agreed to take all the heat.[19]

Of the eighty-five stuntwomen who had received the survey, forty-four responded. The thirty questions covered their career hopes, their annual incomes (most were in the $11,000–$20,000 range; a few earned $30,000–40,000), safety on the set, drug use, sexual harassment, and SAG's value to them as stuntwomen. Nineteen felt they had a real future as stuntwomen; eighteen checked "not enough work for women as it is," and eleven doubted their future, citing "coordinator control" as a reason; nine complained about the "industry not really caring if we exist or not." When asked about the most frequent causes of accidents, twenty-nine checked "rushing the shot," fourteen cited "improper equipment," sixteen selected "misunderstandings," and eighteen cited "untrained safety personnel." Many revealed they had been on sets or locations with inadequate safety or medical personnel.

Most respondents felt that drug abuse was increasing; most had been offered drugs on the set and had worked with people under the influence of drugs. One noted, "Some people who do drugs also do dealing on the set. They think they're making friends and getting more jobs." Twenty-seven said they'd been sexually harassed on the job, and most of them had lost a job because of it. When asked, "Do you feel the SAG Stuntwomen's Subcommittee is a waste of time," most answered no. But one wrote, "Men control the stunt business and if we [the subcommittee] push, we don't work at all." A New York stuntwoman responded: "Stuntwomen were told [by the SAG representative] that they do not belong in the stuntmen's meetings [during contract negotiations]. The women were told not to try to attend any meetings." Other comments included the following: "Women don't stick together, so nothing is accomplished." "I feel the men keep us apart. I don't know why men fear us when we are together, but I hope we will make it as a team." "The men . . . if they know you're part of the subcommittee, it's one more reason not to hire you. I know this is true."[20]

In late September the survey results landed in front of the SAG Board of Directors. Subcommittee members hoped that once board members read the report, they would take steps to stop "what is happening to stunt-women." But the board was absorbed with the *Twilight Zone* disaster, and it was tackling a merger with the Screen Extras Guild. SAG told Leslie Hoffman that it would "like to help the stuntwomen, but they had all these other problems. But some stuntwomen's careers were on the line. We expected our union to help. That didn't happen." The survey bounced around SAG for a month until information director Kim Fellner sent a memo to the board: "The survey deals with [a] wide range of job related issues . . . the results provide a very provocative view of work as a stunt-woman. The question has now arisen over whether the survey results should or should not be publicized. The stuntwomen themselves are not in agreement and the executive staff felt that because of the sensitive nature of the survey, the decision should rest with the Executive Board." Fellner added that the responses related to drug use had been leaked to TV entertainment reporter Rona Barrett.[21]

Ultimately, the board decided to release the survey. "Safety, Discrimination and Drugs Hot Topics in Survey of Hollywood's Stuntwomen" appeared in *Variety* on November 12, 1982, followed by "Stuntwomen Don't Agree on SAG Results of Survey 1982" on November 26. Reactions to the survey flew back and forth in letters to the editor. Lila wrote that she was "aghast" at the survey. Julie fired back, "Mission accomplished," stating that the survey was intended to raise consciousness and to educate.[22]

In the midst of all this, Leslie Hoffman became the first stuntwoman elected to the board of the Hollywood Screen Actors Guild.[23] "Being the first caused a lot of problems," she said. "The stuntmen did not like my being elected. Had I been an independent stunt*man* elected to the board, they probably would have voted me into the Stuntmen's Association, but I was a woman so they decided to blacklist me. Technically, what happened to Julie and to me was criminal, and the Screen Actors Guild did nothing to protect either of us. Yet stuntwomen today benefit from the things we did at the cost of our careers."

Meanwhile, three lawsuits were inching forward in the courts, adding to the industry's turmoil: Heidi Von Beltz's lawsuit for the horrific injuries she suffered on *Cannonball Run,* the mammoth legal action involving *Twilight Zone,* and Julie Johnson's suit against Spelling-Goldberg for non-payment of residuals, sex discrimination, and unlawful firing. In an unrelated development, EEOC investigators from Washington rode into town in 1984 to study charges of alleged discrimination in the entertainment industry, specifically, "the hiring and promotion of women and minorities," Robb reported in *Variety.* "Many in Hollywood feel the problem of discrimination is still very much alive."[24] *TV Guide* covered it, too: "'There is an idea out there that women can only write and direct certain things; they can't do car crashes, football games or bar brawls,'" screenwriter Carol Roper said. There were no women on the writing staffs of *St. Elsewhere* or *Remington Steele,* two series with major female roles. There were no minority writers, either. Leonard Goldberg, a producer of *Charlie's Angels,* rebutted these charges: "Listen, this business has nothing to do with social consciousness, unless it sells. If Aztec human sacrifices sell, then that's what we'll make."[25]

The *TV Guide* article cited a prime example of a person who spoke up and saw her career go south: "Julie Johnson . . . four years ago [1980], openly complained that studios and production companies all over town were taking away work from minority and women stunt people by putting wigs on stuntmen [to] do women's stunts, and 'painting down' white stuntmen so that they could look black. She filed a class-action suit against the Association of Motion Pictures and Television producers, the Screen Actors Guild and three stunt associations. Julie Johnson has not worked since."[26] Julie's audacious class-action suit, filed "on behalf of all stuntwomen," alleged that "qualified stuntwomen are denied employment solely on the basis of their sex."[27] Julie knew the risks. "I didn't want to bite the hand that fed me, but when it starts feeding poison, you must bite back." Years later she summed it up: "It was, simply, the right thing to do."

A Los Angeles newspaper reported in 1984, "The Screen Actors Guild routinely recommends [that] prospective employers hire stunt persons and stunt coordinators from members of the three main professional organizations—Stunts Unlimited, International Stunts Association and the Stuntmen's Association of Motion Pictures."[28] The year before, Robb had reported the hiring link between stuntmen's organizations and SAG, which was supposed to represent all stunt people. SAG had instructed its "Station 12 (that helps put producers together with actors) *not* to recommend the stuntmen's groups to producers seeking stunt performers," Robb wrote. "SAG affirmative action officer Rodney Mitchell said the guild felt it was inappropriate to refer producers to stunt organizations 'because they don't cover the full range of our members.' Nevertheless, as late as last week, a producer told *Daily Variety* he had called SAG's Station 12 seeking stuntmen and women and he was referred to either the Stuntmen's Association (SAMP) or to Stunts Unlimited."[29] Deliberately or not, SAG's inside referral system perpetuated the industry's institutional discrimination.

Blacklisting can effectively slap a lid on people who are clamoring for change. At least three stuntwomen were blacklisted in the 1980s.[30] A memo written by an assistant of Julie Johnson's lawyer stated that, in his opinion, two stunt coordinators "are primarily responsible for all of the blacklisting that has occurred. Julie, Jean [Coulter] and Leslie [Hoffman] have had run-ins with these guys . . . and [they] have sent the word out to the industry that these ladies are not to be hired in any stunt related work."[31]

Leslie believed that her work on the stuntwomen's survey in 1982 damaged her career. "Virtually, I was blacklisted," she said. Once she was elected to the board of the Hollywood Screen Actors Guild, she created an executive group of "independent" stunt people to keep the board informed of vital issues. "Steve Waddell was the SAG staffer who administered the decisions of that group," Leslie said. "I don't recall how it came up, but I told him I was blacklisted. I wasn't sure he believed me. Later at a meeting of the stunt executive group, Steve asked the stuntmen if I was blacklisted. They said, 'Yeah, she's blacklisted.' They didn't care. No one had the power to touch them."

In 1985 Leslie left the board, but she was still blacklisted and worked on only a few shows a year. Despite her frustrations, she had fun in *The Naked Gun: From the Files of Police Squad* (1988), in which she doubled Jeanette Charles as Queen Elizabeth II for a slide down a fully set banquet table. Stunt coordinator Dennis Madalone, who was not a member of any stunt association, hired Leslie as assistant coordinator on *Star Trek: Deep Space Nine* (1993) and *Star Trek: Voyager* (1995). She began solo coordinating in 1996, working on *Mulligans!* and *ABC Afterschool Specials.*[32]

Jean Coulter survived her jump from the car with Julie, but she did not survive sexual harassment. As Debbie Evans said, "You can't play along with it." Jean didn't play along—she sued. For Jean, it began in 1980 on a two-part episode of *Vega$*, an Aaron Spelling production. "Roy Harrison was running it," Jean said. She had been hired to do car work and double singer Michelle Phillips of the Mamas and the Papas. "I was on the set when Roy Harrison said, 'Why don't you come up to my room with me?' I said, 'Thanks for the compliment, but no thank you.' I knew he was dating a new stuntwoman—she had the room next to mine and I heard them partying. The next day, Roy asked me again. I declined. That night the call sheet listed two people to double Michelle Philips. I went to the production office and asked him, 'What's this?' and he said, 'You're running up to the car and the other woman is driving the car.' That was totally embarrassing. I drove cars on many shows and I'd been hired on this show to do that job. He said, 'If you don't like it, go home.' I said I'd go home. He yelled at everyone in that office, 'She's on the first plane out of here,' and yelled at the unit manager, 'Get her on the plane and if you have problems, call Uncle Aaron,' meaning Aaron Spelling. That's when the nightmare began," Jean said. "I didn't know the power he had. Roy started walking on sets, and in front of everyone he'd tell the stunt coordinator, 'She's blacklisted, get her off the lot.' After that, I heard from other stuntwomen who'd refused him. They'd been blacklisted but had never told anyone, and they never sued."[33] Jean did.

In an exposé of sexual harassment for *TV Guide,* Mary Murphy reported Jean's allegation that she had been "blacklisted after she refused advances of a stunt coordinator employed by Spelling-Goldberg Productions."[34] When another stuntwoman told Jean that "the guys" were going to say she had slept with them to get jobs, Jean was devastated. That other stuntwoman offered Jean her support, saying, "I'll go to court with you because this isn't right." Previously, Jean had worked 199 days a year; now she worked only 12 days a year. "It took me a long time to realize the blacklist was really happening. You can't buy a job or make payments on your house. Friends turn their backs, afraid they'd be run out of town." Harrison denied the charges but would not "comment further on the advice of his attorney retained by Spelling-Goldberg."[35]

"Blacklisting means you lose," Julie said, "but it's up to you if you stay a loser. You learn a lot when you're blacklisted. You learn about survival. In the end, when the issue is safety versus profits, it became a matter of conscience. To me, the producers and the Screen Actors Guild abdicated their responsibilities." Julie kept working with the stuntwomen at SAG, but soon the effort to get her day in court took over her life.

For these activist stuntwomen, their fight for on-the-job safety was hard to separate from their battles against discrimination and harassment. In 1983 some of the changes advocated by minorities and women became part of SAG's basic agreement with producers: "Where the stunt performer doubles for a role which is identifiable as female and/or Black, Hispanic, Asian Pacific or Native American and the race and/or sex of the double are also identifiable, stunt coordinators shall endeavor to cast qualified persons of same sex and/or race involved." The phrase "shall endeavor" had no teeth, and some stunt coordinators didn't "endeavor" very hard. Others did, however, and stuntwomen starting out in the 1980s and 1990s did not face the steep, callous difficulties of the hero-women who had created the first stuntwomen's associations and made "getting the wigs off men" their first priority.

Major challenges remained, including unequal pay and a paucity of female stunt coordinators. Other challenges that arose in the 1990s were quite different and revolved around changes in moviemaking. But by then, stuntwomen were quite different, too.

# 11

# Women's New Attitudes and Ambitions

You must make yourself do things that normally you wouldn't tolerate at all.

—*Donna Evans*

For Hollywood stunt performers, the decade of the 1980s had two faces—the rising incidence of injury and death on productions contrasted sharply with the buoyant profitability marked by expanding professional opportunities on many levels. Evidence of the growing power of Hollywood beyond the box office started in 1980, when SAG member and former California governor Ronald Reagan was elected president of the United States.

That same year, former schoolteacher Sherry Lansing became president of production at 20th Century–Fox. At other studios, women were also on the rise: Paula Weinstein, president of production at United Artists; Barbara Corday, president of Columbia Pictures Television; Dawn Steel, president of Columbia Pictures; and Suzanne dePasse, president of Motown Productions. No longer relegated to the secretarial pool, many women became "assistants" with genuine upward mobility. Two of those who turned their early training into high-powered positions were Amy Pascal, chair of Sony Columbia Pictures, and Nikki Rocco, president of domestic distribution at Universal Pictures. The struggles of the 1970s had started to pay off—not only in the executive suites but also in the hard-hitting arena of stunts.

The rise of American stunt families had begun in the 1930s. In Los Angeles these names included Avery, Canutt, Dashnaw, Deadrick, Elam,

Ellis, Epper, Evans, Kahana, Kingi, Happy, Leavitt, Leonard, McDancer, Rondell, Washington, and Wyatt. Stunt work as a familial enterprise thrives wherever films are made. Handy as it is to have relatives in the business, building a successful career depends on skill. Those without it won't get very far.

Between 1980 and 1990 the number of stunt performers tripled—from 629 to 1,954. Most of them were white men. African Americans were still a minority, totaling just 329 (only 32 of them women), as were stuntwomen, whose numbers increased from 85 to 306.[1] These increases resulted from the type of movies being produced, publicity about stunts, and changing social views that led to greater acceptance of women's action roles. In the business of stunts, there had been a time when women were not allowed to do certain kinds of stunts, but that was beginning to change.

Stuntwomen entering the business in the 1980s had been raised by moms who often worked outside the home; they had grown up watching *The Flying Nun* and *Wonder Woman,* and many of them were college graduates. Stuntwomen of the past had been brave and determined, but this new generation was armed with a new kind of confidence—they had expectations, not just hopes. The press repeatedly announced, "Women are breaking the glass ceiling," but as Gloria Steinem later noted, gender had not yet been identified as "probably the most restricting force in American life."[2] Even so, these stuntwomen had a better chance of making it than any previous generation.[3] If they had to prove themselves, that was fine with them.

A new generation of fathers was a big part of that change. Traditionally, dads helped their sons' careers; now they also supported their daughters. "Our dad figured we could do anything sons could do," Donna Evans said. A factory-sponsored motorcycle racer, David Evans raised both his daughters to ride dirt bikes competitively. With his encouragement, Donna's older sister Debbie became a motorcycle champion before she started performing stunts in the 1970s. In high school Donna didn't know what she wanted to do with her life, "but there was my sister, one of the few women flipping cars. I thought it was insane, but the more I saw what she did, the more I thought of giving it a shot." When Debbie got Donna a job riding a motorcycle on the TV series *CHiPs* (Debbie was a regular on the show), Donna discovered how much she liked stunts.

Donna recalled talking to Jeannie Epper about the old days, when a stuntman might have to jump off a wagon just before it went over a cliff.

Donna Evans, who learned early what it takes to do stunt work. (Courtesy of Donna Evans)

"Sometimes a stuntman froze and went over the cliff with the wagon and died," Donna said. "I learned there are two kinds of people in stunts—those motivated by fear that go into hyperdrive to do whatever is needed. Others are paralyzed by fear. I thought I'd be motivated, but wasn't sure. After *Christine*, I knew I had what it took." *Christine*, a 1983 movie directed by John Carpenter and based on a Stephen King novel, is about a death-dealing 1958 Plymouth Fury. In one scene, the killer car chases Donna into a closed garage—with no way out. But there are racks of tires hanging above her head. To escape the fury of the Fury, she leaps up and clings to the rack by her hands and feet. "They'd welded two bars hidden among the tires," she said, "one for my hands and one for my feet. I jumped up, grabbed the bar, swung my feet up on the other bar, and flattened myself against the tires. When I didn't get my feet all the way up on the bar, it made me swing backwards into the path of the car, which was going at a fairly fast clip. I had to get up there. It had to look like the car would run me over. No room for error." She didn't recall how many times she had to do it, maybe ten. "I was absolutely determined to do a great piece of action."

At age eleven, Donna had learned that in addition to having mental concentration and athletic ability, "you must make yourself do things that normally you wouldn't tolerate at all." She and her dad were racing their motorcycles in the desert, passing different checkpoints. "About fifty miles out from the finish, my hands gripped the throttle and it became very painful. I couldn't open my hands, I had to slide them off sideways and peel my fingers open. It really hurt, but I couldn't tell him because we were riding and riding. Finally we got to a checkpoint. I said my hands hurt so much I couldn't ride anymore. He said, 'We're halfway up. It's either ride it or push it.' He was right, we were in the middle of nowhere, I couldn't leave my bike out there—it was my favorite! I had to come up to the bar, go through pain even if I didn't think I could. I shut up and did it. That's the mentality you must have to do stunts."

Years later, Donna attributed her ability to finish a stunt to her dad. One night, while doubling Linda Hamilton on the TV pilot for *Beauty and the Beast* (1987–1990), she was supposed to fall, as if unconscious, out of a moving van. The van would be traveling parallel to a curb, edged by a grassy downhill slope where the camera was placed. "They wanted me to fall out and roll right up to [the camera], but it isn't easy to roll across, not down the slope. I had to roll [in] the wrong direction. The first time gravity took over—I rolled straight down the hill. The next was better, and the third time I rolled right up to the box at the base of the camera. But my dress flew up, my flesh-colored tights made me look naked, and this was for TV!" There was one other little problem: when she fell out of the van the third time, she hit the curb and separated her shoulder. "That fourth time I had to land on my separated shoulder, but many stunt people do things like that. I don't know if it's toughness or stupidity."

Kym Washington has an air of elegance and energy, but, she admits, "I was my father's tomboy 'son.'" Growing up, she excelled in gymnastics, and she thought her dad's work as a stunt coordinator looked like fun because it "wasn't your normal everyday job." Her father, Richard Washington, discouraged his daughter. "I thought she could do something else, and the work had a certain amount of risk. I stretched her training to well over a year." Thanks to Jadie David and other stuntwomen of color, Kym would not experience the same obstacles. "Jadie was special, she was a real mentor," Kym said, "and so were Donna and Debbie Evans. They and my dad tried to teach me about motorcycles. I wanted cars." Her first stunt, on the pilot of a Universal TV series called *Cliffhangers* (1979), was to fall from a rafter into a bed of stacked boxes. Stunt coordinator Tony Brubaker had

Kym Washington knew what she wanted. (Courtesy of Kym Washington)

hired Kym, but she wouldn't do the stunt until her dad was there. "He arrived just as they called 'Action!'" Richard remembered, "She was sweating bullets, but she did it. I told my wife, 'Kym's going to be a stuntwoman.' She said, 'She just got one job.' I said, 'Wait till she gets the check!' Kym hasn't looked back since."

For those who are new to the business, every stunt has a survival lesson. "The bridge on the Universal Studios tour is called the collapsing bridge," Kym said. "It shakes so hard it seems about to fall apart." In one scene from *The Nude Bomb* (1980), frightened tourists leap off the bridge into the lake below. "People say they can do a job because they need work, but one 'tourist' couldn't swim," Kym recalled. "He jumped off, then I jumped, I'm on my way down, but he panics, walks totally over me, pushes me to the bottom. Each time I got near the surface, he'd walk over me. The safety divers pulled him out. I was so new it was scary. My dad said you never know what someone else will do. You have to look out for yourself." That key advice has been passed down from stunt veterans to rookies through the decades. It was vital in the 1980s, as stunts became more complicated and "realistic."

Kym's dad had learned that lesson on *The Deep* (1977). In addition to being one of the stunt coordinators, Richard Washington was doubling Lou Gossett; stuntman Howard Curtis was doubling Robert Shaw. During an underwater fight, one of them was supposed to be pulled head-first toward an opening where a deadly eel lurked. "For a practice to block things out," Rich said, "they asked me to put my head in the opening to see the angle on the eel. It was on a track, its hydraulic jaws were to close to six inches, enough space for my head to fit in. For some reason I pulled back and they just ran the eel. Out it comes, mouth wide open, it reaches the spot, and the jaws slam shut! Those hydraulic jaws would have popped my head like a melon. I was shaking. I was lucky to let them try it first, but it wasn't just luck. It's always smart to say, 'Let's do a test.'"

When she first started accompanying her father to the set, Kym would hear remarks like, "'Richard's got his "chickie" with him today.' The crew thought I was my dad's girlfriend, they didn't believe I was his daughter. I used to think that was pretty funny." Richard looked out for his daughter: "I told her what to do with producers or directors who want to cast you on the couch, or the stunt coordinators who want to take you on loca-tion—as a location girl. I told her everything that happened and every bit is true. On location, guys will go for it. Some of them were not nice. I told the guys I knew [who] were a bit devious, 'That's my daughter, so don't even try it.' They heard me."

Kym's mother didn't want her to do stunts. "I couldn't blame her," Kym said. "If I'd been a son it might have been different." One day, Kym's mother came to the set of *Airwolf* (1984–1986) to watch her daughter run through a minefield. Special effects had told Kym where the mines were placed, but once she started running, "I couldn't remember where all the mines were. One or two caught me by surprise. Suddenly I dived because the big boom was coming." She disappeared into the smoke, and when she reappeared, she had powder burns from head to toe. She wasn't hurt because she was wearing the proper gear, but her mother didn't know that. "I remember the look on my mom's face as she said, 'Don't ask me to come with you again. I don't want to know what you're doing until you are home.' I understood."

Typically, children follow their parents into stunts, but Annie Ellis said, "I didn't come from your usual stunt family." Merry and vibrant, Annie planned to be a veterinarian until her brother David, a surfer and motor-cycle racer, talked her into trying stunts.[4] After that, their dad, Richard,

As planned, Annie Ellis's horse rears up on *Dr. Quinn Medicine Woman,* but during one take, he fell over on top of her. (Courtesy of Annie Ellis)

joined them. "Dad was my best friend," Annie said, "an artist, an architect, a pro surfer, a motorcycle racer, and he was a huge influence on me."

New to stunts but not to horses, Annie doubled Glenn Close in *Jagged Edge* (1985), a film about an attorney (Close) seduced by her client (played by Jeff Bridges), who is on trial for murder. "He uses horses as foreplay,"

Stuntwoman Annie Ellis—as great in a car as she is on a horse. (Courtesy of Annie Ellis)

and the two of them gallop full speed across a luscious meadow pock-marked with treacherous gopher holes. "When a coordinator asks, 'Can you ride?' you better know horses," Annie warned. "If I had not, tripping on those gopher holes would throw most people off." During the ride, the two come to a tree that has fallen across the path, and Annie's horse is supposed to stop and rear up. "I rode two horses" for the stunt, Annie recalled. "Both came off the racetrack, and one loved to jump. A mile away, she'd get ready to jump. There was no way to stop her. I told everyone; they didn't believe me. Take two, we're near the tree, I yank her head around, she's looking at me the way camels do, and even though she can't see what's ahead she leaps over the tree! An overhanging branch catches my wig, I'm still holding the reins, my butt comes down behind the saddle, I jump back into it, and she never stopped galloping."

Stunt work can be dangerous, because no one knows "what will happen till it is happening." But some stunts turn out to be fun. By 1992, Annie had graduated to car work and was doubling Jamie Lee Curtis in *Forever Young*; Annie's brother David was stunt coordinator. In one scene, she was supposed to skid a car down a mountain road, dodge in front of a semi, and plow through a fence—with Mel Gibson and Elijah Wood in the back-seat. "David told me, 'now don't crash.' He was serious, but I laughed. I wasn't going to crash. He said, 'You've got real actors in your car.' Like I didn't know that. I took off, three or four cars came at me, I cut around them, did head-ons and near misses with people and cars. After the first take I turned around to see if the 'real actors' needed medical attention. Elijah Wood with those huge blue eyes, and Mel Gibson—they were both grinning, like, 'Oh, can we do that again?' Priceless."

Marguerite Happy, a rodeo rider turned stuntwoman in the 1980s, described the satisfaction she gets from doing stunts: "My aunt and uncle owned a stable in Salinas, California," she said. "I used to ride there with my cousins. We wanted to really run them [the horses], but we were always told, 'Don't come back with sweaty horses.' That got us in trouble. Imagine my joy as a stuntwoman to do chase scenes on horses or in cars without getting into trouble! I'd spent years learning how to stay in a saddle. Now I get to fall off! I get to crash cars, jump cars, and go 110 miles an hour! I'm not a high-fall person, but sometimes I get to be pushed or shot off buildings—it's in the script. We get to hit the decks in explosions, fire automatic weapons, play cowboys and Indians, cops and robbers. We get to play aliens!"

Marguerite married stuntman Clifford Happy, whose parents, Don and Edith, had been top rodeo riders. "My mother-in-law, Edith, was one of the few women inducted into the Pro Rodeo Cowboy Hall of Fame," Marguerite said. "And my sister-in-law, Bonnie Happy, a great trick rider, is president of USA, the United Stuntwomen's Association."[5] Like Kym Washington's mother, Bonnie's didn't want her to do stunts. But in 1980, when her brother Clifford urged her to give it a try, twenty-five-year-old Bonnie took his advice. Since then, she has done all kinds of gags that had nothing to do with her prowess on a horse.

There is considerable lore about horses and stunt work, and in a very real sense, horse and rider are partners in a gag. While working on *Dr. Quinn Medicine Woman* (1993–1998), Bonnie was supposed to do a "hippodrome"—ride through town, shooting both her pistols, while standing on the back of the galloping "101," wrangler Rudy Ugland's great stunt horse. "You have to set the pattern of the stunt for the horse," she said, "but the director and others kept changing it." Finally, they got it on the fourth take. "Afterward, I thanked the director for 'waiting until my horse gave me the trick so that I could do what you wanted me to do.' You're only as good as what your horse gives you, and you have to set him up for it so *he* doesn't fail either."

Bonnie Happy, an expert trick rider, is currently president of the United Stuntwomen's Association. (Courtesy of Bonnie Happy)

One of Bonnie's first stunts on *Matt Houston* (1982–1985) proved that anything can happen, as her stunt partner Jimmy Nickerson knew from his experience with horses and fast cars.[6] In the scene, a runaway horse was supposed to drag Jimmy for a short distance, and then Bonnie was supposed to save him. "On a drag like that," she said, "you're holding a release gizmo, you push the button and that releases you from the drag. Before the stunt, I'm watching a special effects guy run tape around it and I can't figure how, with all that tape, the release trip will work. But I was new; I thought the guy must know what he's doing. We start the stunt and suddenly Jimmy's horse goes wild, dragging him over rocks, around the exercise rings, and Jimmy's not releasing the trip. I'm behind him and he yells, 'Bonnie, stop me! It's not releasing.' I go to the right so he doesn't hit the parking lot as the wranglers try to rope him from the left. The horse looks up and slows down enough for me to grab him." Who knew the horse would go berserk and Bonnie would have to save Jimmy for real?

Other surprises aren't as dramatic, but they can be taxing. When Donna Evans and Tracy Keehn Dashnaw began to do stunts in 1983, they were

In *Dr. Quinn Medicine Woman,* Bonnie Happy shoots up the town on "101." (Courtesy of Jeff Ramsey)

amazed that their good looks worked against them. Because coordinators often hired their girlfriends to do easy spots, it was widely assumed that any pretty "stuntwoman" who showed up on the set couldn't do anything. "Tracy and I had to show we were the real thing, we could get the job done," Donna said. "We really hung it out there, and if we got hurt, oh

Tracy Keehn Dashnaw—a lot
tougher than she looks. (Courtesy of
Tracy Dashnaw)

well." When a scantily clad Donna calmly and deliberately submerged herself in icy river water, the coordinator gushed, "I haven't seen anyone
tougher!" But Donna later said, "You want to see *tough?* Tracy's a top rodeo
rider, and those cowgirls are *really* tough."

The delicately pretty Tracy doesn't look tough, but in the 1980s, stuntwomen gave *tough* a whole new meaning and proved that pretty and tough
are not incompatible. (In earlier decades, stuntwomen were rarely hired to
do stunts that would prove how tough they were.) Tracy's stepfather, a
rodeo cowboy, had taught her to ride and rope, and with two older brothers, she was a tomboy. At age ten, Tracy rode motorcycles; by eighteen, she
was working as an extra, doing little stunts, barrel racing in rodeos, and
attending Pierce College in the San Fernando Valley, majoring in theater
arts. "Came a time I had to decide if I went to class or made money. I chose
money. Today I drive cars, but horses got me into the business."

Tracy was off and running in 1983 in Veracruz, Mexico, riding a horse
hard and fast in the opening sequence of *Romancing the Stone* (1984). The
big-budget production hired two other stuntwomen: Jeannie Epper and
her daughter, Eurlyne. Jeannie was one of the founders of the first
Stuntwomen's Association and a mentor to many. In 1983 she was forty-

two years old and had worked for thirty years, but never as a stunt coordinator. Her friend Terry Leonard, also forty-two, was a rough, tough, six-foot-plus cowboy. In 1981 he had performed an iconic stunt on *Raiders of the Lost Ark*—a truck drag á la legendary Yakima Canutt's stunt in John Ford's *Stagecoach*. Terry and Vince Deadrick Jr. co-coordinated *Romancing the Stone*.[7]

Unlike her mother, Eurlyne loved high work. "But I wasn't sure I wanted to do stunts," she said, "because I'd go on sets with my mom and it was so boring." *Romancing the Stone* wasn't boring for Eurlyne or anyone else. One of Jeannie's stunts became a classic, even though it seemed ordinary enough in the script. According to Jeannie, "It was anything but simple. It took two and a half weeks, every day, three or five times a day, riding a mudslide 200 feet down the side of a mountain." Because the slope was so steep, the crew had to put down cargo nets about every 50 feet to stop Jeannie and Vince Deadrick from sliding all the way to the bottom. Then the crew would lay down another net, and they'd do another slide. Being stopped by the nets gave them a chance to reposition themselves. "It was very hard to stay in the position we had to be in for the ride down," Jeannie said. "We'd get jumped around, upside down, and I almost drowned once when I went down headfirst and got a mouthful of water, rocks, and dirt." Stuntwoman Caroline Day wrote that Jeannie's careening plunge down the mountainside "hurt just to watch. They were beat up, it was cold, they were wet."[8] Charles Champlin, arts editor of the *Los Angeles Times,* called it "a tumbling, rumbling, cascading fall down a mud slide." Vince Deadrick told him, "It was the most physically demanding stunt I've ever done."[9]

Before leaving for Mexico, Jeannie had questioned another stunt in the movie: a jump out of a car as it went over a waterfall. "The waterfall was very high, the water was rough. I'd never done anything like it before. I wanted the chance to turn it down if I felt it was more than I could do." Jeannie, who is deeply religious, said: "I went to my hotel room and actually got on my knees before God and said, 'I don't know what to do. What should I do?' The answer I heard: 'Do not do it.' I went downstairs and told Terry I couldn't do the gag. He said he was never going to let me do it anyway. I could have gone back to Hollywood and told everybody he didn't let me do it, but he made me say no! I used to call decisions like that my gut feeling," she said, "but after that movie I started to call it my God feeling." Terry and Vince did the now famous waterfall gag, and it was voted the year's most spectacular stunt.[10] *Romancing the Stone* became a top grossing film of 1984.

When Jeannie got home from Mexico, she found that her husband had decamped with her brother's wife. One person observed ruefully, "He must have had a death wish. You don't do that to the Eppers." Her former husband lived, and Jeannie kept working, but she was at a crossroads that had nothing to do with her domestic trials. "There's a transition before you realize that you should *not* do a stunt versus doing it and coming out the hero," she said. "You begin to think you're invincible. And you're not." She wanted to stop hitting the ground and use her experience to stunt-coordinate—a common path for men but not for women. It never happened for Jeannie, but it would for others who came later.

Mary Albee was the first woman to sustain a career as a stunt coordinator. She had no family in the business and didn't know much about the film industry. She was working as a movie extra to help pay her tuition at California State Northridge, where she was a music major. When director Walter Grauman asked her, "Can you talk?" she said that she could.[11] "He gave me dialogue with Leslie Nielsen [on *Crisis in Midair* (1979)]. Afterwards people congratulated me. I was clueless, but of course, getting those lines meant I could join SAG." That break launched her remarkable career. In 1986 Mary began to stunt-coordinate episodes of *L.A. Law* and *Leo & Liz in Beverly Hills*. Later, the largely male International Stunt Association (ISA) interviewed her as a potential member. Mary has a sweet smile but the composure of one who cannot be intimidated. "I guess I got in," she said, "because when I was asked, 'What would you do if you don't get in the group?' I said, 'It's not going to hurt my career. Maybe it'll hurt your career.' The president then was an old cowboy, and he goes, 'Well, how come I never worked with you?' I said, 'How come I never worked with *you*?'"[12]

The popular TV series *Murder, She Wrote* (1984–1996) ran during the golden age of affirmative action, but the show rarely hired female writers, directors, or stunt coordinators. Slowly, that began to change. "It's always who you know," Mary said. "My boyfriend then told me production executives at Universal wanted to interview female coordinators. Someone had realized, 'It's a girls' show!'" They found a girl assistant director, a girl writer, and a girl stunt coordinator—Mary—who worked on more than 100 episodes.

Although women rarely stunt-coordinated, the industry was increasingly hiring them in other positions. "Alice [West] was a secretary in a

New York film company," Mary said. She "came to LA, got into the DGA training program, became a production manager, a first assistant director, then a producer."[13] West hired Mary to coordinate *Ally McBeal* (1997–2002). "*Ally McBeal* was a blast because writer-producer David Kelley inspired us," Mary said. "He challenged us creatively. We had a great team that blended together wonderfully"—special effects, visual effects, and stunts. "On one episode Kelley wrote, 'Christina Ricci, wearing a teddy with a G-string, goes into her bedroom and her bed is a swimming pool with a diving board! John's on the bed, she walks up, does a full one-and-a half somersault dive off the board in pike position and lands on all fours with her head in his crotch.' Now that's a great stunt! We had two days to figure out how to do it physically and visually," Mary said. "We designed a special harness, the seamstress made the matching G-string and laced the harness, and we hired a stunt girl, a high-diver. Usually the actor falls into the shot at the tail end of the take. I didn't want that because if we're going to go through all this, I wanted Christina to drop from six or eight feet and come out of the somersault so we know she actually did it. She's in the harness, the operator tips her over, and [she] lands on her back with her legs up over her face. We thought it up in one day, built the harness, tested it the next day, and shot it the third day."

When Mary began to do stunt work, her parents "were not thrilled with it," but her mother took pictures the first time Mary did a high fall with Tom Morga on *Scarecrow and Mrs. King* (1983). Later, while Mary was working on *Murder, She Wrote,* her father was still encouraging her to go back to school and get a real job. "I told him how much I made. He was rather surprised. I asked him how much he made, and that was the end of the conversation. He was a geology professor at Cal Tech. He's a good guy but didn't understand you can have a great career without going to school for a piece of paper to qualify for a job." As it happened, a few years later Mary felt burned out and, in a unique move, left the business to study medicine. She was slaving away at UCLA when a producer for David Kelley called. "Did I want to do a new series? Did I want to get my director's card? Absolutely!" The series, *Snoops* (1999), didn't last long, but Mary was back in the game.[14]

As good as the 1980s were for some stuntwomen, SAG statistics in 1985 were not encouraging: men performed 86 percent of all stunt work; stuntwomen performed 14 percent, and most of that involved doubling

Whoopi Goldberg and Kym Washington working together—a rare opportunity for women. (Courtesy of Kym Washington)

actresses.[15] For African American stuntwomen, the opportunities were bleak, to say the least, but Kym Washington made a career anyway. Her big break came on *The Color Purple* (1985), when she doubled Whoopi Goldberg and Oprah Winfrey.[16] "When the movie was released it had been shaved down from what we shot," Kym said, "but it had a sequence of teaching driving to 'Miss Daisy,' as we called her." Kym learned how to drive cars, which became her specialty, and the film began her long association with Whoopi Goldberg. "Many stuntmen doubling actors in action movies become part of a family," she said. "It's a good working relationship for both, but it is so rare for women. Whoopi had a loyal friendship with us—her stand-in, her hair, makeup, costume, and I was her stunt double. Few of us have a family like that. Jeannie Epper had it with Lynda Carter on *Wonder Woman*, Jadie David had it with Pam Grier, and I had it with Whoopi."

A couple of years after *The Color Purple*, Kym was working on *Airwolf* (the show she'd invited her mother to see), which was known for its explosions and cars crashes. "It was great to work on," Kym said, "but it did have its problems," including injuries and deaths. The year 1985 was a particularly bad one for stunt performers: stunt coordinator Ron Rondell's twenty-three-year-old son, Reid, was killed in a helicopter crash on *Airwolf;* on the same show, stuntwoman Desiree Kearns suffered severe burns and sued Universal; stunt pilot Art Scholl was killed on *Top Gun;* Max Maxwell was injured on *Invasion USA;* and stuntwoman Carol Daniels, who had worked since 1960, sued Warner Bros. for multiple injuries suffered when she was buried under ten tons of sand on *Shadow Chasers.*[17]

"In the quest for realistic movie and television thrills," Michael Szymanski reported in 1987, "10 people have been killed and 4,998 injured in California productions since 1982." According to stunt coordinator Kim Kahana, "Stunts in movies are looking more real because they are, and stunt people are being hurt and killed because of that. It's the realism that's killing us."[18] Regulations helped, but in 1987, five years after the *Twilight Zone* disaster, industry sources observed that, "aside from a different atmosphere, little has actually changed in the way movies are made." Regulations were proposed by labor and management groups and presented at hearings before the California legislature. Few were enacted, however, "after many directors, actors and producers argued that further regulation of the industry would do more harm than good."[19]

Meanwhile, stuntwomen were taking the usual risks and working hard in the mid-1980s. One of them, Eurlyne Epper, pulled off a dicey swan dive from the side of a steep hill in *Hot Pursuit* (1987).[20] She had never done anything like it, but Eurlyne had always been good in the air. Only when she got to the site of the dive in Mexico did she find out that the water below was only about eight feet deep, barely covering huge chunks of coral. "I had to judge the angle of the dive to miss the coral," Eurlyne said. "I couldn't push off too hard. It had to be a shallow dive, and if I'd missed, it would have killed me."

Around the same time, in a scene from *The Witches of Eastwick* (1987), Donna Evans and Christine Baur were being blown out a door at the top of a staircase. Actually, when they stepped on the pedal of a hydraulic device called an air ram, it hurled them forward into the air. "Donna came off an air ram," Chris said, "crashed into the wall, hit the landing, and went into a stair fall. I jumped off a ram into the air, did a cartwheel over the landing, and hit the ground."

Elsewhere, Tracy Keehn Dashnaw and Annie Ellis staged a glorious fight in *Fatal Attraction,* raging from room to room and ending in the petrifying bathtub scene.[21] Kym Washington doubled Whoopi Goldberg,

Marguerite Happy's exciting times in *Remote Control* (1988). (Courtesy of Marguerite Happy)

playing a narcotics cop in a series of hilarious disguises, in *Fatal Beauty* (1987). That same year, on the pilot for *Beauty and the Beast,* Donna Evans jumped from a car, dislocated her shoulder, but finished the stunt. And Marguerite Happy made sure there was enough room between the train and the trestle before she agreed to hang out the train window.

The 1980s ushered in greater danger and somewhat wider opportunities for stuntwomen. In many ways, the stunt business held fast to old restrictions, but the attitudes and ambitions of these rookie stuntwomen set a standard that women in the 1990s would expand. As these stunt performers were gaining experience, however, the career of a great stuntwoman who had started twenty years before them—Julie Johnson—was coming to an end.

# 12

# Julie Johnson's Day in Court

Julie Johnson is history.

—*Anonymous stuntman*

Julie Johnson wasn't the only stunt person to file a complaint with the Equal Employment Opportunity Commission, and she wasn't the only one to sue her employer. However, most stunt performers' lawsuits dealt with injuries suffered on the job. Julie, a stunt coordinator, was suing for wrongful termination.

Julie's pretty face gave no sign of her steely determination. She had known her complaints about unsafe working conditions and drug use might bring reprisals, but that did not stop her from speaking out. By 1984, she had filed three lawsuits. Two were eventually dismissed, but her suit against Spelling-Goldberg Productions, charging discrimination and unlawful firing, had legs. The press avidly followed her legal maneuvers. Columnist Heidi Yorkshire reported that Julie had lost her house in 1984 and "was not optimistic about how she will survive the three to five years the lawsuit is expected to take."[1] Julie was in "no-person's land," as she called it. It got worse when an ominous voice on the phone told her, "'There's a bullet with your name on it.' Each time I walked out the door," she said, "I felt the scope of the rifle on my head. Sometimes I wished they'd hurry up and get it over with. Other times I thought I'd catch the bullet in my teeth and spit it back. One of my lawyers said he was surprised I hadn't been found dead on Mulholland Drive."

From about 1983 to 1987, when she wasn't alternately dreading or welcoming sudden death, Julie was dealing with lawyers. "They became the

Julie Ann Johnson faces
the conflicts ahead.
(Courtesy of Julie Ann
Johnson)

bane of my existence. Sixty-eight attorneys interviewed me; four separate firms took my case, then dropped it. On the eve of my trial, one said the Mafia had told him to get off the case. The judge gave me thirty days to find another attorney." She was hoping to find a firm that had already represented a plaintiff against Spelling-Goldberg. In courthouse archives she found Simke, Chodos, Silberfeld and Anteau, and five days before the deadline, she met with one of that firm's best attorneys, Richard Grey. "I felt numb," she said. "He was my last hope."[2] Grey wanted to win the case on the merits; Julie wanted to reclaim her career and her integrity.

On the afternoon of August 11, 1987, seven years after she had been dropped as stunt coordinator of *Charlie's Angels*, *Julie Ann Johnson v. Spelling-Goldberg Productions* began in the Superior Court of Los Angeles. The trial turned into an introductory course about the stunt business, taught by experts. It lasted more than three weeks, and twenty-four witnesses were called. Whether testifying for or against Julie, they described how stunts are set up and performed, and they sometimes revealed inside information about the traditions of the stunt community. Collectively, the testimony showed that stunts are deeply embedded in the film industry's production process and that the creation of successful stunts requires the input of professionals of all kinds; directors, writers, producers, designers, special effects experts, camera operators, and specialists in wardrobe, transportation, and props all contribute to the onscreen magic. The tradition is as old as *The Perils of Pauline*. This time, Julie's career was the cliffhanger.

The handsome defense attorneys, William Koska and Kenneth Anderson, represented Spelling-Goldberg. Julie sat at the plaintiff's table with pleasing poise as her attorney introduced her as a cofounder of the Stuntwomen's Association and the Society of Professional Stuntwomen. Grey said her 400 film and TV credits read like a "prime-time catalog," and he told the jury that although her case might resemble a TV soap opera, it was a true-life drama "about a woman who worked for nearly 20 years in the stunt field, a person we contend was wrongfully terminated as the stunt coordinator . . . who was too outspoken, too critical, too visible on safety matters." Then he cited budget issues—the pressure to "get the job done quickly and don't go over budget" was balanced against the desire to "get the job done safely and make the stunt look thrilling." Grey's third point was problematic—drugs. He told the court that Julie and another stuntwoman had been in "a very dangerous predicament . . . their lives were at risk because of someone else's use of illegal drugs in the perfor-

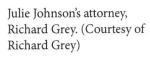

Julie Johnson's attorney, Richard Grey. (Courtesy of Richard Grey)

mance of that stunt." Koska, the lead attorney for Spelling-Goldberg, jumped to his feet. "I object to this, your honor." Judge Leon Savitch overruled his objection. Still, drug use would be hard to prove. Grey had to link Julie's complaints about drugs and safety to her being labeled "a troublemaker, a person to be gotten rid of. . . . To terminate somebody's employment in retaliation for speaking out about safety would be considered a very serious violation of the California public policy," he said.[3] That charge was the key to Julie's case. Before the trial, Grey had decided to eliminate the sex discrimination complaint. "It detracted from the strength of the case," he said, "which was whistle-blowing, complaining about safety or drug use, and retaliation for those things. Sex discrimination was iffy—did they do this to Julie because she was a woman? But you can see cause and effect when she complained and then was not renewed as stunt coordinator."[4]

The Spelling-Goldberg legal team charged that, among other faults, "Miss Johnson's work as a stunt coordinator was mediocre," she had "a problem understanding how to place cameras," and she overpaid stunt performers. "Lastly, the evidence will show that Miss Johnson developed an attitude problem during the time she was coordinator."[5]

This would be a tough endurance test for Julie, sitting in court day after day and listening to Koska tear apart her career. Trials are theatrical dramas staged by players on both sides of a high-stakes contest. Witnesses in this trial would include producers, an assistant director, and a director of photography of *Charlie's Angels,* as well as second-unit directors, stunt coordinators, stunt players, and SAG board members, many of them well-known actors with substantial stage and screen credits.

Actress and SAG vice president Norma Connolly described Julie as "one of the most respected women in the stunt community." Connolly testified that Julie and other stuntwomen had approached her about their employment problems. She did not name the other women "to protect them." She told the court, "Men were doubling for women, causing less employment for the women. They were deeply concerned about safety conditions on the set. As an officer of the guild I was on the stunt committee to represent stuntwomen, to be a voice for them." Grey asked her about the minimum qualifications for a stunt player. "Only [to be] a paid-up member of the Screen Actors Guild," Connolly replied. He asked whether Spelling-Goldberg had any minimum requirements for the stunt players it employed, or whether a person had to have a certain amount of experience to qualify as a stunt coordinator. She knew of no such requirements. He asked Connolly whether Julie and the other stuntwomen who had approached her in the late 1970s were concerned about reprimands. "Yes, Julie was very concerned about her own employment as were all the other women."[6]

Joe Ruskin, an actor for thirty-seven years, was vice president of the SAG Hollywood board and had cochaired the Stunt and Safety Committee from 1977 to 1982. He "knew something about stunts," he said, but when Grey asked him if he'd ever performed stunts in his acting career, Ruskin answered, "No, I always sit down and say, 'Where is the [stunt] man?'" Ruskin knew Julie from SAG committee meetings. "The stunt community was developing a rating system for stunt people in an attempt to guarantee safer stunt work in the industry," he testified. Julie wanted to require "equipment—rolling stock, cars, or trucks used in a stunt—to be in good shape . . . safe to work in." According to Ruskin, she "felt the cars were dangerous and that's what she wanted fixed."[7]

In his pretrial deposition, Ruskin talked about situations involving drug use that did not come out in court. In meetings with stuntmen, he'd heard references to drug or alcohol use, such as, "'Well, crap, he was stoned again,' and someone else said, 'Cut it out. You don't know that.' They were referring to [the] TV show *The Dukes of Hazzard*," which was notorious for alleged drug use on the set. He added that in committee meetings, "Some of the women were complaining that it was very difficult to get work unless they were willing to be the girlfriend on location." It took the women a long time, he said, "to screw up their courage to talk about what was wrong." Ruskin also expressed Julie's safety concerns more clearly in his deposition: "She thought the actors would be put in danger. She told me, 'The actors are going to get badly hurt sooner or later and it is happening too much, too often.' Conrad Palmisano, a stunt coordinator, called her a pioneer, saying words to the effect that she is now suffering as many pioneers do." Ruskin said that he and Palmisano thought Julie was right to make safety demands and that even the industry was now admitting her demands were correct.[8]

When Aaron Spelling appeared in court with his entourage, the press turned out in force. To Julie's attorney, any case that put Aaron Spelling on the stand was a "David and Goliath adventure. I love those cases." Spelling testified that not even the "stars" of the series had "run-of-the-series" contracts. The decision not to rehire "Miss Johnson" as the stunt coordinator of *Charlie's Angels* had been made in February or March of 1980, after the fourth season had been filmed. The program's ratings had dropped; the network had rescheduled the series for a different night and was aiming for a younger audience that would be looking for more exciting stunts and more action. The producers "were of the opinion that the plaintiff [Julie Johnson] was not able to produce the desired level of stunt work and wished to hire a new stunt coordinator." Spelling denied that retaliation had been a factor in their decision.[9]

"Aaron Spelling was a challenging witness because he was—Aaron Spelling!" Julie's attorney said. "He was a celebrity with a mixed reputation, a producer of many popular TV shows, and he was viewed as a wonderful person. I knew the other side of him. I wanted to bring him down a peg. On the stand Mr. Spelling's attitude was, 'I treat everybody fairly, I'd never do anything I'm being accused of here, they were never brought to my attention.' He testified Julie was on a one-year contract, renewable annually; they decided her work wasn't up to standards, so they didn't renew. That was the big defense. They hadn't violated the law because 'we have the right *not* to renew her . . . contract, and she didn't have the right to continue.' In cases of unlawful firing," Grey emphasized, "the defense always falls back on 'her contract was terminable at will, end of discussion.' But when we can bring in the legal protections, they can't hide behind the 'we-can-terminate' argument. If retaliation against a whistle-blower was the real reason she was let go, it's unassailable. That's when the legal protections kick in and take over. That's what we were trying to prove in Julie's case."

Assistant producer Elaine Rich and second-unit director Ron Rondell were important witnesses. On *Charlie's Angels,* Julie had worked for Rondell, and he had worked for the producers, including Rich, who was one of two female producers on the series. She testified she had supported Julie as stunt coordinator because so few women had a chance to do the job. Rich described the accelerated pace of TV productions and the time required to turn a script into a filmed episode. She said there were usually seven working days to prepare for an episode of a show, then seven days to film that show. Preparation for the next episode began on the first day of shooting the previous episode. According to Rich, it cost about $800,000 to produce one episode.[10]

Ron Rondell, a respected professional, had been an actor and stuntman in the 1950s and a stunt coordinator and second-unit director since the 1970s. In court, he summarized the complicated job of a stunt coordinator: he breaks down the script; isolates action sequences; talks with art directors, special effects, anyone "involved in the stunt sequences"; gets "the director's input, how he'd like the sequences to work . . . makes a general stunt budget for the show, and basically puts it all together." But a stunt coordinator's biggest responsibility, Rondell said, "is to make sure he could do the sequence the director requested. Safety was always a major factor to determine whether the stunt can be pulled off the way the director requests." Coordinators are always under a lot of pressure, and *Charlie's Angels* was no exception. The first-unit director was "concerned with getting the words out of his actors, getting them 'off the clock,'" Rondell said. That meant the stunts were delayed "until the actors are finished. Then, when they have an hour left, they apply pressure to . . . get the stunt people in, get the job done, and get out."[11]

A great deal of contradictory testimony swirled around the episodes of *Charlie's Angels* that Julie had performed in and stunt-coordinated. One, a double episode shot in Vail, Colorado, in the fall of 1978, supposedly showed Julie's "attitude" problem. A witness claimed she had stomped off to a snowcat to sulk; Julie said she'd been sent there to wait until they were ready to shoot the scene. There was a more lengthy examination of Julie and Jean Coulter's jump from a moving car in January 1979. Both Rondell and Rich testified about the car jump, as did Julie and Jean. The two stuntwomen's version of events conflicted with other accounts, such as whether the performers had taken a break that morning, who controlled the speed of the car, whether the stuntwomen did the jump properly, Julie's differences with the director of photography, and whether drug use had contributed to the accident. Jean and Julie said that during rehearsals, the driver of the car, Bobby Bass, was not paying attention; "he was kind of not there," Jean testified.[12] They swore that, for safety reasons, they had all agreed the car would be going twelve to fifteen miles per hour, but when the scene was shot, Bass was driving twice as fast, which was why the women had been injured. Others testified they were hurt because they hadn't jumped correctly. Julie and Jean insisted that during a short break just before the stunt, they had heard that Bass and others might have used drugs. No one else recalled taking a break or anyone using drugs.

Bobby Bass and Julie Johnson both began stunt work in the mid-1960s, and both started to stunt-coordinate in 1978; he later became a second-unit director. Car work was one of Bass's specialties, "spinning cars around in reverse 180's, doing forward 180's, 90-degree slides left and right, performing stunts from a car." At the trial, he delivered a short course on the subject: "To get the noise, burn of rubber, screeching and other effects, you must know the surface. On a standard street surface, you'd use chlorine bleach or W.D.-40 on the tires, put the car in gear, push down the accelerator, and it will smoke and make the tires squeal." To spin a car in a forward or reverse 180, he said, speed is important, but the deciding factor is the composition of the ground and whether it is flat or slanted. The easiest surface is standard asphalt or street paving; the most difficult is gravel or dirt. He admitted that Julie had regularly criticized the cars supplied to the show by Spelling-Goldberg as "buckets of bolts." After citing his solutions for missing or inoperative seat belts, Bass noted that some passengers might not use seat belts if they "wanted to climb out when the car was moving."

About the 1979 car stunt, Bass testified that he had driven "very slowly . . . to accommodate the girls at a comfortable speed [so] they felt capable of jumping out of the vehicle." He said that Jean Coulter hadn't done this kind of jump before, so he told her the best way was to "get herself in position where she could stay as low as possible and parallel to the ground, to look in the direction we were driving . . . [because] if something went wrong she could pull her legs in." Bass testified that Julie had been planning to step out, turn her back, and do a rear roll, but he thought that was unsafe. He denied that they had agreed beforehand on a particular speed, claiming he had left it up to Julie to tell him how fast to go. He had slanted his rearview mirror to see the angle of the door "in case Julie Ann came out and something happened I could either apply the brakes or do a swerving action and not run over her or crush her legs or drag her." "Isn't it true," Grey demanded, "that you and other stunt players were all aware that the camera would be under cranked so you could drive at a slower speed and it would appear that the car was going faster than it actually was going?" Bass denied knowing that.[13]

Roy Harrison, a supervising stunt coordinator for Spelling-Goldberg, had been driving the car chasing Bass. Harrison testified that he saw "both ladies exit the vehicle." He reiterated Bass's advice that the right way to fall out of a car "is facing the direction you are going. The momentum takes you forward . . . I felt both ladies exited wrong, wrongly, because . . . they were facing the wrong way." He estimated the car had been going about fifteen miles an hour.[14]

After Julie and Jean returned from the emergency room, the crew was having lunch. Jean said, "Bobby . . . didn't even come over to ask how we were and this was not like him."[15] Bass's recollection of the lunch break was different. "I was already in line with some of the stunt people," he said. "They came back from the hospital or wherever they went and they—wait a minute—we just went over to them right away and asked them how they were and all . . . we were concerned."

"Who was 'we'?" Grey asked.

"The stunt people like Howard Curtis, perhaps Roy Harrison," Bass said. "I went over to see how she was and if she was okay."

"Did anyone accompany you . . . ?"

"I know I made the effort," Bass said. "It could have been . . . I think Roy Harrison was with me in line and he went with me."

"Please, Mr. Bass, don't speculate or imagine what would have happened. If you remember, tell us."

"I remember I went to see how they were," Bass said. "I was focused on their welfare."

Continuing his testimony, Bass said that after lunch he had to complete a 180-spinout, and Jean and Julie were waiting to finish their scene. Grey asked, "Didn't you try to spin the vehicle four or five times and you couldn't do it?"

"No."

"Isn't it true that Ronnie Rondell had to do it for you that day because you were not in condition to make that vehicle spin?"

"No," Bass said. Harrison backed him up, stating that Bass had done the spin, not Rondell.

On cross-examination, Koska asked who usually set the speed of a car in a stunt like the one done by Julie and Jean. "The person performing the stunt . . . has the say-so," Bass answered. "It's most important that [the driver] follow to the letter that issue."

"Was this particular stunt a typical type of basic stunt?"

Bass replied, "It might be typical for a man, might not be typical for women, however."[16]

Since the defense was citing Julie's lack of "camera sense" as one reason for her failure to be rehired, Koska put Richard Rawlings Jr. on the stand. Rawlings had started in 1965 as a camera loader and later moved up to second and then first assistant cameraman. He had been hired as a camera operator on *Charlie's Angels,* and three months later, during the last half of the third season (1978–1979), he had been promoted to director of photography. He testified that his responsibilities were "to be able to interpret what the director wants, 'the look of the show,' and get it done in the amount of time and money the producer has." Rawlings defined "camera sense" as "knowledge of optics and lenses" and other factors.

"To perform your job in the filming of a stunt," Koska asked, "what is necessary for a stunt coordinator to do?"

"To communicate with me. To explain themselves properly so that I and everybody listening understand what we're going to be doing in that stunt."

"Did you have any problems working with Julie Johnson?"

Rawlings responded, "Yes." Overall, he attributed her inability to communicate what she wanted to "her lack of experience as a stunt coordinator." He said her ideas often wouldn't work because of camera angles or because the sun would be in the lens; she had no camera sense, and he didn't have the time to show her. "And towards the end of the season, I think she more or less gave up . . . she just allowed me to go ahead and do it. . . . She would give the set-up and if I had to change it, I'd change it, and that's the way the pattern went after that."

Grey asked Rawlings if a director of photography "generally had the final word as to camera placement, camera angles and things of that nature on the set?"

"Yes," he said. But when there were disagreements about camera placement, the director had the final responsibility for the way a sequence would appear, not the director of photography. "I really and truthfully think that Julie Ann was a very good stunt person," Rawlings said, "but I don't think she was cut out for being coordinator, and I felt that maybe she recognized that. That is my personal opinion, sir."[17]

The issue of drug use remained on the periphery of the trial, only hinted at or mentioned indirectly. Julie's attorney was eager to bring it in, but the Spelling-Goldberg legal team seemed keen to keep it out. Stunt coordinator Roy Harrison denied using or selling cocaine on the set; he also claimed he had never seen an unsafe car on a Spelling-Goldberg production.[18] Everyone denied that Bobby Bass used drugs. Only Jean and Julie, who had been in the car with him, had a different view. Producer Elaine Rich testified that she didn't know of any safety or drug-related complaints Julie had made to people above her in the chain of command. Rich contended that Spelling-Goldberg's policy was that anyone seen using drugs would be fired on the spot. Asked whether that policy had been adopted before or after Julie had been let go, Rich said she didn't know exactly when, but she "would have thought it would have been there all the time."[19]

After two weeks of sometimes devastating testimony against her, Julie believed her case was lost. The next day, Koska called Gary Epper, who had replaced Julie as stunt coordinator for the 1980–1981 season. Like his sister Jeannie and brother Tony, Gary had started working in 1950s TV shows, when the production manager handled "the business that a stunt coordinator now does." Epper had "put in hundreds of days as a stunt coordinator," whose duties he described as follows: "The bottom line is he's the man who has read the script. He is the man that has sat in the production meetings. . . . It's his responsibility to tell the director what will or won't work, what's dangerous, what isn't. . . . He needs a calm disposition; not take whatever is said to heart because there are so many egos on movie sets." Koska asked Epper's opinion of Julie's "ability to do the job of stunt coordinator."

Julie had hired Epper to perform stunts on the 1979–1980 season of *Charlie's Angels,* and he said her reputation as a stuntwoman was "very good." He continued, "Julie had the ability to handle the mechanics of running the show as far as attending meetings, making sure the stunt people were hired. If—I mean, she lacked in a number of areas and I figured, you know, it was nothing but being new and a little inexperienced." About her camera sense, he said, "Well, there was an ongoing battle [with] Richard Rawlings, and I believe I understand what Julie was trying to convey to Richard . . . keep the action crisp and moving." Epper's experience had taught him to "make suggestions to a director and to the D.P. [director of photography]. If they want to buy them, fine; if they have faith in you as a coordinator . . . they will give you the right to place cameras where they belong."

On cross-examination, Grey asked Epper to describe the on-set problems more specifically. "When there is a communication problem between the stunt coordinator and those in key positions on a television show," Epper responded, "there's going to be a problem not only in performance, but in creativity. When you don't have a working knowledge of camera[s], there's going to be a communication problem with the director of photography. You have to know your stuff . . . you cannot be fooling anyone. Either you know it or you don't."

Grey asked whether the "ongoing battle" between Rawlings and Johnson was "a usual circumstance."

"It absolutely is. I have had my run-ins with D.P.s, and believe me if one of us goes, it won't be the D.P."

When asked whether he had he been told to make the stunts more exciting than Julie's had been the previous season, Epper replied that it was clear they planned to add more action sequences, but "the only thing said to me was that the argumentative attitude [of the last season] they didn't want to see that."

Epper reported that he had asked Julie to double the new Angel, Tanya Roberts, on the first shows of the new season, which were being shot in Hawaii. Julie turned him down, partly because she was tired of hitting the ground. "You have to remember at that time Julie was a hot stunt lady," Epper said. "I wanted the talent with me, and not only that, she was a friend . . . I knew she was hurt because she had lost her job . . . we were all concerned for Julie, we were all feeling 'Hey, the best way to get Julie over this is to keep her working.' But Julie turned people down when they gave her a call, including myself."[20]

"Gary was a good guy," Julie said, long after the trial. "Back in 1980, I was emotionally overwrought, in shock. . . . He told me that given the same circumstances of the show that I had had, he could not have done any better. When I was coordinating, I felt I was working with one hand tied behind me." Stuntman Bob Minor observed that, back then, women and minority stunt people "did not get the chance to fail." They had to be perfect. Ron Rondell, Gary Epper, and, to some extent, Richard Rawlings took into consideration Julie's learning curve as a new stunt coordinator. At the time, women could learn from supportive male mentors, but they couldn't shout or sulk or exhibit any of the bad behavior men could.

A pillar of the Spelling-Goldberg defense was the quality of the stunts on the shows Julie had coordinated. Producer Elaine Rich judged them "just adequate. No, not exciting." When asked whether some of her criticisms might have been attributable to the cinematographer or to camera placement, Rich claimed that part of the stunt coordinator's "expertise [is] to advise a D.P. where to place the camera to get exciting stunts on film." Grey brought up the shot of the 1979 car jump that showed only one side of the car—a flaw that Julie had predicted. He also pointed out that, according to Rawlings, the director had ultimate responsibility for camera placement when disputes occurred, and Rich later conceded the point. When Julie's lawyer asked whether the camera angle determined the distance between vehicles when seen on film, Rich was unable to answer. She was more forthcoming on the issue of safety. It is the stunt coordinator's job to make sure the equipment is in working order "for a safe stunt, for a good stunt," she said. When asked how Julie could have done that if she had no access to a car before it arrived on the set, Rich responded, "I find it very hard to believe a stunt coordinator has never seen a car . . . before filming. That's something that has never happened to my knowledge." Rich was asked: If the transportation director did not give a stunt coordinator access to cars, would that be a serious deficiency in his responsibilities? "It would not reflect upon the transportation captain," Rich said. "It would reflect on the stunt coordinator's lack of assertiveness . . . to say, 'I want it prepared such and such a way. It's my responsibility for the safety of those people.' Therefore, it is the stunt coordinator's responsibility."[21]

Earlier, Ron Rondell had testified that Julie had complained about "cars showing up not only without seat belts, but without seat belts that actually worked. If you looked in the car and saw seat belts, you'd assume they'd work, but in some cases they did not. Transportation neglected to check on these things." He admitted that Julie had been frustrated by these improperly equipped cars. "But in a sense," Grey asked, "isn't that a shared responsibility when a stunt coordinator depends on other people for the proper preparation of equipment?"

"Of course," Rondell said.[22]

Declining ratings during the fourth season of *Charlie's Angels* influenced management decisions. The slump was blamed on the stunts. It was Julie's "responsibility as stunt coordinator to . . . make an exciting stunt," Rich said, "to make it appear very dangerous, but not be dangerous, obviously." Grey asked whether Julie had been warned that her job was in jeopardy. Had Rich spoken to Julie about the lack of excitement in her stunts?

"Yes, I did."

"When was that?" Grey asked.

"When the season was over."

"Who asked for that meeting?"

"Julie Ann did."[23]

Rondell testified that he'd had no warning that Julie might not be brought back. He hadn't participated in the decision, and no one in management had consulted him. "When Elaine told me they didn't want to rehire Julie . . . I asked was she sure we couldn't keep her on. I felt Julie could probably do that job."[24]

After the trial, Julie's attorney summed up his impressions of the proceedings: "The most successful witness was Julie, obviously. The jury did not sympathize with her, they empathized with her, and it was not possible for Mr. Koska to make inroads into Julie's credibility. If you're a truthful person and all you're doing is telling the truth, nobody can trip you up. Her strong testimony was believed and it discredited what the people opposing her were trying to say. The truth is consistent; it doesn't deviate. Julie is so principled, she will sacrifice her own financial interest in favor of doing the right thing."

At the end of a trial, a plaintiff has the opportunity to rebut damaging or contrasting testimony. "In your opinion," Grey asked Julie on the witness stand, "what does it take to have good, exciting stunt work on a television action series?"

First, she said, it takes "a producer's willingness to allow and to insist on excitement." Next, the director needs "to confer with the writer to put the initial stunts on paper." Exciting stunts "come down the line and end with the coordinator—*if* the coordinator is allowed to take part in designing that action."

"Were there any limitations in your work as stunt coordinator that made it more difficult for you to get a high level of excitement in your stunts?"

"Time. Limitations with creativity. Creativity takes time. Limitations of the directors, and time. Always no time. Also, limitations of cameras. Often we had only two cameras and that contributes to the lack of exciting stunts."

"Did anyone tell you that your work as coordinator did not result in exciting stunts?"

"No, sir."

During the testimony, one witness had implied that Julie was unprofessional because she hadn't carried a briefcase. But she had, she said. "It contained what I needed . . . production reports, pictures of stunt people, little toy cars. . . . We use the cars to map out certain stunts to show the stunt people what they're going to do, to show camera and the director, once he tells us what he wants us to do."

As a stunt coordinator, had she leaned too heavily on Gary Epper, as some witnesses had claimed?

"On a few occasions I asked him to talk to Mr. Rawlings to try to make a shot what you call 'more exciting.'"

"Why did you use Mr. Epper rather than talking to Mr. Rawlings yourself?"

"Because the communication basically had stopped with Mr. Rawlings."

"Did you have any serious confrontations or heated arguments with the D.P.?"

"Frustrations, yes, but I can't think of any arguments. Just frustrations."

"What did you do in order to alleviate your frustrations?"

"Basically, I let him do his job as he saw it."

"So you just backed off and gave up, as has been described by some other witnesses?"

"Yes, sir."

"Why?"

"Because I felt that, as my experience again dictated, if someone doesn't want to listen or doesn't want to take the time, and if it doesn't involve safety you let them go ahead and do their job."

"In your work relationship with Mr. Rawlings or others on the set, did you ever become overly sensitive or moody?"

"No, sir." Then, after a moment's hesitation, she asked, "May I say one more thing?"

"Go ahead," Judge Savitch allowed.

"With the frustration—possibly 'oversensitive' runs with frustration."

"That is in the eye of the beholder, wouldn't you say?"[25]

Shortly after that, the jury began its deliberations.

On May 30, 1987, three months before Julie's case began, the *Twilight Zone* jury had found John Landis and four other defendants not guilty of involuntary manslaughter. Jubilation reigned in court, but one union executive snapped, "Nobody can believe that nobody was responsible."[26] Years later, few of the safety regulations proposed by labor and management groups had been enacted, so the Screen Actors Guild "stepped into the breach, negotiating into its collective bargaining agreements the safety requirements it had requested from the Legislature," including seat belts in stunt cars.[27]

On September 2, 1987, after almost four days of deliberation, the verdict in *Johnson v. Spelling-Goldberg* arrived. It was a stunner. The jury awarded $1.1 million to Julie Johnson. "I heard the words and could not believe it," she said. "At that moment, I realized I'd never expected to receive justice. But I wouldn't lie down. I had to put up a fight." The courtroom erupted. Her ecstatic attorney hugged her, got on his phone, and shouted, "We got 'em!" But Spelling-Goldberg planned to appeal the verdict. The battle was far from over.

# III

# New Professionals in Better Times

## *1990s–2000s*

# 13

# High Falls

Risks build my character, my confidence, and make me stronger.
—*Leigh Hennessy*

Doing a fall is one of the riskiest stunts. It goes against every instinct, and each fall is different—height, obstacles, landing, and, for women, wardrobe. In the early 1990s five-foot-ten Shawnna Thibodeau was new to the stunt business. She crammed everything she might need into her stunt bag, including pads to protect her. "There was a small back pad in it," she said, but "I never wore it because wardrobe put me in such teeny, tiny clothes the pad would show." On one stunt, she suffered three slipped disks in her neck after a tandem jump with a stuntman who had landed on top of her. She managed to walk away, and no one knew she'd been hurt. "You keep your mouth shut because you have other jobs lined up and you hope it will be okay." A week later she agreed to do a fall from three and a half stories, even though it was for a music video that paid almost nothing. On the day of the stunt she learned it was a *backward* fall with no wires (wires make high falls safer). "My generation usually does falls on wires," Shawnna said. "I sort of panicked. I was in excruciating pain from the last fall, and why was I doing this?" She didn't back out. Luckily, the stunt gods were watching out for her. "I landed flat on my back, it realigned the disks in my neck, and I felt like a new woman!"

Padded and unpadded, stunt players have fallen into rugs, nets, blankets, and mattresses to cushion their landings. In 1945 Babe DeFreest and Polly Burson took a seventy-five-foot fall into a net held up by "some grips." Over time, experience changed the way they landed. For falls of forty feet or less, stunt performers used to fall into stacked cardboard boxes (called box rigs). In the 1960s they fell into crash pads filled with foam rubber and then into airbags, which became bigger and better. In the 1990s a high-faller wore a full harness attached to a rig by wires, and a computer braking system controlled the rate of the fall. Today, stunt-women rarely do high falls without wires.[1]

Backward or forward, 15- to 50-foot stunt falls have been done by just about everyone: gymnasts, acrobats, high-divers, and martial artists who are "good in the air"; riders or drivers who aren't so good in the air; and rank amateurs.[2] Only a few have done falls of 90 to 1,500 feet. These dangerous stunts can make awesome contributions to a movie, but even little falls can cause big injuries. Jeannie Epper's daughter, Eurlyne, was thirty-seven when she suffered a severe neck injury in a four-foot fall. "She has a plate in her neck and never really regained her career," Jeannie recalled sadly. "I don't like to call it the luck of the draw, but our business is not safe. For a major stunt, every safety precaution is taken. The whole crew and cast seem to be in sync and you can feel the energy on the set, but on small stunts no one thinks a four-foot fall can cause a bad injury. Eurlyne was just going over a railing in a little fight, but she landed on her head. If she'd been doing a forty-foot fall, she's so good in the air she would have been able to turn over and land right. But at four or six feet, you can't turn. You just fall."

Two talented women—Melissa Stubbs from Canada and Sophia Crawford from England—developed their skills and their grit before coming to America in the 1990s. Melissa Stubbs's first stunt was a two-story fall from a window in Vancouver, British Columbia. "I had no plan of how I was going to land. I thought I'd figure it out on the way. I'm sort of like a cat, I save myself. But I had to wear a dress, heels and carry a purse, and that sure threw me off. I'm not a dress-heels-purse kind of girl." In high school Melissa worked as an extra in the Vancouver film industry. She knew Betty Thomas, a stunt coordinator and second-unit director who, with her husband, owned Thomas FX—a special effects company.[3] Melissa kept stopping by Betty's office to ask for advice, and one day Betty hired her to jump out that window, doubling Donna Mills in *The Lady Forgets* (1989). "I'd never done a high fall, but I'd done every sport possible and I was fearless. My attitude was 'Give me anything, I can do it.' Betty really helped start my career." There were more female stunt coordinators in the dynamic Canadian film industry than in the States, and in the 1990s, to avoid rising costs in Hollywood, American productions flocked to Canada.

Melissa Stubbs. (Courtesy of
Melissa Stubbs)

Melissa has presence—she's calm, competent, and enterprising. She started her own stunt equipment business "long before we did wiring and rigging." She was twenty-three when second-unit director Michael Joy gave her the chance to co-coordinate the 1994 TV movie *Snowbound: The Jim and Jennifer Stolpa Story*. Glenn Randall, "a legend," engaged her stunt equipment company and hired her to double Mia Sara on *Timecop* (1994), the Jean-Claude Van Damme action movie.[4] "Glenn made me his co-coordinator. I was by no means ready, but he backed me."

Showing up in Betty's office had worked, so Melissa tried it again. Fresh from stunt-driving school, she heard that the likable, witty stunt coordinator Conrad Palmisano was in Vancouver to set up *Carpool* (1996). "I walked in, said, 'Hi, my name is Melissa Stubbs, I'm a stunt driver, you need drivers, and I'm your girl.' He smiled. I was probably the age of his daughters and I hadn't really done any stunt driving. He said, 'How about I make you one of my special skills drivers?' I didn't know what that was— it's basically a background car—but I learned a lot from Rick Seaman, Betty Thomas, and other great stunt drivers." On *Carpool*, Melissa doubled Rhea Perlman as the meter maid on a scooter. "Any movie is hilarious with Conrad," she said, laughing. "It was probably more fun to make than to watch." Since 1995, Melissa has stunt-coordinated movies and television shows. In 2004 she became a second-unit director, a route few women have traveled.[5]

Melissa always knew what she wanted, but Sophia Crawford did not. She did not set out to learn martial arts, high falls, or wirework, and her journey into stunts was a remarkable one. Born in London, Sophia was one of triplets, plus she had an older brother and sister. Her mother died when she was twelve, and her father, a well-known economist and journalist, commuted to London from their home in Kent every day. "He left at seven in the morning and didn't come back until midnight," Sophia recalled. "We had so much freedom, no direction or discipline, and we got into trouble. I was expelled from four or five schools. In the mid-1980s I was sixteen and knew if I stayed in London I'd go down the wrong path." To avoid that, Sophia and her sister Ingrid embarked on a bus trip to India that retraced the route taken by "hippie" buses in the 1960s. The idea was to see how much had changed in twenty years. From India, the sisters went on to Thailand, where Sophia taught English, worked as an extra in American films being shot on location there, and met film crews from Hong Kong—a burgeoning production center that churned out pictures filled with flying fists and feet and plenty of falls. There, in the Hong Kong–based film industry, "I finally found something I felt I could do well—action." Sophia had no martial arts skills, but she applied herself and trained with members of legendary Jackie Chan's stunt team. Her first years in Hong Kong were rough. The city was undergoing major social, political, and cultural changes. Sophia recalled:

Hong Kong was a British colony, everyone knew the lease was up, and they felt empowered. Toward me the team had two faces. Sometimes I went to karaoke bars with them, but as much as I practiced martial arts and studied Cantonese, on the set I felt quite segregated. No one would talk to me; it wasn't the right thing to do. I was the *gweilo*—white ghost. The pay was crap, no union, no adjustments, no overtime, but I was thankful to be there. I trained hard and I learned. The girls fascinated me, Yukari, Moon Li, Sibelle Hu—I wanted to be like them. I didn't care if people were unfriendly. One director screamed in my face, swearing, spitting. They were hard on us *gweilos*. I was so new they lost patience. Why did they bother with me? A director told me I didn't have the

Sophia Crawford.
(Courtesy of Sophia Crawford)

best technique, but I had heart, I fought with passion. In a fight you have to get into that moment just as a good actor gets into the moment of the scene. Over those five years I improved dramatically. I was tenacious, I stuck it out.

Female action star Yukari Oshima (*Story of Ricky, Fighting Madam*) invited Sophia to join her all-Asian stunt group, Yukari's Funky Action Crew. "She was a real stuntwoman and she inspired me," Sophia said. "She created her unique fighting style out of her personality and taught me a combination of martial arts, stunt skills, and acting." Sophia became known for her fights, but she did plenty of high falls, too. "The Hong Kong action teams used an early form of wirework. The equipment we now have was not available then," she said. "We used ropes, leather harnesses, and a very thin aircraft cable. It couldn't carry a lot of weight; it often snapped in a fight or fall, and there were a few bad accidents." But Hong Kong stunt performers were creative—what they didn't have, they improvised. "In the early 1990s they brought better cable from the U.S. and the newest harnesses marketed by AMSPEC in California." The rest is history. The wirework invented in Hong Kong changed movies and stunts around the world. For Americans, the best-known example is probably *Crouching Tiger, Hidden Dragon* (2000).

Sophia performed in more than thirty Hong Kong films, including "girls with guns" action flicks such as *Yes Madam*. But she had no idea that these films had been exported to the West or that some of them had a cult following. When she arrived in Los Angeles in 1993, her modest manner gave no indication of her fast, ferocious fighting style of runs, jumps, and combat moves. Her skills got attention, however, and martial artist and stunt coordinator Jeff Pruitt asked her to join his stunt team on the TV series *Mighty Morphin' Power Rangers* (1993–1996). In 1998 she doubled TV star Sarah Michelle Gellar in *Buffy the Vampire Slayer* (1997–2003). Drawing on her Hong Kong experience, her vigorous martial arts moves became Buffy's fighting style in at least 300 fight and stunt scenes. "Jeff Pruitt and I pushed hard to give the action sequences more of a Hong Kong style, sometimes at the expense of pissing people off. As the seasons progressed, Jeff was able to create a fighting style for each character that worked well, though we still wanted a little more artistic expression."[6]

One stunt in an episode of *Buffy* ("Phases") was not planned as a high fall, and Sophia's training and strength saved her. Falls usually start on top of something; they don't involve being hurled *up* from the ground and then *down* into a fall. Sophia described the stunt: "In a forest, Buffy stepped on a capture net that was supposed to fold up around her and lift her about six feet off the ground." The special effects team worked to rig the net, but the production crew ran out of time, and when they got to the gag with the net, they had to shoot the rehearsal. "The net was made out of rope, big squares woven together. I stepped into position, the net captured me, then, like a slingshot, flung me with great power over and beyond the camera on the crane." She had one elbow hooked inside the net, but her body was outside of it, and she had been hurled fifty feet into the air. "I saw treetops below me. If I hadn't grabbed onto the net as it was coming down, I don't know how I would have landed. It was terrifying." Too late, the riggers realized that the sandbags providing the counterweight for Sophia's 110-pound body had been left outside in the rain. They were too heavy, and as a result, she had been flung into the air like a rag doll. Unfortunately, the shot wasn't good enough. "My woolly hat flew off. They couldn't use any part of the shot," Sophia said. Suffering from whiplash, and shaking from head to foot, Sophia had to do it again. She went into her trailer to com-

Sophia Crawford's jump kick at *Buffy* stunt coordinator Jeff Pruitt. (Courtesy of Denise Duff)

pose herself, and stunt coordinator Jeff Pruitt, who seemed even more shaken than she was, followed her. He asked her to marry him. She said "yes," coolly walked back to the set, and did the stunt again.[7]

Sophia Crawford survived her unintended high fall, but others weren't as lucky. The movie *Vampire in Brooklyn* (1995) starred Eddie Murphy and Angela Bassett; Wes Craven directed, and Alan Oliney, Murphy's double on *Beverly Hills Cop II*, stunt-coordinated. Oliney hired almost every stuntwoman of color working at that time—Kym Washington, LaFaye Baker, Sharon Schaffer, and Sonja Davis, who doubled Angela Bassett.[8] Thirty-two-year-old Sonja, a member of the United Stuntwomen's Association (USA), had only about three years' experience, but she was considered *the* up-and-coming African American stunt performer. She'd done a high fall from a Ferris wheel in *Beverly Hills Cops III*. "Sonja was a perfect size, great to get along with, had high morals, and was in top shape," said Bonnie Happy, president of USA. The young performer was ambitious, and she wanted to be written into Bassett's contract as her regular double. Any stunt person with career aspirations is willing to take risks, and Sonja was no exception.

On November 14, 1994, Sonja's mother and brother were in downtown Los Angeles to watch her do a backward high fall from a ledge near the top of a four-story apartment building. She was supposed to land in an alley between two buildings, but the alley was only fourteen feet, ten inches wide—a narrow space for a fall and a big problem. The ledge Sonja stood on jutted out from the building about a foot, using up precious inches she needed because "a falling body tends naturally to drift out a few feet before landing."[9] She couldn't simply push off the ledge; she had to "melt" off it, being careful to fall safely within the limited space of the alley and landing in the bag positioned on the ground below. "Typically, the rectangular bag would be positioned so that Davis would fall into it lengthwise," Holly Millea wrote for *Premiere*. "The bag procured was fifteen feet, more than an inch too long to fit in the alley. It had to be placed so that Sonja would not fall into its *length* but into its *width*, which was only twelve feet."[10] Disastrously, the bag was set against the wall of the building from which Sonja jumped. That left three feet of exposed pavement between the far edge of the bag and the adjacent building. Anyone familiar with high falls would have questioned that placement, but no one did. The bag was pressed against the wrong wall, no boxes or pads covered the bare pavement between the far edge of the bag and the other wall, no safety spotters were in place, and none of the required drop tests or practice jumps were done.[11] At the time, techniques were changing, and some high falls were done using wires—descenders—that can make falls safer. The *Vampire in Brooklyn* production team decided not to use safety wires.

According to Kym, at one point, she was supposed to do the jump. "I wouldn't have done it," Kym said. "It's like, why do I have to go off backward that high? A lot of guys in the business won't do those [falls]! You can't be afraid to turn something down."[12] At the last minute, Sonja asked if she could do a different kind of fall. The director declined; he wanted a backward fall.[13] The cameras rolled, the director called "Action!" and Sonja dropped into empty space. The back of her head hit the cement alley eight inches beyond the edge of the airbag. A nurse was on set, but there was no ambulance or doctor. In that Los Angeles alley, surrounded by lights and camera crew, Sonja Davis suffered the injury that caused her death thirteen days later, a calamity that still resonates today.

"Most people like to keep their feet on the ground," said stuntwoman Nancy Thurston. "I like to be airborne." Nancy, who began working in 1994, quickly became an admired high-fall performer. "It's important to have the right people on the ground," she told *Inside Stunts*, "people you trust to set the bag the way you want it. Measure the distance from the wall to the bag and fill in the gap with boxes." High-fall specialist Jon Epstein said that anyone doing a fall "has to be able to coordinate his own high fall. He's got no business doing it if he can't. A stunt coordinator is just an extra pair of eyes on the ground."[14]

Like Nancy, Leigh Hennessy, Jill Brown, and LaFaye Baker started doing stunts in the 1990s.[15] They did not have family in the business, but they all excelled at sports, high-diving, trampoline, and gymnastics. Gymnast Lynn Salvatori had no industry connections either when she began in the late 1980s, but her independence and adaptability suited stunt work. Since her father worked for Conoco, she had grown up all over the country, eventually graduating from a college in Colorado with a degree in physical education. She had appeared in a commercial as a student and got her SAG card, which helped her pick up work in Los Angeles on low-budget horror flicks such as *Chopper Chicks in Zombietown* (1989). "I thought of myself as the B-horror stunt queen," she said. "High falls always get your attention. On a Honda commercial, I was to jump off the roof of a building, but when I scouted the location I saw the telephone wires were about ten feet below me and about ten feet out from the building. I went home to practice off the eighty-foot tower set up in my backyard. I worked to keep myself as vertical as possible for the first part of the fall before positioning myself to fall into the bag. People don't realize in high falls your body will go out a few feet and then down. It's physics."

The type of high fall dictates where the bag below should be positioned. The week before Sonja's accident, Lynn had used the same airbag for a backward fall from about forty-five feet on the TV series *Earth 2*. "I set the center of my bag twelve to fourteen feet *out* from the building because I knew how far out I normally go. If I'm doing a header, which is a forward somersault to land in the bag on my back—that puts your head closest to the building. Therefore, to protect my head, I move the bag *in* toward the building. If I do a back fall, take off backwards from the building, I'll land in the bag on my back, but my head will be farther from the building, so I move the bag out from the building. For those falls, I usually set the center of the bag about fourteen feet from the building. Sonja fell into an alley that was less than fifteen feet wide, next to impossible to do."

On another stunt, Lynn fell off a balcony.[16] Again, she couldn't jump or push off; she had to step off just enough to "sit down" and keep falling.

"Even doing that, I was still twelve feet out when I landed. If you're going down vertically, lengthwise, and land twelve feet out without pushing off, and the space between buildings is only fifteen feet, your head is going to hit whatever is not padded on the ground. Sonja had practiced backward falls off a trapeze board into a net about fifteen feet below, but that wasn't the forty feet she had to go, and no one measured how far *out* she went."

Known as the "high-fall girl from Peoria," Nancy Thurston grew up watching *Wonder Woman* and *Charlie's Angels*. "Those strong women inspired and encouraged me," she said. Nancy trained as a gymnast, rode horses, dreamed of being a jockey or a stuntwoman, and taught herself how to dive. "My dad was a retired colonel in the army, and he'd challenge me: 'If you learn a two-and-a-half forward pike off the three-meter, I'll take you to Six Flags in St. Louis.'" Each summer she learned a new diving skill and went to Six Flags, where she saw the high-diving show and told her dad, "I can do that." Her college coach helped prepare Nancy for her interview with the U.S. High Diving Team. "When I was hired, my dad looked at what I'd be paid, added up the costs of living in LA, and kept shaking his head. 'You're not going to make any money—but you're going to have a lot of fun!'" High-diving and gymnastics led Nancy into stunts. She doubled Kathy Long, five-time world-champion kickboxer, in *Knights* (1993) and worked with high-fall experts Jon Epstein and Bob Brown.[17]

From her experience on *The X-Files* (1993), *Titanic* (1997), and the TV series *Charmed* (1998–2006), where she doubled Holly Marie Combs for eight years, Nancy learned the "tricks" that are often thrown in at the last minute to make a fall different or exciting. "First they say it's a twenty-foot fall. Great. Then they throw in the curveballs. 'We need you to jump out a window.' Fine. 'You're going to be barefoot, or naked, or on fire when you go through glass.' Why not blindfold me, too? It's not just the fall, it's all the things that come with it. Then there's wardrobe—skimpy. Stuntwomen know that going in. They accept it or get out. You can't complain." Her parents didn't always like what she did, but they never said, "Don't do that." They *would* say, "'You like getting hit by a *car?* You want to be lit on *fire?*' Yeah, it's great!"

Lynn Salvatori and Nancy Thurston expected to be called for stunts involving falls, but Bonnie Happy didn't normally do falls. She was faced with a choice: "not do the fall and have Chris Howell, the coordinator, tell the story behind my back the rest of my life, or suck it up and do it." A stately five-foot-nine blonde, Bonnie sought the advice of her brother,

Nancy Thurston does a handstand on the perch leading to a sixty-foot fall with American acrobats Karen and Danny Castle at the Chico County Fair. (Courtesy of Danny Castle)

Clifford. He told her, "If you're really scared you shouldn't do the stunt. It should just get your attention." Bonnie's fall in *The Fisher King* (1991) got her attention.[18] "I was to sit on a barstool next to Robin Williams, not all bad," Bonnie said. "A guy shoots up the place, blows the back of my head off, and I fall off the barstool." Then the complications started. "The director was a Monty Python type of director," she said. "He wanted me to fall backwards from a distance so he could slow the shot to make it look like slow motion onscreen. That meant I had to fall about twenty feet. I told Chris I don't do high falls. 'Sorry, babe, you've already got the job,'" he told her. So off they went to Chris's barn. Bonnie climbed into the scoop on the front of his tractor, and Chris hoisted her higher and higher toward the top of the barn. "In an hour he had me going backwards off the roof," she said. On the day of the stunt, they stuck a blood pack under her wig that was rigged to pop open when she fell off the barstool, spraying blood everywhere. "Now I love falls," Bonnie said happily, "but I'm not a high-fall girl like Nancy Thurston or Leigh Hennessy. I'd never go as high as they do."

"Nancy is the most supportive stuntwoman I know," Leigh Hennessy said. "Must be something about high-fallers. We're confident of who we are." Leigh's website shows her at age one, balancing on one leg while standing on her father's hand. She was an athlete throughout her academic career. Her father taught physical education at the University of Southwestern Louisiana, and "he pioneered and coached the sport of trampoline." Leigh competed in events and achieved international status as a trampoline champion. Stunts were never part of her plan, but after working for Louisiana congressman James A. Hayes in Washington, D.C., Leigh realized she needed a more physically active life. She resigned her Capitol Hill job in 1991, bought a used car, and drove to Los Angeles. "The first three years were hell, but I got my SAG card quickly. I was in a gym, some guys saw me doing flips on a trampoline, [and] my name went into a pile for a Ralph Lauren ad."[19]

On one of her first stunt jobs, Leigh learned what a good coordinator can achieve. While doubling Téa Leoni in *Bad Boys* (1995), Leigh was supposed to jump out of a moving car and hit the pavement wearing a miniskirt and a midriff. "Dar Robinson's son, Troy, taped pieces of neoprene, the spongy stuff wetsuits are made of, to my hipbones and tailbone. That was it." Then the stunt changed, and the jump was replaced by a little movie trickery. "A cameraman lay on the ground to shoot the scene: a stunt driver in the car takes off, I run very fast, dive over the cameraman and his gear

Leigh Hennessy flying high. (Courtesy of William Bradford)

to land lengthwise in the center of the frame so they can see my entire body. I didn't have to jump out of the car because as the car sped past the cameraman, the stunt driver opened the door as I dived over the cameraman. It looked like I jumped from the car. It was a creative and clever decision. Kenny Bates designed the gag, and it worked."[20] Diving out of a moving car can be dangerous, but this stunt faked the jump and delivered the same effect.

After that, Leigh's stunt work picked up. "I'm never called to 'fall this way and hit the ground.' I get these calls: 'Will you jump off the Sixth Street Bridge?'" Or how about playing a mother forced to leap with her daughter from a four-story building? With a heavy dummy strapped to her back, Leigh was supposed to break through a candy glass window, take a step, and jump. "A lot of preparation went into that stunt," she said. "Safety meetings are often held even for little gags, but when it's a big gag everyone on the crew is in the meeting to hear what's been set up." That fall had its quirks. When Leigh was inside the room, she couldn't see the airbag below. "Once I crashed through the glass, I had to step on a precise spot on the ledge. I couldn't step over it or I'd miss the bag below. I could only see the airbag when I leaned over one second before the jump. That's a leap of faith. All one take. Before the stunt, I leaned against the glass, stood on tippy-toes to see the bag and tell the crew to move it right or left until they got it right. I have to trust my experience, judge the distance, judge the bag, take three steps back, then go for the fall. It's all about me trusting me."[21]

In 1999, on the energetic remake of *Charlie's Angels* (2000), Nancy Thurston, Leigh Hennessy, and Lisa Hoyle doubled the three stars.[22] They were on the roof of a ten-story building, preparing to do a ninety-five-foot fall. "I looked down at the bag nine or ten stories below," Leigh remembered, "and I was muttering to myself, 'Never take a job like this again.'" She had never done a fall that high; at the time, her biggest fall had been a seventy-five-foot training jump. Nancy and Lisa had jumped sixty-five feet, and Lisa had trained for falls up to ninety feet. "The jump was shot in a unique way because at that height no airbag is big enough to accommodate three or even two people," Leigh said. "We each jumped individually, one right after the other, so that when it was edited together the sunlight wouldn't change." The backdrop of their jump was supposed to be an explosion; therefore, in editing, the footage of their separate jumps would make it seem like the explosion had blown them into the air.

Each of the women determined where she wanted the bag, and the riggers on the ground blocked off its placement for each jump. After one woman jumped, the crew quickly moved the bag to the next place and refilled it with air. "It was a forward fall, a fireman's jump," Nancy said. "You jump, kick out, and then drop. You're not poised in the air, it's like you have no choice except to jump. I wasn't scared, but I did have butterflies. I call them respectful butterflies." Just standing on the roof looking down was riveting. Because the women had to be off-camera, they couldn't watch each other jump. "As you're waiting, anticipation drives through you," Leigh said. "In those eternal minutes before it's your turn, you learn about your own character." Lisa was up first. They heard, "Rolling, action!" and then heard her fall into the bag. Nancy was next. "I'm ready, I'm looking down, I hear 'Rolling camera, 1, 2—Hold the roll!'" She was one second from pitching herself into the air. "There was some technical problem," she said calmly. "I backed up. After a while it was fixed, and I was back at the edge of the roof." She heard, "Rolling camera! Action!" and Nancy hit the bag. "My turn," Leigh said. "My heart was about to beat out of my chest, but as soon as I heard the director, 'One, two, three, action!' anxiety flowed out of my body. I was confident, and I jumped. I remember rolling out of the bag and wanting to climb up there and do it again right away."

Behind every stunt is a unique story—the performers' different techniques, their emotions before and after the stunt, the kind of characters they're doubling. In this case, after all the preparation, this spectacular stunt ended up on the cutting-room floor. That was very disappointing, but Nancy, Lisa, and Leigh had performed perfectly. They had taken the risk, executed the vital act that, Leigh wrote, "builds my character, my confidence and makes me stronger."[23]

# 14

# Stunt Fights

In a fight today it's a fine line between aggression and femininity.
—*Shauna Duggins*

The movie remake of *Charlie's Angels* launched that saga into the twenty-first century.[1] Stuntwomen had been struggling for decades to secure their place in the action, and they were still far from equal in number and position. But more than ever before, new and seasoned stuntwomen were crashing cars, jumping off buildings, and taking part in slam-bang, kick-ass fights.

"Women's roles aren't sidekicks or wives or girlfriends or damsels in distress—we're action heroes," declared stuntwoman Shauna Duggins. She began working in 1998 and was too young to have seen *Charlie's Angels* on television, but she knew that "all the women who'd worked so hard in the last twenty years—*they* made it possible for us to work today." They had certainly made a difference. Sometime during the 1990s, being a feminist had became old hat, but young women like Shauna had grown up in that world. "My mom said, 'You want to be a *nurse?* Be a doctor! If a guy can do it, so can a girl,'" Shauna recalled. "There were no limits, go after what you want. That's how I grew up." Raised in the Imperial Valley east of San Diego, Shauna was a gymnast and a high-diver. For fun, she, her brother, and her dad had jumped off thirty- or forty-foot cliffs into the water. "My mom was a pilot for recreation," Shauna said. "We'd land somewhere, the ground crew asked my dad if we needed fuel, and he'd say, 'I don't know, ask the pilot.' It's hard to believe that in the 1990s people were shocked a woman was flying the plane!"

On the new *Charlie's Angels* movie, Shauna worked with Donna Evans, who was known for her skill as well as her generosity. "She was an amazing mentor for me," Shauna said, "so professional, so talented—and she's mar-

Shauna Duggins.
(Courtesy of Shauna Duggins)

ried with two kids. How does she do all that?" Compared with the many martial arts clashes in *Charlie's Angels,* Shauna and Donna's "gnarly, messy" fight on a stone staircase is short and vivid. Shauna doubled Kelly Lynch (playing the evil Vivian), and Donna doubled the star, Cameron Diaz. Shauna's long-sleeved black leather suit was made of rubber "as thin as a balloon," she said. "They had to put baby powder all over it and me, then roll the suit on me." Wardrobe told her she couldn't wear any pads because they would show. "I was so green, I just nodded." Donna's low-cut, sleeveless outfit wasn't much better. "Behind the double doors at the top of the stairs, we stepped on apple boxes to give us some lift as we came out," Donna said. "After that, Vic Armstrong, the coordinator, said we could come down the steps however we wanted to do it." Donna proposed that instead of tumbling down the stone stairs separately, like "sausage rolls," they stay together all the way to the bottom, one person rolling over the other—a much tougher stunt. "Some girls get afraid; they want to do it the easy way. Shauna was up for it," Donna said. "I couldn't grab her because her suit encased her like an inner tube, but she could hang on to my lapels." In the scene, they come flying through the doors, airborne, and hit the steps as intertwined bodies, head to head, legs flying, clutching each other in a cruel, tumbling roll to the ground. "Then," Donna said, "it's over! But Shauna wouldn't get up. I thought she was hurt." Everyone shouted, "Get the medic!" Shauna, however, didn't need the medic. "I need wardrobe!" she yelled. She'd snagged her pants on the stairs. "The back of the suit had popped and my bare butt was completely exposed. I knew I'd never hear the end of it—they had it on playback. And for years I'd go on shows and the coordinator, Vic Armstrong, would say, 'You haven't popped any pants, have you?'"[2]

Since the 1950s, stuntman Loren Janes has punched his way through scores of fights. "What makes one fight better than another is the way it fits the characters," he said. "Are they furious or just mad, are they insane, are they protecting someone? Sometimes a fight goes on and on, other times it's over in three punches. The greatest stunt in the world is worthless if it doesn't fit the story."[3] For years, jealousy seemed to be the only motive writers could cook up for a fight between women. In *Destry Rides Again* (1939) Una Merkel's jealous rage started the unprecedented barroom fight with Marlene Dietrich. In *Gone with the West* (1968), nearly thirty years later, not much had changed as Polly Burson and Julie Johnson brawled over a man. Today, when two women duke it out, their characters' motivations vary greatly, and the popularity of martial arts has changed their fighting style. Action heroines may be altruistic champions, merciless villains, or betrayed victims bent on revenge. "Male coordinators used to stage fights for women that imitated the way guys fought," said stunt coordinator Mary Albee, "but girls didn't grow up learning how to fight, they don't square off and start punching. Their fights have a whole different flavor." Today, women are much more likely to be expert fighters of the take-no-prisoners school.

A stunt fight in the science fiction movie *Total Recall* (1990), starring Sharon Stone and Arnold Schwarzenegger, brought these changing images into focus. Stone's character, Lori, kicks Schwarzenegger's character, Hauser, in the groin and snaps, "That's for making me come to Mars." Then she delivers the punch line along with a punch: "You know how much I hate this fucking planet!" Donna Evans, who doubled Stone, explained, "In features, they often shoot things over and over. Arnold is one of the most professional actors I've worked with. I must have kicked this poor guy in the balls fifty times." At least his wardrobe allowed him to wear lots of protective pads. Donna continued, "In another shot he's lying on the floor, I'm wearing spike heels, and I'm supposed to stomp on his privates

Donna Evans, doubling Sharon Stone, battles it out with Arnold Schwarzenegger in *Total Recall* (1990). (Courtesy of Donna Evans)

again as I walk out. After that, I listed 'ball-kicking specialist' on my résumé. All thanks to Arnold."[4]

"In this new century, it's fun to see real women's fights," Mary Albee said. "They are heroes holding their own, the guy is not coming to their rescue or even to their defense. We can save ourselves. Ain't that grand?" It is. But in fact, this trend is a revival from two earlier periods in film history: one from the days of the silent movie serials, when fearless heroines like Helen Holmes saved themselves week after week, and the other from 1970s TV shows and blaxploitation films, which had Jadie David (doubling Pam Grier in *Foxy Brown*) ramming a taxiing airplane into a drug shack to knock off the bad guys. "In fights today it's a fine line between aggression and femininity," said Shauna Duggins. "You're not a big, burly woman; you're the feminine hero, and you want her to read as powerful. I love the choreography for a one-on-five fight. I'm kicking their butts, I'm running in high heels, and they're all on the floor. That's empowering."

"Fights make you feel good," stuntwoman Ming Qiu said, "they make you feel special." Ming, a great wushu (Chinese martial arts) stylist, has been competing since age eight in Nanjing, China, and in 1998 she was awarded the title Black Belt Female Competitor of the Year.[5] Ming's fight-

Ming Qiu leaps up as the train explodes in *Ecks vs. Sever* (2002). (Courtesy of Ming Qiu)

ing style is a mix of martial arts and dance. She is from a family of dancers, gymnasts, and acrobats, and her mother was a national gymnastics champion. "She is my idol," Ming said. "She's tough, and she was tough on me. Even when I took first place, she said I could do 'better than that.' I didn't have a lot of confidence when I moved here. My first friend in the stunt business was Chad Stahelski, Keanu Reeves's stunt double. I trained with him. He gave me courage. He said, 'You're better than a lot of guys.'" While doubling actress Nia Peoples on *Walker, Texas Ranger* (1993–2000), Ming flew to Los Angeles to audition for *Charlie's Angels* and meet the film's three stars, Lucy Liu, Drew Barrymore, and Cameron Diaz. "Lucy saw me and said, 'Yes, you are my double.'" Japanese martial artist Michiko Nishiwaki also doubled Lucy Liu.[6] "I respect her very much," Ming said. "Michiko was an actress and is a very skilled fight choreographer." She changed the stereotype of the docile Japanese woman, and she created a bodybuilding boom in Japan when she became the first women's bodybuilding and power-lifting champion.

Movie fights display all kinds of martial arts, but Ming advises stunt people to start with wushu "because it involves jumps and kicks and the low stances. You learn many styles, hard and soft, different kinds of weapons, and then it's easy to learn other martial arts."[7] Ming's entire career had been martial arts fighting—until *Charlie's Angels.* "My first scene was in an explosion and I had no clue how to land. I'm pretty much a ground person. Learning new things on the set is the scary part of the work—and the most exciting. Without the help of Donna Evans I don't think I could have done it. I had to do wirework and high falls. I had to hang outside a helicopter." That memorable aerial sequence won a Taurus World Stunt Award.[8]

"When I tell stuntwomen to get through that wall," Danny Aiello III said firmly, "they *will* get through the wall, and they do it in gowns or bathing suits—no protection. In my experience, they're tougher than the men." Like his famous actor-father (*Do the Right Thing* [1989]), Danny had appeared in front of the camera, but he focused on stunts and became a respected stunt coordinator and second-unit director in New York City.[9] "Being a stuntman lets you be a child forever," he said happily. "You get to do things they arrested you for when you were young, and now those same cops are holding back traffic so you can do your stunt!" During filming of the sci-fi thriller *The Invasion* (2007), Danny spotted martial artist Li Jing in the hotel lobby, arms crossed, looking really mad.[10] He asked her what was wrong. "She said, 'Four men asked me what I was doing here, I told them I was in a movie, and one said, "A porno movie?" I was so mad. I was going to beat them up.' I said, 'Li Jing, could you beat up all four guys?' She said, 'Oh, absolutely.' To me, that sums up everything," Aiello said. "Being a stuntwoman is probably like being a [female] cop years ago when there were so few women, trying to be as tough as the guys, trying to be accepted. It's the same in stunts. These attractive girls, decked out in gowns, looking great, and a minute later they run in front of a car and go into the windshield! It's fascinating to see the dynamic things stuntwomen do compared to what the world thinks they can do. It's better now, but it's still hard for them to be accepted."

Danny stunt-coordinated scores of episodes of *Rescue Me* (2004–2011), an action-packed soap opera about family and firefighters. "We did a fight scene between two women, and it's the most vicious fight I've ever seen," he recalled. "A couple of women behind the monitor were crying, that's how ferocious it was. Stuntwoman Stephanie Finochio took a real beating."[11] "That was a really fun fight," Stephanie yelled. "The actress was beating me up!" That's hard to believe, given that from 2002 to 2005 Stephanie was known as "Trinity," a professional wrestler on the World Wrestling Entertainment circuit. She's not the only stuntwoman who has

Stephanie Finochio, the target of the ferocious fight. (Courtesy of Stephanie Finochio)

climbed into the ring; Caryn Mower, Jwaundace Candece, and Elle Alexander have been there too. "Wrestling is like a big stunt," Stephanie said. "Men often do crazier stunts than women, but they can pad up. We are in tank tops and heels—no pads. That's the fun difference! I love the physicality of stunt fights. It's probably why I got into wrestling." Stephanie grew up on Long Island, where her dad owned a motorcycle shop, so she and her two sisters learned to ride early. Stephanie also Rollerbladed, raced Jet Skis, and did gymnastics and martial arts. Despite having three college degrees, she couldn't decide on a career until a friend from California mentioned the stunt business. That sounded ideal—beat people up, rappel down buildings, crash cars—what could be better?

In the "vicious" *Rescue Me* fight, Stephanie doubled Callie Thorne (playing Sheila Keefe). Her opponent was actress Brette Taylor (playing Debbie). "Sheila and Debbie had gone over to the other side for a while," Stephanie explained, "a lesbian affair that turned sour." The women were dressed in summer skirts, tank tops, and flip-flops—no pads. Because the fight was filmed in the foyer of a real home—complete with hardwood floors and a staircase—"they couldn't rig it or put down pads for us to land on," Stephanie said. "Sheila, the role Callie played, is girly. Her girlfriend,

Danny Aiello and Vince Cupone, co–stunt coordinator, take a break after the har-
rowing fight scene. (Courtesy of Chrys Cupone)

Debbie, is the tomboy. Sheila wants to end the relationship. Debbie
screams, runs up behind Sheila, slams her against the front door, and suddenly they're in a big fight." The fight had been rehearsed, but then things
changed. "In any stunt, I take my bumps and bruises, but the actress playing Debbie wasn't a stunt person. Actors get so into their parts. She slams
me into the door, grabs the back of my head, hammers on me, we're flying
around that small space, she throws me to the floor. I'm down, she slams
my face against the floor, banging away." According to Stephanie, it might
have seemed more realistic than a Hollywood stunt fight "because it was
quick and brutal in a confined space, very like a fight that could have happened in someone's home."

Stunt performers—and actors—can get carried away, but not all fights
are that grueling. Some are challenging in completely different ways. For
instance, a comic fight on *Mr. Deeds* (2002) was short and sweet compared
to the time and effort it took to create it. Stunt coordinator Mary Albee
doubled Conchata Ferrell, and Dorenda Moore doubled actress Winona
Ryder.[12] "Conchata is a wonderful actress and rather large," Mary said, "a
good contrast with Winona Ryder, who is petite. We were not on a set; we

were in a practical location. The coordinator, Gregg Smrz, brought his equipment to rig the pizza parlor for us to work. In the scene, Conchata wanted to protect Adam Sandler (Deeds) from Winona, and the fight was on." Mary was wearing a wig, a full prosthetic face mask (because Conchata's character had jowls), and a full body suit that added seventy-five pounds. "Then they dumped sixty pounds of birdseed in the boobs to make the weight jiggle right," Mary said. "The problem doing the stunt wasn't the fight; it was what it took for me just to move. My knees were at least a foot apart, walking or standing, and I had to sit down a lot because the suit was so heavy. Once we're into the fight, it escalates fast. I was to lift Dorenda over my head, spin her around—she was on a cable that held her over my head—and then I threw her into a table. She picked up a circle of pizza dough and tossed it over my head. I had the fat suit on, the prosthetics, pizza dough over my face, and now I couldn't see. At that point, Dorenda was to jump up, kick me in the chest, and send me backward into the tables."

The reaction to a kick or a punch can be crucial in a staged fight; it intensifies the ferocity of the attack. Mary was on a ratchet, wearing a full harness and a jerk vest attached to the cable. When triggered, the ratchet was supposed to jerk her back over the tables—a physical reaction to the kick in the chest. "By the time I put on the vest and zipped up the fat suit, the pressure . . . squeezed my carotid arteries," Mary recalled. "I could stand up for only a few minutes before the lack of blood flow made me dizzy. On the first take, Dorenda did a flying stunt kick, but I couldn't see it coming—pizza dough over my head—and with the birdseed boobs, the vest, the harness, the fat suit, I didn't even know she'd done it. I was still waiting for the kick. When you get ratcheted, you have to know it's coming to keep your balance, and her kick was the cue to start the ratchet." Once they figured out how to make it work, Mary flew wildly across the tables and into the chairs. "Not your standard fight, but it was comedy, and comedy is great!"

That fight worked because all involved knew what they were doing, but sometimes a crazy stunt turns out to be impossible to perform. Tall, dark-haired Shawnna Thibodeau was doubling Charlize Theron in fight scene for *Hancock* (2008) that was filmed underwater.[13] "We're in a tank, we go way, way down, breathing in a regulator," she said, "and then they take it away because we had to look like we were flying through the sky. They didn't want bubbles to show and wouldn't take them out digitally.

We're fighting, spinning around, throwing punches, which isn't really hard underwater. For some reason, we had to keep our eyes open. It didn't bother me, but Will Smith's double, his eyes were so red he couldn't see the punches coming. It was all so freaky." When it was over, Shawnna still had to make it to the surface, but wardrobe had put her in high-heeled, thigh-high boots that had filled up with water. "I thought, 'Oh, man, I'm stuck down here.' It was so hard to stay down with no air." Finally someone noticed, and the safety divers pulled her out. That stunt didn't get past the testing stage—and they did a lot of tests. It just didn't work.

Most fights work amazingly well, and stuntwomen have turned in some memorable brawls in *The Matrix* franchise, *Mr. and Mrs. Smith, G.I. Jane, G.I. Joe: Rise of the Cobra, Wanted,* and *Transformers.* But Quentin Tarantino's two-part action thriller *Kill Bill* gave new meaning to the phrase "a couple of broads throwing down."[14] In *Kill Bill Vol. 1* (2003) stuntwomen Zoe Bell (doubling Uma Thurman) and Angela Meryl (doubling Vivica A. Fox) have a violent and deadly fight inside a house. Thurman plays the bride who was shot at her wedding by Bill's assassination squad. Once she recovers, she seeks revenge and begins with former squad member Vernita (Fox). Combat starts the moment Vernita opens the door of her pretty suburban home. Their ferocious battle wrecks the living room, rages into the kitchen, and returns to the living room—until Vernita's young daughter comes home. Instantly, both women hide their weapons and turn into Mom and Mom's friend. Murder takes a sedate time-out. The child goes upstairs, and the two enemies adjourn to the kitchen for coffee. Their chatty tone seems normal—until Vernita takes a cereal box from the cupboard, reaches inside it, and fires the hidden pistol at the bride. She misses, and instantly the bride flings a knife into Vernita's chest.[15]

For Angela Meryl, who began doing stunts in the 1990s, that fight was "the ultimate experience."[16] To prepare, she trained with Master Wu-Ping doing what she loves best: all-out action. "I had to jump backward over a couch into a glass coffee table, which was blown about 12 inches before I hit it. Of course, you have your eyes closed, but your equilibrium is a little off since you don't know exactly when you're going to hit it. If you don't land right you can break your neck."[17]

In *Kill Bill Vol. 2* (2004) New Zealander Zoe Bell took part in another rugged and inspired fight—this time with Monica Staggs, a gymnast and dancer from Arkansas. She was a college student when she played a maid

Monica Staggs, from raging stunt fights to stand-up comedy. (Courtesy of Monica Staggs)

in the low-budget film *Shelter*. Stunt coordinator Gary Wayton was having a hard time finding stunt people in Arkansas, and it turned out that Monica was the same size as actress Brenda Bakke. "I was a passenger in a car that goes over an embankment. It required no skill, but it was scary and I had to be brave." That made Monica eligible to join the Screen Actors Guild. "I was trying to get acting roles in little theater. I asked my agent if I should join SAG. 'Oh, no, honey. How much is it, a thousand dollars? You buy yourself a nice dress.' That was the mentality." Monica joined SAG anyway. A few months later the coordinator offered her a job in Los Angeles—falling backward into a creek. "I'm best known for hitting the ground really hard," Monica said. "I found that out in LA. I was a skinny five-nine, and a guy said, 'I want you for this movie because I hear you do the big banger stunts nobody else will do.'" Once she moved to California, she gravitated to a gym because, as a college gymnast, "every gym was like home." The stuntmen there taught her martial arts; she taught them gymnastics. "No one ever said I couldn't do something because I was a woman. They expected me to do the job I was hired to do. I wanted to hit the ground as hard as a guy and make it look just as good." Once, when Monica heard someone say she punched like a ballerina, she felt embarrassed. "My fear of embarrassing myself helped my career," she said. "My dad was an architect, my mother was a teacher. She was strict, she demanded As, so I was performance based, which didn't serve me until I got here. I did whatever a coordinator wanted, trusting they knew more than I did. Later, you may find out you're working for idiots and have to stick up for yourself. Some people back out of a stunt. Even if I'm frightened, I'm more scared of embarrassing myself, and that got me through a lot of terrifying stunts."[18]

Around 2000, Zoe Bell was doubling Lucy Lawless on the TV series *Xena, Warrior Princess* (1998–2001) when she met Jeannie Epper and filmmaker Amanda Micheli.[19] They had teamed up to make a documentary about two stuntwomen of different generations, *Double Dare* (2004).[20] Amanda was "attracted to the idea of women who make a living putting their bodies in danger. Doing crazy things with your body, that's drama right there, and then you put tits on that body, well, it opens up a bunch of other issues!"[21] Zoe, the "wide-eyed newcomer," joined Jeannie, the "seasoned pro," in the documentary, which described their separate stories and how they both carried on the traditions of superwomen heroines. The film included lively comments from Steven Spielberg, Quentin Tarantino, Lynda Carter, and others. "Quentin had all kinds of advice for us," Jeannie said. "He remembers his days working in a video store and wanting to be a moviemaker. He gave us the last $60,000 to finish *Double Dare.*" About the film, Zoe said, "I got to meet Jeannie and Amanda, two stunning women . . . and I got to do *Kill Bill.*"[22]

Monica Staggs called her celebrated cage fight with Zoe in the trailer in *Kill Bill Vol. 2* "a huge brawl with all those gnarly thrasher stunts. We spent about six weeks doing it. I thought I'd broken my ribs and for a year and a half I didn't know I had a compression fracture in my back." She was in tremendous pain but didn't want anyone to know it. Doubling Daryl Hannah as the venomous Elle Driver, Monica wore a black eye patch to match her skin-tight black leather outfit and boots; Zoe, again doubling Uma Thurman, wore white slacks and a blouse and was barefoot. In the movie, Elle has just killed Bill's brother by putting a black mamba in the cash-filled suitcase she has brought to his dilapidated trailer. She gathers up the money, lifts a samurai sword, and opens the door. A pair of naked feet punch her back inside. The bride has found Elle. Having no weapon, the bride uses kicks and punches to prevent Elle from unsheathing her sword. Elle jams the hilt of it into the bride's face and clobbers her with it. The bride rips out a TV antenna and whips it like a rapier, sending Elle crashing into some dishes on the counter. They lock together, inches apart, each holding Elle's sheathed sword. Elle smashes her head into the bride's nose, but the bride fights back with anything she can find—a pole, a curtain rod, a guitar, a can of bacon fat. With murderous kicks and blows, they bounce each other off the walls of the confined space. Then Elle grabs on to a ceiling beam, raises her legs, and sends the bride across the room into a couch; her face is bloody and she is semiconscious. Screaming for vengeance, Elle charges forward and lifts herself into a beautiful killer leap—one leg straight out, one knee bent—as she sails through the air to give the bride the coup de grace. Just in time, the bride rolls off the couch. Elle misses her mark and crashes feet first through the wall and into the bedroom. The bride comes after her, grips her in a choke hold, and rides her down to the floor. Their furious battle goes into overdrive until the bride is knocked out. A triumphant Elle strides down the hall to retrieve her sword. Whipped and groggy, the bride spies a samurai sword in a set of golf clubs, unsheathes it, and leaps into the doorway, renewed. At the end of the short hall, Elle is armed and ready. In classic samurai stance, they rush each other and engage, swords crossed, faces inches apart. The bride jabs two straight fingers into Elle's one good eye. Shrieking, Elle falls to the floor as the ragged, bloody, barefoot bride holds the eyeball between her fingers. She drops it and paces down the hall, passing the hissing black mamba on her way out.[23]

Every fight depicts different characters with different motives, action styles, and weapons of choice. Choreographing or performing a stunt fight is an art, but the argument persists that violent movies (at which Tarantino excels) feed the audience's unwholesome appetite for savagery. But what's a movie without conflict? Some spectators still object to women being punched out or thrashed with a TV antenna, but movies and action are no longer the exclusive terrain of men. For centuries, real-life women have been well acquainted with violence in their homes, on the streets, and in war; they've been raped, beaten, tortured, and murdered. Now, onscreen and off, women do not suffer in silence; they take action. The horrific movie stunt fights described here represent a blend of aggression and femininity, an equal match of strength and skill in combat that is both intimate and lethal as it destroys everything around them in the most satisfying way.

# 15

# Car Stunts

Basically, you stand in the road and get hit by the car!
—*Chrissy Weathersby*

When women began driving cars in the early 1900s, they didn't have educational, financial, employment, or voting rights. However, the heroic female characters in silent movies implied the possibility of very different lives. By 1915, action-oriented women were famous for their driving skills. But when moviemaking became a real business in the 1920s, Hollywood's short-lived egalitarian era bit the dust. Except for glamorous actresses with star power, women were pushed aside. In the decades that followed, stuntwomen performed as swimmers or riders; they did falls and occasionally some fights, but it wasn't until the 1970s that they worked their way back behind the wheel of a stunt car. Today, like their silent movie predecessors, they jump cars over fences, hurtle them into rivers, and do power slides that stop inches from a ravine. They are full-fledged professionals. If something goes wrong, how a stuntwoman adapts to the misadventure reveals a lot about her courage, her skills, and her character.

Tall, blonde Shauna Duggins grew up jumping off cliffs with her dad and her brother. Her mother, a pilot, told her she could do anything. When Shauna got behind the wheel of a car for a stunt in 2002, that maternal reassurance would be tested. "I did a car jump into a lake," Shauna said. "It was to sink down about eighteen feet, and when the pressure equalized, I'd get out." That's what everyone thought, but when the car hit the water, the impact damaged the front end, and the doors and windows didn't open. Shauna couldn't see three inches in front of her in the murky water, and she wasn't sure the five cameras in the car would be able to record anything. "About a minute later I realized, 'I'm going to die in this car.' That's panic, and when it happens, it's good to know you've got what it takes." She pushed the panic aside and went through all the "what-if" plans she'd made in case the stunt went wrong. "Being able to do that comes from survival instincts and from being a competitor when the stakes are high." Plan A: get air. "I had an air tank," she said, "but finding the ten-foot hoop line floating in the dark water was not easy." Plan B: try the door and window again. "You keep going through your plans until you get out. Once I had air, I grabbed the steering wheel, used that and my body weight to press against the door until finally I broke the seal, cracked the door open, and worked my way out." The safety divers were looking for her some distance away, and in fact, no one on land knew what was actually happening beneath the surface. "Dimly on camera, they saw me moving around in the car and felt it was perfect. Only *I* thought I was going to die in that car." That stunt wasn't part of a big movie; ironically, it was for an episode of *Worst Case Scenarios,* a 2002 TV documentary series, intended to show how easy it is to get out of your car if it ends up underwater.

Tracy Keehn Dashnaw, a tough rodeo rider turned stunt driver, had learned the limitations of cables while doing a car stunt in *Cherry 2000* (1987). Years later she was in Canada doubling Kim Basinger in a little horror movie called *Bless the Child* (2000), and that's when Tracy simply insisted on saving her own life.[1] The script called for her to drive a car through a guardrail on a bridge spanning a river. The back wheels were supposed to get stuck, leaving the front of the car hanging over the edge, nose down, 200 feet above the water. Ever careful, Tracy went to the special effects shop with stunt coordinator Matt Birman. "I requested three cables," she explained, "independent of one another, attached to three different parts of the car, and I wanted each cable hooked to different parts of the bridge. Cable doesn't stretch, it can snap. If one failed, we had the other two." She also asked for a test run with the car, but when they finally got to her sequence, the producers wanted to do it right away. When the car was brought out, it had three cables on the places Tracy had specified, but all the cables led through one big ring attached to one part of the bridge. Tracy wanted to reattach the cables and do a test, but it was late, and everyone was in a rush. "I knew the ring would not hold," she said, "so I got in the car, put my foot on it pretty good, going faster than I would have, barreled straight down the bridge, not through the guardrail. The ring snapped!" Tracy had proved her point. "That was pretty sobering for everyone. Even when the pressure is on, you have to stop and say, 'Here's what we need to do.' If I had not, that would have been the end of me. You always need a safety, you always need backup. The next day I wanted five cables for my own peace of mind."

A precision-level driver with twenty-five years of stunt experience, Kym Washington (who doubles Whoopi Goldberg) has only been injured twice. "Flying a car, spinning a car, being in midair—there's nothing like it. In stunts you do things you never thought you'd do. How often do you get the chance to do a reverse 180 in the middle of Wilshire Boulevard and crash into a police car?" It can be fun, but even experienced stunt performers are not immune to accidents or incompetence. On an episode of *Rescue 911* (1989–1996), Kym drove an out-of-control car that was impossible to stop. "I drive into the median, the car goes up and airborne, sails over the oncoming traffic lanes. It's supposed to land on a flatbed truck, a shot that was inserted later by dropping the car from a crane." Kym's car went over the traffic, but it landed nose first on the pavement, crunching the grille and hood. "It caused my torso to contract," she said. "Right after it I was fine, but the next morning I couldn't stand up. They stuck me in a neck brace for four months." The car had not been properly weighted to keep the back end down. Kym said, "On every stunt you have to know what's being done. You have to look out for yourself and never totally trust somebody else."

By 2003, May Boss had fifty years of experience. Before retiring and concentrating on her golf game, she agreed to do one last gag—a car hit on the movie *Hulk*.[2] "They sort of glossed through the stunt," May said. "I wasn't going to drive much, just be hit. They wanted someone my age because the director needed a close-up in the main cameras. They did not tell me I was going to be hit head-on and then back-ended." May went to San Francisco for the big shoot, which was being directed by Ang Lee of *Crouching Tiger, Hidden Dragon* fame. After she was introduced to Lee she went to wardrobe, where she was padded up for the hit. Back in the intersection, the assistant director said, "Now, May, we only have two cars. That means you only get two takes." May wasn't worried. She got into the car, and the director yelled, "Action!" May recalled that after she got moving, "I look up and see a *cable car* is tearing down the hill right at me. 'Oh, man, I'm going to wear the engine in my lap.' I did a header right into it, a real cruncher, and right after that a car rear-ends me—makes an accordion out of me and the car! When they eventually pried me out of the car, Mr. Lee ran up and hugged me. I'd never been hugged by a director, I didn't expect it. He's kind of reserved and such a big name. That was pretty nice."

Donna Evans had eighteen years' experience when she was injured doing an unusual car stunt on *Gloria* (1999). "I broke my nose on that show!" she said. The first shot called for her to swerve off the freeway. The second shot required her to jump the car down a "stairway" constructed of concrete railroad ties embedded in a sloping embankment. "Those stairs looked like they'd been built for the fifty-foot woman," Donna said. A plywood ramp was placed at the top of the embankment, so Donna would have to come in fast to start bumping the car down those ties. At the last minute they decided to add an extra bump on the ramp to increase the lift of the car. "That's when I asked for a shoulder harness," she said, "because I'd be coming off the ramp with force. But they were losing the light. I agreed to go ahead" without the harness. She roared off the ramp and down the embankment, but the car got stuck in one of the railroad ties. Her face slammed into the steering wheel and she broke her nose, but that didn't stop her from finishing the ride. "I got unstuck, kept going down those ties one after another, bang, bang, bang. The blood's running down my nose, and I'm trying to suck it up because a bloody face might ruin the shot." Somehow she got through it, but there was still one more shot to do. The crew told Donna to go to the hospital. "They were going to put in one of the guys," she recalled. "I said, 'I'll finish the shot.' They said, 'You're kidding.' I told them I didn't need my nose to drive."

Like careening cars, motorcycle stunts have been winners since the silent movie era. In 1917 serial heroine Helen Gibson gunned her bike onto a train station platform, went full speed through an open boxcar, and then emerged onto the flatcar of a moving train.[3] Few remember the fearless Helen Gibson today, but Debbie Evans, her sister Donna, and a few other stuntwomen have performed some amazing stunts on motorcycles.

LaFaye Baker is a five-foot-three whirlwind of high spirits and action. Her previous jobs included elementary school teacher and probation officer at a boys' camp facility. One of the few African American stuntwomen, LaFaye cut a career out of the granite of physical danger and racial prejudice. She did falls, car work, and, her favorite, fire burns. Because she had showed the producers footage of her motorcycle stunts, she wound up in

LaFaye Baker, founder of the Diamond in the Raw Action Icon Awards. (Courtesy of LaFaye Baker)

a 1996 music video, *Ready or Not,* doing a stunt that was billed as a "very easy motorcycle jump." On a narrow uphill road in a canyon, she revved the high-powered Enduro dual sports motorcycle, hit a small hidden ramp to gain some height, landed back on the road, and sped off. She did it three times—no problem. On the fourth take she came up the hill and, without warning, met a wall of smoke—an addition no one had bothered to mention. "I couldn't see the ramp. The only thing I recalled about the road ahead was a drop on the left and another on the right of Latigo canyon. I hit the ramp, but I was a little to the left. My chin hit the speedometer. I broke both jaws at the joints and fractured my mandible." She was on the ground, still unaware she'd been hurt. "I could move my arms and legs, but they said blood was coming out of my mouth. I felt something was wrong with my teeth and screamed, 'No more pretty teeth!'" The production was deep in the canyon. Fortunately, they had a helicopter on call, and LaFaye was airlifted to UCLA Hospital. She had a broken nose and facial nerve injuries, and it took ten hours of reconstructive surgery to reset her jaw. Today, she has three screws on each side of her face and a plate in her chin. But that didn't stop her from getting back into the stunt game. "I was like a football player on the injured reserve. I had to reclaim my spot. I'd worked so hard to be a stunt person, I wasn't about to give that up."[4]

To newcomers, driving looks easy and fun, and they clamor to do it. But veterans like Shauna, LaFaye, Donna, and Tracy know better. "Oh, man, it's so much pressure because a lot can go wrong," Donna said. "If you're not a proficient stunt driver, you can literally take out a crew." Only through experience can stunt performers learn to adapt quickly to the inevitable last-minute changes. "You're told it's a simple kick," Donna said, "but soon you're in spike heels, you're at this angle, your foot doesn't really bend that way, but they want it to bend that way. Then they want you to hold a chain saw in one hand and grab the rabid dog with the other. They always complicate everything."

"That's what stunts are!" exclaimed Christine Baur, who started out with the crazy Baxley Bunch. "They tell us, 'You're driving the Ferrari, we only have one, you can't wreck it, but when you get near that cliff, we want you to slide the car sideways and stop two inches from the edge.'" Enter the wardrobe department to add to the stuntwoman's difficulties. In *Hellhole* (1985) Christine rode a 1200 BMW motorcycle, a big touring bike. The stunt coordinator, Sandy Gimpel, had hired six stuntmen and twelve stunt-women—one of the few times there were more women than men. "I'm only five-four," Christine said. "My legs are short, and I had a passenger on the back—a big gal, stuntwoman Laurie Creach. We were in Malibu, riding up hills on a twisty road. I made a big turn, came back down, stopped the bike for a beat, took off again. That was great until wardrobe put me in a tight miniskirt, fishnet stockings, and, I swear, four-inch high heels. That woman said to me, 'Isn't it going to be a fabulous look on the motorcycle? So Malibu!' I stared at her. I couldn't ride a motorcycle in four-inch heels. Naturally, I had to do it anyway. 'So *Malibu?*' Moron. It's like, 'Let's put the actress in lingerie because she'll look so hot when the car hits her!' What is *that* about?"[5]

Hitting a pedestrian is a traditional car stunt that has been refined for decades, but it comes down to this: see the Buick hit the pretty girl in the bikini. It's a thrill with salacious undertones, and it's a much bigger crowd-pleaser than hitting a guy in overalls. Kimberly Shannon Murphy—a tall, blue-eyed blonde who is a gymnast, acrobat, and dancer—did a radically different kind of car hit in the science fiction movie *I Am Legend* (2007).[6] "To do stunts," she said, "you need to be able to go with whatever happens."

Kimberly was playing a pedestrian on the street who is caught in a trap: "I'm in a full harness ready to do a ratchet and be tossed into the air. I lean back, the ratchet yanks me forward and up over the cars. But when the trap springs, it drops a big tarp like a bag over me. I can't see anything. Special effects tested it with a dummy, but they wanted the movement of someone struggling inside the bag." She knew she might get hurt, but she trusted the riggers; otherwise, she would never have done it. "I went over the hood of one car, was thrown into the windshield of a van, breaking the glass, and I couldn't see what was coming at me before it happened. I just had to suck it up and hope for the best. I ended up swinging upside down on a ledge, blind, covered in the tarp." She credits stunt coordinator Vic Armstrong and George Aguilar, who gave Kimberly her start—both of them part of the New York stunt community. "They'd been stuntmen, they know their stuff. They understand what you're going through."

When Kimberly did that wild car hit in *I Am Legend* she had only two years' experience, but she had been a member of Anti-Gravity for longer than that. The celebrated New York group is composed of professional athletes who perform unique combinations of athletics, acrobatics, and aesthetics.[7] Kimberly credits her family for her success: "I wouldn't be nearly as tough had it not been for my dad, a marine in Vietnam. He had four daughters, and in his mind we were all marines. We grew up very hard core. Crying was not allowed. My mother taught me mental toughness." Stuntwomen need that kind of toughness. "Stunt people don't go to work, get our wardrobe, do the stunt, and go home," Kimberly said. "It's a twelve-hour day, and finally at some ungodly hour you throw yourself off the balcony. You need to be tough, you have to be prepared for anything."

"To go against a car," New York stuntman Vince Cupone said, "you're going head-to-head with 2,000 pounds of metal. It doesn't give too much. When a stunt guy does that, he's well padded. But that's just for the hit itself. Even if a woman without pads applies perfect technique going into a car and gets up on the hood right, she still has to deal with hitting that windshield, and then she's going for a ride—up and over the windshield, spinning in the air, and she's going to land where she's going to land. At that point, technique doesn't matter. You're simply an object flying in the air. When you come back to the ground and you're not padded, that's the scary moment because the ground doesn't give either."[8]

A conventional pedestrian hit involves a stunt person and a car. But like everything else in stunts, each hit is different. When Nancy Thurston was hired to do a car hit on the TV series *Nash Bridges* (1996–2001), the first question she asked was, who's driving the car? "You want someone with experience, who maintains the speed, someone like Dwayne McGee. The stunt coordinator, Merritt Yohnka, said I'd be doubling a counselor and I could pad up. That's rare." Nancy got to the set early so that she and the coordinator could look at the car, a newer Mustang without a hood ornament. Her previous car hits had been "accidents"—the driver slams on the brakes and the pedestrian spins off to the right, left, or front. "I asked [the coordinator] if he needed me to go off a certain way. He said, 'Oh, no, you go over the whole car, it's not stopping.' . . . That stunt was a new one for me." Nancy and stunt driver Dwayne McGee (*Glory, Zoolander*) practiced at different speeds and settled on fifteen miles per hour, even though she had once cracked a windshield doing a near miss at eleven miles an hour. In the scene in question, the counselor (Nancy) and a boy are walking across a pier. The bad guys in the car intend to run over the boy, but he jumps out of the way, and they hit the counselor instead. Dwayne came toward Nancy at a steady speed; she got up on the car, hit the windshield, went over the roof, and flipped off the back. "How you get off the car is different every time," she said. "It depends on the driver holding his speed or if your clothes catch on something. On this one, having aerial awareness saved my life. When I came off the back end, my head was low, my feet were high. I was coming to the ground fast, but I rolled just right and landed. After they yell 'Cut,' they ask, 'Are you okay?' and you do a thumbs-up. Instead of jumping up, I lay there a moment, fully aware my gymnastics had saved me. Some things you don't mind doing over—not car hits."

"Basically, you stand in the road and get hit by the car," Chrissy Weathersby said brightly. "I didn't say that to my mom, and anyway, I didn't know what to expect. Jeannie Epper gave me a bunch of pointers, but you can't practice a car hit. You just do it." Chrissy did her first car hit in *The Brave One* (2007), where she doubled Zoe Kravitz (playing Chloe), who had just been rescued from a pimp by Jodie Foster (playing Erica). As the two women walk down the middle of the street, the enraged pimp barrels after them in his car. Erica fires off a few shots and kills the driver; the car veers, Chloe looks back, and bam! The car hits her. Chrissy described a basic car hit: you "go up on the hood, hit the windshield, and the momentum throws you off the side or the back." The secret, Chrissy said, is that "the car doesn't really hit you, because at the last second you jump up on

The exuberant Chrissy Weathersby Ball. (Courtesy of Michael Helms)

the hood. If you don't, the car can take you under it. If you make your move too early you have egg on your face—it looks like you jumped on the car, not like it hit you."[9]

That same year, Chrissy felt lucky to work on *Grindhouse,* writer-director Quentin Tarantino's action ode to stunts of the 1970s consisting of two story-connected features titled *Planet Terror* and *Death Proof.* "He [Tarantino] understands it's hard for women and even harder for minority women to get experience," she said. He also understands stunts. In the films, Jeff Dashnaw, Terry Leonard, Buddy Joe Hooker, and others represent different generations of stuntmen who had designed or performed "old-school," 1970s-style fights and car chases.[10] Zoe Bell and Tracy Keehn Dashnaw serve up a remarkable stunt sequence in *Death Proof,* with Tracy using her considerable driving skills to protect Zoe, who is lashed to the hood of a white 1970 Dodge Challenger. "Zoe was vulnerable out there," Tracy said, "especially when she was hanging onto the front grille or the windshield wipers. I felt very mother-hennish." At times, Zoe's struggles

*Above:* Buddy Joe Hooker, Quentin Tarantino, and Tracy Keehn Dashnaw. *Below:* The car chase sequence in *Deathproof* (2007). (Courtesy of Tracy Dashnaw)

on the hood kept Tracy from "really seeing ahead as I raced down the road." Chasing the Challenger is the mean, squirrelly Stuntman Mike (played by Kurt Russell, doubled by Hooker), who uses his "black charger," a Chevy Nova, to assault the women's car. He sideswipes it, rear-ends it—it's all sport to him. But when he slams into the Challenger, Zoe flies off the hood and into a field. Then the fun's over, but not for Tracy's character, Kim. She shoots Stuntman Mike in the arm; he dives into his car and takes off. Roles reversed, the women chase after him with Zoe riding post, straddling the window. He runs them off the road, they run him off the road; they rear-end him and then T-bone him. His car flips over. They drag him and the steering wheel he's clinging to out of the car and take turns punching him, but he remains standing until Zoe delivers the kick that finally takes him down. It's brutal, but also very satisfying; their onscreen revenge is the perfect payback.[11]

The *Grindhouse* features, jammed with 1970s-style stunts, were released a decade after movie gags had become "new school" and stacked with visual effects. But some traditions never die. To figure out how a car sequence will go down, stunt drivers and coordinators still hunch over a table and play out the sequence with little toy cars. The toy cars were brought out for the giant production of *The Matrix Reloaded* (2003). "There were seventy stunt guys and four or five girls," said Annie Ellis, and she was one of them.[12] She spent four months on a naval air base on Alameda Island, near Oakland, California, where they had built a long freeway set with eighteen-foot walls for the car sequences. On a film that big, planning and filming the action sequences is a huge undertaking that requires juggling thousands of different pieces. Annie began to make her maps. "I'm a continuity freak," she said. "The second units kept asking me, 'Scene 56A—what car was I in? Which way were we going?' Let's say a car is jumped off a bridge, goes with traffic, turns around and goes against traffic. Two months later on the freeway set no one remembers which car they were in. I did maps—color or make of car and the drivers' initials. Basically, it's about the color. If the white van is next to the hero car in a certain spot and weeks later they want the actors in the hero car to look back, a white van should be there. Soon script supervisors on both second units are calling about the cars in a scene. I went to my maps: 'Red car here, blue car here, limo there.' I was one of the stuntwomen; I wasn't paid to do maps. It should be part of continuity or coordinating. It should be a whole new job."

Debbie Evans was on that freeway set doing tour-de-force car and motorcycle work in traffic and doubling Carrie-Anne Moss (as Trinity), particularly in the fourteen-minute chase sequence.[13] "Our directors, especially Andy Wachowski, were so excited about what we were doing," Debbie said. "That meant the world to us because stunt people don't get paid all that we should, considering the risks involved. The work was quite intense and it took weeks." In one scene, with a passenger on the back, Debbie gunned her Ducati motorbike, going full out as she dodged cars and a semi that almost creamed her. "I like all the physical stuff," Debbie said. "I'm a perfectionist. I was very hard on myself when I started out, but I find a lot of people who really excel are perfectionists, especially in the beginning. I constantly tried to learn new skills and analyze them. A lot of

Debbie Evans won her third World Stunt Award, for best overall stunt by a stunt-woman, for *The Matrix Reloaded* (2003). (Courtesy of Debbie Evans)

people on the set chat or read a book and they're not tuned in to what's going on. I want to know where's my car, how we're doing this as safely as possible, what's going on in the scene and the story line behind it. Is the actress mad, sad, glad? I need to know how to play the role." Even in a car, a stunt double is visible, and how she drives tells a story. "Is she drunk? How drunk? I have to know how much weaving to do. Is she a good driver or not? You can do all kinds of subtle things with your body," Debbie explained, "because you're performing as the character whether you're doing a physical stunt or a vehicular stunt."[14]

Whether a gag involves a fall, a fight, or a car, it usually revolves around a character at a pivotal moment. When watching the action onscreen, it's easy to forget that the true art of stunt doubling is giving a performance on two very different levels: physically doing the stunt *and* acting the part. Stunt players have done both simultaneously for more than a hundred years.[15] Doubling hasn't changed much, but moviemaking has changed radically in the last twenty years. A digital revolution is under way, and the consequences for stunt people seem to be both a gift and a curse. As Terry Clotiaux, the visual effects producer of *The Matrix Reloaded,* pointed out, "Chad Stahelski, an accomplished stuntman, doubled Keanu Reeves. He works regularly because Keanu is continually doing action films, so there's likely to always be some stunt work. Everything else, or what movies may look like in fifty years, that's a huge question mark in my mind."

IV

# The Digital Age

*1995–2010*

# 16

# Computer-Generated Imagery and the Future of Stunt Work

It's a new world of visual effects and CGI. It's the old world of
stunt coordinators—not many dames.

—*Anonymous stuntwoman*

A veteran in the field of visual effects, Terry Clotiaux was part of the biggest change in the movies. Early on, he had worked with Douglas Trumbull,
the visual effects pioneer of *2001: A Space Odyssey* (1968) and *Blade
Runner* (1982). "The process Doug was developing was seminal," Terry
said. "He was and is always pushing the envelope."[1] In 1975, George Lucas
founded Industrial Light and Magic to create special effects for *Star Wars*
(1977). When the digital revolution hit in the mid-1990s, moviemaking
entered a mysterious and disconcerting new realm. "Eighty thousand dollar optical printers became boat anchors," Terry said. He had just been
hired as the visual effects producer of Roland Emmerich's *Independence
Day* (1996). "For me, it was right time, right place, but as I recall, nobody
else wanted the job because *Independence Day* had already started, and it
was in trouble." Later, Terry worked on *Godzilla* (1998) with the same
director. "It was the transition period in the industry between digital and
physically filming models we'd created. There was not a lot of confidence
about what we would be able to do digitally, so we were kind of hedging
our bets. For instance, we shot a giant hydraulically controlled scale model
of the Godzilla torso. I think it's in the movie for three seconds."

Terry explained the difference between special effects and visual effects: "When you blow up a car on a movie set, it's called special effects," he said. "When you blow up a miniature car on another stage, it's called visual effects. The special effects department serves production while you're filming the movie. Those scenes are generally captured by the production camera—first unit or second unit or sometimes by a special effects unit that's picking up elements to be used later for visual effects. When a crew films a snowy Boston city street, special effects provides fake snow on the ground and the snowflakes falling from the sky. If you build a miniature of that same street to create the same effect, we'd shoot it as a miniature—that's visual effects, and it's a postproduction process."

As visual effects became a larger part of filmmaking, special effects became a smaller part. This had an impact on stunt work because stunt coordinators have always worked closely with special effects departments. Terry said, "In the past, special effects would blow up a building in full scale, filmed by the second unit. We don't even do that in miniature anymore, we create it fully in CG—computer graphics. The explosion would be CG, the debris would be CG. Everything is CG." One result of all these technological innovations has been to enhance stunts. "Visual effects makes it possible for the stunt world to pull off much more complicated action," Terry said, "because in postproduction we're able to hide how a stunt's done, such as paint out the wires and rigs that fly stunt performers around. That would have been very difficult if not impossible before." He gave an example: "For the battle between the characters Neo and Agent Smith in *The Matrix Revolutions* in 2003, the actors are able to do twists and turns, and then we paint out wires and even replace materials like cloth. In some cases, when a stunt is considered too dangerous for the actor and the stunt person, we create what we call digital stunt doubles—digital humans to do the gags. The stunt people are bypassed altogether. We can fly actors without wires by making them digital, but it depends on how close an actor is to the camera and if an actor's face must be seen. As good as the digital work is, it's still expensive to get it to look as good as the real deal. Today, most movies use a digital stunt double somewhere in it."

Digital effects can also make stunt work safer. For instance, stunt people don't have to do a full burn when visual effects can torch a character in postproduction. "With computer tools we can make scenes more realistic than we could before," Terry explained. "We can animate the progressive destruction of a fire, we can show the face of an actor on fire—if you have the time and the money." Stuntwoman Jeannie Epper's son Richard did stunts on *Bad Boys II* (2003). She said, "They drove cars off a transport carrier, turned cars over, and exploded them in flames using CGI [computer-generated imagery] for safety because at times it can keep people alive. That's genius. None of us really want to get killed. We're not that dumb."

At the same time, the use of digital effects decreases job opportunities for stunt performers, and women are often the first to feel the impact. "It may not exist as a career in the future," said stunt coordinator Mary Albee. "In the past, a very tight group ran stunts. Now the film industry is international, more of it's done by computer than by human beings, and for stunt people it's more difficult to make a living."

Motion capture is the process of using sensors attached to an actor's body to record his or her movement, style, and even facial expressions. The data collected by the sensors are then used to create digital models that produce animated characters that require no human presence—computer-generated characters. Not even the environment is real: often the action is recorded in a studio against a green screen, and the backgrounds are inserted later. This is a direct threat to the unique, real-world nature of stunt work, and some stunt people won't accept lower-paying motion-capture work. "Producers want you to do a commercial online for $100 a day, no residuals," said stuntwoman Sophia Crawford, who learned her bold fighting style in Hong Kong. "I don't recall what I was paid for my first motion-capture job, but they put what you do into a database. You're not performing falls or acrobatics for that one show; your work becomes part of many shows. They make millions. You earn nothing."

A more subtle consequence of the digital revolution is its effect on a film's credibility, which is often an essential component of its power. What if a CG heroine fights off five men with swords and leaps out a window? Is her life really at risk? "Audiences are savvy," Sophia said. "They look forward to seeing real stunt people doing real stunts. They know computer-generated characters are not real, so there's no risk in the fight or the fall. Without risk, where's the thrill? It's like animation; it takes away the excitement." That thrill has been the engine of the movies since the nickelodeon days.

Sophia Crawford and Shauna Duggins worked on *G.I. Joe* (2009). It was "a fantastic experience," Sophia said, "but a lot of action was CG—computer generated. We'd begin a stunt, the CG director would say, 'Let's do a lighting reference for CG characters who are going to fly around.'

There goes our stunt adjustment. We did lots of action in front of blue screens. The guilds have no jurisdiction over anything used online. Our residuals make a huge financial difference to us. If those disappear, a lot of careers will end."

But there may be hope. "Most things in this great culture of ours are money driven," observed Terry Clotiaux. "Therefore, if it's cheaper and easier, why not put an actor or stunt person in there to do the action on camera? There will always be the need for stunts. The wirework has lasted this long because now we can see the actors doing it. The kung fu movies gave us a wire look that appealed to filmmakers and to audiences. On *Crouching Tiger, Hidden Dragon,* the people flying in the canyon are clearly on wires, but seeing that whole floaty thing as they flew about was a fantasy world and we were willing to suspend our disbelief. Wirework may stay in movies and stunts because it's more economical, and in post we're better at the cleanup, painting out the wires and rigs needed to do those stunts."

Many stunt performers, especially women, feel like they're being carried along by a surge of change that can't be stopped. In recent years, Nancy Thurston has done fewer high falls. "For a forty-foot fall on *Charmed,* we did it hanging on a wire, fell in front of the green screen, they put the plate of the building behind it, [and] got rid of the wire. I'm happy to do wirework, but it's a bummer to lose high falls, and we get a lower adjustment. That's where technology is going, green screen, wirework, and CGI." That's true, but it's hard to ignore the other side of the issue: "These effects have opened a new world. You can go wherever your imagination takes you," reported stunt coordinator and second-unit director Danny Aiello III. "With CG we can do bigger stunts, it makes us rethink stunts we've done." But he also believed that stunt people would always be needed.

"In some ways," Terry Clotiaux added, "all phases of filmmaking have become more [of] a postproduction process. In visual effects, because we can manipulate images and create moments onscreen, directors will postpone their decisions as long as they can, embrace the extension of the process into postproduction. Moviemaking today is a director's dream, because if he or she can imagine a scene and has the time and the money, we can do it. The only challenge to filmmakers' imagination is not the technology but the kind of money they have. *Benjamin Button* [2008] is a perfect example. Years ago, our Holy Grail was to create a fully digital human actor that could withstand up-close scrutiny and give a performance. We have crossed the uncanny valley. That's where we are today." The digitally generated tiger in *The Life of Pi* (2012) is another example of how new visual effects technology can create scenes in which a real actor appears to be in genuine danger but is actually totally safe.

The fate and future of stunt work as we know it may depend on gags that can be done more cheaply by stunt players doubling actors or on the new generation of low-budget productions distributed online. Whatever new methods emerge, stunt coordinators will be a significant part of the process. The question is, will there be more female stunt coordinators in the twenty-first century? When the danger to stunt performers becomes more benignly digital, will that make stunt work less macho?

Today, when scripts call for stunts, women—not men in wigs—double the actresses.[2] Without a doubt, times are better when a stuntwoman with years of experience can say, "Being a woman hasn't affected my career at all." Tall, sleek Shawnna Thibodeau has done falls, fights, and stunt driving from *Law & Order* in 1990 to *The Dark Knight Rises* in 2012. She enjoyed stunt-coordinating some music videos and a movie called *The Clique* (2008), but she's ambivalent about doing more of it. "I don't want to watch people playing basketball—I want to play! At the same time, I want to keep my options open. When they're older, many men coordinate, but you don't see any older women coordinating. Those women are experienced, they're ready, and it hasn't been easy for them."

Not everyone wants to stunt-coordinate, and not everyone can handle it. The job was already complicated before digital effects came along. Coordinators are the link between stunt players and directors and producers; they are the link to special and visual effects. They need political and management skills as well as current technical knowledge. The few women who regularly stunt-coordinate in the United States began their careers in the 1990s. For Canadian Melissa Stubbs, *Double Jeopardy* (1999) was her first coordinating job in the States. "Second-unit director Glen Randall helped make that happen for me," Melissa said. "As a Canadian, I had to apply for a work visa. You or the production company must prove to U.S. immigration that you are tops in your field. That is quite difficult, since there are many talented stunt performers and coordinators in the U.S. It certainly wasn't easy for a female coordinator from Canada, and normally it's almost impossible to be granted entry into the U.S." After obtaining four visas over ten years, Melissa applied for citizenship.[3]

Melissa Stubbs, assistant stunt coordinator for *The Last Samurai* (2003). (Courtesy of Melissa Stubbs)

During that time, Melissa trained with Nick Powell (*Gladiator, Braveheart*), whom she called "the best fight choreographer in the world." In 2002 Powell was preparing to work on *The Last Samurai;* he didn't know who the stars were going to be, but he asked Melissa to be assistant stunt coordinator. "I had no idea the scale of that film once Tom Cruise signed on," she said. "I began a nine-month journey with hundreds of Japanese men, fighting. Here I am, a stunt coordinator, this young blonde woman shouting at them, and in their minds, they're real samurai. I had fifty men on charging horses and I'm yelling, 'You've got to stay behind Tom Cruise! He wins the race!' Or I had to say, 'You can't control your horse. Sorry, you're not in the charge.' It dishonored them, but they all were very respectful to me. Quite an adventure, that one."

Melissa's skills are widely acknowledged, but she, too, has faced an uphill battle to be hired. "I walk into an interview with two guys, I have a better plan, more experience, and as soon as we're in the room, I can feel it. The producers and the director wonder, 'How can she possibly know what she's doing? Is she better than this six-one, forty-year-old guy that looks like a stunt coordinator?' Basically, it's playing a role. Guys with less experience get the job because it's perceived [that] stunt coordinators are strong male figures." You are what you are perceived to be.

While working on *New York Minute* (2004), Melissa hired thirteen stuntwomen, including Jennifer Lamb, Kym Washington, Angela Meryl, Shawnna Thibodeau, and Alison Reid from Canada.[4] One car-chase sequence in the movie required thirty drivers. Director Dennie Gordon (*30 Rock* [2006–2013]) "was great at comedy and with actors," Melissa said, "but not familiar with action, so I wrote the car chase." When Warner Bros. and the production company, DiNovi Pictures, wanted a big-name second-unit director, Melissa recommended Conrad Palmisano, who had hired her for *Carpool* (1996).[5] In the end, Palmisano was unavailable, but he returned the favor and suggested that Melissa direct the second unit. That was an important break. "We closed off Fifth Avenue in Manhattan," she said. "I'd storyboarded all the beats, like the guy on the bike with one

Stunt coordinator on *Terminator Genisys* (2015), Melissa Stubbs plays the role of a soldier from the future. (Courtesy of Melissa Stubbs)

of the Olsen twins, Mary-Kate or Ashley, when the bicycle rides over the top of the cars. *New York Minute* was my big introduction to second-unit directing." Conrad recalled, admiringly: "All those people in the car sequence, [and] Melissa's out there [saying], 'I want it to go farther. Can they go faster? Get it sideways?' She's fantastic. When she isn't working, she's training, taking editing or directing classes. She is a true stuntwoman. There were times that a stuntwoman had to hand the wig to a guy to roll a car over. Those days are long gone."

Other obstacles remain, but despite the odds, Shauna Duggins is a stunt coordinator and second-unit director.[6] Doubling actress Jennifer Garner on *Alias* (2001–2006) boosted her career, and in 2005 Duggins began to stunt-coordinate the show. One stunt sequence in an episode titled "Reprisal" illustrates how much stunts were changing. The gag begins when Sydney (Jennifer Garner) stops her new Jaguar at a guard gate and a huge crane seizes the Jag, lifting it 200 feet into the air. "The crane is supposed to be magnetized," Shauna said. "The bad guys want her to talk; if she doesn't, they'll drop the car." Newcomer Stacey Carino, doubling actress Rachel Nichols, is in the trunk of the car. She knocks out the paneling and crawls into the backseat. Jennifer grabs her hand, reaches through the sunroof, and sticks a James Bond–type gadget to the magnet, which allows both women to lift safely out of the sunroof as the car falls away from them. "That's the look they wanted," Shauna said: "a brand new Jag falls 200 feet to the concrete, leaving the girls dangling from a cable." As stunt coordinator, it was Shauna's job to make that happen. "The challenge was . . . getting them safely through the sunroof. I wanted to cut off the roof of the car and have it drop as the girls grabbed the cable, but they wanted to shoot from above and needed to see them emerge from the sunroof. The sequence had to be done in sections." Shauna knew that the best coordinators rely on teamwork and aren't afraid to ask for ideas. "I talked to my riggers, I talked with stunt coordinators I respected, and we came up with the idea." She explained, "For the shot of the girls hanging from the cable, we ratcheted them off the roof of the car and tipped the camera. It looked just like the car fell away from the actresses, who, for close-ups, were hanging about fifty feet on a stage in front of the green screen. After, in postproduction, they were hanging against a background of shipping cranes." For other shots of the car dropping away, Shauna and Stacey were really hanging from the crane, 200 feet up, on a descender linked to a rig that controlled their movement up and down. The car was on a separate special

Stacey Carino, making it work out.
(Courtesy of Stacey Carino)

effects rig. In 2006 Shauna became the first woman nominated for an Emmy as best stunt coordinator for this episode of *Alias*.[7]

The stuntwoman in the trunk of the Jag, Stacey Carino, had only two years' experience at the time. She had been a competitive gymnast and a teacher in Cleveland, Ohio, until she took a ski trip with friends. She didn't know how to ski, so she climbed to the top of the hill and then fell all the way down. One of her friends said she should go into stunts. Stacey looked it up on the Internet and found a stunt school in Seattle that operated in the summer—three weeks of spinning cars, climbing rocks, and learning how to fight and fall off horses. Then Stacey moved to Hollywood and got to hang from a crane.[8] After that, she worked on a TV series that was a standout for women behind the camera: *Crossing Jordan* (2001–2007).

Although the power of stunt coordinators stems from their ability to hire, they often have a lot to teach rookie stunt players. Mary Albee, a stunt coordinator and second-unit director since the 1990s, has employed many people, among them stuntwomen Stacey Carino and Luci Romberg on *Crossing Jordan*.[9] Both said it was awesome to work for Mary. Luci was very tense and didn't want to screw up. "It was one of my first jobs," she said. "I had to get shot and fall down, but I was so anxious. Mary was mak-

Luci Romberg's stunt work led her to the art of freerunning. (Courtesy of Brady Romberg)

ing fun of me like, 'Are you nervous?' so then I learned to relax a little more." One day, Stacey forgot to bring her stunt bag to the set. "Mary really drilled me," she said. "She scared the crap out of me. We laugh about it now. I realized she was looking out for me to make sure I was prepared." Luci was amazed at how few female stunt coordinators there are. "Jill Brown and Mary are the only ones I've worked for—and that's crazy!"

Whether that number will increase is anyone's guess. Will Luci or Stacey become coordinators? Maybe—if they want it enough. Luci certainly showed her determination at an early age. As a three-year-old, she decided to climb a neighbor's fence. She was halfway up when the woman next door rushed over to her and cried, "Little girl, let me help you!" Luci said, "I don't need help. I'm tough." Her parents were college athletes, and she grew up playing sports with her brother and sister. Luci was a champion gymnast at Texas Women's University when a former teammate, stuntwoman Natascha Hopkins, talked her into trying stunt work.[10] On January 1, 2005, Luci's mother drove her from their home in Colorado to California. Her first real stunt was doubling an elderly woman as a tractor-trailer going thirty miles an hour jackknifed. Luci and stuntwoman Jennifer Caputo did a barrel roll under the semi. "We hugged the ground, rolled together, and, yes, we did it five times."[11]

Female coordinators may become more common in the future, but hardened stuntwomen are skeptical. One with twenty years' experience snapped, "Someday I'm going to coordinate a show and hire thirty-eight girls and two guys." Thirty-year veteran Annie Ellis said, "We want a fair shake at stunt-coordinating. Women are camera operators, grips, producers—women, women, women! They've smashed through that glass ceiling. But in stunts we have not."[12]

Mary Albee, Jill Brown, Shauna Duggins, and Melissa Stubbs have regularly been hired to stunt-coordinate or direct the second unit on TV series and films. Since the late 1980s, it is estimated that only about twenty to thirty other women have stunt-coordinated. The reasons are both simple and complicated.

In 2008 SAG listed 8,079 stunt people; only 1,499—less than 19 percent—were female. It's still an old boys' network in which talented stuntmen are mentored and trained; talented stuntwomen usually are not. Thus, the typical stunt coordinator is a six-foot-one, forty-year-old guy, not a five-foot-six blonde. In addition, the longtime hiring system of the stunt business remains intact. Hiring often involves a series of reciprocal favors. For example, thirty people are needed for a nondescript (ND) scene of a scuffle; the coordinator confers with the director and hires the stuntmen he trusts, who are often the same guys he owes favors to. The power to hire determines the distribution of work; it is the currency of the business. When a hundred women, not four or ten, have the power to hire, to reciprocate, to be part of the chain, then the players in the system will begin to change. "Because we don't coordinate many shows," one stuntwoman said, "we're not hiring and we can't say, 'I'll hire you on this movie, because you hired me on that one.' This industry is unique. You're the boss today; tomorrow you work for the person you hired yesterday. When only a few women are the boss, it's hard to return that favor."

A lot of the reciprocal hiring by coordinators involves the large category of stunts called nondescript, which would seem to encourage or even require the use of female and minority stunt performers. But a few years ago, a stuntwoman and a friend were in New Orleans when they came across a film crew preparing to shoot a chase scene of a bus driving erratically and sliding down a street. She was delighted to see about thirty old friends on the public bus, stuntmen and coordinators she knew in Los Angeles. But her friend was shocked because, in his experience, most people riding buses in New Orleans are not white men. "There were two black guys, an Asian guy, and a couple of minority women," she said, "but it didn't represent a true picture of bus riders in a southern city."

One stuntwoman analogized the progress in civil rights—or the lack thereof—to a pendulum, swinging from bad to better to worse. She thinks sex discrimination and racism are "at an all-time high, and I have thirty years in this business."

"The Screen Actors Guild could do more to help," said Annie Ellis. "Our SAG contract with the producers states that people in a crowd must reflect 'the American Scene,' a variety of men and women, African Americans, Asians, Hispanics. Then, if you look up 'minority groups,' which one leads the list? Women! I've tried to get ND work, but the coordinators said there's nothing for me because 'it's an army thing.' Well, it happens that a lot of women are in the army! They're in the police force! There are women in SWAT! Coordinators should be forced to hire more women and minorities."

Resistance to hiring women for ND work is still an active attitude. When a scene in *Alias* needed ten guards, Shauna Duggins had to fight the same battle that "great stunt coordinators like Gregg Smrz and Jeff Habberstad had fought because most directors, producers, and coordinators still want the guards to be men. For a scene without guards, like [one with] six ND club-goers, we'd ask for four women and two men. In other crowd scenes, I'd say, 'I want to ratchet the girl and she'll hit the deck in her little skirt and high heels!' When a girl takes a hit in a crowd scene, it has impact." But, she added, a lot of men don't like to see a woman take a hit like that.

To explain the resistance to giving ND work to women, just follow the money. "Nondescript work really supports the men," one stuntwoman said. In 2013 the SAG minimum daily rate was $859. On a two-day job for three people to stage a fight on a broken-down truck, each will earn $1,718, plus health and pension benefits. The work brings other advantages, too. Rookies gain experience from every stunt they do, and they can learn from the older stunt performers they work with. In addition, they can make contacts, which are crucial to freelancers—and all stunt people are freelancers. To stunt players, hanging out all day in an ND crowd and getting to know the stunt coordinators is as important as schmoozing at dinner parties is to writers and directors. That's where the deals are made.

The crowd work on the film *Titanic* (1997) was an exception. "That was the first and last time I worked with many ND stuntwomen," said high-fall expert Nancy Thurston. "Women from the Czech Republic, Hungary, England, Spain, South Africa, and the U.S. were jumping off the side of the ship. One great movie for women on ND work—out of how many?"

Jadie David nailed the consequences when most nondescript work goes to men: "They're the ones who will get the most experience, and that experience is what qualifies them for the next job." Because ND scenes often involve people in a car or a crowd, it's very hard to identify anyone by gender—it's just a mass of bodies in a huge blur of action. "That's how people get away with paint-downs and men doubling women," Jadie said. In her career, Jadie has dealt with all the roadblocks to equal employment, and once she joined the fray, there was no way to stop. "If you didn't participate you were going to be left out anyway, so you had to jump in, and it wasn't all about *you* getting more work, it was about helping make things better for everybody."

Like sexism in the stunt business, race is still an issue with muscle. In 1991, of the more than 4,500 male stunt performers, 4,016 were Caucasian and 277 were African American.[13] In 1994 Jadie David and stuntman Marvin Walters cofounded the Alliance for Stunt Performers of Color, a subcommittee of SAG's Equal Employment Opportunity Committee. The group addressed the "underemployment problems" of all ethnic minorities. It also compiled statistics showing that some studios and independent production companies had been "engaging in unfair hiring practices . . . [such as] men stunt doubling for women."[14]

Five years later, in September 1999, Walters charged film and television producers with a continuing "pattern of discrimination." He said, "When you have paint-downs, you're taking jobs away from African Americans." The alliance wanted SAG to "face the issue" and enforce its nondiscrimination clause. That summer, SAG members filed a dozen complaints about paint-downs. "Underemployment among minority stunt workers is a 'huge issue,'" said SAG spokeswoman Katherine Moore. 'Only about 6% of stunt work last year [1998] went to African Americans, compared to about 80% for whites."[15] For women of color, who faced gender discrimination as well, the impact was much greater.[16]

Stuntwoman Chrissy Weathersby Ball hadn't experienced many race-related problems—until she moved to Los Angeles in 2000. "It is humbling and very hard to watch someone painted down in front of you," she said. "Sometimes it is necessary, but usually it isn't. That's the golden question we all struggle with." At first, she agonized about it. Should she protest? "I did my job, but it was very frustrating." Her ninety-five-year-old grandmother, who had lived through segregation, told Chrissy to focus on her work; the rest would evolve and change. "My grandmother was the first African American public school teacher to get a contract in the state of Colorado. I appreciate my opportunities more because many were not there for my grandmother."[17]

Along with race and gender discrimination comes the issue of sexual harassment. "If more women coordinated shows," Lynn Salvatori said, "men wouldn't have the power to get away with that, and women wouldn't have to depend on those guys for jobs." Sexual harassment is not as rampant today as it once was, but it's still an issue. Not long ago, Lynn heard from some women who "were very upset about a guy who insisted they try on harnesses. He made them strip to their underwear, saying, 'I have to see how it fits under the clothes for wirework.' They don't officially report it because anyone who talks of sexual harassment can get blackballed."

Happily, women's attitudes—and some men's—have changed. "Now it's about you handling it yourself," said Sandra Lee Gimpel, a stunt coordinator and second-unit director since 1980. "It's the way you conduct yourself, the way you look at them. They back down fast. I told a guy, 'You don't want to mess with me.' You want that message to get around because guys tell other guys, 'Don't mess with her. She's a fourth-degree black belt.' And I can take them down."

One reason for the scarcity of female stunt coordinators has nothing to do with the system: mothers with small children can't work eighteen-hour days on location for three weeks. Donna Evans, winner of two World Stunt Awards, has young children.[18] "The challenge of stunt-coordinating sparks my creative side in a different way than stunts," Donna said. She coordinated the TV series *Freaks and Geeks* (1999) because "a brilliant producer thought the moms [of the teenaged actors] would feel better if a mom set up the stunts for the kids and made sure no one was hurt. Stunt-coordinating is time-intensive; they always give you rewrites at the last minute, you're away a lot, and I had to make a choice. My career is on hold until my children are older. By then, the window of opportunity may have closed—but maybe not!"

Women everywhere balance motherhood and work, but most jobs

Nicole Callender, looking forward to making more changes. (Courtesy of Nicole Callender)

don't require them to jump off a building lit up like a torch. After performing a stunt like that, stuntwomen go home and make dinner. For Nicole Callender, balancing her roles as stuntwoman, wife, and mom is like "moving mountains on a daily basis to make it all happen. When I started to work I was amazed at the attitudes about wives and mothers. There's a taboo about refusing a job just because you had a baby, and there are assumptions, like, 'You had a baby so you're not coming back.' I was on *Strangers with Candy* [2005] eight weeks after a C-section. Nor do they want to hear, 'Let me check with my babysitter.' I know it's better for women today. I also think you have to make it that way."

"Women need both careers and family," Debbie Evans said. "When I got married, the guys said, 'Marriage and this business don't work.' I said, 'Yeah, maybe for *you*.' My husband and I have been married twenty-five years. Then they said, 'When you have kids, you won't work anymore.' I had kids, and guess what? I still worked! As I get older I guess I'll hear my career's over. We'll see about that. I love passing those barriers they set."[19]

Zeal is both admirable and necessary when the obstacles are erected by those in your own camp. One long-standing issue is that women often don't hire other women. That subject came up in a 1993 interview of stuntwomen Jeannie Epper and Linda Fetters-Howard. "Look at *Thelma and Louise*," Jeannie demanded. "That was about women, but they had a male stunt coordinator." Linda cited *A League of Their Own* (1992), directed by Penny Marshall. "You had, basically, an entire female cast," she said. "She [Marshall] hired a guy."[20] Jeannie and Julie Johnson had tried to convince female producers and directors to hire stuntwomen as coordinators. "We thought they'd look at our body of work," Jeannie said, but "that didn't happen a lot. Of course, women directors don't get that much work. They're just as forgotten as we are."[21] The numbers bear that out. Dr. Martha Lauzen's research into women's employment in the TV industry revealed that in 2013–2014, women directed 13 percent of the TV shows (up from 12 percent in 2012), produced 43 percent (up from 38 percent), wrote 25 percent (down from 34 percent), and edited 17 percent (up from 16 percent); the percentage of female cinematographers decreased from 3 percent to 2 percent. Overall, women's employment in these positions has been virtually unchanged since 1997. According to Lauzen, "44% of television programs employed 4 or fewer women in the roles considered. Only 1% of programs employed 4 or fewer men."[22]

By 2005, stuntwoman Lynn Salvatori had coordinated fifteen movies and TV series. "At that time, Shonda Rhimes ran *Grey's Anatomy*," Lynn said, and "I'd worked with the woman who line-produced." The show needed someone to coordinate a stunt with a motorcycle. "'Do you ride motorcycles?'" they asked Lynn. "I said, 'Every weekend.' I sent in my credits. They hired a guy to coordinate, and he hired me for the stunt because the production wouldn't pay for two people. I coordinated myself, I rode the motorcycle, but he [got credit for] the show. That happens at lot." From 1999 to 2005, Lynn tracked who was hired to stunt-coordinate shows about women. Of the 263 films and 35 TV shows on her list, only 22 women had stunt-coordinated. For example, Callie Khouri wrote the screenplay and directed *Divine Secrets of the Ya-Ya Sisterhood* (2002); there were female executive producers, and the movie had a cast of women. Yet "they hired a man to stunt-coordinate," Lynn said. "On that show, a top stuntwoman, Donna Evans, doubled Sandra Bullock, and she could easily have handled the coordinating."[23]

Doing a few shows doesn't make a person a stunt coordinator, but considering the size of the rock they had to roll uphill to do the work at all, the following women on Lynn's list deserve recognition: Mary Albee, Joni Avery, LaFaye Baker, Christine Anne Baur, Liza Coleman, Kerri Cullen,

Shauna Duggins, Jeannie Epper, Donna Evans, Glory Fioramonti, Cindy Folkerson, Sandra Lee Gimpel, Marian Green, Jennifer Hewitt, Sonia Jo Izzolena, Donna Keegan, Alison Reid, Debbie Lynn Ross, Lynn Salvatori, Jodi Stecyk, Melissa Stubbs, Betty Thomas.[24]

Hollywood bestows both mighty and modest awards. The Academy still declines to award an Oscar for stunt work, but other new entries in the twenty-first century do recognize stunts—the World Stunt Awards, the Emmys, and the SAG Awards. Another celebration of stuntwomen came about because the women proposing it just wouldn't quit.

Three years after LaFaye Baker was seriously injured while doing a motorcycle stunt, she learned that Martha Coolidge was preparing to direct *Introducing Dorothy Dandridge* (1999), starring Halle Berry. "They were looking for women in key positions," LaFaye said, and "second-unit director Eddie Watkins recommended me."[25] LaFaye had co-coordinated before, and she got the job—making her the first African American woman to stunt-coordinate a show of that size. The HBO special won several awards, including the Emmy and Golden Globe. LaFaye did coordinate other shows, but "it's hard," she said, "for women to get that job. I learned networking and establishing relationships are crucial to success as a stunt coordinator."[26]

In 2005 LaFaye and stuntwoman Jadie David cofounded Diamond in the Raw, a nonprofit foundation to educate at-risk teens about professional opportunities in the entertainment industry. Then, in 2008, Jadie and LaFaye formed the Celebrity & Stuntwomen's Awards "to recognize unsung heroes—women behind the scenes in the industry." Stunt coordinator Mary Albee received its Special Achievement Award in 2009.[27] Her acceptance speech went directly to the heart of the matter: "First I would like to recognize the stunt coordinators that came before me—Donna Garrett, Jeannie Epper, Julie Ann Johnson, and Sandy Gimpel—and I want to congratulate the stunt coordinators working today. For the rest of you talented women, I pose a challenging question—why is it that on shows I still hear these words—'I've never worked with a female stunt coordinator before.' Get to work, ladies." A year earlier Albee had written:

At least it's no longer a shock to see a woman as the stunt coordinator. It's more acceptable in the corporate world now for women to be in positions of power, and I believe that's translating to the

Mary Albee, Julie Ann Johnson, and Jadie David at the Diamond in the Raw Awards, 2010. (Courtesy of Julie Ann Johnson)

film industry. Kids coming out of college are used to working with women, minorities and multinationals without prejudice, without the limitations of the past. Directors today may be just out of film school and they don't have a problem working with women. That change didn't come from within the industry, it's from the way they grew up and what our attitudes are nationally. In the movies or on TV today women don't have to be heroines, they can be heroes.[28]

It is true that times have changed and will continue to change, but women as stunt coordinators—that's still a chasm to be crossed.

# 17

# Controversy and Progress for Stuntwomen

*The more fearless you are in what you do, the fewer regrets you'll have.*
*—Jadie David*

For a few weeks in 2000, it felt as if the 1970s had returned. Many of the stuntwomen on the set of the remake of *Planet of the Apes* were too young to recognize the resemblance, but they knew what had happened was wrong.[1] A blast from the "bad old days" came thudding into the present when a stuntman was assigned to double a woman. "That [movie] was a bad experience from the get-go," one stuntwoman said. "People got injured right and left, like broken ankles, or wranglers doing stunt work when they're not supposed to, things like that. Then a stunt coordinator replaced a woman with a man, and when someone complained, he threatened to fire all the stuntwomen."

To double Helena Bonham Carter, who played the ape Ari, a number of terrific stuntwomen were interviewed: Simone Boisseree, Eliza Coleman, Leigh Hennessy, Gloria O'Brien, Eileen Weisinger, and Darlene Ava Williams.[2] Body type, size, and weight were important, as was the structure of the double's face because of the facial prosthetics involved. Two doubles were selected: Simone Boisseree and Eileen Weisinger. Simone, a horsewoman, gymnast, and all-around stuntwoman, doubled Carter in the riding scenes; Eileen is also a versatile stuntwoman but doesn't do horse work. The other stuntwomen could double the actress as needed.

In a battle sequence between the apes and the humans, Ari was supposed to be thrown into the air, and Simone was called in to do the stunt. However, when she arrived at the makeup trailer, she was told that the young stuntman sitting in her chair would be replacing her because "he did tumbling." Other women on the set "did tumbling," and they were concerned about how Simone had been treated. One was trampoline champion Leigh Hennessy, who had jumped ninety-five feet off a building in *Charlie's Angels* (2000). "Simone had been called to do a stunt, hadn't been alerted she wouldn't do it, and basically she'd been dismissed. Looking back, there are lots of ways to make a situation controversial, and this small issue turned into a big issue." Additional facts about the stunt surfaced later in the day. "It turned out to be just a ratchet!" Leigh said, amazed. "Simone could do it, I could do it, other stuntwomen there could do it. We were gymnasts, we were in the original interviews, and a ratchet is a fairly simple stunt. We say you're 'going for a ride.' The challenge for the stunt person is whether the rigging has been done properly. You're in a harness attached to a cable and on a cue you're jerked off your feet into the air." This ratchet stunt was a little different because when the big ape tossed Ari into the air, she was supposed to do a flip. "You have to have skill," Leigh said, and "it helps to have acrobatic experience, but you don't need to be a college-level champion gymnast."

"At the end of the day, the coordinator has to get the shot," another stuntwoman cautioned. "He'll use a woman, but not if he has to dial down the stunt." On the set, news spread about the ratchet that "women couldn't handle." A couple of women in the crew said the stunt didn't look very hard and they didn't understand why a guy was doing it. "I told them the coordinator just decided to use the new kid instead of Simone," Leigh said, "but that was against SAG rules—it wasn't right to put a man in arbitrarily for a woman." Leigh had worked for the stunt coordinator, Charles Croughwell, on *Deep Impact* (1998) and *Inspector Gadget* (1999).[3] "I got along well with him," she said. "Maybe he thought Simone couldn't do a ratchet because she was more of a horsewoman."

By evening, it had become a politically hot issue. Leigh called Bonnie Happy, president of the United Stuntwomen's Association (USA). Bonnie contacted Jadie David, a charter member of USA who was now working for SAG as a stunt and safety representative. Both women had been in the front lines of the battle over men doubling women. Jadie suggested that Bonnie get in touch with Sandy Kincaid, a SAG national director with experience in interpreting and enforcing contracts; she also worked closely with the Stunt and Safety Committee.[4] Bonnie called Sandy not to make a complaint but merely to clarify SAG's current policy. That led to a rumor that the stuntwomen were "complaining" to the guild.

"There were five of us," Leigh said. "One stuntwoman was dating the assistant coordinator and one was dating the stunt double for Mark Wahlberg, so those two girls were safe. But three of us were not safe and essentially we were fired." Stunt people are not fired in the usual way; they just don't get called back to do another stunt. For those working on a daily contract, theoretically the contract terminates at the end of the week; a stunt person on a weekly contract usually works to the end of the production. "In this case, we didn't get a new call time to come in to do a stunt," one stuntwoman said. "Day after day you keep asking, 'When do I come back,' and finally you realize you're not on the show anymore. That's what happened to some of us on *Planet of the Apes*." No one had filed a complaint with SAG, even though a rookie stuntman had replaced a seasoned stuntwoman.

Leigh Hennessy was a member of the Stunt and Safety Committee, and she eventually did call the guild. She was referred to Anne-Marie Johnson and Gretchen Koerner, active board members at the time. "They are strong advocates for women's and minority rights," Leigh said. "They're the women I want to be when I grow up."[5] Since this was 2000, not 1975, SAG responded promptly (the guild was also just a few weeks away from negotiating its next theatrical contracts). Mary Albee, Jeannie Epper, Jadie David, and others formed an ad hoc committee to work with Johnson and Koerner to turn what had been merely a policy into a rule. For that significant change, USA inducted Jadie David and Anne-Marie Johnson as honorary members. Essentially, the rule states that when trying to find a double for a minority actress, for example, a stunt coordinator has to call SAG, which checks its database to find a stuntwoman of the same minority as the actress. If one can't be found, then the job can go to a woman of a different minority race or, if necessary, to a Caucasian woman; only after exhausting those options can a man double a woman.

"Get the wigs off men" had been a slogan, a battle, and a goal since the 1970s. It had taken SAG and dozens of stuntwomen thirty years to override the entrenched custom of men doubling women. The controversy on *Planet of the Apes* had some positive effects. It exposed weaknesses in the SAG policy, brought about change, and made it known that a man doubling a woman was no longer acceptable.

Three years later, a stuntwoman who had fought in the trenches walked onto Stage 27 at Sony Pictures. Dan Bradley, stunt coordinator and second-unit director of *Spider-Man 2* (2004), had hired Julie Ann Johnson to test flying sequences and double Rosemary Harris, who was playing Peter Parker's aunt.[6] "She was delightful," Julie said, "and it was simply wonderful for me to work again."

Julie had been suspended from hot-air balloons, balconies, and roofs; she had leaped through breakaway windows. But, as it turned out, the most dangerous thing she'd done was complain about unsafe stunt vehicles and widespread drug use in the industry. When Spelling-Goldberg Productions failed to rehire Julie in 1980 to coordinate the fifth season of the TV series *Charlie's Angels,* she sued. A jury awarded her $1.1 million in 1987, but Spelling-Goldberg appealed. Five years later, in June 1992, the court of appeals ruled against her, based on a technicality that had changed the statute of limitations in wrongful-termination cases. That little bomb had been buried in another case, *Foley v. Interactive Data Corporation.* "No one realized in reading *Foley* that it was going to destroy Julie's case on appeal," said her attorney Richard Grey.[7] "Never in thirty-five years of practicing law have I seen anything like that happen," he claimed. "It was outrageous, unbelievable. I tell this story often to prospective new clients—don't expect justice out of the judicial system because bad things can happen beyond your control. The result for Julie was unbelievably bad, worse than Murphy's Law."

Julie survived, but not as a stuntwoman. She was blacklisted from 1985 to 1998, when she finally began to work again—in *Mystery Men* (1999) and *The Animal* (2001). Then in 2003 Julie was on Sony Pictures' Stage 27 doing a type of stunt that was completely new to her—wirework. She was in a harness, suspended by cables, about forty feet above the studio floor. "That doesn't sound very high," she said, "but when you're hanging by these thin cables with no safety net and looking down at that hard floor, it's high!" By that time, computers were largely in control of these elaborate, sometimes dangerous stunts. A keystroke on a computer keyboard could fly Julie up and down with amazing speed or sail her around the three-story building on the huge set. In one scene, Julie found herself on the ledge of the building. Above her, a statue of an angel was perched under the roof. "They called the facing of that building the 'war wall,'" she said. "I was waiting for the test, and suddenly I was catapulted about fifty feet straight up." She swung past and barely missed the angel, then jerked violently to a stop. "It took the wind right out of me. Scary as hell. Someone at the computers below said, 'Oops, sorry, are you okay?' I gave thumbs-up, but my rib cage felt pulverized. Port-a-pits had been left on the floor. I was glad to see the pads, but a fall would still kill me if I didn't hit them just right."

When Julie declined to do a forty-foot fall, stuntwoman Leigh Hennessy was hired. In the end, the fall was canceled, "but I got to hang out with Julie Johnson!" Leigh said. "It was quite an honor. She'd been one of the founders of the first stuntwomen's association. I'd heard about her lawsuit and how much she'd suffered to pave the way for younger women like me. She stunt-coordinated when almost no women had. I'm coordinating, too, but so few women do." Despite coming from different generations—Julie had started in the business in 1965, Leigh in 1995—they had much in common. Both had helped revise SAG contract language about men doubling women; both had worked on *Charlie's Angels*—Julie on the TV show, Leigh on the movie remake; Leigh is a high-fall artist (*Teaching Mrs. Tingle* [1999]), and Julie's high work included straddling the wing of a biplane and the skid of a helicopter high above the San Fernando Valley in *The Cat from Outer Space* (1978). Both of their fathers were great influences. Leigh's dad was her sports coach and trainer; Julie's was an athletics coach who taught her all about sports. Most of all, they shared the bond of their unique profession—once a stuntwoman, always a stuntwoman.[8]

"It's like we're in a sports league. We're in the same NFL," Sophia Crawford said of the connection. "We can meet, talk, look at each other, and know exactly what that person is going through. We share the same conflicts, challenges, pressures of work, age, wardrobe—all the different factors we experience as women in stunts. We're part of an elite group, a small, tough group, and it unifies us."

They were certainly unified when Jeannie Epper became the first woman to receive the Taurus World Stunt Lifetime Achievement Award in 2007. On the stage that night, stuntwomen were recognized collectively and publicly. These days, stuntwomen win Taurus and SAG Awards, but Mary Albee observed, the awards "may not be about recognition as much as they're about perceptions, such as the sense that some women coordinators do actually exist."

Besides awards, acknowledgment can take other forms that are just as meaningful. Before Stacey Carino dangled from a crane on *Alias* in 2005, she had been a teacher with a normal lifestyle. When she told her parents she was moving to Hollywood, where she didn't have a place to live and didn't know anyone, "that did not appeal to them," she recalled. "They'd heard about Hollywood and drugs and rock and roll. My dad, [who worked] in engineering sales, was not in favor of my move at all." About three years later, her father was having lunch with some clients, and one of them mentioned that his son was in Hollywood. "My dad said his daughter was there doing stunts. A laptop was on the table. The client pulled my name up on the Internet Movie Database and said, 'My gosh, she's worked on this show, that show, and my favorite, *My Name Is Earl*.' My dad was astonished. He didn't know the IMDb website; he just knew I was here doing something weird—stunts. He called me right after that lunch, telling me what they'd said, like, 'Oh my gosh, it's so cool.' I could tell he was finally the proud dad."[9]

In the movie business, dressing rooms symbolize status, respect, and recognition. At best, the stunt people are usually relegated to one or two small rooms, and sometimes they are downright insulting. But *War of the Worlds* (2005) was different.[10] When Stephanie Finochio (a participant in the "vicious" *Rescue Me* fight) and the other stunt players converged on the film's various locations, they were asked if they wanted separate trailers or one big room. "To be *asked* what we'd like to have—that doesn't happen often," she said. "We began joking about a big room with a big-screen TV, a couple couches, a card table, and everyone kept adding to it because being asked what we wanted was so rare it was funny. The next day we were led to a big room with a big-screen TV, couches, a card table, a dartboard, a Play Station, plus *separate* dressing rooms for the men *and* the women! That was a first for me and for most of us. Big actors get big trailers. We're the stunt people. We're important to a movie too, but this time we were treated that way. And on that show we got to hang out with stunt people from all over the world!"

Affirmation can also come from a surprising or kind gesture. "Few leading women are five feet tall and black," said New York stuntwoman Nicole Callender, "so I don't do a lot of doubling, but I can double kids, and that's not open to my five-foot-ten stuntwomen friends." *War of the Worlds* was on location in Newark, New Jersey, where Nicole and another stuntwoman from Los Angeles were waiting on a street. A short distance away, Steven Spielberg was talking to an assistant director. "The LA stuntwoman was very talented and amusing," Nicole said. "She'd brought a camera on the set, which is not permitted. We shouldn't take pictures of the stars, but we can take pictures of our own work. She handed me the camera, glanced back, then faced me and held out her arm. 'Line it up so I look like I've got my arm around Steven Spielberg.' I laughed, started lining it up, and the next thing I knew, Mr. Spielberg was walking toward us. I froze. I got ready to be fired. He stopped in front of us. 'I'm sorry I messed up your picture. Here, let me help you.' He put his arm around the girl and let me take the picture. For a moment I wanted to hand the camera to someone else and get in the picture, but I didn't want to ruin it for her. When would she have this chance again?"

"Being acknowledged can travel through generations," Jadie David said. "Women had no voice and now they do." After performing stunts for twenty-four years, Jadie badly injured her back and had to rethink her options. In the 1990s, after working for the Screen Actors Guild, she supervised safety programs at Paramount Pictures. "My mother's family was from Texas," she said, "and her uncle, born in the early 1900s, went through really hard times as an African American. In his old age he played dominoes with friends, and one day he told them, 'Can you imagine what I went through as a kid? And now look at my grand-niece—she can actually shut down a movie if she has to.' For him, that was awesome. I felt special that a member of my family was proud to have come that far. Families know the past, but recognizing what occurs in the present is part of the achievement—when they can see the distance traveled. What we do has consequences to the past and future generations."

As a small group inside a little-known profession, stuntwomen have come quite a distance, too. Before 1970, all stunt players who doubled the stars had to hide their identities and keep away from the press. Today, they have websites that list their stunt specialties and the stars they double.

Many of today's stuntwomen praise the work they've chosen for what it has taught them about life and, sometimes, how it has changed them. For Glory Fioramonti, "Stunts gave me the way to live a bigger, braver, more empowered life. I had a dysfunctional childhood. My mother was an alcoholic, she was abusive, and I had to survive. There are different ways to survive. I wanted to confront everything I feared. Learning stunts gave me those tools."

Leslie Hoffman said, "Whether you're doing dialogue in a scene or throwing yourself down a staircase, it takes courage to act. Taking action is one of the keys to life."

Luci Romberg's stunt work led her to a sport that saved her life. A consummate gymnast, she strived for perfection. "I always felt I wasn't skinny enough," she admitted. "I starved myself as much as I could . . . I'd end up eating a ton and purging." When she was working on Clint Eastwood's *Changeling* (2008), her friend, stuntwoman Natascha Hopkins, introduced her to members of Victor Lopez's Team Tempest, the top Los Angeles-based freerunning group.[11] Luci became its only female member, and by 2010, she was the first female athlete in the World Acrobatics Society for Freerunners. These ultimate athletes, who perform in urban environments, must have strength, endurance, agility, and the power to imagine a movement and then achieve it. "The sport is about how we get over or around the barriers in our path," Luci said. "We create what we call art, and movement is our art." Freerunning saved Luci's health and gave her confidence because, unlike gymnastics, freerunning is about individual styles of movement, both on the ground and in the air. "New moves in freerunning are invented every day," she said. "It's whatever you can create in your mind."[12] It seems like a perfect sport for stunt people—improvised, incessant forward motion studded with twists, leaps, and flips propelled with power and style.

"I enjoyed doing something most people would call insane," Jadie David said. "I enjoyed being able to override my body's natural instincts, push the envelope and not allow fear to overtake my judgment. I learned about life. The more fearless you are in what you do, the fewer regrets you'll have. I learned those things from doing stunts."

As a theater major in college, Nicole Callender studied unarmed, hand-to-hand combat and fighting with weapons.[13] "When I picked up a sword, I couldn't believe I hadn't held one before," she said. "It came so easily to me. It informed my work as an actor. That sword was like I'd found a missing link." She worked in New York as an off-Broadway actor and began doing stunt work in 2001. Only later did she realize that her image as a woman armed with sword had impact, especially when teaching fight techniques to young actors. "On one level they know women have more opportunities now, but when they see me physically fight with a broadsword, and then do it themselves, I hear them say, 'I can do anything now—no limits!' They don't have to settle for a job behind a desk."

Taking action, overcoming fear, improvising on the spot, dealing with changing situations, hiding your injuries, saving your own life—that's what stunts are! The work can seem like barely controlled chaos or a new online game or a course in emergency procedures. When Danny Aiello III worked as a stuntman, people kept asking him, "Are you stunt guys *crazy?*" His response: "No. We're probably the sanest people on the set. We're very smart. We have to be. If an actor screws up, all they do is say 'Cut.' If we screw up, people can get seriously hurt."

Stunt performers are not daredevils; they analyze stunts mentally, physically, even geometrically. However, they know that every time they do a stunt, it's going to be different. "A famous stuntman told me that," said one stuntwoman. "'You could do 100 high falls,' he said, 'and each will be different.' The location is different, the wind, the height—something. So each time you work, it's almost like your first time, no matter how many times you've done it in the past. All you can do is prepare yourself and perform the stunt, because it's never going to be the same." Those challenges build life skills. Stunt people always remember the surprises that changed a gag, threw off their timing, crashed the car. The recurring appeal is facing the challenge and succeeding.

This profession can deliver disaster and delight. Despite grueling hours, inequality, and injuries, every stuntwoman embraces the joy of the work in her own way. There are "moments of bliss," said skateboard champ Christine Anne Baur. "You picture the action in your head, you've worked it out technically, studied the actor you're doubling, you're in character for what's happening to her at that moment, which generates the stunt. They roll action, and it all comes together simultaneously in Mach one speed *and* super slow motion. I become what's happening, I'm in the explosion that blew out the window, my body is mechanically performing as I told it to, and at that moment, I literally let go. It is magical."

According to stuntwoman Sharon Schaffer, "The best time is making a moment come alive visually by using your body, mind, and soul to express what's going on in the story."

Mary Albee said with her typical but perceptive brevity, "The joy happens when the stunt comes out just as you visualized it. That's fairly rare."

Melissa Stubbs described how she feels when performing a stunt: "I get the jazz, the adrenaline rush of not knowing how I'll do it, that I might get hurt because the outcome is never certain, but you pull the magic out of your soul and you do it." When she's stunt-coordinating, she creates the idea, works with the actors and the stunt team, brings all the elements together, and orchestrates it. "It's always a gamble," she said. "There are too many shots and never enough time, the cars break down, the stunt guy doesn't show up, we only have the street for three minutes every hour—and yet we prevail! It's like no other feeling."

"When you do a challenging stunt and come out unscathed—to me, that's being 'on top of the train,'" said Monica Staggs. Both she and high-faller Nancy Thurston do live stand-up comedy "for the fun of it." Monica, who has performed at comedy clubs such as the Laugh Factory, said, "After you survive death in stunts, being on a stage and making an ass of yourself is not a stretch." Three weeks after Monica fractured her skull in four places and fractured her eye socket while doing a stunt for *Joy Ride* (2001), she was asked to double a Guess supermodel in a video of American boy band *NSYNC's "Bye Bye Bye." She didn't want to take the job, but "finally I agreed to do it because sometimes if you don't get right back on the horse, you never will." She was supposed to run on top of a moving train, jump the three or four feet between cars, run across the next car, jump, and keep running. "The roofs of the boxcars I ran across were slightly arched, not flat," Monica said. "I was about fifteen feet from the ground that was covered with rocks and gravel on both sides. I knew if I fell off, with my skull fracture, that was it for me. At the end of the day, after all the running and jumping, I was to stand still on top of the train. The helicopters were circling around me overhead, the sun was setting, and I felt really victorious. I'd taken the risk, I got back on the horse, and I'd won."

Victory rewards those who take the risk. One stuntwoman summed up the essence of her profession: "The efforts that really count come from your ability to act on your dreams." Great stuntwomen have what old-timers called "go-ahead." They have heart. They are keen and strong, and they seize opportunities with zeal. They hurl themselves into the moment, betting on their skills to see them through safely.

"What we do is absolutely exhilarating," said stuntwoman Sophia Crawford. "When you get a stunt, you dream about it that night, how it will go the next day, but sometimes [when] you get on set, it's completely different, and that's part of the fun—especially at high-pressure times. It's five in the morning, the stunt is the last shot, got to get it in one take, thousands of dollars at stake, the crew is tired, the actors have gone home, and you're on the line. Here we go, 'Action!'"

More than a century ago, movies were just a flickering novelty. Today, motion pictures and television are considered the most influential form of art and entertainment ever created. Stuntwomen have been there from the start, delivering acting and athletics, action and drama to our dreams on the screen. Despite the danger, despite the discrimination, their perseverance and adventurous spirits took them into the heart of motion pictures, earning them an essential role in our history as women. That is quite a legacy.

# Acknowledgments

I am indebted to many people who helped me research various aspects of this book. In the early stages of my work, three generous and knowledgeable men gave me advice about a period they are well acquainted with— the silent movie era. I knew of author, historian, and film preservationist Kevin Brownlow from his book *The Parade's Gone By*, which I read in film school. He sent me a videotape, a transcript of one of his interviews, and the photograph of John Ford's "Wild Bunch." I was already acquainted with Anthony Slide, noted film historian and author of the seminal *Early Women Directors*. He gave me guidance, recommended archives for further research, and suggested key questions the book might answer. I found William M. Drew (*Speaking of Silents*) through a lively and information-packed website that presented chapters of his *Speeding Sweethearts of the Silent Screen*. He gave me a number of research sources and early news accounts of silent movie stuntwomen.

Many others came to my aid. Bob Birchard provided photographs from the silent movie era that included his handwritten notations identifying everyone pictured. Sue Terry located other photographs from that era in Los Angeles and tracked down myriad references for me, from the budgets of obscure movies in the 1930s to major studio changes in the 1960s.

Staff members of the Screen Actors Guild were always ready to search their archives or suggest where I might find other information: Valerie Yaros, SAG historian; Glenn Hiraoka, national director of stunts, singers, dancers, and safety equipment; and author and former SAG senior staff member Kim Fellner.

Stephen Hanson, director of the USC Cinema-TV Library Archives, put me in touch with valuable advisers, including film critic, historian, and author Leonard Maltin. Ned Comstock, senior library assistant at the USC Cinematic Arts Library, helped me answer questions about stuntwomen in *Destry Rides Again*. Jan-Christopher Horak, director of the UCLA Film and Television Archive; Dr. Linda Harris Mehr, director of the Margaret Herrick Library, Academy of Motion Picture Arts and Sciences; and Karen

Herman, vice president of the Academy of Television Arts and Sciences, also provided invaluable assistance.

I am grateful to many friends. Some read the manuscript—Loraine Despres, screenwriter and novelist; Barbara Blair, executive director; and Diane Baer, producer. They all offered structural ideas and made many notations all over the pages. One of the first readers, film director Lynn Hamrick (*Chess Kids*), exclaimed, "These women are like Olympic athletes without the laurels they deserve." Producer Gale Anne Hurd introduced me to her aunt, Jewell Jordan, a stuntwoman in the 1930s; Debbi Bossi, producer and postproduction supervisor, gave advice and supplied me with a digital recorder for the interviews; and Destiny McCune is the best transcriber ever to be found.

Thanks to other friends who came through with ideas, contacts, and suggestions: Beth Kennedy, Pola Miller, Mary Ledding, Beth Solomon, Johnna Levine, Melissa Miller, and author Cari Beauchamp. Rick Ruiz built the best computer I've ever had; Alison Barrett provided marketing guidance and rebuilt my website; and Teresa Hulme provided super computer support. Reporter Dave Robb's knowledge of legal and labor issues expanded my understanding of the conflicts in stunt work. The intrepid Tracy Burns, lawyer and writer, helped in so many ways—researching, editing, and organizing the endless lists and numerous photos. She made much of the work on this book not only possible but also enjoyable.

Over the years, I had amassed many photographs from stuntwomen and collectors. Writer, director, filmmaker, and friend Jon Wilkman (*Moguls and Movie Stars: A History of Hollywood*) read the manuscript and made lots of notes. Since I know nothing about handling photos online, he spent untold hours manipulating, shifting, numbering, and checking them. I will always be grateful for his skill, patience, and humor.

I want to thank Patrick McGilligan, biographer of Clint Eastwood, Alfred Hitchcock, and others, who introduced me to the University Press of Kentucky, to superb senior acquisitions editor Anne Dean Dotson, and to the very able Bailey Johnson, acquisitions assistant. To my tenacious, tireless, and wise agent Ellen Geiger at the Frances Goldin Literary Agency, I send recognition and gratitude. A respected filmmaker who started working in the 1930s told me in 1973 that everyone needs friends in the trenches. I took in his pronouncement, but I was too young to fully appreciate his advice. Now I do.

*Stuntwomen* exists because stuntwomen were willing to tell me about

Acknowledgments

their work. Their influence on the movies has been hugely underrated; without their stories, we would have no history of this remarkable profession. In the interviews, they spoke to me with vitality, candor, and wit. Many interviews still come back to me: May Boss, Danny Aiello, Jadie David, Donna and Debbie Evans, Christine Baur, Kym Washington. I can hear Leigh Hennessy and Conrad Palmisano patiently explaining how a ratchet works, Polly Burson whooping with laughter, and Bonnie Happy quietly telling me, "The horse has to *give* you the stunt."

I am very grateful to all of you for sharing your experiences with me. You made this book possible.

# Notes

## Introduction

1. The Screen Actors Guild began to recognize the work of stunt players in 2008 at the Fourteenth Annual SAG Awards.

## 1. The Rise and Fall of Female Stunt Players in Silent Movies

1. Helen Gibson, as told to Mike Kornick, "In Very Early Days: Screen Acting Was Often a Matter of Guts," *Films in Review* 19 (January 1, 1968): 28–34. Helen Gibson (1892–1977) was born Rose August Wenger in Cleveland, Ohio. For the stunt described, she was doubling for Helen Holmes in episode 45, "A Girl's Grit." Gibson herself starred in the serial from 1915 to 1917.

2. Eleanor Clift, *Founding Sisters and the Nineteenth Amendment* (New York: John Wiley & Sons, 2003), 3.

3. Shelley Stamp, *Movie-Struck Girls: Women and Motion Picture Culture after the Nickelodeon* (Princeton, NJ: Princeton University Press, 2000), 140, 154–55.

4. Clift, *Founding Sisters,* 10.

5. See Virginia Scharff, *Taking the Wheel: Women and the Coming of the Motor Age* (New York: Free Press, 1991).

6. William M. Drew, *Speeding Sweethearts of the Silent Screen,* chap. 1, at www .welcometosilentmovies.com. See also William M. Drew, *Speaking of Silents: The First Ladies of the Screen* (New York: Vestal Press, 1997); *At the Center of the Frame: Leading Ladies of the Twenties and Thirties* (New York: Cooper Square Press, 1999); and Drew's many articles for *Take One* and *American Classic Screen.*

7. Ally Acker, *Reel Women, Pioneers of Cinema* (New York: Continuum, 1991), 252.

8. Drew, *Speeding Sweethearts,* chap. 3, citing "Helen's Daring Stunt," *New York Dramatic Mirror,* June 9, 1917.

9. A preeminent film historian of the silent era, Slide has published seventy books, including *The American Film Industry: A New Historical Dictionary,* 2nd ed. (Lanham, MD: Scarecrow Press, 2001), and *The International Film Industry: A Historical Dictionary* (Westport, CT: Greenwood Publishing Group, 1989). He has also consulted on a number of documentaries and directed others, such as *The Silent Feminists: America's First Women Directors* (1993).

10. Anthony Slide, *Early Women Directors* (New York: Da Capo Press, 1984), 13, quoting a December 1923 article in *The Business Woman* by Myrtle Gebhart, "a prominent fan magazine writer of the period."

11. Nell Shipman's (1892–1970) movies include *The Girl from God's Country, The Grub Stake, White Waters, Trail of the North Wind,* and *Something New.*

12. Slide, *Early Women Directors,* 106.

13. Anthony Slide, *The Silent Feminists: America's First Women Directors* (Lanham, MD: Scarecrow Press, 1996), 2–3.

14. Carey McWilliams, *Southern California Country: An Island on the Land,* ed. Erskine Caldwell (New York: Duell, Sloat & Pierce, 1946), 331.

15. Robert Sklar, *Movie-Made America: How the Movies Changed American Life* (New York: Random House, 1975), 74–75. See also McWilliams, *Southern California Country,* 333.

16. H. Sheridan Bickers, "Extra Ladies and Gentlemen," *Motion Picture Magazine,* August 1917, 91–96.

17. Frances Denton, "Ride, Swim and Dance," *Photoplay,* May 1921.

18. William M. Drew, "Esther Ralston," *American Classic Screen* 5, no. 4 (1981): 27–28.

19. Kevin Brownlow, *The Parade's Gone By* (Berkeley: University of California Press, 1968), 314. In addition to being an author, film historian, and film preservationist, Brownlow is a producer and director. He received an Oscar from the Academy of Motion Picture Arts and Sciences as "the preeminent historian of the silent film era as well as a preservationist."

20. William M. Drew, e-mail to the author, citing Mary MacLaren's (1896–1985) lawsuit as reported in *Los Angeles Times,* February 15, 1917.

21. Quoted in John Baxter, *Stunt* (New York: Doubleday, 1974), 282–83, citing *Picture Play,* May 1916. Mary Fuller (1888–1973) acted in many films from 1907 to 1917; she also wrote eight shorts, including *The Golden Spider* and *A Princess in the Desert.*

22. Dorothea B. Hering, "The Sensational Feats of Motion Picture Stars," *Munsey's* 71 (December 1920): 412–19; *The Film Index: A Bibliography,* 3 vols. (New York: Museum of Modern Art Film Library, 1941–1985). *The Film Index* was compiled by participants in the Writers Program of the Work Progress Administration, New York.

23. Kalton C. Lahue, *Bound and Gagged: The Story of the Silent Serials* (New York: Castle Books/A. S. Barnes, 1968), 277–78.

24. *Daily Milwaukee News,* January 1, 1860.

25. Sandra Gabriele, "Towards Understanding the Stunt Girl" (paper presented at the annual meeting of the International Communication Association, May 17, 2003), www.allacademic.com.

26. Samuel Butler's February 17, 1878, letter is cited in *Oxford English Dictionary,* 2nd ed. (1989), 16:998.

27. Stamp, *Movie-Struck Girls,* 102–10, 114–15.

28. Ibid., 105.

29. Kathlyn Williams (1879–1960) acted in many other films until 1935; she also wrote six films and directed two of them: *The Last Dance* (1912) and *The Leopard's Foundling* (1914).

30. Quoted in Slide, *Silent Feminists,* 118–19.

31. Mary Fuller, Kathlyn Williams, Helen Gibson, and Ann Little had long lives; Grace Cunard and Helen Holmes died in their sixties.

32. Grace Cunard (1893–1967) was born Harriet Mildred Jeffries, but Universal chief Carl Laemmle renamed her "after the steamship lines he used on his trips home to Germany" (Kevin Brownlow to the author). Cunard starred, produced, and directed from 1913 to 1921 and wrote about a hundred scripts; she acted in the 1930s and did bit parts in the 1940s.

33. Acker, *Reel Women,* 162, citing Gerald Perry, "Sanka, Pink Ladies and Virginia Slims," *Women & Film* 1, no. 56 (1974): 82–84.

34. Francis Ford (1889–1953) acted in scores of films (*The Quiet One, Stagecoach*), as well as writing, directing, and producing.

35. Drew, e-mail to the author, February 23, 2010.

36. The first sequel was *The Exploits of Elaine.* Its chapter titles were as action-packed as the serial itself: "The Clutching Hand," "The Hour of Threes," "The Blood Crystals." White's last serials were *Plunder* (1923) and *Perils of Paris* (1924). See "Death Balks Pearl White Plans for Film Comeback," *Los Angeles Times,* August 5, 1938.

37. See Acker, *Reel Women,* 250–51, regarding male doubles for White.

38. A. L. Wooldridge, "Girls Who Risk Their Lives," *Picture Play,* March 1925, 111, quoting stuntman Bob Rose.

39. John Dreyfuss, "George Marshall, Director, Dies," *Los Angeles Times,* February 18, 1975.

40. Ruth Roland's (1892–1937) company produced several movies in the early 1920s, including *Ruth of the Rockies, The Timber Queen, White Eagle, Ruth of the Range,* and *The Haunted Valley.* See Read Kendall, "Death Calls Ruth Roland," *Los Angeles Times,* September 23, 1937.

41. Helen Holmes (1892–1960) wrote and directed episodes of *The Hazards of Helen* and *The Railroad Raiders.* She and her husband, director John P. McGowan, formed their own production company, Signal Film Corporation. William Drew confirmed Holmes's birth date as 1892 (1900 census).

42. A letter from Leo S. Rosencrans, February 5, 1917, mentions the male double for Helen Holmes in episode 12, "The Main Line Wreck," of *The Hazards of Helen* (file V413, Special Collections, Margaret Herrick Library, Academy of Motion Picture Arts and Sciences).

43. Gibson, "In Very Early Days," 34.

44. Kevin Brownlow, "The Cowboy in Hollywood," in *The War, the West, and the Wilderness* (New York: Alfred A. Knopf, 1979), 290.

45. Hoot Gibson (1892–1962) was a rodeo champ before appearing in *Shotgun Jones, Buckshot John,* and *Action.*

46. Gibson, "In Very Early Days," 29. See also Brownlow, *War, West, and Wilderness,* 253.

47. Clift, *Founding Sisters,* 4.

## 2. Blackface and Wigs

1. Jack Carleton, "Are Women Braver than Men?" *Los Angeles Times,* August 18, 1935, 116, courtesy of Valerie Yaros, historian, Communications Department, Screen Actors Guild (SAG). In 1940 Eddie Cline directed *The Bank Dick* and *My Little Chickadee* with Mae West and W. C. Fields.

2. McWilliams, *Southern California Country,* 337–42.

3. *MGM Studio Tour* (MGM, 1925), aired by Turner Classic Movies, 2010.

4. Slide, *Silent Feminists,* 134–35.

5. See Baxter, *Stunt,* 281–82. For instance, Audrey Scott became the riding double to the stars—Greta Garbo, Rosalind Russell, Clara Bow, Barbara Stanwyck, Bette Davis, Judith Anderson. Scott wrote *I Was a Hollywood Stunt Girl* (Philadelphia: Donovan, 1969).

6. One exception was actress Bebe Daniels (1901–1971), who reportedly performed many of her own stunts. See Eddie Cantor, *My Life Is in Your Hands* (New York: Harper & Brothers, 1928).

7. Wooldridge, "Girls Who Risk Their Lives," 16–18.

8. Swimmers from the 1920s and 1930s included Mary Wiggins, Janet Ford, Loretta Rush, and Elsie Ware; riders were Frances Miles, Evelyn Finley, Vivian Valdez, Vera McGinnis, Winnie Brown, Audrey Scott, Crete Sipple, and Marilyn Mills.

9. Adela Rogers St. Johns, "Stunting into Stardom," *Photoplay,* December 1922, 39.

10. Helen Klumph, "Bust 'Em Cowgirl!" *Picture Play,* January 1925, 17. Winnie Brown's movies include *The Iron Trail, The Prairie Trail, Campaigning with Custer, Trail of the Lonesome Mine,* and *Captain Courtesy.*

11. Ibid., 16.

12. Brownlow, *War, West, and Wilderness,* 292–93. According to Brownlow, Olive Carey told him in a June 1980 interview, "So many tumblers came from lumber towns because as kids they could practice falls on sawdust piles." Brownlow to the author, June 4, 2008.

13. Wooldridge, "Girls Who Risk Their Lives," 18. In the 1920s and 1930s Janet Ford worked on *The Steel Trail, The Sideshow,* and *The Furies.* Loretta Rush's (1906–

1972) credits from the same era include *Flowing Gold, Catalina Here I Come,* Fay Wray's double in *King Kong,* Jean Harlow's double in *China Seas,* and *Three on a Honeymoon.* Rush worked into the 1950s.

14. Carleton, "Are Women Braver than Men?" 116. Mary Wiggins (1910–1945) worked on *Love at First Flight* and *His Unlucky Night;* she doubled Barbara Stanwyck in *Union Pacific* and Claudette Colbert in *It Happened One Night.* In 1940 she appeared in an eighteen-minute Warner Bros. short, *Spills for Thrills,* directed by De Leon Anthony. See "Veteran Woman Stunt Artist Ends Own Life," *Los Angeles Times,* December 21, 1945, 1A.

15. Thomas Schatz, *Genius of the System* (New York: Pantheon, 1988), 127–29.

16. Stuntman Bob Rose (1901–1993) played Rusty McDonald in *Lucky Devils* and did some of the stunts. He started in the business in 1919 and sometimes doubled Ruth Roland in her serials. At the time, no stunt players were credited by name.

17. The following films featured black actors: *Birth of a Nation* (1915), *The Emperor Jones* (1933), *Judge Priest* (1934) with Lincoln Perry, *Green Pastures* (1935) with Rex Ingram, and *They Won't Forget* (1937) with Clinton Rosemond.

18. Gary Null, *Black Hollywood: The Black Performer in Motion Pictures* (Secaucus, NJ: Citadel Press, 1975), 39.

19. Other pre-Code (1933) films were *Duck Soup, Ecstasy, She Done Him Wrong,* and *42nd Street.* See *Complicated Women, 1929–1934* (Timeline Films, 2003), based on the book by producer Mike LaSalle.

20. McWilliams, *Southern California Country,* 333.

21. SAG's founders were Berton Churchill, Grant Mitchell, Ralph Morgan, Charles Miller, Kenneth Thomson, and his wife Alden Gay. Among those who joined in the first year were James Cagney, Robert Montgomery, Fredric March, Jeanette MacDonald, and the Marx brothers.

22. McWilliams, *Southern California Country,* 348.

23. Studios did not recognize the Writers Guild as the collective-bargaining agent for writers in motion pictures until October 1940.

24. Kim Fellner, "Gil Perkins: Union Activist [second of a two-part oral history]," *Screen Actor,* Summer 1981, 32. Fellner was the director of public relations at SAG. This oral history is valuable not only for Perkins's accounts of his own stunts but also for his recollections of the stuntwomen he worked with.

25. Stuntwomen's SAG membership supplied by Valerie Yaros, e-mail to the author, August 19, 2008.

26. According to some sources, the industry began to open up for women in the 1960s. However, the 1970s were the key period for awareness and action. Based on my interviews for *Women Who Run the Show* (New York: St. Martin's Press, 2002), the failure of SAG, the Writers Guild of America, the Directors Guild of America, and other unions to recognize discrimination against women and minorities continued well into the 1990s and persists today to some degree.

27. Jewell Jordan's (1917–2009) films include *Ninotchka, New Moon, Ever since Eve,* and *The Good Earth.*

28. Lila Finn (1909–1996) also doubled Veronica Lake, Olivia De Havilland, and Ida Lupino. She worked on *It's a Wonderful Life, Heart Beeps, Legal Eagles, Suburban Commando,* and *Predator 2.* One of the original Venice bodysurfers and volleyball players, Finn was a member of the USA volleyball team.

29. Author interview with Barry Shanley. He practiced law in Beverly Hills for twenty-seven years, specializing in civil, personal injury, and business litigation.

30. Paul Stader (1911–1991), a stunt coordinator and second-unit director, often doubled Gregory Peck, John Wayne, and Cary Grant.

31. SAG, "Stuntwomen's Oral History Project," April 2, 1981, 7. The interviewer is not credited, but it was probably Kim Fellner. Lila Finn did a stair fall in *The Stunt Girl,* a short produced by Jerry Fairbanks and directed by Robert Carlisle in the 1947 Paramount documentary series *Unusual Occupations.*

32. Lila's knife stunt was for *Just Off Broadway* (1942). *Fall Girls,* a 1987 Group W television short, included stuntwomen Lila Finn, Debbie Evans, and Diane Peterson.

33. David Lamb, "Stuntwomen Stand on Feats," *Los Angeles Times,* November 29, 1971, D1–D3.

34. Murray M. Moler, "Want a Dainty Gal Bodyguard? Helen Thurston Can Qualify," *Waterloo (Iowa) Daily Courier,* February 7, 1945. Lila Finn joined SAG on July 29, 1937; Helen Thurston joined on November 17, 1937.

35. Author interview with Sean and Michele Fawcett, grandchildren of Helen Thurston (1909–1979). Helen married Jimmy Fawcett on January 1, 1929, when she was nineteen years old. Her films include *Star Spangled Banners, Anne of the Indies, River of No Return,* and *The Great Race.*

36. Florabel Muir, "They Risk Their Necks for You," *Saturday Evening Post,* September 15, 1945, 27–35. A former police reporter for the *New York Daily News,* Muir was the Los Angeles correspondent for the *Daily News* and a *Variety* columnist. Muir cited stuntwomen Frances Miles, Betty Danko, Nellie Walker, Jeanne Criswell, Evelyn Smith, Mary Wiggins, Aline Goodwin, Ione Reed, Vivian Valdez, Loretta Rush, and Opal Ernie.

37. Paula Dell's credits include *Camelot, Logan's Run, Above the Law, Circle of Power,* and *Star!*

38. William Witney, *In a Door, into a Fight, out a Door, into a Chase: Moviemaking Remembered by the Guy at the Door* (Jefferson, NC: McFarland, 1996), 202.

39. Herbert Yates, owner of Consolidated Film Industries, formed Republic Pictures to produce and distribute movies.

40. In 1939 Helen Gibson appeared in *Stagecoach* and *The Oregon Trail;* Nellie Walker was in *Born to Be Wild* and *Wyoming Wildcat;* and Babe DeFreest (1907–1986) was in *The Roaring West, The Tiger Woman, Zorro's Black Whip,* and *Perils of Nyoka.*

41. Witney, *In a Door,* 141–43.

42. Stuntman Jimmie Dundee doubled Cary Grant. According to Valerie Yaros, SAG historian, stunt performers received $35 a day in 1937.

43. In the 1950s the gaffer of a stunt was called the "ramrod," and he had to be a strict disciplinarian; a ramrod's original job was "to ram home the charge of a muzzle-loading firearm" (*Webster's Third International Dictionary,* 1971). Today, a gaffer is the chief electrical technician on a film, but the term also refers to a stunt person who runs the stunts.

44. Steven Bach, *Marlene Dietrich, Life and Legend* (New York: William Morrow, 1992), 250.

45. McWilliams, *Southern California Country,* 339–40.

46. Second-unit director Yakima Canutt created the famous stunt in *Stagecoach;* Aline Goodwin doubled Margaret Hamilton, and Betty Danko was a stand-in for the Wicked Witch in *The Wizard of Oz;* Richard Talmadge was second-unit director and stunt coordinator for *Beau Geste;* Marie Bodie and Ione Reed doubled Maureen O'Hara in *The Hunchback of Notre Dame;* and Audrey Scott was the riding double for Bette Davis in *Dark Victory.*

47. Brownlow, e-mail to the author, February 23, 2010.

48. Muir, "They Risk Their Necks," 27.

49. Aline Goodwin (1889–1980) also worked on *The Rainbow Trail, King Kong* (doubling Fay Wray), *The Wizard of Oz, Leatherstocking,* and *The Sky Rider.* Hazel Hash Warp (1914–2008) was a rodeo rider (*Bozeman [Mont.] Daily Chronicle,* www.legacy.com).

50. Bach, *Marlene Dietrich,* 249, 251–52. Finally budgeted at $768,000, *Destry Rides Again* was released three months later, on November 29, 1939. See also the documentary *Marlene Dietrich: Her Own Song* (2001).

51. Jon Wilkman and Nancy Wilkman, *Picturing Los Angeles* (Salt Lake City, UT: Gibbs Smith, 2006), 170–74.

52. Among George Marshall's (1891–1975) many films were *You Can't Cheat an Honest Man* and *The Blue Dahlia.* He also directed the television series *I Love Lucy* and *The Odd Couple.* His granddaughter, Christine Anne Baur, is a stuntwoman today.

53. Una Merkel (1903–1986) acted in silent movies and was a comic character actress. She was in *The Fifth Horseman* and *42nd Street,* was a Tony nominee for *Summer and Smoke,* and appeared on the TV series *The Red Skelton Show* and *Playhouse 90.*

54. Maria Riva, *Marlene Dietrich* (New York: Galantine Books, 1992), 493–94.

55. Quoted in Roy Pickard, *Jimmy Stewart: A Life in Film* (New York: St. Martin's Press, 1992), 38. See also Charles Higham, *Marlene: The Life of Marlene Dietrich* (New York: W. W. Norton, 1977), 192–93.

56. Muir, "They Risk Their Necks," 34. She did not reveal Una Merkel's double.

Among the stuntwomen who might have done it were Betty Danko, Mary Wiggins, Aline Goodwin, and Loretta Rush.

57. Ibid., 27. Frances Miles (1907–2004) worked on *The Hunchback of Notre Dame, Scarface,* and *The Devil Is Driving.*

## 3. Television

1. Muir, "They Risk Their Necks," 34. Betty Danko (1903–1979) probably doubled actress Binnie Barnes, playing the Anne Bonney role. Danko's other credits include *45 Fathers, All American Toothache, Slightly Static,* and *Made in Hollywood.*

2. Moler, "Want a Dainty Gal Bodyguard?"

3. Lila Finn, recalling Polly in the program book "The Perils of Polly," presented by the United Stuntwomen's Association and Burbank Elks to Honor Polly Burson, March 15, 1986. See also Barbara De Witt, "Ride 'em Cowgirls," *Los Angeles Daily News,* March 7, 1995.

4. Polly Burson (1919–2006) was born Pauline Shelton in Ontario, Oregon. Her credits include *Abbott and Costello Meet the Keystone Cops, The Crimson Ghost, Barefoot in the Park, Heller in Pink Tights, Vertigo, Some Like It Hot, McLintock! Spartacus,* and *How the West Was Won.* She received the Golden Boot Award from the Motion Picture and Television Fund and was inducted into the Pro Rodeo Hall of Fame, the Hollywood Stuntmen's Hall of Fame, and the National Cowgirl Museum Hall of Fame.

5. Bill Mayer, "Living Dangerously—By Design," *Daily Variety,* Forty-Fourth Anniversary Issue, 1977.

6. Arthur Rosson (1886–1960) directed the second unit on *Unconquered* and probably coordinated the stunts with DeMille, who knew the action and the stuntmen he wanted. *Unconquered* opened on October 10, 1947. Rosson worked with DeMille for years as associate director and second-unit director; their collaborations included *Ten Commandments* and *King of Kings.*

7. Actor and stuntman Ted Mapes began working in 1929 and often doubled Gary Cooper.

8. Mayer, "Living Dangerously."

9. Finn, "Perils of Polly." Lila Finn also doubled Paulette Goddard in a dive off a ship into the ocean in DeMille's *Reap the Wild Wind.*

10. See Sklar, *Movie-Made America,* 274–85.

11. "Stunt Rider Prefers Denim to Chintz," *Omaha Evening World-Herald,* September 19, 1966, 15. May Boss worked on *Marnie, Mary Poppins, The Hallelujah Trail, Fort Dobbs, Nevada Smith, The Way West, Westbound, The Last Sunset, How the West Was Won,* and *Mackenna's Gold.*

12. Among the stuntwomen listed with Teddy's in 1954 were Helen Thurston, Loretta Rush, Lucille House, Lila Finn, Stevie Myers, Polly Burson, May Boss,

Sharon Lucas, Shirley Lucas, Evelyn Finley, Martha Crawford, Opal Ernie, Donna Hall, and Evelyn Smith. William Gordon Collection, folders 551 and 453, Margaret Herrick Library, Academy of Motion Picture Arts and Sciences (Gordon was a casting director at 20th Century–Fox). Teddy's service still operates today; other similar services are Joni's, Bill's, and Missy's.

13. John D. Ross and Mark Ivis, "Robert Herron: 80, Unbreakable and Still Going Strong!" *Inside Stunts,* Summer 2004, 15.

14. The stuntwomen in *Westward the Women* were Opal Ernie, Evelyn Finley, Polly Burson, Donna Hall, Edith Happy, Lucille House, Sharon Lucas, Stevie Myers, and Ann Roberts. Others were credited as "pioneer women." There were nineteen stuntmen.

15. Quoted in *Challenge the Wilderness* (1951), a thirteen-minute short produced by MGM. Charles Schnee wrote the screenplay for *Westward the Women.*

16. Edith Happy doubled Dorothy Malone in *The Last Sunset.* Her daughter, Bonnie Happy, is president of the United Stuntwomen's Association.

17. During our interview, Polly Burson didn't mention stunt-coordinating on *Westward the Women* to me. Nor does a 1986 tribute book cite her as stunt coordinator for the film. Since she didn't coordinate all the stunts, she may have felt she wasn't entitled to the credit. No stunt coordinator is listed in the film credits.

18. William Wellman Jr. was featured in 180 movies and TV shows; he is the author of *The Man and His Wings* (Santa Barbara, CA: Praeger Publishers, 2007) and *Wild Bill Wellman: Hollywood Rebel* (New York: Pantheon Books/Random House, 2015). In the 1930s and 1940s Evelyn Finley (1915–1989) worked on *The Diamond Queen, Sheriff of Medicine Bow, Gunning for Justice, Valley of Vengeance,* and *The Texas Rangers.* "The great female equestrians of the movies included Nell O'Day and Betty Miles. Evelyn Finley was one of the top riders, far better than most of the male cowboy stars of that period. Finley played the heroine in dozens of 1940s westerns, but her best work was stunt doubling and riding for many of Hollywood's famous lady stars" (Stunt Players Directory Memorial).

19. Sharon Lucas (1928–2006) doubled Jane Russell in *Paleface;* in the 1960s she did stunts in *The Great Race* and *Once You Kiss a Stranger.* In the 1950s her sister Shirley Lucas (ca. 1924–) worked on *The Cisco Kid, Blood Alley,* and *The Story of Will Rogers.*

20. Chuck Roberson with Bodie Thoene, *The Fall Guy: 30 Years as the Duke's Double* (Vancouver, BC: Hancock House, 1980), 41. Roberson (1919–1988) was an actor, stuntman, and expert rider on his famous horse Cocaine; he doubled John Wayne, Clark Gable, and Robert Mitchum.

21. Lucille House (1910–2008) also doubled Maureen O'Hara in *Flame of Araby* and *McLintock!* Her other credits include *The Great Gatsby, It's Great to Be Alive,* and *Spencer's Mountain.*

22. Robeson, *Fall Guy,* 41–44.

23. Hal Needham, *Stuntman! My Car-Crashing, Plane-Jumping, Bone-Breaking, Death-Defying Hollywood Life* (New York: Little Brown, 2011), 42.

24. Roberson didn't know that Polly had no children.

25. Roberson, *Fall Guy*, 149–50.

26. Instead of *The Tall Men*, Polly Burson worked on *The Rains of Ranchipur* and *Some Like It Hot*.

27. Muir, "They Risk Their Necks," 27.

28. Regis Parton (1917–1996) appeared in *Night Passage, Planet of the Apes, Hooper, The Stunt Man*, and *Alien Nation*. His daughter, Regina Parton, became a stuntwoman in the mid-1960s.

29. See also Finn interview in SAG, "Stuntwomen's Oral History Project," 1.

## 4. Stunt Performers Organize

1. Richard Setlowe, "Hollywood's Hitmen," *Variety*, July 23, 1992.

2. Saul David, *The Industry: Life in the Hollywood Fast Lane* (New York: Times Books, 1981), 129. Saul David (1921–1996) produced *Fantastic Voyage, Von Ryan's Express, In Like Flint, Skullduggery*, and *Logan's Run*.

3. Loren Janes has appeared in 500 movies and more than 2,200 television shows. He qualified for two Olympic teams in the pentathlon and raised two children as a single parent. In 1964 and 1990 he ran for Congress. He is a member and past president of the Adventurer's Club of Los Angeles and the Explorers Club of New York. He was a board member of the Hollywood Screen Actors Guild and national chair of the SAG Stunt and Safety Committee. The many credits of actor-stuntman Dick Geary (1925–2000) include *Bullitt, The Great Race, Hopscotch, Star Trek, Mannix*, and *The Rawhide Trail*.

4. *Everything's Ducky* (Barbroo Productions, Columbia Pictures, 1960).

5. Nathaniel Freedland, "The Danger Biz," *Los Angeles Times*, June 29, 1969, 21.

6. Sara Terry, "Stuntwomen Go Full Throttle," *Christian Science Monitor*, April 25, 2003.

7. Marilyn Moe Stader (*Mission Impossible, The Poseidon Adventure*) was an expert swimmer and diver like her husband, Paul Stader.

8. Patty Elder's (1936–1984) credits include *Highpoint, Ice Castles, Hooper, Paint Your Wagon*, and *Quick before It Melts*. Eddie Hice, a stuntman and stunt coordinator, worked on *Get Smart, Dante's Peak, Sweet Justice*, and *Repo Man*. Their son, Freddie, is a stuntman and second-unit director today.

9. Regina Parton worked on the TV shows *Charlie's Angels, The Rockford Files, Hart to Hart*, and *Legal Eagles*. See Karen E. Willson, "Stuntwomen the Invisible Superheroes of Hollywood," *Starlog* 30 (January 1980).

10. Julie Johnson's early credits include *Star Trek, The Girl from U.N.C.L.E., Dr. Doolittle, Gone with the West, Eye of the Cat, Magnum Force, Caprice*, and *Nickelodeon*.

11. The Stuntwomen's Association announced its formation on February 12, 1969, with twenty-four charter members. Its first board of directors consisted of Regina Parton, president; Sharon Lucus, Stevie Myers, and Helen Thurston, vice presidents; Marilyn Moe Stader, secretary; and Patty Elder, treasurer. Board members at large were Polly Burson, Lila Finn, and Donna Hall. Information courtesy of papers from Paula Dell's collection.

12. Edward Smith (1924–2005) worked on *Halls of Anger*, *The Dogs of War*, *M\*A\*S\*H\**, *Dirty Harry*, and *Scarface*; he was stunt coordinator for *Youngblood*, *Roots*, *Across 110th Street*, and *Do the Right Thing*.

13. Helen Thurston doubled Ethel Merman in *It's a Mad, Mad, Mad, Mad World*; other stuntwomen who worked on the movie were May Boss, Carol Daniels (her credits range from *Gunsmoke* to *Desperate Housewives*), and Stephanie Epper.

14. Quoted in Tod Longwell, "Breaking Bones and Barriers," *Los Angeles Times*, June 7, 2002.

15. Calvin Brown's credits include *I Spy*, *The Split*, *Will Penny*, and *Mission Impossible*; he was stunt coordinator for *Exiled*, *Across 110th Street*, *Man and Boy*, and *Live and Let Die*. Marvin Walters worked on *RoboCop 2*, *Star Trek*, *Glory*, *What's up Doc? Blazing Saddles*, and *The Front Page*; he was stunt coordinator for *The Dogs of War*, *The River Niger*, *Magnum P.I.*, *Keaton's Cop*, *Heart of Darkness*, *Eve's Bayou*, and *Shaft's Big Score!*

16. Donald Bogle, *Toms, Coons, Mulattoes, Mammies and Bucks: An Interpretive History of Blacks in American Film* (New York: Continuum, 1973), 195.

17. Mike Davis, *City of Quartz: Excavating the Future of Los Angeles* (London: Verso, 1990), 42–43. Chester Hines's books are *If He Hollers Let Him Go* and *Lonely Crusade*.

18. Screen Actors Guild, "History," www.sag.org.

19. Longwell, "Breaking Bones," 3.

20. "Edward Smith, Stuntman," obituary, June 2005, www.lastlinkontheleft.com.

21. Longwell, "Breaking Bones." Henry Kingi's many credits include *R.P.M.*, *Predator 1* and *2*, *K-9*, *Daniel Boone*, *The A-Team*, and *Action Jackson*; he stunt-coordinated *Let's Do It Again*, *In the Heat of the Night*, and *Matter of Justice*. He won a Taurus Award in 2004 for *Bad Boys II* and worked on *Taxi* in 2005, performing an add-on sequence doubling Queen Latifah.

22. Evelyn Cuffee's credits include *The New Centurions*, *Hooper*, *Melinda*, *Mandingo*, *The Nude Bomb*, *Paris Blues*, *Roots: The Next Generation*, *The Learning Tree*, *The Great White Hope*, *Mission Impossible*, *Mannix*, and *Room 222*. Louise Johnson worked on *Mandingo*, *Halls of Anger*, *D.C. Cab*, *Hooper*, *Earthquake*, and *Coffy*. The Harvey Parry Collection (folder 35), Margaret Herrick Library, Academy of Motion Picture Arts and Sciences, contains two circa 1970s directories for the Stuntwomen's Association.

23. Longwell, "Breaking Bones," 3.

24. Tod Longwell, "Real Double Troubles," *Hollywood Reporter,* May 18–20, 2001.

25. "Edward Smith, Stuntman."

26. Longwell, "Real Double Troubles."

27. Among other films, Polly Burson worked on *Heller in Pink Tights, The Last Train from Gun Hill,* and *El Dorado;* she doubled Jean Simmons in *Elmer Gantry, Guys and Dolls,* and *Spartacus.*

28. *Gone with the West* (Synergy Entertainment, 2007), DVD. It was also titled *Man without Mercy* or *Little Moon and June McGraw.*

29. According to Julie Johnson, she and Polly were both "nondescript" characters and were not specifically doubling anyone; in the roster of cast members, they are listed as "townswomen." Boyd Stockman is credited as stunt coordinator.

30. Screenwriter Marguerite Roberts's (1905–1989) credits include *5 Card Stud, The Bribe, Ivanhoe, The Rampage,* and *Norwood.* Joel and Ethan Coen wrote the screenplay for the 2010 remake of *True Grit.*

31. The 1969 version of *True Grit* employed twelve stuntmen and one stuntwoman—Polly Burson; no stunt coordinator was listed. The 2010 remake used seventeen stuntmen and three stuntwomen—Cassidy Hice, Jennifer Lamb, and Ruth Morris; the stunt coordinator was Jery Hewitt.

## 5. Social Turmoil Brings New Opportunities for Women and Minorities

1. Quoted in Jerry Roberts, "Fall Girls Getting the Drop on Stuntwomen," *Torrance (CA) Daily Breeze/News-Pilot,* April 25, 1986.

2. Jadie David's credits include *Friday Foster, Drum, Convoy, Hooper, Bustin' Loose, The Star Chamber, Legal Eagles, Colors, Grand Canyon, Zooman, Escape from New York, Hunter, Car Wash, Logan's Run, Earthquake, Mambo Kings, Above the Law, Exit to Eden,* and *The Color Purple.* Denise Nicholas appeared in *Room 222, Ghost Dad, The Cosby Show,* and *One Day at a Time.* Fred Williamson acted in *Julia, Black Caesar, Fast Track, Police Story,* and *Life Outside;* he was director-producer of *South Beach, On the Edge,* and *Steele's Law,* among many others.

3. Bob Minor worked as a stuntman on *2 Fast 2 Furious, Blues Brothers 2000, Come Back Charleston Blues, Buffalo Soldiers, O. J. Simpson Story, Ocean's Eleven, Without a Trace,* and *National Treasure;* as stunt coordinator for *Glory, Set It Off, Unlawful Entry, Love Field, Boyz in the Hood, Poetic Justice,* and *Mo' Money;* and as second-unit director for *Posse, Lord Help Us, Body and Soul, Dirty Tricks,* and *Crunch.* On *Magnum P.I.* Minor stunt-doubled for Roger E. Mosley, and from 1982 to 1988 he was stunt coordinator and second-unit director of the series.

4. Melvin Van Peebles's *Sweet Sweetback's Baadasssss Song* was released by Roger Corman's New World Pictures in April 1971. In July 1971 Gordon Parks

directed *Shaft*, for which Isaac Hayes composed the score. "Theme from Shaft" won an Oscar, a Golden Globe, and a Grammy.

5. "NY Beauty Gets Kicked, Slugged," *Jet*, August 26, 1954, 60–61. One of Jones's credits was an episode of *Studio One* (CBS), "Man behind the Badge."

6. Films from the 1970s featuring blacks include *The Great White Hope* (starring James Earl Jones and Jane Alexander; directed by Martin Ritt), *Cotton Comes to Harlem* (written by Chester Himes; directed by Ossie Davis), *They Call Me Mister Tibbs! Lady Sings the Blues, Sounder, The Autobiography of Miss Jane Pittman, Conrack, Claudine, Buck and the Preacher, Super Fly* (directed by Gordon Parks Jr.; score by Curtis Mayfield), *Black Caesar,* and *Saturday Night.*

7. Quoted in Isaac Julien's TV documentary *Baadasssss Cinema* (IFC, Minerva Picture Co., 2002), starring Jim Brown, Larry Cohen, Tamara Dobson, Pam Grier, and Fred Williamson. Julien is an award-winning director whose credits include *Derek, Looking for Langston, Black and White in Color,* and *The Dark Side of Black.*

8. Gloria Hendry's 1980 repertory group was called Women in the Performing Arts. Her film and TV credits include *Black Kissinger, Seven Swans, Doing Time on Planet Earth, Black Caesar, Love American Style,* and *Falcon Crest.*

9. In the early 1960s, before the BSA was formed, Wayne King Sr. was probably the first black stuntman to become well known and in demand; he worked on *Omega Man* and *Cleopatra Jones.* Calvin Brown doubled Bill Cosby on *I Spy* and Jim Brown in *The Split.* Jophery Brown worked on *I Spy, Coffy,* and *Live and Let Die;* he became Morgan Freeman's regular double. Stunt coordinator Alan Oliney worked on or coordinated *Die Hard* and *High Crimes* and doubled Eddie Murphy. Marvin Walters coordinated *Shaft's Big Score, The Dogs of War, Heart of Darkness,* and *Eve's Bayou.* Stuntman Tony Brubaker worked on *There Was a Crooked Man, Melinda, Escape from New York,* and *Midnight Run;* he stunt-coordinated *Slaughter's Big Rip-off, Sugar Hill,* and *Devil in a Blue Dress.* Wayne King Jr. worked on *Blue Knight, Wholly Moses! D.C. Cab, Glory, Rush Hour,* and *Minority Report.* Henry Kingi Jr. worked on *Man Called Hawk, Baywatch, Money Train, Dante's Peak,* and *Mr. and Mrs. Smith;* he stunt-coordinated *V.I.P.* and directed *Redemption.*

10. Hill's comments on *Foxy Brown* (MGM Home Entertainment, 2001), DVD.

11. Among Pam Grier's first roles were *Women in Cages; Black Mama, White Mama; Greased Lightning;* and *Cool Breeze.* Jadie David doubled Grier in *Coffy, Foxy Brown, Drum, Friday Foster,* and other films.

12. Quoted in Julien, *Baadasssss Cinema.*

13. Mabel Normand's movie was *Mabel at the Wheel* (1914); Mary Pickford's was *A Beast at Bay* (1912).

14. The stuntwomen in *Coffy* and *Foxy Brown* included Jadie David, Stephanie and Jeannie Epper, Peaches Jones, and Louise Johnson.

15. Richard Washington's stunt credits include *Glory, Die Hard: With a Vengeance, Blown Away, The Abyss, Seven Hours to Judgment, Mississippi Burning,*

*Disorderlies,* and *The Goonies;* he stunt-coordinated *Fortune Dane, Some Kind of Hero, The Nude Bomb, The Deep, Sheba Baby, Fox Style,* and *The Sword and the Sorcerer.*

16. Peaches Jones (1951–1986) also worked on *Halls of Anger, The Strawberry Statement, Melinda, Black Samson, Buck and the Preacher, Freebie and the Bean,* and *Earthquake.*

17. David Lamb, "Stuntwomen Stand on Feats," *Los Angeles Times,* November 29, 1971, D1–D3. Lamb estimated there were 200 stuntmen, but not all of them belonged to the Stuntmen's Association.

18. Minutes of the Stuntwomen's Association, February 5, 1972, from the collection of Julie Johnson.

19. The March 1977 directory of the Stuntwomen's Association of Motion Pictures lists the following members: Susan Backlinie, Pam Bebermeyer, Paula Crist, Evelyn Cuffee, Paula Dell, Rita Egleston, Lila Finn, Donna Garrett, Donna Hall, Rosemary Johnson, Marilyn Moe, Stevie Myers, Audrey Saunders, and Kim Ward. Honorary life members were Polly Burson, Babe DeFreest, Sharon Lucas, and Helen Thurston. Not all stuntwomen were members of the Stuntwomen's Association, the new Professional Society of Stuntwomen, or the Black Stuntmen's Association. Janet Brady and Kitty O'Neil were the only female members of Stunts Unlimited.

20. Needham, *Stuntman!* 169.

21. Jock Mahoney (1919–1989) was an actor, stuntman, and stunt coordinator from the 1940s to 1980s.

22. Richard Setlowe, "Biz's Fall Guys Join Hands," *Variety,* December 6, 1996.

23. Needham, *Stuntman!* 169–70, 181. In 1980 stuntman Alan Gibbs left Stunts Unlimited to organize the International Stunt Association, which currently has forty-four male members and one female member. In 2010 Stunts Unlimited had fifty-three members. In 1992 stuntman Tony Epper formed the National League of SAG Stunt Performers to unite all the groups, including the Stuntwomen's Association and Drivers Inc., under one umbrella to achieve common goals, such as safety.

24. A third organization was founded in 1984, the United Stuntwomen's Association (USA). In 2002 Darlene Ava Williams and Gloria O'Brien Fontenot formed V10 Women Stunt Professionals.

25. Janet Chase, "Women Daredevils," *Cosmopolitan,* July 1980.

26. Author interview with Dave Robb.

27. Dave Robb, "Okay on the Job, but No Room for Women in Two of Three Stuntmen's Orgs," *Daily Variety,* December 28, 1983.

28. Robb interview.

29. Robb, "Okay on the Job."

30. Suzanne Stone, "Numbers Don't Lie," *American Premiere* [ca. 1981], 13.

31. Washington was hired to stunt-coordinate a Universal production: a remake of *Two Minute Warning.* His other coordinating credits include *The Nude Bomb,*

*Bustin' Loose,* the TV series *Buck Rogers, Seven Hours to Judgment, Fortune Dane, The Sword and the Sorcerer, Sheba Baby,* and *The Deep.*

32. Bob Minor served on the board of the Stuntmen's Association and was a second vice president. In 2010 the fifty-member association had black, Asian, and Hispanic members. When Minor stunt-coordinated *Glory* (1989), he hired seventy-two stunt people; thirty-two were African American.

33. Kim Fellner, "Stuntwomen: Breaking Through," *Screen Actor* 23, no. 1 (Summer 1981).

34. Quoted in Robb, "Okay on the Job."

35. Quoted in Longwell, "Real Double Troubles."

36. In 1973, after serving several terms, Kathleen Nolan became the first woman to serve as first vice president on the SAG board.

37. Gregory, *Women Who Run the Show,* 114; "SAG-WGA Joint Women's Committee Goals," archives of Kathleen Nolan. The Directors Guild formed its Women's Steering Committee in 1979; not until 1994 did it establish the African American Steering Committee.

38. The Black Stuntmen's Association and the Hollywood branch of the NAACP pressured studios to hire black stunt doubles for African American actors in the TV miniseries *Roots* in 1977. Members of the SAG-AFTRA EEO and Diversity Committee and the Coalition of Black Stuntmen and Women (headed by Maria Walters), which succeeded the BSA in the 1980s, won a settlement when a studio violated the agreement to hire more minorities.

39. See also the Forty-Second Anniversary Issue of *Variety,* November 1, 1974, 130, covering the release of a new SAG survey revealing that men held a three-to-one lead over women in prime-time roles on television.

40. Stone, "Numbers Don't Lie," 13–14. This study revealed that each succeeding age group had similarly unequal jobs and earnings.

41. Robb, "Okay on the Job."

42. Stone, "Numbers Don't Lie," 14.

43. Gregory, *Women Who Run the Show,* 123.

44. William Panowsky, "Irish Street Fighter Wanted SAG to Be Part of the Cultural Revolution," *Los Angeles Herald Examiner,* November 27, 1975.

45. Gregory, *Women Who Run the Show,* 123–24.

46. Gloria Henry said she did some of her own stunts in *Black Belt Jones,* "but I also had the privilege of a stuntwoman. I think it was Evelyn Cuffee."

47. Robert Clouse (1928–1997) was a writer, producer, and director (*Enter the Dragon, Ironheart, The Game of Death*).

## 6. The Women's Movement and Female Action Heroes

1. Molly Haskell, *From Reverence to Rape: The Treatment of Women in the Movies* (New York: Holt, Rinehart & Winston, 1973), 1–2, 370–71.

2. *Honey West* was the first prime-time TV series with a female detective as its main character. Sharon Lucas and Marilyn Moe doubled Anne Francis.

3. Rita Egleston worked on *Blade Runner, Dallas, Cliffhangers, Big Foot, When Time Ran Out, Cutter's Way, Tron,* and *Ghost Story.* Other stuntwomen of the 1970s included Pam Bebermeyer, Janet Brady, Dottie Catching, Ann Chatterton, Denise Cheshire, Jean Coulter, Paula Crist, Kerrie Cullen, Debbie Evans, Marneen Fields, Glory Fioramonti, Dorothy Ford, Leslie Hoffman, Marcia Holley, Louise Johnson, Rosemary Johnston, Debbie Kahana, Mags Kavanaugh, Kay Kimler, Wendy Leech, Joyce MacNeal, Beth Nufer, Kitty O'Neil, Mary Peters, Diane Peterson, Sherry Peterson, Lee Pulford, Glynn Rubin, Tanya Russell, Audrey Saunders, Victoria Vanderkloot, and Sunny Woods.

4. Carolyn Day, "Jeannie Epper a Real-Life Wonder Woman," *Inside Stunts,* Winter 2007, 11–12. A gymnast, acrobat, and trick rider, Day performed stunts in *Drive, Threshold,* and *Lost;* she stunt-coordinated *Dockweiler, Sanctuary, Death in Charge, Paying for It, Stacy's Mom, Make It or Break It, Karl Mulberry,* and *Redemption.*

5. Fellner, "Stuntwomen: Breaking Through," 34.

6. Day, "Jeannie Epper Real-Life Wonder Woman," 12–13.

7. Author interview with Jeannie Epper. In the 1970s she also worked on *Emergency, The Rockford Files, Charlie's Angels, Bionic Woman, Eaten Alive, The Poseidon Adventure,* and *The Don Is Dead.*

8. "Person of the Week: Jeannie Epper," ABC News Internet Venture, May 12, 2007.

9. Chase, "Women Daredevils."

10. Roberts, "Fall Girls Getting the Drop."

11. Jean Coulter worked on *Cujo, Time Bomb, A View to Kill, The Quest, Remington Steele, The Paper Chase, Airport '77, Kojak, Stunts, Beach Patrol, Hart to Hart, Charlie's Angels, Bionic Woman, Wonder Woman, The Rockford Files, Harry-O, Baretta, The Villain,* and *The Children of Times Square* (as stunt coordinator). Jean's son, Shawn Coulter, also did some stunt work and was a producer on *Uninvited.* Jean's sister, Lori Martin, appeared in *Cape Fear* and *The Chase.*

12. Chase, "Women Daredevils." Julie Johnson's many stunt performances include work on *Doctor Doolittle, The Strawberry Statement, Women in Chains,* and *Pete 'n' Tillie.*

13. Vince Cupone's credits include *Castle, All My Children, Meet Dave, Sex in the City, The David Letterman Show, Rescue Me, Law & Order, Dirty Sexy Money,* and *The Sopranos;* he was assistant stunt coordinator for *Cupid, Law & Order: Criminal Intent, Rescue Me,* and *The Beautiful Life: TBL* and stunt coordinator for *How to Make It in America, Nexus, Pan Am,* and *Golden Boy.*

14. Regina Parton doubled Stephanie Powers on *Hart to Hart* and Jaclyn Smith on *Charlie's Angels.* Donna Garrett worked on *Lost in Space, Star Trek, Police Woman, Cagney & Lacey, Twins, Ghostbusters,* and *Hero.*

15. Willson, "Stuntwomen the Invisible Superheroes," 53. Debbie Evans's 1970s credits include *Rock 'n' Roll High School, The Concorde . . . Airport '79, The Dukes of Hazzard, CHiPs,* and *Wonder Woman.*

16. Christine Anne Baur worked on *Maximum Overdrive, Over the Top, Mannequin on the Move, Eye of the Tiger, Hellhole, Sudden Impact, The Witches of Eastwick, The Singing Detective,* and *Thicker than Water.* In 2005 she was among the group that won the World Stunt Award for best specialty stunt, for *Taxi.*

17. The Baxley Bunch stuntmen were Al Wyatt Sr., Bobby Orison, Jerry Summers, Henry Kingi Sr., Al Wyatt Jr., Henri Kingi Jr., and Paul Baxley's son Craig and nephew Gary.

18. Fellner, "Stuntwomen: Breaking Through," 34.

## 7. Disaster Movies and Disastrous Stunts

1. *The Poseidon Adventure* (1972) employed forty-one stuntmen and nine stuntwomen, including Lila Finn, Paula Dell, Jeannie Epper, Marylyn Bower, Carol Daniels, Donna Garrett, Marilyn Moe Stader, and June Ioma Wilson. The sequel, *Beyond the Poseidon Adventure* (1979), employed sixteen stuntmen and six stuntwomen. *King Kong* (1976), with an estimated budget of $24 million, used twelve stuntmen and four women; in comparison, the 1933 version of *King Kong* was budgeted at $670,000 and used eighteen stuntmen and six stuntwomen. *Logan's Run* (1976) employed eighteen stuntmen and fifteen stuntwomen. *The Hindenburg* (1975) had about forty stunt players, including Rosemary Johnston, Regina Parton, Dottie Catching, and Evelyn Smith. *Apocalypse Now* (1979) employed five stuntmen. More than fifty stunt people worked on *1941,* including stuntwomen May Boss, Denise Cheshire, Eurlyne and Jeannie Epper, Leslie Hoffman, Mary Peters, and Regina Parton. *The Black Hole* (1979) had twelve stuntmen and three stuntwomen. *Meteor* (1979) had eighteen stuntmen and six stuntwomen.

2. *Airport* (1970) employed two stuntwomen, *Airport 1975* had one stuntwoman, *Airport '77* had five stuntwomen, and *The Concord . . . Airport '79* had eight stuntwomen. These were small gains, but they were better than *The Planet of the Apes* franchise: 1968, twenty-nine stuntmen and no stuntwomen; 1970, thirty stuntmen and no stuntwomen; 1971, three stuntmen; 1972, forty-three men and two women, Paula Crist and Regina Parton; 1973, thirty-two men plus Crist and Parton.

3. Six stuntmen worked on *Jaws* (1975), and eighteen stuntmen and two stuntwomen worked on *Star Wars* (1977).

4. *Blazing Saddles* employed sixty-two stuntmen and eleven stuntwomen.

5. Of the seventy-three stunt people hired for *The Towering Inferno,* eleven were women, including May Boss, Paula Crist, Paula Dell, Jeannie and Stephanie Epper, Lila Finn, Regina Parton, Glynn Rubin, and Marilyn Moe Stader.

6. Glynn Rubin's credits include *The Chase, Independence Day, Private Benjamin, Cutter's Way, RoboCop 2, The Sting II, Foul Play,* and *Hard Target.*

7. Sandra Lee Gimpel's early credits include *Lost in Space, Time Tunnel, Land of the Giants, Man from the 25th Century,* and *The Poseidon Adventure.*

8. *Hollywood Reporter,* May 10, 1974, cited 141 stunt people working on *Earthquake.* The Internet Movie Database lists more than 100, including Richard Washington, Henry Kingi, Bob Minor, and three other African American stuntmen, along with twenty-four stuntwomen, among them May Boss, Polly Burson, Evelyn Cuffee, Carol Daniels, Paula Dell, Patty Elder, Jeannie and Stephanie Epper, Lila Finn, Donna Garrett, Louise Johnson, Peaches Jones, Stevie Myers, and Regina Parton. The quake effect was produced by the "Shaker Mount" camera system developed for the movie.

9. As a dancer, Paula Dell worked with Martha Graham, Jose Limon, and choreographers Jerome Robbins, Jack Regas, Busby Berkeley, and Nick Castle. As an acrobat, she toured with the Russ Saunders Trio in the 1950s and worked in Ted DeWayne Brothers Circus and DeWayne's acrobatic shows, performing an adagio-teeterboard act and circus acrobatics that involved a trampoline, Arabian pyramids, and aerial work. This was great experience for her stunts on *Logan's Run, The Poseidon Adventure, Silent Movie, In Harm's Way, The Towering Inferno, Death Race 2000, Swashbuckler,* and *Star!* In 2003 she was inducted into the U.S. Sports Acrobatics Hall of Fame Gallery of Honor.

10. Willson, "Stuntwomen the Invisible Superheroes," 53.

11. Finn interview in SAG, "Stuntwomen's Oral History Project."

12. De Witt, "Ride 'em Cowgirls."

13. Finn, "Perils of Polly."

14. *Stunts* employed stuntwomen Lee Polford, Deanna Dae Coleman, and Jean Coulter; its stuntmen included Dar Robinson, A. J. Bakunas, Gary David, and Paul Nuckles. Deanna Dae Coleman was the only stuntwoman in *The Stunt Man.*

15. One year earlier Needham had directed his first picture, the surprise hit *Smokey and the Bandit* (1977).

16. The stuntwomen on *Hooper* included Janet Brady, Jadie David, Patty Elder, Regina Parton, Mary Peters, Pamela Bebermeyer, Louise Johnson, and Bonnie McPherson. Bobby Bass was the stunt coordinator. High-fall expert A. J. Bakunas leaped a record 232 feet from a helicopter into an airbag.

17. Sammy Thurman's credits include *Diabolique, Misery, Peacemaker, American History X,* and *The War of the Roses.* Janet Brady's credits include *Cannonball!, Silver Streak, Smokey and the Bandit, Blade Runner, Beverly Hills Cop, Fatal Attraction, The War of the Roses, Terminator 2, Basic Instinct, Rain, Gone in 60 Seconds, Evolution, Say It Isn't So, Orange County, Showtime,* and her favorite, *The Kitty O'Neil Story.*

18. Alan Gibbs (1940–1988) was a stuntman, stunt coordinator, and second-

unit director. His credits include *Chinatown, The Deerslayer, Scorpio, The Stone Killer, Jigsaw John, Cannonball Run II,* and *Legal Eagles.*

19. In *Steamboat Bill, Jr.* (Buster Keaton & Joseph M. Schenck Productions, United Artists, 1928), Louise Keaton is credited as the stuntwoman doubling Marion Byron.

20. In 1980 sportswoman Kitty O'Neil held the land speed record for women at 512 miles per hour; she was also the fastest woman on water skis, at 105 miles per hour, and a champion drag boat racer. She doubled Lee Grant in *The Omen II,* was set on fire in *Airport '77,* and did a six-story fall in a 1975 episode of *Baretta;* on *Eschied* she set a world record of 127 feet for a fall, then broke her own record with a 180-foot fall. Amazingly, Kitty was deaf, but her remarkable mother taught her how to talk and how to play the piano and the cello. She gave Kitty "a dime or a quarter to try to jump off the high dive or master a new athletic skill," according to Janet Chase's 1980 article in *Cosmopolitan.* Her husband, stuntman Duffy Hambleton, appeared in *Midway, Bound for Glory,* and *Cleopatra Jones.*

21. In contrast, the Stuntmen's Association retained its all-male membership until March 2002, forty-one years after its founding, when Jeannie Epper was made an honorary member.

22. John D. Ross, "Jophery Brown: This Guy's Something Else," *Inside Stunts,* Summer 2007, 23–25. Brown's credits include *Bonfire of the Vanities, Kiss the Girls, The Flood, Along Came a Spider, Sum of All Fears,* and *Dreamcatcher.*

23. *King Kong's* four stuntwomen were Kelly Nichols, Beth Nufer, Diane Peterson, and Sunny Woods (Woods and Nichols doubled Jessica Lange). Sunny Woods's other credits include *Logan's Run, Witchboard, Charlie Chan and the Curse of the Dragon Queen,* and *Bustin' Loose.*

24. Ronnie Lippin, "Women Who Fall for Their Jobs," *American Way,* June 1977.

25. Day, "Jeannie Epper Real-Life Wonder Woman," 11.

26. Susan Backlinie's other credits include *The Fall Guy, 1941,* and *Quark.* The stuntmen in *Jaws* were Richard E. Butler, Howard Curtis, Frank James Sparks, Dick Warlock, Fred Zendar, and Dick Ziker; Ted Grossman was the stunt coordinator.

27. Chase, "Women Daredevils."

28. Glory Fioramonti's stunt credits include *Carrie, Rocky, Escape from New York, Thelma and Louise, The Abyss, Alien Nation,* and *Groundhog Day;* she was stunt coordinator for *The Client, Till There Was You, Earthly Possessions, Kalamazoo? Hush, The Craft, Bam Bam and Celeste,* and *If These Walls Could Talk 2,* among other films.

29. Chris Nashawaty, "Danger Is Their Middle Name," *Entertainment Weekly,* October 19, 2007, 96.

30. Chase, "Women Daredevils."

31. In addition to Jadie David, *Rollercoaster's* stunt players were Diamond

Farnsworth, James W. Gavin, Bob Herron, Larry Holt, Tanya Russell, and Jesse Wayne. John Daheim was the stunt coordinator.

32. "Stunters Are Injured," *Variety*, November 1, 1976.

33. By 1979, Debbie Evans's credits included *General Hospital*, *Deathsport*, *Rock 'n' Roll High School*, *CHiPs*, *The Dukes of Hazzard*, and *Smokey and the Bandit II*. Other stuntwomen on *The Jerk* were Diane Peterson and Jeannie Epper.

34. Conrad E. Palmisano's other credits include *Police Story*, *Kung Fu*, and *Cat Ballou*; he stunt-coordinated *Grand Theft Auto*, *Thunder and Lightning*, *Spenser: For Hire*, *Stakeout*, and *War and Remembrance* and was second-unit director for *Red Dragon*, *X-Men*, *The Peacemaker*, and many other films.

35. Willson, "Stuntwomen the Invisible Superheroes," 53. In 1979 Debbie Evans was also the highest-placed woman in the National Motorcycle Trials Championship.

## 8. Stunt Safety and Gender Discrimination

1. Stuntwoman Donna Garrett worked on *Logan's Run*, *Laverne and Shirley*, *Melvin and Howard*, *Cagney & Lacey*, *Airport*, *Ghostbusters*, *Hero*, *Tron*, and *Footloose*, among many others. In addition to stunt-coordinating, Sandy Gimpel doubled the lead in *Mrs. Columbo* (Kate Mulgrew). She was also stunt coordinator for *A Vacation in Hell*, *Otherworld*, *Population: 1*, *Timescape*, *Seinfeld*, *Any Day Now*, *State of Grace*, *Seven Hours to Judgment*, *Montana Amazon*, *Tourist Trap*, *Hellhole*, *These Old Broads*, *Diamond Confidential*, *Luis*, *Immortal Combat*, *Double Cross*, and *Adventures of the Dunderheads* and was second-unit director on *Harts of the West*.

2. Interview with Beth Kennedy in Gregory, *Women Who Run the Show*, 65–66. As a senior vice president of business development and administration at Universal Studios/MCA, she developed systems and hired and trained administration, information systems, and telecommunications personnel.

3. Interview with Gale Anne Hurd in Gregory, *Women Who Run the Show*, 217–18. Hurd's other credits include *Very Good Girls*, *Choctaw Code Talkers*, *The Wronged Man*, *The Walking Dead*, *Gaiking*, and *The Nameless*.

4. Freedland, "Danger Biz," 21. For Ron Rondell's stunt, see also Kevin Conley, *The Full Burn: On the Set, at the Bar, behind the Wheel, and over the Edge with Hollywood Stuntmen* (New York: Bloomsbury, 2008).

5. Julie Johnson coordinated seventeen episodes of the fourth season of *Charlie's Angels*; she also doubled the stars in nine of those episodes. Darlene Tompkins doubled Cheryl Ladd, and Hilary Thompson doubled Kate Jackson.

6. Jean Coulter married in 1961, had two children ten months apart, and divorced soon after. A few years later she remarried, divorced, and became a single mom again. In 1981 she married and is still married to Ray Marek, a high-wire walker, human cannonball, and professional water-skier (his stunt credits include

*Witchboard* and *Fletch*). Jean and one of her former husbands developed, financed, and ran Camera Cars Unlimited.

7. Bobby Bass (1936–2001) stunt-coordinated *Hooper, The Cannonball Run, Rocky V, Corvette Summer, Lethal Weapon, Excessive Force,* and *Warning Signs;* he was second-unit director for *Thelma and Louise* and *Black Rain.* Howard Curtis's credits include *The Deer Hunter.*

8. Testimony of Jean Coulter-Marek, August 14, 1987, summary of reporter's transcript, *Johnson v. Spelling-Goldberg Productions,* vol. 5, 929–30.

9. Transcript of attorney Richard Grey's pretrial interview with Julie Johnson, March 1987.

10. Coulter-Marek testimony, 936–39.

11. Grey-Johnson interview, 1–2.

12. Author interview with Julie Johnson.

13. Coulter-Marek testimony, 939–42.

14. Grey-Johnson interview, 3.

15. Coulter-Marek testimony, 941.

16. Grey-Johnson interview, 3.

17. Coulter-Marek testimony, 949.

18. Author interview with Jean Coulter.

19. Coulter-Marek testimony, 952.

20. Author interview with Johnson. At the trial in 1987, Blair Gilbert testified that she didn't see the dailies.

21. Grey-Johnson interview, 4.

22. Coulter-Marek testimony, 939.

23. Grey-Johnson interview, 6–8.

24. Ibid.

25. Ibid.

26. Coulter-Marek testimony, 971, 976.

27. Grey-Johnson interview, 9–10.

28. Author interview with Johnson.

29. Grey-Johnson interview, 11–15.

30. Ibid.

31. Author interview with Johnson.

32. Dave Robb, "Stunt Community Intensifying Efforts for Ratings System," *Hollywood Reporter,* September 14, 1981, 4.

33. SAG Stuntwomen's Facts, August 8, 1984.

34. Minutes of Stunt and Safety Committee, February 27, 1982.

35. Jeffrey Hansen, "Business Is No Joke to Movie Fall Guys," *Los Angeles Times,* September 20, 1981, 10.

36. In 1983 the SAG board turned down the ratings system because it was based only on the number of days a stunt performer worked. In the 1983 contract nego-

tiations, versions of "getting the wigs off men" and eliminating the practice of "painting down" were accepted, but as one stuntwoman said, "The guild has some pretty sketchy language that has to do with who you hire as a double. It's not really clearly defined." In 2001 the definitions were improved.

37. Henry Wills, "Ego Has No Place in the Matter of Safety," *Film News International,* September 1984. Wills's forty-seven-year career began in 1935; he was president of the Stuntmen's Association in 1974–1975. His secret for safety on the set: careful preparation.

38. Robb, "Stunt Community Intensifying Efforts," 4.

## 9. Danger, Drugs, and Death

1. Stuntwoman Paula Moody (1951–2007) also worked on *Action Jackson, Lisa, RoboCop 2, The Wizard,* and *The Blob.* Other stunt players on *Airplane!* were Janet Brady, Paula Dell, Mary Peters, Diane Peterson, and Dar Robinson.

2. Dean Jeffries stunt-coordinated.

3. Michael London, "The Stunt Man: Issue of Safety vs. Spectacle," *Los Angeles Times,* February 7, 1983, 1.

4. Stuntwomen in *The Blues Brothers* included Pam Bebermeyer, May Boss, Janet Brady, Jean Coulter, Carol Daniels, Jadie David, Jeannie and Stephanie Epper, Karen McLarty, Stevie Myers, Kitty O'Neil, Lee Pulford, Tanya Russell, and Sharon Schaffer.

5. In addition to *The Blues Brothers,* Janet Brady worked on *Hunter,* both shot in Chicago. She said: "On *Hunter,* we were doing fights on the train and shooting guns. It was much more fun because Steve McQueen was awesome. That was the last show he did. McQueen was doubled by Loren Janes; talk about a gymnast, that man is the ultimate."

6. Frank Swertlow, "It's Snowing in Hollywood Every Day," *TV Guide,* March 7, 1981, 38–40.

7. Frank Swertlow, "Hollywood's Cocaine Connection," *TV Guide,* February 28, 1981, 9–12.

8. Swertlow, "Snowing in Hollywood," 40.

9. Andy Furillo, "For LAPD 'Entertainment Squad' Narcs, Coke Is It," *Los Angeles Times,* Metro edition, March 22, 1985.

10. Will Tusher, "Drug Abuse Serious and a Growing Problem among Pic and TV Workers," *Variety,* December 29, 1986.

11. Grey-Johnson interview, March 1987. The incident related by Julie Johnson took place on January 24, 1980. A few interviewees stated that drug use on the set was common knowledge, but they called it "recreational." Two said that by the fourth season of *Charlie's Angels* (1979–1980), "the drugs came out." The smooth-running show began to fall apart, and season five was its last.

12. Baxter, *Stunt,* 12.

13. Odile Astié performed stunts in many French and U.S. films, including *The Great Race, The Southern Star, Bluebeard,* and *The French Connection II.* She doubled Brigitte Bardot, Claudia Cardinale, Ursula Andress, and Jeanne Moreau.

14. Minutes of the SAG Ad Hoc Stuntwomen's Subcommittee meeting, December 6, 1980, from Julie Johnson's collection. Glory Fioramonti's source for the report was stuntman Ralph Carpenter; stuntmen Ernie Orsatti and Chuck Couch were allegedly present as well.

15. Michael Szymanski, "Gag Work Takes Its Toll in Injuries—and Lives," *Torrance (CA) Daily Breeze/News-Pilot,* April 25, 1986. Other deaths in 1981 included director Boris Sagal (*The Omega Man, The Diary of Anne Frank*), who was killed on May 22 on the set of *World War III* "when he walked into a rotating helicopter blade," and stuntman Jack Tyree, who died in August "when he missed the air bag that was to break his fall from an 80-foot cliff on *The Sword and the Sorcerer.*" Michael Szymanski, "Film, TV Accidents on Rise," *San Fernando Valley Sunday Daily News,* October 25, 1987.

16. Michael London, "Safety, First, Last, Ever?" *Los Angeles Times,* February 6, 1983.

17. Jack Slater, "On the Risk of Filming Stunts," *Los Angeles Times,* July 14, 1981.

18. According to Needham, *Stuntman!* 261, *Cannonball Run* cost $15 million and had a thirty-two-day shooting schedule.

19. Heidi Von Beltz with Peter Copeland, *My Soul Purpose: Living Learning and Healing* (New York: Random House, 1996), 9–11.

20. Dave Robb, "When a Stunt Goes Wrong: One Victim's Tragic Aftermath," *Hollywood Reporter,* September 4, 1981.

21. Dave Robb, "Needham Stands Alone in Stunt Car-Crash Suit," *Variety,* January 10, 1983.

22. Von Beltz, *My Soul Purpose,* 14–16.

23. Robb, "Needham Stands Alone."

24. Von Beltz, *My Soul Purpose,* 186. Heidi sued and won $3.2 million on June 13, 1986, almost six years after the accident.

25. London, "Safety, First, Last, Ever?"

26. Robb, "Needham Stands Alone."

27. SAG membership numbers courtesy of Glenn Hiraoka, SAG stunt and safety director.

28. Minutes of the SAG Ad Hoc Stuntwomen's Subcommittee meeting, December 6, 1980. Among those present were Dottie Catching, Paula Dell, Jeannie Epper, Lila Finn, Glory Fioramonti, Sandy Gimpel, Leslie Hoffman, Louise Johnson, Diane Peterson, Sherry Peterson, and Sharon Schaffer.

29. The report was circulated by the SAG Women's Conference Committee, December 11, 1980.

30. SAG Stuntwomen's Fact Sheet, September 8, 1984.

31. Karen Lustgarten, "Stunt Women Speak Up," *Reel News* 3, no. 2 (April 1993): 16.

32. Gregory, *Women Who Run the Show,* 21–23.

33. Author interview with Julie Johnson, and excerpts from Johnson's written memorandum about the EEOC.

## 10. Breaking the Code of Silence

1. Stephen Farber and Marc Green, *Outrageous Conduct: Art, Ego and the Twilight Zone Case* (New York: William Morrow, 1988), 16.

2. Originally cited in the minutes of the Stuntwomen's Subcommittee meeting, December 6, 1980, and reiterated in the minutes of February 25, 1982. In 1982 subcommittee members included Jeannie Epper, Diane Peterson, Leslie Hoffman, K. C. Nichols, Dottie Catching, Debbie Kahana, Sherry Peterson, Paula Dell, Rita Egleston, Lois Gaines, and Debbie Porter.

3. Ibid.

4. In 2015, thirty-three years later, the second stuntwomen's survey was prepared and distributed. Julie Johnson and Jadie David spearheaded that effort.

5. Finn interview in SAG, "Stuntwomen's Oral History Project," 3–4, 6, 8–9.

6. Grey-Johnson interview, 18–20.

7. Joe Dante, George Miller, and Steven Spielberg directed the other three segments of *Twilight Zone.*

8. Farber and Green, *Outrageous Conduct.* See also London, "Safety, First, Last, Ever?"

9. London, "Safety, First, Last, Ever?"

10. Farber and Green, *Outrageous Conduct,* 169. Stunt people who worked on *Twilight Zone* included Eurlyne Epper, Debby Porter, Terry James, Thomas Byrd, Eddy Donno, Joseph Hieu, and Al Leong. Gary McLarty stunt-coordinated.

11. Ibid., 107–12.

12. Ibid., 169.

13. Ibid., 106, 168–70, 207.

14. SAG Stunt and Safety Committee minutes, February 27, 1982.

15. Szymanski, "Gag Work Takes Its Toll." In a later article, Szymanski noted that 10 people had been killed and 4,998 injured in California productions since 1982. Szymanski "Film, TV Accidents on Rise."

16. Deborah Caulfield and Michael Cieply, "Twilight Aftermath: It's Caution on the Movie Set," *Los Angeles Times,* May 20, 1987.

17. See Von Beltz, *My Soul Purpose,* 188, for the usual handling of stunt injuries.

18. Both Jean Coulter and Leslie Hoffman claimed they were blacklisted for

their work on the survey. Coulter was also blacklisted because of her sexual harassment suit against stunt coordinator Roy Harrison. Julie Johnson blamed her blacklisting on her work on the survey, her complaints about unsafe and inadequate stunt cars, her EEOC complaint, and her subsequent suit against Spelling-Goldberg.

19. Norma also wanted Julie to present the stuntwomen's survey results to the L.A. City Commission on the Status of Women, which she did on March 25, 1987.

20. Stuntwomen's Survey, 1982, archives of Julie Johnson. One respondent wrote that the New York group had thirty stuntmen (ten of whom were coordinators), seven stuntwomen, and one female stunt coordinator.

21. Interoffice communication from Kim Fellner to the SAG Board of Directors, November 3, 1982.

22. Letters to the editor, *Variety*, December 17, 1982, quoted by committee members D. K. (Debbie) Kahana and K. C. Nichols, who agreed that the survey's goal had been accomplished.

23. Leslie Hoffman served on the SAG board from 1982 to 1985. She was cochair and later chair of the board's Stunt Committee and also served on the national and Los Angeles boards of the American Federation of Television and Radio Artists (AFTRA).

24. Dave Robb, "EEOC Searchlight on Hollywood," *Variety*, April 27, 1984.

25. Michael Leahy and Wallis Annenberg, "Discrimination in Hollywood: How Bad Is It?" *TV Guide*, October 13, 1984, 8–10. Carol Roper is an award-winning writer whose credits include *Orphan Train, The Lady Killers*, episodes of *Knot's Landing, Kaz*, and *All that Glitters*.

26. Ibid. In the 1980s Johnson worked on *Heartbeeps, Bare Essence, The Thorn Birds*, and episodes of *St. Elsewhere, Scarecrow and Mrs. King*, and *MacGyver*, but these jobs amounted to much less work than in her earlier career.

27. Julie Johnson filed her class-action suit on February 21, 1984. In April 1984 the California Department of Fair Employment and Housing allowed the case to go to trial. The suit alleged that SAG's referral of producers to the stunt associations "perpetuated discrimination."

28. Maria Denunzio, "Stunt Woman Claims SAG, Other Groups Discriminate," *Los Angeles Herald Examiner*, February 22, 1984.

29. Robb, "Okay on the Job."

30. It is unknown how many others were blacklisted. There is no doubt that blacklisting was used as a threat.

31. Memo from Tom Gleason, assistant to attorney Matt Byron, to Jean Coulter and Julie Johnson, April 26, 1984, from Julie Johnson's collection.

32. From 1999 to 2008 Leslie Hoffman stunt-coordinated *The Innocents Mission* and six episodes of *Star Trek: New Voyages: Phase II*. Her other coordinating credits include *Never Land, Safe Journey, Everything Put Together, As Far as the Eye Can*

*See,* and *Daybreak Berlin;* she was fight coordinator on *Dead Ballerina* and she was a stunt rigger on *Dead above Ground.*

33. Author interview with Jean Coulter and e-mail from Coulter, August 19, 2007. The two-part "Golden Gate Cop Killers" episode of *Vega$* aired in March 1980. Stunt credits included Coulter and Sherry Peterson; Roy Harrison was not listed as coordinator.

34. Mary Murphy, "Sexual Harassment in Hollywood," *TV Guide,* March 29–April 4, 1986, 3–5.

35. Ibid., 4. According to Murphy, the judge rejected Jean Coulter's lawsuit because the statute of limitations had expired. In her interview with the author, Jean said her lawyer had missed the filing deadline.

## 11. Women's New Attitudes and Ambitions

1. Statistics supplied by Glenn Hiraoka, SAG.

2. Gloria Steinem, "Women Are Never Front-Runners," *New York Times,* January 8, 2008.

3. New stuntwomen in the 1980s included Julie Adair, Joni Avery, Simone Boisseree, Eliza Coleman, Kelsee King Devoreaux, Annie Ellis, Cindy Folkerson, Sarah Franzl, Marian Green, Bonnie Happy, Marguerite Happy, Sy Hollands, Barbara Anne Klein, Tina Mckissick, Caryn Mower, Patricia M. Peters, Alison Reid, Debby Lynn Ross, Sharon Schaffer, Patricia Tallman, Kim Wade, Cheryl Wheeler-Dixon, and Boni Yanagisawa.

4. Annie Ellis's credits include *Fatal Attraction, Burglar, Lethal Weapon, Point of No Return, Made in America, The Matrix Reloaded, True Blood, Green Lantern, Fast Five, The Green Hornet,* and *The Lone Ranger.* In 2009 Ellis and others performing in *Iron Man* won the SAG Award for outstanding performance by a stunt ensemble. David Ellis was stunt coordinator or second-unit director for *Patriot Games, Gorky Park, Fatal Attraction,* and *The Perfect Storm;* he directed *Cellular* and *Snakes on a Plane.*

5. Clifford Happy's credits include *Patriot Games, 2 Fast 2 Furious, Rules of Engagement,* and *The Fugitive;* he regularly doubles Tommy Lee Jones. Edith Happy was a stunt rider in *Westward the Women, After the Sunset,* and other films. Bonnie Happy was a trick rider for eleven years in the Professional Rodeo Cowboys Association. Her stunt credits include *Crank, Problem Child 3, Home Invasion, Hellhole, Silverado, Dynasty,* and *Die Hard: With a Vengeance.* The United Stuntwomen's Association was formed in 1984 by stuntwomen Tonya Russell, Christine Anne Baur, and Faith Minton.

6. In *Matt Houston,* Jimmy Nickerson doubled Lee Horsley, and Bonnie Happy doubled Pamela Hensley. Nickerson began in the business in 1970 and started stunt-coordinating in 1976; his many credits include *Rocky, The Deep, Rocky II, Raging Bull,* and *Dynasty.*

7. *Romancing the Stone* was directed by Robert Zemeckis; Diane Thomas wrote the screenplay, with contributions from Treva Silverman, Lem Dobbs, and Howard Franklin. Jeannie Epper's other work in the 1980s included *The Blues Brothers, Used Cars, Smokey and the Bandit II, Cannonball Run, The Sword and the Sorcerer, Dynasty, Poltergeist, Terms of Endearment,* and *Blade Runner.* Terry Leonard stunt-coordinated *A Man Called Horse, The Fugitive,* and *Die Hard: With a Vengeance;* he was second-unit director for *Cowboys and Aliens, Expendable,* and *The Fast and the Furious.* Vince Deadrick Jr. started in the business in 1978 and began stunt-coordinating in 1983. His credits include *Avenging Angels, MacGyver, True Grit* (2010), *Victorious,* and *Star Trek: Enterprise;* he was second-unit director for *Arlington Road* and *The Hat Squad.*

8. Day, "Jeannie Epper Real-Life Wonder Woman," 12–13.

9. Charles Champlin, "The Adrenalin Junkies," *Los Angeles Times Magazine,* March 16, 1986, 18.

10. The 2002 Taurus World Stunt Awards cited the car jump over the waterfall as one of the five most memorable stunts in motion picture history.

11. Walter Grauman was producer-director of *The Untouchables, Blue Light,* and *The Streets of San Francisco.*

12. Formed by Alan Gibbs in 1980, the International Stunt Association (ISA) has about forty members. Mary Albee is the only woman.

13. Alice West's credits include first assistant director–coordinating producer of *L.A. Law;* first assistant director of *Murder, She Wrote;* co–executive producer of *Ugly Betty, Ally McBeal, Snoops,* and *Picket Fences;* and producer of *The Practice.*

14. Mary Albee's credits include second-unit director for *Snoops* and *Crossing Jordan* and stunt coordinator for *L.A. Law; Murder, She Wrote; Border Line; Brooklyn Bridge; Perfect Couples; George Lopez; Tucker;* and *Weeds.*

15. Statistics courtesy of Glenn Hiraoka.

16. *The Color Purple* was adapted from Alice Walker's prize-winning novel. Greg Wayne Elam was stunt coordinator for the movie.

17. Kim Murphy, "Injured Stunt Woman Sues Warner Bros.," *Los Angeles Times,* November 16, 1986. Carol Daniels's other credits include *The Rifleman, The Untouchables, That Girl* and *Desperate Housewives.*

18. Michael Szymanski, "Stunt People Risk Injuries, Death on Set," *Torrance (CA) Daily News,* October 25, 1987.

19. Caulfield and Cieply, "Twilight Aftermath."

20. *Hot Pursuit* was stunt-coordinated by Ted White; the second-unit director was Max Kleven. There were four stuntmen plus Eurlyne Epper, whose other credits include *Scarface, Acapulco, HEAT, Bitch Slap, True Blood, Con Air, Side Out,* and *Murphy's Law.*

21. In *Fatal Attraction,* Tracy Dashnaw doubled Ann Archer, Annie Ellis dou-

bled Glenn Close, and Freddie Hice doubled Michael Douglas. Other stuntwomen in the film were Laurie Shepard and Janet Brady.

## 12. Julie Johnson's Day in Court

1. Heidi Yorkshire, "Stuntwoman Claims that Fight for Equality Has Tripped Her Up," *Reader*, April 25, 1984, 3.

2. Author interview with Julie Johnson and excerpts from her memoranda, supplied to the author.

3. Plaintiff and defense opening statements, August 11, 1987, transcript, *Johnson v. Spelling-Goldberg Productions,* from the archives of Julie Johnson (unless otherwise noted, all testimony cited is from this source). Witnesses testified on different dates during the three-week trial, so their testimony is not necessarily presented in chronological order. In some cases, testimony has been summarized for clarity.

4. Author interview with Richard Grey. Subsequent quotations from Grey that are not part of the trial transcript are from this interview.

5. Plaintiff and defense opening statements.

6. Testimony of Norma Connolly, August 11, 1987, 445–82. Connolly's Broadway theater credits include *A Streetcar Named Desire, The Love of Four Colonels,* and *Angel Street.*

7. Testimony of Joe Ruskin, August 14, 1987, vol. 5, 1039–50. Ruskin's film credits include *Prizzi's Honor, The Magnificent Seven,* and *Oh God.*

8. Deposition of Joe Ruskin, August 12, 1987, 11–13, 29, 31–37, conducted by Kenneth G. Anderson, defendant's counsel, and Jennifer B. Kaufman, plaintiff's counsel.

9. Testimony of Aaron Spelling, August 12–14, 1987, 687–786, 876–982; excerpts from appellant's opening brief, June 29, 1990, 824–46.

10. Testimony of Elaine Rich, August 17, 1987, vol. 3, 1054–128.

11. Testimony of Ron Rondell, August 12–13, 1987, vol. 3, 565–70, 623–95, 760–92. Rondell's extensive credits include stunt coordinator for *Sphere, Hart to Hart, Dynasty,* and *Mod Squad* and second-unit director for *Baywatch, Midnight Rider,* and *McQ.*

12. Testimony of Jean Coulter-Marek, August 14, 1987, vol. 5, 929–30.

13. Testimony of Bobby Bass, August 18, 1987, vol. 6, 1190–251.

14. Testimony of Roy E. Harrison, August 18, 1987, 1326–32.

15. Coulter-Marek testimony, 949.

16. Bass testimony, 1264–88.

17. Testimony of Richard Rawlings Jr., August 26, 1987, vol. 11, 2340–85.

18. Harrison testimony, 1322–25.

19. Rich testimony, 1137–46.

20. Testimony of Gary Epper, August 25, 1987, vol. 10, 2104–89. Epper's stunt

work included *Annie Oakley, Fury, Rin Tin Tin* (1950s), *L.A. Confidential, Eraser, Jurassic Park, Starsky & Hutch,* and *Scarface.* He was stunt coordinator for *Charlie's Angels, Witness,* and *Night of the Hunter,* among other shows.

21. Rich testimony, 1069–1124.

22. Rondell testimony, 662–64.

23. Rich testimony, 1073–1134.

24. Rondell testimony, 635–39.

25. Rebuttal testimony of Julie Johnson, August 27, 1987, 2455–87.

26. Deborah Caulfield and Michael Cieply, "Elation, Anger Greet Outcome of 'Twilight Zone' Trial," *Los Angeles Times,* May 30, 1987.

27. Sharon Bernstein and Robert W. Welkos, "In the Line of Duty," *Los Angeles Times,* February 18, 1996.

## 13. High Falls

1. Dar Robinson and Vic Armstrong created and refined various systems to control the speed of high falls. Armstrong won a technical achievement Academy Award in 2001 for his Fan Descender, which safely arrests the descent of a stunt person doing a high fall; he won the Michael Balcon Award from the British Academy of Film and Television Arts in 2002. Robinson, who started out on a trampoline, did the 100-foot cliff jump into the river in *Papillon,* set a free-fall record from a helicopter (311 feet into an airbag) in 1979, and performed a 220-foot free fall in *Sharky's Machine* and a 700-foot free fall from the CN Tower in Toronto, Canada. In 1980 he jumped 1,170 feet from the same CN Tower using a steel cable that stopped him a few feet from the ground.

2. John D. Ross, "High Fall Basics," *Inside Stunts,* Summer 2004. There are four high-fall categories: the face-off, the header, the suicide, and the back fall. Ross interviews with experts Jon Epstein, Nancy Thurston, Scott Leva, Leigh Hennessy, Bob Brown, and Andy Dylan.

3. The credits of Betty Thomas Quee (not Betty Thomas the actress-director-producer) include *Once a Thief, Jumangi, The Edge, Excess Baggage, The Boy Who Could Fly,* and *Romeo Must Die.*

4. Michael Joy is a well-known production designer in Canada; his credits include *Alice, The Tin Man,* and *Resurrection.* Stuntwoman Corry Glass (*Carpool, X-Men: The Last Stand*) also worked on *Snowbound.* Glenn Randall was the stunt coordinator–second-unit director on *Raiders of the Lost Ark.*

5. Melissa Stubbs's stunt-coordinating credits from the 1990s–2000s include *Power of Attorney, Once in a Blue Moon, Bounty Hunters, To Brave Alaska, Perfect Body, A Cooler Climate, Romeo Must Die, Mission to Mars, Along Came a Spider, Ballistic: Ecks vs. Sever,* and *X2;* she was second-unit director for *New York Minute, Hunt to Kill, License to Wed,* and *My Bloody Valentine.*

6. Sophia Crawford's credits include *Kung Fu: The Legend Continues, U.S. Seals II, Sword of Honor, Fifteen Minutes,* seventy-eight episodes of *Buffy the Vampire Slayer,* and sixty episodes of *Power Rangers.* She has expertise in numerous areas: trampoline, martial arts, wirework, weapons (broadsword, staff), ratchets, stair falls, fight choreography, and hitting the ground. Jeff Pruitt's credits include *The Hunter, Timecop, The Berlin Decision, Red Skies, Deadly Target, Sheena,* and *Sword of Honor.*

7. Sophia Crawford and Jeff Pruitt were married on January 15, 2010.

8. Kym Washington's credits include *Sister Act; Ghost; One False Move; Corrina, Corrina; Boys on the Side; Die Hard: With a Vengeance; Asunder; The Forgotten; The Invasion; Madea Goes to Jail; Live Free or Die Hard; War of the Worlds; Taxi; The Break-up; The Interpreter,* and *King's Ransom.* LaFaye Baker worked on *Grand Canyon, Metro, Con Air, True Crime, Made in America, Hannibal,* and *Fat Albert.* Sharon Schaffer's credits include *Blood Work, Hollow Man, Next Action Star, Lost in Plainview, Article 99, D.C. Cab, In the Line of Fire,* and *Burglar.* Sonja Davis worked on *Deep Cover, Class Act, Timecop, Live Wire, Ballistic, The Fear,* and *Hearts and Souls.*

9. Ross, "High Fall Basics."

10. Holly Millea, "After the Fall," *Premiere,* January 1996.

11. Bernstein and Welkos, "In the Line of Duty."

12. Millea, "After the Fall."

13. Bernstein and Welkos, "In the Line of Duty."

14. Ross, "High Fall Basics," 40–41.

15. In addition to the stuntwomen mentioned in this chapter, others who began to work in the 1990s were Elle Alexander, Jane Austin, Zoe Bell, Cheryl Bermeo, Nicola Berwick, Dartenea Bryant, Danielle Burgio, Crystal Dalman, Shauna Duggins, Mary Fallick, Stephanie Finochio, Alisa Hensley, Eunice Huthart, Sonia Jo Izzolena-McDancer, Jennifer Lamb, Angela Meryl, Heidi Moneymaker, Heidi Pascoe, Jodi Pynn, Dana Michelle Reed, Bridgett Riley, Catherine Robert, Lori Seaman, Karin Silvestri, Jill Stokesberry, April Weedon Washington, Cheryl Wheeler-Dixon, and Darlene Williams.

16. Lynn Salvatori's tricky fall from the balcony was for *Pure Luck* (1991). Her other stunt credits include *Switch, Strange Days, Titanic,* and *The Jackal;* she was stunt coordinator for *The Robber, Stranger in My House, Drive In, The Rose Technique, Nancy Drew, Girltrash: All Night Long, Séance, D.E.B.S., Lois and Clark, Kiss of a Stranger, Murderous Affair,* and *Prey for Rock and Roll.*

17. Nancy Thurston, a graduate of Illinois State University, doubled Hayden Panettiere in the pilot of *Heroes* and did stunts on *Ally McBeal, Scrubs, Six Feet Under, Saving Grace, Sun of Morning, Transformers: Dark Side of the Moon, Terminator: The Sarah Connor Chronicles, Beowulf, The Invasion,* and *Twilight.* Jon Epstein's credits as second-unit director or stunt coordinator include *Miami*

*Medical, CSI, Jake in Progress,* and *Alien Nation.* Bob Brown, a world-champion high-diver, started in 1985; his credits include *Death Race, Dark Water, Man on Fire, True Crime, Because I Said So, Underdog,* and *Babylon AD.*

18. Terry Gilliam directed *The Fisher King,* which was produced by Lynda Obst and Debra Hill, with associate producers Stacey Sher and Tony Mark. The highly praised film starred Robin Williams, Jeff Bridges, Mercedes Ruehl, and Amanda Plummer. Chris Howell had been a stunt coordinator since 1980 (*Urban Cowboy*) and a second-unit director since 1985 (*Moonlighting*).

19. Leigh Hennessy has a master's degree in communication and was cited in the *Guinness Book of World Records* for being the U.S. woman with the most national trampoline championship titles and for having the highest score in the women's double mini-trampoline event at the World Trampoline Championships (that record has since been broken). A member of the United Stuntwomen's Association, Leigh's stunt credits include *Planet of the Apes, The Guardian, Artificial Intelligence: AI, Charlie's Angels, What Lies Beneath,* and *The 13th Warrior;* she doubled Demi Moore in *G.I. Jane* and Leelee Sobieski in *Deep Impact.* Janet Orcutt, who did high falls, mentored Leigh early in her career.

20. Kenny Bates was stunt coordinator for *Transformers* and *The Italian Job* and second-unit director for *G-Force, The Hours,* and *Training Day.*

21. Leigh Hennessy performed this stunt for the "Fly Away" episode of *Cold Case,* which aired November 30, 2008.

22. Lisa Hoyle's many stunt credits include *Zombieland, Lost, Buffy the Vampire Slayer, Alias, Charlie's Angels: Full Throttle, Spider-Man 2,* and *Battle Los Angeles.* She won the Taurus World Stunt Award for best fight in 2008 for *Pirates of the Caribbean: Dead Man's Chest;* she was nominated for *Pirates of the Caribbean: At World's End, Spider-Man 2,* and *National Treasure.*

23. Leigh Hennessy, "The Risk Gene: Stunt Performers and Borderline Personality Disorders," *Inside Stunts,* Fall 2005.

## 14. Stunt Fights

1. Stuntwomen who worked on *Charlie's Angels* (2000) included Lesley Aletter, Laura Alpert, Nina Armstrong, Jennifer Badger, Roberta Brown, Jennifer Caputo, Marta Cases, Laurie Creach, Lisa Dempsey, Annie Ellis, Donna Evans, Dana Dru Evenson, Courtney Farnsworth, Tanya Garcia-O'Brien, Dana Hee, Lisa Hoyle, Michiko Nishiwaki, Ming Qiu, Cheryl Wheeler-Dixon, and Boni Yanagisawa. Stuntwomen on *Charlie's Angels: Full Throttle* were Jennifer Caputo, Eliza Coleman, Annie Ellis, Debbie Evans, Anita Hart, Alisa Hemsley, Leigh Hennessy, Lisa Hoyle, Heidi Moneymaker, Julia Morizawa, Ming Qiu, Gloria O'Brien, and Boni Yanagisawa.

2. Donna Evans and Shauna Duggins won the 2001 World Stunt Award for

best specialty stunt. Their fight was intercut with a fight and fall off a decrepit structure in Carmel by Lucy Liu (doubled by Ming Qiu and Michiko Nishiwaki). Shauna's earlier stunt work included *That's Life, Stop at Nothing,* and *Nash Bridges.* After *Charlie's Angels* she piled up the credits, stunt-coordinating *13 Going on 30,* doubling Jennifer Garner in *Alias* from 2001 to 2005, and stunt-coordinating the show in 2005–2006.

3. Loren Janes, "SAG Stunt Performers: The Professionals," *Screen Actor,* Fall 1992.

4. Vic Armstrong was stunt coordinator for *Total Recall.* In addition to Donna Evans, stuntwomen May Boss, Simone Boiseree, Jeannie and Stephanie Epper, Chere Bryson, Dana Dru Evenson, Marcia Holley, and Cherie Tash worked on the movie. Evans also doubled Sharon Stone in *Casino, Diabolique,* and *Basic Instinct.*

5. Ming Qiu's stunt credits include *Angels & Demons, Rush Hour, Transformers, The King of Fighters,* and *The Last Airbender.* In 1996 she won the Forms and Weapons Division of the Grand National Karate Championships. Other stuntwomen with expertise in martial arts include Karen Shepard, Li Jing, and Caryn Mower (also a professional wrestler).

6. Michiko Nishiwaki, stuntwoman and fight choreographer. Her credits include *Red Corner, Collateral, Brave New World, Rush Hour 2,* and *Kill Bill Vol. 1* and *Vol. 2.*

7. "Ming Lui [Qiu] Wushu Athlete," WushuKicks.com.

8. Stuntwomen Donna Evans, Shauna Duggins, Ming Qiu, Dana Hee, Eileen Weisinger, and Marta Casey and pilots Joey Box and David Paris won an award for best aerial work for the helicopter sequence in *Charlie's Angels.*

9. Danny Aiello III (1956–2010) was an actor (*The Wanderers, The Natural*) and a stunt coordinator or second-unit director for many films and TV series, including *Sex and the City, H.E.L.P., The Job, Life on Mars, Royal Pains, Diabolique,* and *Angels in America.* He directed and produced the TV series *Dellaventura* and *The Untouchables* and the feature film *18 Shades of Dust* (aka *Hitman's Journal*).

10. Stuntwoman and martial artist Li Jing has worked on *Entourage, The Fast and the Furious: Tokyo Drift, Rush Hour 3,* and *The Last Airbender.*

11. Aiello was referring to a scene in "Happy," from the second season of *Rescue Me.* Stephanie Finochio, who is also a professional wrestler, has a BBA in accounting, a BA in psychology, and a master's degree in education; she was a member of Psi Chi Honor Society. Her stunt credits include *Burn after Reading, Awake, The Bourne Ultimatum, Sex and the City, Taxi, War of the Worlds, Spider-Man 2, Duplicity,* and *Indiana Jones and the Kingdom of the Crystal Skull.*

12. Dorenda Moore's stunt credits include *Ritual, Strange Ways, The Convent, Thor,* and *Planet of the Apes;* she stunt-coordinated *Kamen Rider: Dragon Night, RCVR,* and *Serial Killing 4 Dummys.* On *Mr. Deeds,* Moore and Albee were nominated for a World Stunt Award for best overall stunt by a stuntwoman.

13. Shawnna Thibodeau's credits include *Rabbit Hole, Rum Diary, She's Out of My League, Men in Black III, Premium Rush, Spider-Man 3, The Interpreter, Oz,* and *New York Minute.* She was also in *The Bourne Ultimatum,* which won a SAG Award for outstanding performance by a stunt ensemble in 2008.

14. Actor-writer-director Quentin Tarantino's other credits include *Reservoir Dogs, Pulp Fiction, Grindhouse, Death Proof, Jackie Brown, True Romance,* and *Four Rooms.*

15. The fight was nominated for two World Stunt Awards in 2004: best fight and best overall stunt by a woman. Other stuntwomen on *Kill Bill* were Ming Qiu, Lisa McCullough, Cheryl Bermeo, Michiko Nishiwaki, Jeannie Epper, and Shauna Duggins.

16. Angela Meryl has also doubled Gabrielle Union, Vanessa Williams, and Beyoncé. Meryl is an expert in tae kwon do as well as explosions, high falls, and precision driving. Her credits include *Coyote Ugly, Shaft, Cradle 2 the Grave, Alias, Freedomland, Ugly Betty, Law & Order, Heroes, NCIS: Los Angeles,* and *Pirates of the Caribbean: At World's End.*

17. Shanti Sosienski, "Women Who Love Danger," *Marie Claire* 10, no. 9 (September 2003): 117.

18. Monica Staggs, a graduate of the University of Arkansas at Fayetteville, has performed stunts in *Red Dragon, Bug, Thieves, The Glass House, Swordfish, Angel's Dance, Transformers: Dark of the Moon, Cedar Rapids, Isolation,* and *True Blood;* she was stunt coordinator for *White Oleander, Out for Blood, War Eagle, Arkansas,* and *Hard Times.* She also writes poetry and screenplays.

19. Zoe Bell's other credits include *Inglorious Bastards, The Extreme Team, Bitch Slap, Death Proof,* and *Grindhouse.*

20. *Double Dare* was produced by Danielle Renfrew and Karen Johnson.

21. Jason William McNeill, "Zoe Bell: Dying for Her Close-up," *Inside Stunts,* Summer 2007.

22. Amy Murphy, "Inside the Head of Zoe Bell," www.whoosh.org/issue 87/bell1.html (March 2004).

23. For *Kill Bill Volume 2,* Woo-ping Yuen was fight and stunt coordinator; Keith Adams was stunt coordinator. In 2005 Monica Staggs and Zoe Bell won the World Stunt Award for best fight and best overall stunt by a stuntwoman.

## 15. Car Stunts

1. Tracy Keehn Dashnaw also doubled Kim Basinger on *The Getaway, My Stepmother Is an Alien, Cellular, The Real McCoy,* and *Cool World.* Her other credits include *Iron Man 2, Final Destination, 12 Rounds, The Fast and the Furious, Death Proof,* and *Grindhouse.* Other stuntwomen in *Bless the Child* were Debbie Lee Carrington, Kym Kristalie, Jessica Meyer, Alison Reid, and Jennifer Vey.

2. *Hulk* was produced by Gale Anne Hurd, who has delivered action roles for women in many films, including *Terminator, Terminator 3: Rise of the Machines,* and *Adventure Inc.*

3. Acker, *Reel Women,* 254.

4. LaFaye Baker trained with Greg Elam, stunt coordinator–second-unit director of *Deep Cover, The Color Purple,* and *The Ghosts of Mississippi.* LaFaye's first stunt, a near-miss with a car, was for the TV series *In the Heat of the Night* (1988–1994). In the music video she was doubling actress Lauren Hill (*Entourage*). Baker's other credits include *Set It Off, The Nutty Professor, Lawnmower Man 2, Don't Be a Menace to South Central While Drinking Your Juice in the Hood, Mission Impossible III, What's Love Got to Do with It, The Thin Line between Love and Hate, Angels & Demons, True Crime, Hannibal,* and *Green Lantern.*

5. Laurie Creach's credits include *Breathless* and *Seabiscuit.* The other stunt-women on *Hellhole* were Pamela Bebermeyer, Chere Bryson, Cheryl E. Duncan, Glory Fioramonti, Linda Lee Franklin, Bonnie Happy, Candy Hoskins, Deseree Kerns, Paula Moody, and Dianne L. Wilson.

6. Kimberly Shannon Murphy's other credits include *Enchanted, Star Trek* (2009), *One Shot, Savages, Premium Rush, Men in Black III, The Hunger Games, Chuck, Iceland, Wonder Woman* (2011), *Salt, The Box, Oblivion, Happy Endings,* and *Revenge.* Other stuntwomen on *I Am Legend* were Jill Brown, Shawnna Thibodeau, Nicole Callender, Caroline Leppanen Vexler, Nina Armstrong, Angelina Cruz, Cheryl Lewis, and Jodi Pym; Wendy Leech Armstrong, Joey Box, and Douglas Crosby were assistant stunt coordinators.

7. Anti-Gravity, based in New York, was founded by Christopher Harrison in 1990. The group has performed in theatrical and sports productions in twenty-five countries.

8. Vince Cupone's stunt credits include *Meet Dave, Sex in the City, The David Letterman Show, The Sopranos,* and *Spider-Man 2;* he was assistant or co-coordinator for *Cupid, Castle, Dirty Sexy Money,* and episodes of *Rescue Me* and stunt coordinator for *Nobody's Perfect, Pan Am, Adrift, Ring the Bell, Nexus, Curb Your Enthusiasm, Royal Pains,* and *Blue Bloods.* Cupone has two Emmy nominations: in 2010 (with Danny Aiello) and in 2011 for stunt coordination.

9. Chrissy Weathersby was nominated in 2008 for the World Stunt Award for her work on *The Brave One.* She began in the business in 2001; her credits include *One on One, Mr. St. Nick, The Fast and the Furious, Wanda at Large, Wonder Woman* (2011), *X-Men: First Class, Larry Crowne, NCIS: LA, Hawthorne, The Undercovers, Man of the House, Terminator Salvation, Iron Man, Due Date, Memphis Beat, Takers, Inception, Southland, Big Time Rush, American Horror Story, Larry Crowne,* and *Californication.*

10. Conley, *Full Burn,* 115–18.

11. In *Death Proof,* Tracie Thoms played Kim (doubled by Chrissy Weathersby

and Tracy Keehn Dashnaw), Rosario Dawson played Abby (doubled by Crystal Santos), Mary Elizabeth Winstead played Lee, Monica Staggs played Lanna Frank, and Zoe Bell played herself. Other stuntwomen who worked on the two-feature *Grindhouse* were Dina L. Margolin, Malosi Leonard, Dana Reed, Boni Yanagisawa, and Karin Silvestri.

12. Other stuntwomen on *The Matrix Reloaded* were Debbie Evans, Kelsee King-Devoreaux (doubling Jada Pinkett Smith), Danielle Burgio, Leesha Davis, and Tawny Marie Ellis. R. A. Rondell was supervising stunt coordinator; David Ellis was second-unit director, U.S.; Freddie Hice was stunt coordinator, second unit; Glen Boswell was stunt coordinator; and Chad Stahelski was martial arts stunt coordinator. In 2003 Annie Ellis also worked on *CSI: Miami* and thirteen other movies, including *2 Fast 2 Furious* and *Charlie's Angels: Full Throttle.*

13. See Conley, *Full Burn*, 107–12.

14. Debbie Evans has won several World Stunt Awards: best work with a vehicle in 2011 for *Date Night,* best overall stunt by a woman in 2007 for *Superman Returns,* best specialty stunt (shared with Anita Hart, Christine Anne Baur, Jill Brown, Henry Kingi, and others) in 2005 for *Taxi,* and two awards for *The Fast and the Furious* in 2002—best stunt by a stuntwoman and best driving.

15. Other splendid stuntwomen who haven't been mentioned here include Jill Stokesberry (who doubles Jodie Foster), Eunice Huthart and Nicola Berwick (who double Angelina Jolie), Corry Glass, Jeri Habberstad, Jennifer Lamb-Hewitt, and Kelly Dent.

## 16. Computer-Generated Imagery and the Future of Stunt Work

1. The other credits of Douglas Trumbull, a director, producer, and special photographic effects supervisor, include *The Andromeda Strain, Close Encounters of the Third Kind, Silent Running,* and *The Tree of Life.* Terry Clotiaux worked for the Showscan Company's visual effects entity, the Chandler Group, as executive producer of *The Shadow, Batman Returns,* and *Batman Forever.* He also served as visual effects producer on *ID4, Godzilla, The Matrix Revolutions, Alexander, Volcano, Monkeybone,* and *Spider-Man 3.* In 2009 he became president, visual effects worldwide, for Prime Focus Group; in 2013 he became president of Digital Domain 3.0.

2. Stuntwomen who began in the 2000s include Nicole Callender, Kimberly Shannon Murphy, Stacey Carino, Ming Qiu, Luci Romberg, Chrissy Weathersby Ball, Candace Jwaundace, Carolyn Day, Lahi Gelera, Angela Uyeda, Jeri Habberstad, Natascha Hopkins, Li Jing, Caroline Leppanen-Veder, Karine Mauffrey, Jade Quon, and Ramsey Scott.

3. Melissa Stubbs's recent credits as stunt coordinator include *Alcatraz, Mr. Young, Missing, Marmaduke, The Secret Circle,* and *Hellcats;* she was second-unit director for *Hunt to Kill, License to Wed, New York Minute,* and *My Bloody Valentine.*

4. Alison Reid was stunt coordinator for *Phase One, Beauty and the Beast, Skins, King, Being Erica,* and *Combat Hospital;* she was second-unit director for *D.C. 9/11: Time of Crisis, Highlander, The Raven,* and *The Third Twin;* and producer-director of *Seccubus* and *The Baby Formula.*

5. Denise DiNovi produced *Edward Scissorhands, Little Women, Sudbury, Catwoman, New York Minute, You're Not You, Crazy Stupid Love,* and *Life as We Know It.*

6. Shauna Duggins was second-unit director for *What about Brian?* She coordinated episodes of *Brothers and Sisters, Fringe, Family Man, The Madness of Jane,* and *Anatomy of Hope.*

7. Other stuntwomen on the "Reprisal" episode of *Alias* included Karin Silvestri, Lisa Hoyle, and Heidi Pascoe.

8. Stacey Carino also duked it out with Zoe Bell in "Solo," a 2005 episode of *Alias.*

9. On *Crossing Jordan,* Luci Romberg worked on "Dead Again" in 2007; Stacey Carino doubled Jill Hennessy for eight episodes in 2005–2006.

10. Natascha Hopkins's credits include *Transformers, Project X, Venom, Sky High, Spider-Man 3,* and the TV series *ER, The Shield, American Heiress,* and *Heroes.*

11. Luci Romberg's credits include *Zombieland, Ten, Run, Sparks, Project X, Dragon Age: Redemption, Green Lantern, Parenthood, Castle, Trance,* and *Indiana Jones and the Kingdom of the Crystal Skull.* Jennifer Caputo has worked on *Charlie's Angels, The Fast and the Furious, Catwoman, Thor, War of the Worlds,* and the TV series *Monk, Cold Case,* and *Crossing Jordan.*

12. Annie Ellis stunt-coordinated *Bare Knuckles, Snakes on the Plane, Park,* and *Homeward Bound 2.*

13. In 1991 the Screen Actors Guild also included 101 Asian Pacific, 160 Latino/ Hispanic, and 34 Native American stunt performers. By 2005, SAG had 6,595 stunt performers; of these, 5,295 were Caucasian, 511 were African American, 319 were Hispanic, 317 were Asian, and 40 were Native American. Seventy-five percent were male.

14. SAG statement regarding the Alliance for Stunt Performers of Color. Marvin Walters wrote *Awakening Giant* (1995), an informative history of African Americans in the film industry. His stunt-coordinating credits include *The River Niger, The Dogs of War, Shaft's Big Score, Eve's Bayou, Flag,* and the TV series *Nobody's Perfect, Delta House, Magnum P.I.,* and *Heart of Darkness.*

15. Soraya Sarhaddi Nelson, "Protestors Say White Stunt Workers Favored," *Los Angeles Times,* September 28, 1999; Marvin Walters, "The Coalition of Black Stuntmen and Women Inform Black Press of Hiring Bias," October 5, 1999, www .exodusnews.com. According to Walters's 1999 press release, of SAG's 2,227 stunt people, only about 65 were African American.

16. Here is a sampling of the African American stuntwomen who began working in the 1980s and 1990s: Kelsee King-Devoreaux's credits include *Hawthorne, Clueless, The Italian Job, American Dreams, Terminator Salvation, Collateral,* and *The Matrix Reloaded.* She coproduced *Hollywood at Its Best* and regularly doubles Jada Pinkett Smith. Sharon Schaffer started in 1980 and did stunts for twenty-five years, including her work on *Crossing Jordan, Freedom Writers, Another Stakeout, Colors, Out for Justice, D.C. Cab, Burglar, The Pineapple Express, Metro, Kindergarten Cop, Lambada, American Me, Alien Nation, Scarface,* and *The Star Chamber.* She is also an accomplished swimmer, scuba diver, surfer, and stunt driver. Since 1996, April Weeden-Washington has worked on *Eraser, Crash, Minority Report, True Blood, Ugly Betty, My Name Is Earl, Drive, Lethal Weapon 4, Baggage Claim,* and *Community;* she stunt-coordinated *Hidden Blessings, Show Stopper,* and *Billie's* and regularly doubles Tamala Jones, Robin Givens, and Regina Hall. In 2004 she won the Trailblazer Award from Cine Noir.

17. Chrissy Weathersby Ball's grandmother wrote a book at age ninety-four titled *Every Child Can Learn.*

18. Donna Evans also coordinated *A Single Rose.* She won two World Stunt Awards in 2001 on *Charlie's Angels;* she was nominated for *The Punisher* in 2005 and for the SAG Award for outstanding performance by a stunt ensemble for *Iron Man* in 2009 and *Transformers: Revenge of the Fallen* in 2010. Her recent stunt credits include *Haywire, The Avengers, Iron Man 2, Sleeper Cell, In the Valley of Elah, Bird in the Air,* and *The Artist.*

19. Debbie Evans is married to Lane Leavitt, a U.S. motorcycle champion who invents, designs, and builds stunt equipment. He has been nominated three times for an Academy Award for technical achievement for his Airramp, Leavitator, and High Speed Descender. Debbie stunt-coordinated *Distortions, Beauty and the Beast, Private Debts,* and *Danika.*

20. Karen Lustgarten, "Reel Endangered Species: Stuntwomen Speak Up," *Reel News* 3, no. 2 (April 1993): 3. Linda Fetters-Howard (*Peacemaker, Another 48 Hours*) has been a stuntwoman since the 1980s; she is a precision driver and also does high falls, fights, and burns. She was president of the Stuntwomen's Association in 1994–1996. Born in Memphis, Tennessee, she is married to Emmy- and Tony-winning actor Ken Howard.

21. Author interview with Jeannie Epper. Epper stunt-coordinated *Extremities, Before Women Had Wings, Amy & Isabelle, Hairless* (with Mary Albee), *November,* and *American Son.*

22. Dr. Martha M. Lauzen, "Boxed In: Employment of Behind-the-Scenes and On-Screen Women in 2013–2014 Prime-Time Television" (2014). Lauzen is executive director of the Center for the Study of Women in Television and Film, San Diego State University. The report also included comparative percentages of female characters in network TV programs.

23. M. James Arnett stunt-coordinated *Divine Secrets of the Ya-Ya Sisterhood.*

24. Christine Anne Baur's coordinating credits include *Unholy Matrimony, The Comeback, Not Quite Human 2, Fathers and Daughters, Little Man Tate,* and the *Perry Mason* movie of the week. Glory Fioramonti coordinated *The Client, The Craft, Til There Was You, Hush, Anywhere but Here, Earthly Possessions, Bam Bam and Celeste,* and *Kalamazoo.* Donna Garrett stunt-coordinated *Streets of L.A., Private Benjamin, Women in Prison, Invisible Women,* and episodes of *Cagney & Lacey.* Marian Green's many credits include stunt-coordinating *Crackerjack, Savannah, Killing Uncle Roman, Breaking at the Edge, The 7th Lie,* and *The Learning Curve.* Donna Keegan regularly doubled Jamie Lee Curtis and stunt-coordinated *The Jimmy Show, Twin Peaks, L.A. Heat, Virus, Stat,* and others.

25. Eddie L. Watkins was stunt coordinator for *Friends with Benefits, For Colored Girls,* and *Family Matters;* he was second-unit director for *Scary Movie 2, Thicker than Water, First Sunday,* and *Gang Tapes.*

26. LaFaye Baker assisted or stunt-coordinated *Man in 318; My Wife and Kids; Sister, Sister; Thicker than Water; Guess Who; The Janky Promoters; First Sunday;* and the TV series *EVE.* She coproduced *Kujo, My Love,* and *On Sundays* and produced the documentary *Hollywood at Its Best II,* profiling African American stuntwomen and featuring Kelsee King-Devoreaux, Sharon Schaffer, Kym Washington, and April Weeden-Washington. Baker cofounded the stunt production group Stone Cold Action. LaFaye Baker and Jadie David were recognized by the African American Film Market for their pioneering accomplishments, including establishing Diamond in the Raw. They will be inducted, along with the Black Stuntmen's Association, into the Smithsonian African American Museum in 2015.

27. Stuntwoman Kym Washington won the Special Achievement Award in 2011.

28. Mary Albee, "Reality Check Revisited," *Inside Stunts,* Spring 2008. This is a valuable article about the lives and work of stunt performers.

## 17. Controversy and Progress for Stuntwomen

1. Stuntwomen on *Planet of the Apes* (2001) included Joni Avery, Cheryl Bermeo, Simone Boisseree, Eliza Coleman, Shauna Duggins, Deborah Habberstad, Christie Hayes, Leigh Hennessy, Alisa Hensley, Lisa Hoyle, Sonia Izzolena, Dorenda Moore, Carol Neilson, Gloria O'Brien, Pamela Rittelmeyer, Shirley Smrz, and Darlene Ava Williams.

2. Simone Boisseree's credits include *The Singing Detective* and *Poodle Springs.* Eliza Coleman's include *Men in Black III, Hugo, True Grit,* and *Inception.* Gloria O'Brien worked on *Spider-Man 3, New York Minute,* and *Death Row.* Eileen Weisinger's credits include *Charlie's Angels, Analyze That, Iron Man 2, Anger Management,* and the TV series, *ER, Oz,* and *Great Performances.* Darlene Ava

Williams, a founding member of V10 Women Stunt Professionals, has worked on *Timecop, V.I.P.,* and *Desperate Housewives.*

3. Charles Croughwell was stunt coordinator for *Life of Pi, Flight,* and *Knight and Day;* he was second-unit director for *Aeon Flux* and the TV series *The Pacific.* Sonny Tipton was assistant coordinator on *Planet of the Apes.* The first *Planet of the Apes* (1968) employed no stuntwomen.

4. Sandy Kincaid became national director of SAG's Stunt, Safety, and Music Committee in 2002 and SAG-AFTRA's national director of commercials, corporate/educational, and nonbroadcast contracts in 2013.

5. Actress Anne-Marie Johnson appeared in *In the Heat of the Night, In Living Color,* and *Melrose Place;* at SAG she was first vice president of the Hollywood Division and then first national vice president of the board of directors. Gretchen Koerner, a film and stage actress, appeared in *Strong Medicine, Pit Stop,* and *The Tempest;* she chaired SAG's National Legislative Committee.

6. Dan Bradley stunt-coordinated *The Bourne Ultimatum* and was second-unit director for *The Bourne Supremacy.* Actress Rosemary Harris's career began in 1952; she appeared in *Studio One, Being Julia, Tom and Viv, Crossing Delancey,* and *Strange Interlude.* Stuntwomen on *Spider-Man 2* included Julie Adair, Jill Brown, Lisa Cohen, Debbie Evans, Stephanie Finochio, Jeri Habberstad, Claudette Jones, Rachel Kinsey, Dana Lupo, Jane Oshita, Ming Qiu, Darlene Roberts, Katie Rowe, and Boni Yanagisawa.

7. The Spelling-Goldberg appeal, as Grey wrote in rebuttal, hung on the issue of a state court requiring direct evidence and eliminating circumstantial evidence as "proof of evil motive. To require direct evidence of motive (i.e., a confession) before the burden shifts to the defendant would disembowel the only guardian standing between arrogance and the common citizen—the threat of a punitive damage private lawsuit." On appeal to the Second Circuit, the jury verdict was reversed. Julie Johnson appealed to both the California Supreme Court and the U.S. Supreme Court, but her appeals were denied.

8. Leigh Hennessy stunt-coordinated *Slaughter House of the Rising Sun, Mask Maker, Monsterwolf, Scream of the Banshee,* and *The Somnambulist.* The Taurus World Stunt Awards nominated her for best specialty stunt in *The Guardian* (2006). After *Spider-Man 2,* Julie Johnson worked on *I Heart Huckabees, Smokin' Aces,* and *Crank.*

9. Stacey Carino's credits include *The Twilight Saga: Breaking Dawn, True Blood, The Cape, Jack the Reaper, Ghost Whisperer, Transformers, Transformers: Revenge of the Fallen, Dark Moon Rising, The Hunger Games, Catching Fire,* and *Alice in Wonderland.*

10. Stuntwomen on *War of the Worlds* were Laura Alpert, Nina Armstrong, Robin Lynn Bonaccorsi, Nicole Callender, Jennifer Caputo, Stacey Carino, Eliza Coleman, Laura Dash, Annie Ellis, Dana Dru Evenson, Lena Fennema, Stephanie

Finochio, Claudette James, Karine Mauffrey, Heidi Moneymaker, Ming Qiu, Crystal Santos, Shawnna Thibodeau, and Kym Washington. Steven Spielberg directed, Vic Armstrong was second-unit director, and Joey Box assisted and stunt-coordinated the second unit.

11. Freerunning developed from parkour, which Dave Bell originated in France in the late 1990s. Parkour involves running, leaping, and climbing across, around, or over obstacles to get from point A to point B. Parkour and freerunning have been featured in the movies *Casino Royale, Live Free or Die Hard, Breaking and Entering,* and *Paul Blart: Mall Cop.*

12. Rachel Heller, "Queen of Freerunning, an Extreme Sport that's Like Running but More Awesome," October 25, 2012, LA Weekly Arts and Culture Blog.

13. Nicole Callender earned an MFA in theater from the University of Cincinnati, College Conservatory of Music. She has acted off-Broadway in *Joan of Arc* and *Henry VI.* Her stunt credits include *Indiana Jones and the Kingdom of the Crystal Skull, American Gangster, Zombieland, The Dictator, Salt, Spider-Man 3, Confessions of a Shopaholic,* and *Freedomland.* Nicole was nominated for the SAG Award for outstanding performance by a stunt ensemble in 2007 and 2008. She trained with the Society of American Fight Directors and is a certified teacher.

# Selected Bibliography

Acker, Ally. *Reel Women, Pioneers of Cinema*. New York: Continuum, 1991.

Bach, Steven. *Marlene Dietrich, Life and Legend*. New York: William Morrow, 1992.

Baxter, John. *Stunt*. New York: Doubleday, 1974.

Bogle, Donald. *Toms, Coons, Mulattoes, Mammies and Bucks: An Interpretive History of Blacks in American Films*. New York: Continuum, 1973.

Brownlow, Kevin. *The Parade's Gone By*. Berkeley: University of California Press, 1968.

———. *The War, the West, and the Wilderness*. New York: Alfred A. Knopf, 1979.

Clift, Eleanor. *Founding Sisters and the Nineteenth Amendment*. New York: John Wiley & Sons, 2003.

Conley, Kevin. *The Full Burn: On the Set, at the Bar, behind the Wheel, and over the Edge with Hollywood Stuntmen*. New York: Bloomsbury, 2008.

David, Saul. *The Industry: Life in the Hollywood Fast Lane*. New York: Times Books, 1981.

Davis, Mike. *City of Quartz: Excavating the Future of Los Angeles*. London: Verso, 1990.

Drew, William M. *Speaking of Silents: The First Ladies of the Screen*. New York: Vestal Press, 1997.

Farber, Stephen, and Marc Green. *Outrageous Conduct: Art, Ego and the* Twilight Zone *Case*. New York: William Morrow, 1988.

Gregory, Mollie. *Women Who Run the Show*. New York: St. Martin's Press, 2002.

Haskell, Molly. *From Reverence to Rape: The Treatment of Women in the Movies*. New York: Holt, Rinehart & Winston, 1973.

Higham, Charles. *Marlene: The Life of Marlene Dietrich*. New York: W. W. Norton, 1977.

Lahue, Kalton C. *Bound and Gagged: The Story of the Silent Serials*. New York: Castle Books/A. S. Barnes, 1968.

McWilliams, Carey. *Southern California Country: An Island on the Land*. Edited by Erskine Caldwell. New York: Duell, Sloat & Pierce, 1946.

Needham, Hal. *Stuntman! My Car-Crashing, Plane-Jumping, Bone-Breaking, Death-Defying Hollywood Life*. New York: Little Brown, 2011.

Null, Gary. *Black Hollywood: The Black Performer in Motion Pictures*. Secaucus, NJ: Citadel Press, 1975.

Pickard, Roy. *Jimmy Stewart: A Life in Film*. New York: St. Martin's Press, 1992.

Riva, Maria. *Marlene Dietrich*. New York: Galantine Books, 1992.

Roberson, Chuck, with Bodie Thoene. *The Fall Guy: 30 Years as the Duke's Double*. Vancouver, BC: Hancock House, 1980.

Scharff, Virginia. *Taking the Wheel: Women and the Coming of the Motor Age*. New York: Free Press, 1991.

Schatz, Thomas. *Genius of the System*. New York: Pantheon, 1988.

Sklar, Robert. *Movie-Made America: How the Movies Changed American Life*. New York: Random House, 1975.

Slide, Anthony. *Early Women Directors*. New York: Da Capo Press, 1984.

———. *The Silent Feminists: America's First Women Directors*. Lanham, MD: Scarecrow Press, 1996.

Stamp, Shelley. *Movie-Struck Girls: Women and Motion Picture Culture after the Nickelodeon*. Princeton, NJ: Princeton University Press, 2000.

Von Beltz, Heidi, with Peter Copeland. *My Soul Purpose: Living Learning and Healing*. New York: Random House, 1996.

Wilkman, Jon, and Nancy Wilkman. *Picturing Los Angeles*. Salt Lake City, UT: Gibbs Smith, 2006.

Witney, William. *In a Door, into a Fight, out a Door, into a Chase: Moviemaking Remembered by the Guy at the Door*. Jefferson, NC: McFarland, 1996.

# Index

Haskell, Molly, 93
Hathaway, Henry, 56, 73, 75
Hawks, Howard, 33, 35
Hayes, James A., 214
Hays, Will "Deacon," 29
Hays Commission. *See* Motion Picture
  Production Code
Hayward, Little Chuck, 54
*Hazards of Helen, The* (movie serial,
  1915), 7, 8, 15, 20–21, 22, 82,
  279n1, 281nn41–42
*Hellhole* (movie, 1985), 238, 312n5
Hendry, Gloria, 81, 84, 91, 291n8,
  293n46
Hennessy, Leigh, 203, 211, 214–17,
  265, 266, 267, 269, 309n19,
  309n21, 317n8
Henreid, Paul, 41
Henry, Norm, 134
Hepburn, Katharine, 33, 35
Heston, Charlton, 89, 90, 112
Hewitt, Jennifer, 263
Hice, Eddie, 66, 288n8
Hill, Jack, 81, 82
Hill, Leslie, 158
*Hindenburg, The* (movie, 1975), 109,
  295n1
Hines, Chester, 68, 289n17
*Hi-Riders* (movie, 1978), 136
Hoffman, Leslie, 271, 303n23;
  blacklisting, 161, 162–63,
  302–3n18; as stunt coordinator,
  163, 303–4n32; stuntwomen
  survey, 152, 153–54, 159, 160,
  302–3n18
Hollywood, 13–14, 25–26. *See also*
  drug use
*Hollywood Reporter*, 86, 110
"Hollywood Ten," 47
Holmes, Helen, 10, 11, 12, 16, 20–21,
  22, 222, 279n1, 281n31, 281n41

*Hondo* (movie, 1967), 65
*Honey West* (TV show, 1960s), 94,
  294n2
Hong Kong, 206–8, 249
*Honky Tonk Freeway* (movie, 1981),
  138, 300n2
Hooker, Buddy Joe, 241, 242 *Hooper*
  (movie, 1978), 100, 113–14, 115,
  116, 296n16
Hopkins, Natascha, 256, 272, 314n10
horror movies, 152, 211, 234
horse-riding stunts, 43–44, 46, 47, 48,
  50–51, 53–54, 282n5, 282n8;
  1960s, 65, 66–67, 73–74; 1980s and
  1990s, 171–73, 174, 175, 176; early
  stuntwomen and, 21–22, 26–27
*Hot Pursuit* (movie, 1987), 181,
  305n20
House, Lucille, 53, 54, 287n21
House Un-American Activities
  Committee (HUAC), 47
Howell, Chris, 212, 214, 309n18
Hoyle, Lisa, 216, 217, 309n22
*Hulk* (movie, 2003), 126, 235–36, 312n2
*Hunchback of Notre Dame, The*
  (movie, 1939), 36, 285n46, 286n57
Hurd, Gale Anne, 126, 298n3
*Hurricane, The* (movie, 1937), 32, 33,
  50, 94–95
Hutton, Betty, 43, 44, 45

*I Am Legend* (movie, 2007), 238–39,
  312n6
*Independence Day* (movie, 1996), 247
*In God We Tru$t* (movie, 1980), 106–7
*Inside Stunts*, 211
*Inspector Gadget* (movie, 1999), 266
International Stunt Association (ISA),
  162, 178, 292n23, 305n12
*Introducing Dorothy Dandridge*
  (movie, 1999), 263

BOOKS IN THE SERIES

*Mae Murray: The Girl with the Bee-Stung Lips*
    Michael G. Ankerich
*Hedy Lamarr: The Most Beautiful Woman in Film*
    Ruth Barton
*Rex Ingram: Visionary Director of the Silent Screen*
    Ruth Barton
*Von Sternberg*
    John Baxter
*Hitchcock's Partner in Suspense: The Life of Screenwriter Charles Bennett*
    Charles Bennett, edited by John Charles Bennett
*Ziegfeld and His Follies: A Biography of Broadway's Greatest Producer*
    Cynthia Brideson and Sara Brideson
*The Marxist and the Movies: A Biography of Paul Jarrico*
    Larry Ceplair
*Dalton Trumbo: Blacklisted Hollywood Radical*
    Larry Ceplair and Christopher Trumbo
*Warren Oates: A Wild Life*
    Susan Compo
*Crane: Sex, Celebrity, and My Father's Unsolved Murder*
    Robert Crane and Christopher Fryer
*Jack Nicholson: The Early Years*
    Robert Crane and Christopher Fryer
*Being Hal Ashby: Life of a Hollywood Rebel*
    Nick Dawson
*Bruce Dern: A Memoir*
    Bruce Dern with Christopher Fryer and Robert Crane
*Intrepid Laughter: Preston Sturges and the Movies*
    Andrew Dickos
*John Gilbert: The Last of the Silent Film Stars*
    Eve Golden
*Stuntwomen: The Untold Hollywood Story*
    Mollie Gregory

*Saul Bass: Anatomy of Film Design*
    Jan-Christopher Horak
*Hitchcock Lost and Found: The Forgotten Films*
    Alain Kerzoncuf and Charles Barr
*Pola Negri: Hollywood's First Femme Fatale*
    Mariusz Kotowski
*Sidney J. Furie: Life and Films*
    Daniel Kremer
*Mamoulian: Life on Stage and Screen*
    David Luhrssen
*Maureen O'Hara: The Biography*
    Aubrey Malone
*My Life as a Mankiewicz: An Insider's Journey through Hollywood*
    Tom Mankiewicz and Robert Crane
*Hawks on Hawks*
    Joseph McBride
*William Wyler: The Life and Films of Hollywood's Most Celebrated Director*
    Gabriel Miller
*Raoul Walsh: The True Adventures of Hollywood's Legendary Director*
    Marilyn Ann Moss
*Charles Walters: The Director Who Made Hollywood Dance*
    Brent Phillips
*Some Like It Wilder: The Life and Controversial Films of Billy Wilder*
    Gene D. Phillips
*Ann Dvorak: Hollywood's Forgotten Rebel*
    Christina Rice
*Arthur Penn: American Director*
    Nat Segaloff
*Claude Rains: An Actor's Voice*
    David J. Skal with Jessica Rains
*Buzz: The Life and Art of Busby Berkeley*
    Jeffrey Spivak
*Victor Fleming: An American Movie Master*
    Michael Sragow
*Hollywood Presents Jules Verne: The Father of Science Fiction on Screen*
    Brian Taves
*Thomas Ince: Hollywood's Independent Pioneer*
    Brian Taves
*Carl Theodor Dreyer and Ordet: My Summer with the Danish Filmmaker*
    Jan Wahl